Günther Schlee (ed.)

Imagined Differences

Market, Culture and Society

edited by
Hans-Dieter Evers
Rüdiger Korff
Gudrun Lachenmann
Joanna Pfaff-Czarnecka
Günther Schlee
Heiko Schrader

Volume 5

Günther Schlee (ed.)

Imagined Differences

Hatred and the construction of identity

LIT VERLAG
Palgrave

Cover Picture: „Uighur peasant paying market dues in a village near Kashgar"
(Foto von Chris Hann) und „Uighur peasant with visiting Chinese scholar" (Foto von Ildikó Bellér-Hann)

First published in Germany by

LIT VERLAG

Grevener Str. 179 D-48159 Münster

Die Deutsche Bibliothek – CIP-Einheitsaufnahme

Imagined Differences : Hatred and the construction of identity / Günther Schlee
(ed.). – Hamburg : LIT, 2002
    (Market, Culture and Society ; 5)
    ISBN 3-8258-3956-7

Library of Congress Cataloging-in-Publication Data

Imagined differences : hatred and the construction of identity / edited by Günther
Schlee.
    p. cm.
    Includes bibliographical references and index.
    ISBN: 1-4039-6031-3 (cloth)
    1. Ethnic conflict. Ethnicity. 3. Political violence. I. Schlee, Günther.
    HM1121.I43   2002
    305.8–dc21   2002020636

First published in the United States of America 2002 by

Palgrave
175 Fifth Avenue,
New York, N. Y. 10010

ISBN: 1-4039-6031-3

© 2002 LIT VERLAG

All rights reserved. No reproduction, copy or transmission of this publication may be made without
written permission.
    Any persons who does any unauthorized act in relation to this publication may be liable to criminal
prosecution and civil claims for damages.

Printed in Germany

IMAGINED DIFFERENCES: HATRED AND THE CONSTRUCTION OF IDENTITY

Günther Schlee (ed.)

Preface

The present volume on 'Imagined Differences: hatred and the construction of identity' appears at a time when old political entities are dissolving and new, generally smaller ones are emerging. These processes tend to be associated with considerable degrees of violence. While violence is not new in the context of emerging or decaying statehood or changing shapes of states, some of the ways of dealing with it are: international organisations like the UN, the EU and NATO assume new roles in actively intervening in crisis spots in different parts of the globe. Matters of ethnicity, nationhood and comparable forms of social identity and the conflicting loyalties they demand are of a new dimension of importance not only to those who -through the growing global interdependence and the new responsibilities assumed by governments outside crisis areas in the field of conflict management and intervention- are indirectly concerned with such matters.

Since the 1990s we have witnessed the breakdowns and periodic resumption of a number of carefully managed "peace processes" like in Israel/Palestine and Northern Ireland. Part of the problem seems to be that the approaches to conflict resolution still fail to recognise local factors. These local and regional social networks and political dynamics are related to the identities and motivations of the local actors who largely organise political violence. This volume reasserts local perspectives and a comparative theoretical focus.

TABLE OF CONTENTS

LIST OF CONTRIBUTORS

Ildikó Bellér-Hann: Orientwissenschaftliches Zentrum (OWZ), Martin-Luther-Universität Halle/Wittenberg, Halle/Saale, Germany

Georg Elwert: Institut für Ethnologie, Freie Universität Berlin, Berlin, Germany

Georg Haneke: Max Planck Institute for Social Anthropology, Halle/Saale, Germany

Mark Hobart: Department of Anthropology and Sociology, School of Oriental and African Studies, University of London, London, United Kingdom

Birgit Mara Kaiser: Comparative Literature Department, New York University, New York, United States of America

Mary Catherine Kenney: The Sociology of Development Research Centre, University of Bielefeld, Bielefeld, Germany

Philip Quarles van Ufford: Department of Anthropology and Development Sociology, Free University of Amsterdam, Amsterdam, Netherlands

Thomas Rieger: COMO Consulting GmbH, Hamburg, Germany

Günther Schlee: Max Planck Institute for Social Anthropology, Halle/Saale, Germany

Purnaka L. de Silva: Leadership Academy, United Nation University, New York, United States of America

Bernhard Venema: Faculty of Social-Cultural Sciences, Free University of Amsterdam, Amsterdam, Netherlands

Petra Weyland: Führungsakademie der Bundeswehr (General Staff Academy of the German Army), Hamburg, Germany

Part I

Introduction and theoretical approaches

INTRODUCTION
Günther Schlee

Approaches to 'identity' and 'hatred': some Somali and other perspectives

The political map of the world in the 1990s has undergone changes which in their speed and extent may be comparable to the amount of re-colouring and re-naming necessitated by the acceleration phase of decolonisation in the 60s but to no other phase of human history. Even the establishment of the post World War II order affected smaller areas and the fall of the Roman Empire was slower. Eastern Europe, South Eastern Europe, parts of the Middle East and adjoining North-East Africa show the features of political/territorial change: contested areas, the rise of new states or the reshaping of the constituent parts of states. If one shades these areas on a map one can see a wide belt of instability among the hitherto accepted states stretching from one end of the Old World to the other.

One of the basic ideas of the 'nation' state is that a group based on common ethnicity (no matter how much ideological effort is required to construct it), defined by an open list of criteria (which tend to comprise historical, linguistic or other cultural features in complex combinations) should be able to claim a common territory. In the most developed parts of the world this idea has once again already lost some of its importance through the transfer of competences from the national to supra-national (e. g. EU) and infra-national levels (although the nation state remains the basic structure and the point of reference by which the other levels are defined). On the margins of Europe and in other parts of the Old World it is, however, celebrating gruesome triumphs right now.

Those empires which survived the First World War, namely the Russian Empire in the shape of the Soviet Union and Ethiopia, are now disintegrating along 'ethnic' lines, while fragments of those empires which did not survive that war (namely the Habsburg and Ottoman ones) are now undergoing processes of further fragmentation. Besides bloody un-mixing (Bosnia) these can take the form of relatively peaceful separations (Czech and Slovak republics). Alongside these fragmentation processes one can observe the formation of supra-ethnic units, some of which take ethnicities as their constituent units (various forms of ethnic federalism, sometimes as a line of retreat of the old central powers) or are reminiscent of political units of earlier periods (if one thinks of the Black Sea Conference which comprises an area so strangely reminiscent of the Ottoman Empire). Turanian, Islamic and other ideas provide similar supra-ethnic and supra-national identifications and some people even revive the 'Occident' by claiming that it is at stake in Croatia.

This *tour d'horizon* describes part of the political context in which 'identity' and 'hatred' are placed today and much of the destruction we see on our television screens stems from this context. A collection of papers on 'Imagined differences: hatred and the construction of identity' will therefore be judged by what it has to contribute to the analysis of these world issues. We accept this challenge. Our aim is to contribute to the understanding of the formations of social identities and of the articulations - hostile and other - of these identities with each other. The papers, however, have not been selected to refer to the geographical regions outlined above as problem areas. Ethnicity and related forms of identity do not lend themselves particularly well to study in those periods when they express themselves through physical violence. The authors therefore have taken their case studies from those areas which they know best, irrespective of whether they are at the moment politically 'hot' or not (some of them are). Spreading from Morocco to Indonesia, these case studies provide many variations on the theme and also some re-current elements which will be relevant for a theory of conflicting identities.

In this introductory chapter I shall try to outline our shared concepts and give an overview of how the papers complement each other and which parts of them offer themselves to mutual comparisons. This is not unusual for an introduction. I depart, however, from the general pattern from time to time by clarifying a point through reference to examples from my own research area, which is North-East Africa.

The theme of the book was proposed by a British contributor[1] and this may not be coincidental. Particularly in British anthropology there has been some interest in the dark side of human life before. A conference at St. Andrew's in 1985 resulted in the volume *The Anthropology of Violence,* edited by David Riches. Even earlier there was a series of seminars at SOAS which resulted in Parkin's reader *The Anthropology of Evil.* A book with 'hatred' in its title seems to fit this pattern.

If we look at the history of British social anthropology, not only is this interest understandable but also the fact that it comes up as a wave, at a certain point of time with a massing effect. Early anthropology in Britain was interested in functional wholes, balanced systems, and the rationality of practices which appear strange at first glance (something we always find if we look for it long enough and which disqualifies us as ethnographers if we don't find it; in other words: something which is empirically void). We can summarise this preoccupation of the early British anthropologists as the quest for harmony, regulation, the pragmatic and practical aspects of strange customs and as the quest for things which are good and sound and reasonable. This may be sickening in the long run. We therefore understand the reorientation of our British colleagues towards evil, violence, hatred and everything dysfunctional.

But there are other possible explanations for why social scientists, British or not, once a beginning is made, are fascinated by topics like 'violence', 'evil' and 'ha-

---

[1] The person in question is Mark Hobart to whom I also owe several ideas expressed in this introduction. Philip Quarles van Ufford has also given valuable hints. H.-D. Evers has gone through an earlier version of this introduction.

tred' and join the debate. Western bourgeois academics are unused to violence. All the aggression they can muster is just enough for tawdry little exchanges in journals. In Germany there was a time when one could recognise an academic by the scars on his face from sword duels, but these days are fortunately gone. (Even then these duels were highly ritualised and involved little actual danger, but they did require a different attitude to one's body and an ideology of toughness, especially since the student culture associated with them also involved, apart from militarism, teutomania and loud songs, competitive drinking on a level which was certainly more harmful than the duels.) Today's academics are more hesitant in the expression of their own violent feelings and they are rather helpless when confronted by the violence of others - even at a safe distance, through the media. It is easy to estimate that in Africa and some other parts of the 'developing world' more development efforts have been rendered ineffective by violence - shelling, massacres, displacement of populations - than by any other single factor. Nevertheless, development studies continue to be preoccupied almost exclusively with economic issues and hardly discuss war. The term 'violence' has been incorporated into this development discourse, but with reference to 'structural violence' (*strukturelle Gewalt*), meaning economic relationships which are geared to harm certain groups and their chances of survival in a regular and continuous form. This is a very legitimate concern, but it surrounds direct physical violence, i.e. violence per se, violence unadorned by adjectives which explain a metaphorical use, by a layer of pseudoviolence, special-type violence, violence which requires an explanation for why it is violence. This layer seems to work like an insulator, it enables us to deal with violence in the form of violence clad in adjectives rather than with naked violence. Dealing with the latter is almost like a taboo - like hard pornography, something most academics would not watch or not admit to watching, although in our societies in general there seems to be a market for video tapes which combine just these two elements - physical violence and hard pornography. If violence or hatred are addressed in academic discourse at all, people hasten to morally condemn them. No doubt that this condemnation is justified. But does it help our analytical needs? If we want to find out how, why and under which circumstances normal people, who are husbands, fathers, sons and lovers in other contexts, commit genocide, massacres and gang rapes, there is a little we can learn from hearing for the umpteenth time that all these things are very bad. If anything, this wrapping in moralism reduces our direct analytical grip on the matter. Another way of pushing violence away from us is by treating it as abnormal or pathological. This helps us identify it as belonging to another department - let the psychiatrists deal with it. Or we push it even beyond the limits of what we define as human: we declare it to be animality, beastly actions etc. This is plainly contrafactual since no other primate species has developed violence against its own kind to the same level as humans (chimpanzees sometimes come close to it), but again, it helps us to push the phenomenon away from us. Making violence a taboo theme does not reduce its fascination, on the contrary, it increases it. Somehow we keep on managing to come back to the topic.[2]

'Imagination' and 'Construction'

The other concepts in the title also have their own history or at least an ancestry of related ideas. Imagined differences, of course, evoke the title of Anderson's work on the nation state, namely *Imagined Communities.* Mark Hobart in his contribution establishes this connection quite explicitly. Differences, of course, are a key concept in modern (or, some would say: postmodern) philosophy, and *la differance*, spelled with an *a*, has become the collective symbol and sign of recognition (i. e. the boundary or 'differance' marker) of the group of philosophers around Jacques Derrida. In the anthropological context a rather common and closely related concept is that of the *boundary* - the reader *Symbolising boundaries,* edited by Anthony Cohen (1986) which deals with the establishment of differences between the subethnicities of Britain, may serve here as an example for this line of thought, together with Cohen's book *The social construction of community* which takes up a concept also found in the title of this volume: 'construction' which, in turn, evokes various derivates from constructivism to deconstructionism all of which are reactions to structuralism and thus are part of poststructuralist lines of reasoning. (If there are too many derivates of the Latin verb *struere* in the last paragraph, it is not our fault but characteristic of the debates we summarise here.)

The recent wave of 'imagination' in book titles can be explained by the pleasure derived from the, mostly implicit, play with two meanings of the term. Constructionism comes in here, too, because of one of these meanings being more 'realist', the other more 'constructionist'.

'Imagination' with a realist ring to it occurs in phrases like "I imagined you to be taller than you are", which might be uttered by someone who meets for the first time a famous person he has so far only read about. The person in question is real enough; he or she had only been associated with a putative characteristic which is now rectified. 'To imagine' here means to form an image of something which exists independently of this process of imagination and which is not imagined to be, but only imagined to be a certain way.

---

[2] Armon-Jones (1986: 71) discusses "sinful emotions". She raises the question whether "hatred, envy and jealousy" are "by definition undesirable". She then enumerates "cases in which 'hatred' can be identified as a response which is deemed by members of a society to be warranted in certain contexts". Her examples, Nazis, Apartheid, American anticommunism, are rather remote in time or space from people living today. Middle class citizens of industrialised countries are not required or encouraged to mobilise their capacity to hate on a day-to-day basis. It remains a clearly undesirable or even sinful emotion.

Imagination in creative writing is something different; it has a more constructionist ring. Here whatever is imagined has not existed before it was imagined; the
process of imagination has created the entity in question.

Imagination in sociological contexts oscillates between these two meanings,
and this may be the cause for the fascination of this term and its undoubted popularity
in book titles. Objects of collective imagination may or may not have existed before,
or they may not have existed in the same shapes defined by the same features and
marked by the same symbols.

Entire subcontinents can be imagined in this ambiguous way. There are two
books entitled *Imagining India*, one by Richard Cronin (1989), the other by Ron Inden
(1990). The first is an analysis of the images of India in creative writing, a book which
must make delightful reading especially for all those who, unlike myself, have been
brought up in a British or anglophone literary tradition and are more familiar with the
works discussed. The other one, by Inden, is of more direct concern here.

'Imagination' for Inden is about the social construction of reality and how it
works in practice. In the case of India it was initially philosophers (Hegel, Mill, Marx),
then successive generations of scholars and civil servants, who imagined an India they
partly made to exist.[3] Inden raises the Gramscian question of the position of intellectuals in imagining differences. This raises questions of who defines the hegemonic discourse and how. We shall come back to Inden and the role of intellectuals.

For Africa the role of administrators, anthropologists and missionaries in creating or reshaping ethnic units was often stressed in the 1980s, although the fact that the
tribes or ethnic groups of Africa were often projections of European ideas resulting in
administrative creations, has been noted since the 1930s (Rattray 1932 cited by Elwert
1989: 444), i. e., a part of the colonial system was aware of what it was doing.

In some cases, units that were to become the 'ethnic groups' of the colonial and
postcolonial times, could not be described as ethnic groups at all in pre-colonial days.
There were no ethnic groups in certain areas, a finding which may be hard to swallow
for 'ethnologists' (as anthropologists are often called in continental Europe) who assume all of mankind is subdivided into 'ethnic groups' and this category therefore is
suitable as a universal definition of the unit of study. The absence of 'ethnic groups' in
such cases was not due to the absence of the raw materials from which 'ethnic' definitions are made. Of course, people there had culture, including language, history etc.,
concepts and attitudes about 'we' and 'other' and all the other things ethnicity is made
of. Rather it was due to the fact that any entities which could be defined by such 'ethnic' criteria lacked the characteristics of 'groups', that there were no 'ethnic groups' in

---

[3] Imagination in this sense of social construction also plays a role in yet another book on India, *Lions
of the Punjab*, by Fox (1985). Fox shows how Singh identity as a 'warrior race' developed in an inter-
active process with the colonial power.

many pre-colonial settings. People there might consider the village upstream and the village downstream as consisting of people who are 'the same' as themselves and so might those inhabitants of the village upstream and the village downstream: they also include the people adjacent to t h e m in their definition of Self. We thus have a continuum rather than a group, boundaries shifting with the point of reference rather than shared boundaries (cf. Elwert 1989: 445).

A point I wish to dwell on for a couple of paragraphs is the relationship between *difference* and *identity*. I do so because I have found that for some people the term *identity* evokes a whole range of philosophical and psychological ideas, it has an existentialist and essentialist ring to it, an association with authenticity and some form of deeper truth. People are said to '*search for identity*' as if identity was there somewhere before the search. I would be glad if we could all agree to relegate these ideas to the same drawer as *négritude* and *africanité* and *true self* mystifications. They may be part of what we want to analyse but they are not suitable as analytical tools themselves.

However, I want to defend the use of the term identity and I have made frequent use of it myself (Schlee 1989) but in a purely sociological sense, referring to the social ego, the surface, or the interface with others. And, used in this sense, without any vain search for deeper meanings, the relationship between *difference* or *boundary* on the one hand and *identity* on the other, becomes simple: it is a complementary one. *Identity* refers to the *absence of a difference*, the absence of a difference along any of the dimensions which are used to define social categories: religious affiliation or ethnicity which in itself is not defined by a finite set of criteria but a set which may comprise language, culture (i. e. symbolically loaded elements of sub-systems of culture other than language) and references to a common history. If such identifying features differ, we speak of a difference - or a social boundary - if they do not differ, we speak of an identity. Different criteria, obviously, lead to different identities which may overlap and offer possibilities of optional identification in different situations such as constraint by the forces of the market and the state.

In the present volume 'identity' is used in this relatively simple sense, dispensing with much of its essentialist, moralist or ideological load which is not useful for analytical purposes. Identities are remoulded by individuals who want to make sense of their situation or - as people often live happily or otherwise for extended periods of time in situations which do not make much sense - simply to fit the needs of their economic or social advancement. They are remoulded also by political movements that define different aggregates of people as the target of their policies, or who instrumentalise identifications for the organisation of support. There is no end to the caleidoscopic recombinations of features in this game of identity and difference. In the Horn of Africa – in one of the fragmentation processes characteristic of the 1990s – imperial ideas and wider nationalisms have given way to smaller ones. Two new "nations", Eritrea and Somaliland, derive their boundaries from those of former colonies. Within

Ethiopia ethnic states have replaced former ethnically mixed provinces. Linguistic and cultural similarities and differences are carefully traced to raise "ethnic" consciousness (Schlee 2000 b). Inevitably 'ancient histories' grow out of the newly constructed ethnic identities: they grow their roots. 'Roots' grow from the present into the past. (Also in terms of botany the metaphor that something springs or stems or derives from a root is wrong. A plant does not grow out of the root. Both the root and the stem grow out of the seed, one downwards, one upwards. In a similar fashion it is the present societies which grow their roots by describing their links to real and faked, often quite plausible but selected past events.)

Ironically the only 'real' (i. e. linguistic and culturally homogeneous) nation state of the area, Somalia, is the one which has split into the smallest fragments, thus belying assumptions about a causal link between heterogeneity/homogeneity and the likeliness of successful nationbuilding or the prospects of peace and unity. Culture is a raw material of the politics of identity and difference, not more. It can be taken up for use or be disregarded.

The relationship between political ideology, culture and history can be - so it would appear from this regional example - visualised as a supermarket. History fills the shelves with its products: culture in all its forms and shapes, and ideology selects from these shelves whatever it needs. Occasionally, however, ideology does not content itself with what it is offered and projects its own products back into history, it populates pre-national periods with "nations" and other objects of all sorts of invented traditions.

The arbitrariness of such processes, the multiple and mutually contradictory forms the definitions of ethnic groups and nations can take, is reflected by the adjective 'imagined' in the title. Minimal variation in cultural attributes may become symbolically loaded and mark a difference, while rather heterogenous elements may be combined in one entity by stressing what they have in common. It appears indeed that much room is left to the imagination in this process. The products of this imagination, however, are often not lofty dreams that fade after some time but collective identities with their own historical dynamics and with expressions in real life, many of them violent. They may be dreamt up but they are difficult to dream away again.

The example of North-East Africa suggests that the features which mark identities can be arranged as lists of dichotomies like modernist/traditionalist, coloniser/colonised or as dimensions which - in a given setting - only acquire a limited number of values like:

Religion: Muslim, Christian, "traditionalist"

or

Ethnicity: Oromo, Somali, Afar.

Social identities appear (also in the local discourse under study, not only in the language of the analyst) to be marked by a structural matrix in which such features are combined in various ways, mutually exclusive or cross-cutting.

The present volume shows that static pictures of this type (useful as they may be in some contexts) do not reflect the complexities of the social world drawn by Quarles. Some national affiliations are conceived by some people as being mutually exclusive with certain religious ones. In the mind of many Polish people on cannot be a real Pole if one is Protestant or Orthodox Christian, not to mention being Muslim. To be Polish one has to be Roman Catholic (Hann 1996, 1998). Kurdish identity, on the other hand, combines easily with being Sunni or Alevi Muslim or Yezidi, and there are also Alevites and Sunnites among the Turks. There is no law which requires Poles to be Roman Catholic and the de-facto religions and ethnic plurality of Anatolia is hardly recognised by the Turkish state, but the two cases allow us to distinguish two forms of relationships between identities: congruent versus cross-cutting. Polish people and Catholicism in the regional context are congruent. Ideally, Poles are Roman Catholics, the relevant others are not: Prussians tend to be Protestant, Russians to be Orthodox, Ukrainians to be Orthodox or Eastern Catholic. Turkish or Kurdish ethnicity, on the other hand, cross-cuts with Alevi or Sunni Islam. In the first case religion deepens ethnic divides, in the second case it bridges them. In a mixed setting (like among labour migrants and their descendants in Germany) two people of Anatolian origin can stress their identity or their differences. If one of them is a Kurd (which he often does not need to declare anyhow) and the other one a Turk, they can still decide to stress shared religious affiliation rather than ethnic difference. Cross-cutting dimensions of identity provide matrixes of options of identification (Firat 1997). In this example one dimension of identity would be ethnicity with the values Kurdish and Turkish, the other one would be religion with the values Alevi and Sunni.

In northern Kenya the ethnic dimension intersects with clanship in a similar way. As historical processes which have led to the emergence of the present ethnic groups have affected parts of clans in different ways, we here find the same clans in ethnic groups which are clearly distinguished by language and other aspects of culture. In their interaction with strangers, actors therefore often have the option of either stressing ethnic difference or relatedness by clan-links. People who are knowledgeable about such links can seek refuge with clan brothers in other ethnic groups during times of drought or war. This does not imply an immediate change in ethnic identity – they might still be referred to as clan-brothers from another ethnic group – but in the course of a couple of generations such an ethnic re-affiliation might take place. Thus clan-equivalences might serve as bridges between ethnic identities.

In his essay in this volume, Georg Elwert deals with such changes of identity systematically. He distinguishes two types of switching: situational changes in identification by individuals versus the identity in question itself changing the dimension of identity to which it belongs: for example a national identity being re-interpreted in religious terms or a religion being ethnicised.

The papers by Bellér-Hann and Quarles van Ufford have been grouped together under the heading "Unravelling conflicting emotions" because they both deal with emotions associated with social identifications, ranging from local theories of temperamental dispositions, ethnicised gender roles, conflicting feelings of pride and shame to despair and social isolation.

Quarles van Ufford in his paper on *Murder in the cathedral: the death of a high official in an Indonesian church* gives a moving account of the consequences of the betrayal of trust in a relationship phrased in pseudo-kinship terms between Indonesians and Dutch missionaries. It shows how emotions become too strong to be contained through etiquette and lead to accusations of "murder" and to the social "suicide" of the accuser, both to be understood as psychological reality and sociological metaphor, because no blood is actually shed in the whole chain of events described.

The next section, 'Hatred and the boundaries of social identities' is not free of emotions. Some of them can, as Hobart shows, dissolve into laughter. This appears to be one way of dealing with ambiguities and multi-layered identities. In his paper 'Lances greased with pork fat: imagining difference in Bali" Hobart describes facets of Balinese identity emerging from "the activities of people, often grouped as 'complex agents', in public." Hobart's analysis of the theatre play describes the reproduction of the social universe and the self-localisation in it as taking place on more then one level of meaning. It is a play in more than one sense. Balinese Hindus assert their difference from the Muslim Indonesian majority by referring to their own community by an Indonesian Muslim legal term of Arabic derivation[4], *umat*, thereby implying their claim to the status provided to an *umat* by the Indonesian constitution: an assertion of a diffrence and a claim to inclusion in a wider whole at the same time, expressed by a switch of code, by a loan from a language of wider currency. In a similar way, by mimicking the language of their prototypical representatives, modernity, bureaucracy, aristocracy and all other social identities into which one has to fit situationally or with which one is confronted by others, are made fun of or played with in various shades of irony. Nothing is too close to the self not to merit from time to time a more distanced view (Hobart this volume).

While Bellér-Hann deals with a Muslim minority in an agnositic, formerly even aggressively atheist state, and Hobart with a Hindu island amid dominant Muslim neighbours, Petra Weyland's contribution *Religion, modernity, tradition and the construction of difference inside an Egyptian village* is set in a locality marked by reli-

---

[4] In the language of the Oromo, a social identity which has often been described as in opposition to Islam, the words for 'religion', 'faith' and 'law' are all derived from Arab-Islamic terminology. The dominant alien culture may be rejected, but in the very process of asserting one's own culture as equal to it, its categories are accepted as frames of reference. (Schlee and Shongolo 1995, Schlee 1994 a)

gious residential segregation, with Christians and Muslims living in separate neighbourhoods within the same village, the Muslims being the majority in the national society and having the power in the state, but the Christians feeling second to nobody. In her analysis Petra Weyland stresses the centrality of religion for social identification. There are other relevant differences cutting across the social universe of the village, among them the class distinction between absentee landowners and poor peasants who, Muslims and Christians alike, have to eke out a meagre living. When confronted with the researcher (who is Western, educated, female, urban... in addition to an infinite number of other features which might have been regarded as relevant in some context) the village women did not respond by communicating their own contrasting or corresponding identities as Arab, female, rural etc., but they focussed to a degree which at first must have been surprising to Weyland on their shared Christian religion.

What follows is a delightful account of how the researcher was instrumentalised by Christian village women to enhance their own cultural prestige and how she gradually discovered which symbols she conveyed to them. An Arab-style dress which she took as a tribute to her inclination to "go native" was perceived as the epitome of modernity by her environment - it was imported and synthetic! Unknowingly, by being incorporated by the Christians into their ranks and by being "modern" she reinforced the identification of Christianity with modernism and Islam with backwardness.

Another point which struck Weyland is that religion - being the primary social identifier - is hardly ever discussed in religious terms. Religious beliefs or the practices based thereon were not a prominent topic of discussion, although feelings about religious affiliation were intense, amounting in some cases to physical disgust.

We know this phenomenon from other parts of the world where religion is used as a social identifier, e.g. from Bosnia where religiously defined groups with or without equivalent ethnonyms (Muslims, Catholics = Croats, Orthodox = Serbs) have even waged a war of genocidal dimensions, although they have gone through long phases of atheist state ideology, may know very little about their respective religions and are definitely not restrained in their actions by the fear of God or other ideas rooted in religion. All this fits well with our above observation that social identity is something which concerns our surface, our interface with others, not any real or imagined "deeper" aspects of our personalities. If 'identity' is superficial in this sense, so are the 'differences' which constitute it.

Georg Haneke in his contribution, *The Multidimensionality of Oromo identity*, examines the various markers which have been used to circumscribe this contested and highly politicised ethnic identity. The Oromo, in the sense of the speakers of a cluster of dialects, are the largest linguistic group in Ethiopia. In fact, they may be one of the largest in Africa, at least as far as African languages are concerned (thus excluding the colonial languages and Arabic) and in terms of numbers of first language speakers. This puts languages spoken by large numbers of speakers as a second language like

Hausa and Swahili) at a disadvantage. Yet Haneke discusses critically the degree of linguistic unity of the Oromo and asks the question, how good an indicator linguistic unity is for political unity or we-group feeling anyhow. It might be a rather poor one.

He then goes through a list of other elements of 'national unity' as constructed by Oromo nationalists like shared history and the common possession of a *gada* system and finds the situation much more heterogeneous, multi-layered and complex than what is depicted by the proponents of an 'Oromo' identity as the basis of a claim to statehood.

Given the numerical importance of the Oromo and the fact that not all of them were the victims of 'Abyssinian' imperialism, it is surprising how uniformly Oromo nationalists try to derive mobilising power from depicting the Oromo as victims.

Even fairly large and powerful groups sometimes seem to engage in competition for minority status and status in the hierarchies of victims ('Opferhierarchien'): the more disadvantaged, the better. Shongolo and I (work in progress) have recently analyzed a document in which the Boran Oromo, for centuries the most powerful group in northern Kenya, claim "indigenous" status for themselves, thus equating their status to that of the decimated and oppressed non-white minorities of European settler colonies like the Americas Siberia and Australia. This was the setting in which the discourse on the rights of indigenous people has developed, not black Africa where everyone or no-one is 'indigenous'.

A similar point has recently been made by an Oromo writer who takes up the phrase of the Oromo being a "sociological minority", i. e. a group which holds a minority position and /or (?) has adopted for itself a minority discourse, although it is the largest single ethnic group of Ethiopia. Gudina Merera (1994: 915, 925) further stresses that by no means all Oromo have had a disadvantageous position in Ethiopia at all times. Northern Oromo were part of the imperial elite and some of their family histories were intertwined with that of the emperor. History provides examples of Oromo in strong positions and of exploited and humiliated Oromo. Modern Oromo nationalists have chosen the weak Oromo and not the strong Oromo as the basis of their discourse on minority rights and separation. Merera suggests taking part in the central system, and confidence in their own strength, numerical and otherwise, as the more advantageous strategy for the Oromo and Ethiopia as a whole.

In his paper *Writing the Nation*[5] Thomas Rieger analyses how in the prewar Indonesian novel nationalism emerges out of internationalist discourses like socialism and Islamism. He also discusses the roles ethnicity plays in it - Chinese, Malay and as a negatively loaded, contrasting background: Dutch. Ethnicity also competes with

---

[5] The title is borrowed from Bhabha. For a critical note on Bhabha, following Norval, cf. Kaiser, this volume.

'class' as a guiding concept in giving literary expression to what was going on during this period in the future Indonesia.

The Gramscian question of whose definitions become hegemonic, which Inden asks in the Indian context, can be posed here again. Inden finds that the texts "that can be dubbed 'hegemonic' in a Gramscian sense" are those which "scholars and their administrative doubles in the world have used to build and maintain hegemony of their discourses over the other knowledge" (1990: 42), without implying that these discourses are "unitary and imposed by force by a ruler sharply opposed to the completely passive population of the ruled" (Inden 1990: 36). In the Indonesian case Rieger finds that in the phase of emerging nationalism political organisations had a "very limited numerical strength", that the circulation of their papers was limited and their meetings restricted and that novels therefore played a major role in defining the nation. We can thus ascribe a hegemonical role in the Gamscian sense to literature at least as far as Indonesia in the 1930s and 1940s is concerned.

In the case of competing identifications or competing hierarchies of identities (is one first a Muslim, then an Arab and then an Egyptian or is one first an Egyptian and then an Arab --- - rather than a Nubian - and then a Muslim - rather than a Copt - in addition to being a teacher or a nurse ...?), it is an interesting question which hierarchy of identifying features wins in which context, a) in historical processes where the primary allegiance of large aggregates of people may shift from one identity to another, b) in the individual context where one of several identities tends to be put forward situationally, depending on opportunity (it is better to be an Amerindian when there is compensation for native land rigths) or simply on situational context (an American would identify himself as such in Europe but not in America).[6]

---

[6] Cf. Roosens 1989, Eriksen 1993 for a general discussion of such matters, Schlee 1989 for the historical and situational interplay of clanship and ethnicity in northern Kenya.

This paragraph mentions hierarchies of identities. A closer analysis would have to distinguish at least two types of such hierarchies: 1. hierarchies of different criteria for identification, say linguistic versus religious ones. Historically, such hierarchies (= order of application of criteria) may be inverted. In a religious era one has religious classifications (Christians versus Muslims) first, linguistic classifications second (Medievial Christianity divided into still very vaguely bounded linguistically defined proto-nations). In a nationalist age the order is the other way around: nations comprise religious communities in different proportions. Of course, such order of application also depends on situational perspectives. From a church perspective, or the one of the Lutheran World Council, one might perceive a wide community of Lutherans made up of Germans, Swedes and Americans. The above example about 'Muslim' versus 'Arab' etc. is of this kind.

The other example about the American who would identify himself as such in Europe but not in America, where he would specify that he is from Iowa, is of the 'hierarchy of identities' type 2. It corresponds to Eriksen's 'segmentary identities': "The segmentary model may enable us to describe the social identities of a person as, say, citizen of the world, African, Kenyan, Kikuyu, member of clan X, member of lineage A" (1995: 259). Although these identities are well, strictly speaking, defined by qualitatively different criteria: geographical (world, Africa), colonial boundaries culturalised by postcolonial 'nation building' (Kenya), language or dialect, origin myth and administrative classification as 'tribe' (Kikuyu) or descent (clan, lineage), the basic idea in this juxtaposition of identities is both

While in Bellér-Hann's paper 'ethnicity' plays a primary role, in Weyland's the focus is on 'religious' distinctions which are, however, described as linked to a class difference, and in Rieger's 'nationalism' prevails, the following contribution by Venema puts the emphasis on 'class'.

In his paper about Moroccan politics, ethnicity definitely appears as a secondary phenomenon. The French in their definitions and their administrative practice singled out the Berbers as a separate entity and ascribed a customary law to them which was not based on the *shariᶜa,* although in reality Islam and its law were as firmly rooted among the Berbers as among the neighbouring Arabs.[7] Ethnicity was used as a barrier against nationalism, but as history shows, unsuccessfully in the end. After independence, the monarchy coopted Berber elites and this enforced divisions also within the Berbers, because such policies created a priviledged class without profiting the rural poor. Today the young elements of the opposition identify themselves as lower class and are no longer interested in Arab or Berber origins.

The difference between these perspectives is considerable, and the question to which extent these differences are *in re* and to which extent due to the theoretical persuasions of the authors needs to be allowed. If we look beyond this collection of papers, our confusion is not alleviated. Roosens (1989) describes ethnicity as a way of

---

for the Kenyans who classify themselves in this way and for Eriksen who quite correctly cites this example - not one of difference in quality but of one of scale: all these identities are similar enough to be perceived as smaller ones being comprised in larger ones of basically the same kind (the idea of a segmentary lineage system from which Eriksen derives the term). One may also speak of degrees of inclusivity: first order units including second order units, second order ones comprising those of the third order etc.

A key variable for the success of larger scale identifications is the prosperity of the organisational forms to which they demand loyalty: nation states need to reward the efforts people invest in education, in learning the national language by job opportunities. If they cannot reward efforts at integration, they tend to desintegrate into smaller units associated with more particularistic identifications (Gellner 1981, 1983).

[7] Islam and its outer signs have become strong symbols of group identification in the Morrocan context. Arabs and Saharaouis see local Berbers as barbarians who produce daughters to become prostitutes. They are said not to give title to the poor immigrants, on the contrary, even to exploit them. This provokes the wrath of God so that it rains less than before.

The Berbers despise the Arab immigrants. When addressed by one a Berber might respond *raa aarabe* - '[go an] see an Arab', turning his back on him. Berbers see Arabs as 'occupiers' and the only Arabs they respect are the *chorfa* families of noble descent who often act as peacemakers.

Physical characteristics -real or imagined- are also used to express 'racism'. Saharaouis might be called *isnegh,* 'black slave', although one often relies on them for leading the prayers because of their firmer grip on Islamic knowledge. Hospitality is denied to members of other ethnic groups because of their 'intense smell'!

Intergroup relationships become most tense when immigrants become better off than the autochthonous population. A too successful immigrant will be harassed by denying him water, pasture and other resources: 'on ne lui laisse pas le temps de respirer'. (Venema, pers. comm.)

For group relationships in neighbouring Mauritania cf. Ruf 1994, 1999. For the continued existence of the 'Berber' dimension in Algerian politics cf. Kaiser, this volume.

disguising class conflict while Dench (1986) sees certain forms of class struggle as a disguise for an ethnically based movement. The reason given for the disguise is in both cases the same: 'respectability'. But why is 'ethnicity' more 'respectable' than class in one case, so that class creeps into the guise of ethnicity, while in the other case the relationship is the other way round? Is it a difference between America and Britain? Or is the difference between two theoretical persuasions?

Roosens explains, with reference to the USA and Canada, that in the 1930s "there were few advantages...to define oneself visibly as a member of the Sicilian or Polish immigrant community". In "the current North American situation", however, ethnicity has brought strategic advantages. Politicians are prevented from refusing the demands put forward by ethnic groups for fear of "being branded as racists". The ethnic movement seems to have a moral advantage. "Militant ethnic groups can thus be considered pressure groups with a noble face".(Roosens 1989: 14)

In this they differ from social classes. 'Class' provides less attractive identifications. "If one identifies oneself as a member of a lower class, one places oneself at the bottom of the social ladder. The class division is vertical and is thus a hierarchical division of groups of people; the ethnic division is horizontal, and it creates equivalences rather than hierarchies" (Roosens 1989: 14).

In England, at least from Dench's perspective, things are the other way round. Here ethnic movements try to pass as elements of a class struggle, the 'class' discourse seems to be more respectable than the 'ethnic' one. This seems to have to do with the fact that socialism has firmer roots in Britain[8], and "socialists see class as the paramount dimension of consciousness, and ethnicity as dependent and ultimately dispensable". "Socialists old and new are adept at sniffing out the class interests behind ethnicity" and thus discredit it as swindling with labels Dench 1986: 26).

To illustrate the dominance of 'class' values, Dench takes the "Welsh as an example. Until it revived during the middle of this century, Welsh political nationalism had been firmly subsumed to class identity for several generations. [...] As class politics developed in Britain, the Welsh joined in centralised oppositional movements, seeing them as the best available means of securing benefits for Wales. [...] As we have already seen, the language of class is morally superior to that of ethnicity and communalism, as it does not ascribe identity and impose exclusive loyalties to group members". Recently, Welsh protest has become more explicitly nationalistic to fight against regional imbalances, but in this process the Welsh run the risk of being accused as

---

[8] Dench himself suggests similar terms for the explanation of the differences between his perspective and the current views from America, which he terms instrumentalist because they perceive ethnicity "as a framework for a rational and goal oriented mobilisation of group consciousness" (1986: 25). These have underrated "the continuing vitality of universalist [like: class] values and their role in supporting ethnic lobbies". This is partly explained by the fact that "most instrumentalist theories are American, and class has yet to make a significant entry into American politics" (1986: 28).

"inward-looking separatists and historical throw-backs. [...] If anyone tries to accuse the Welsh of these vices, there will be many Welshmen and observers of Welsh ways who can respond that 'really', at root, Welsh solidarity is that of an oppressed class 'which may have acquired a regional quality in response to the Englishness of the capitalist class'. This ability to take cover under a protective class mantle is most important. Without it Welsh nationalism would have had a much tougher job in avoiding portrayal as a negative and retrograde phenomenon" (Dench 1986: 27f).

The relationship between socialism and ethno-nationalism is a complicated one because of the relationships of combination and overlay between the two ideologies. The Soviet Union depicted itself as a country ruled by the proletarian class but it gave itself the regional organisation of a federation of republics based on 'nationalities', thus preserving and institutionalising the forces that made it fall apart.

Similarly the present collection of papers, from Indonesia to Ireland, can be read as so many cases of interaction between 'class' and 'ethnicity', including colonialists from outside who had a 'class' and 'ethnic' identity themselves and had a key role in defining the identities of others.

If 'class' and 'ethnicity' are masks which one puts on depending on which form of identification is more respectable in a given political context, the question emerges how to explain the apparently deep feelings, including 'hatred', which attach themselves to it.

Similar questions can be put with regard to religion. If the Welsh explain that their struggle is not 'really' about ethnicity, but about class, similar statements are made in Ulster about religion. It is said to be phrased in religious terms but to be 'really' about class. In Algeria no one relegates the conflict between Islamism and secularism to the symbolic level. Essentialist readings of each other's positions seem to be at the core of the power struggle. In Sri Lanka, depicting the conflict exclusively along the ethnic divide Tamil/Sinhalese would obscure the view of intra-ethnic and criminal violence and the self-perpetuating potential of violence which needs no reason other than prior violence. In Somalia, both the ethnic and the religious explanation fail, because the rival factions are all Somali, more often than not speak the same dialect or closely related dialects, and are all Muslims[9]. 'Clans' is the label most widely used to desribe the social units in conflict over the appropriation of the State or what is left of it, but we shall see that this inadequately describes the pattern of interclan-alliances of sub-clans and the strategies of war-lords who, to a degree, are caught in the logic of clan identities and differences without being representatives of clans. In all these cases what the conflict seems to be about at first glance differs from what it is about upon closer inspection.

---

[9] There are ethnic minorities and strong dialect differentiation in Southern Somalia, but these did not play a role in the initial stages of the conflict.

These cases, Algeria, Sri Lanka, Northern Ireland, and Somalia, form the empirical background to the following section "The politics of difference: violence, shifting boundaries, and the fragmentation of states".

In her contribution, *Exclusivist rhetorics – the constitution of political identities in present-day Algeria,* Birgit Mara Kaiser takes current globalisation theories which associate increased contacts, easier communication and shortened distances with tolerance of plurality, as a contrasting background to her description of exclusivist identification strategies which draw mortal dividing lines within Algerian society

The partisans in the conflict compete to be true Algerians and depict each other as being under foreign influence: the secularists are said to be under French influence and, in their turn, accuse the Islamic *intégristes* to be under Saudi, Egyptian or Sudanese influence. Another element of mutual description is terrorism. The violence of the other side is depicted as terrorism, one's own violence as resistance to terrorism.

Islamists proclaiming the *jihad* against fellow Muslims face the same problem as Osman dan Fodio did at the beginning of the 19th century in what was to become Nigeria and which many Muslim rulers who base their legitimacy on their purer form of Islamic creed and practice have faced since. According to Islamic law, *jihad* is justified against non-Muslims who oppress Islam and prevent Muslims from practicing their religion. To be able to direct *jihad* against rival Muslims, this rule needed to be circumvented. *Jihad* leaders like Osman dan Fodio or Hajj ᶜUmar Tall further west along the Senegal and the Niger accused their opponents of maintaining alliances with non-Muslims and therefore placed themselves outside the Muslim Gold. Pointing to outside links to discredit one's opponents, as it is done in modern Algeria, thus has a long tradition in this type of discourse (Abun-Nasr 1965, Martin 1967)

We shall come back to this paper briefly below, in the context of a discussion of 'hatred'.

Sri Lanka (de Silva) and Somalia (Schlee) provide two contrasting examples. Whereas the conflict in Sri Lanka is primarily along an ethnic divide, Tamil vs. Sinhalese (although de Silva goes beyond this ethnic dimension and introduces some considerations which complicate the issue), in Somalia there are no ethnic differences between the warring factions. On the grounds of language and culture one would not be able to tell one from the other. One would have to ask them for their clan and political affiliation. The Somali case shows that the formation of violently opposed we-groups does not need much cultural substance. It can also do without religious divisions, linguistic differences or the historical baggage some other movements carry along.

For decades, pan-Somali ideologies and Somali irredentism have worried the neighbouring states and the Organisation of African Unity. Somali nationalists sought to unite the Djibouti and the ethnically Somali territories of Ethiopia and Kenya with Somalia. After the troubles of the 1990s no trace of this is left. Somalia itself has broken into fragments. Former British Somaliland has declared its independence within its colonial boundaries with as good reasons as the other African states which are almost all shaped by boundaries drawn by their colonisers. It has also shown itself capable of providing higher stability and lower levels of violence than the south. Another unilaterally declared state is 'Puntland' at the peak of the Horn. The south has been split into small domains of power by urban war-lords and rural clans. It remains to be seen whether the President elected by a Lybian sponsored conference of faction leaders in Djibouti in 2000 will be able to muster any real power.

Some of the political movements of the 19th and 20th centuries were governed by inclusive ideologies which embraced large parts of continents or the whole world. Think of pan-Slavism, Turanianism or the colonialist *mission civilisatrice*. (They might have had divisive effects however, if they cut across other large-scale identities like the imperial ones of the Habsburg and Ottoman multi-ethnic domains which comprised Slavs and Non-Slavs alike etc.). Nothing is left of this wide gesture of inclusion, of this conquering attitude. In what used to be the Ottoman empire we today find micro-states like Bosnia, Lebanon and Israel where ethno-religious factions are engaged in processes of further subdivision and violent dis-articulation from each other.

One needs to distinguish between inclusive and exclusive identity strategies. Both work, of course, at the same time. Elwert (this volume) mentions the Nazi concept of 'ethnic Germans' which includes minorities of Austrian and Dutch origin in countries with Slavic majorities but excluded Jews, even though Jewish elites had been the main bearers of German culture in Eastern Europe. On the inclusive side of this ideology one might have added that the wider "Nordic" and "Germanic" identification extended to Dutch and Scandinavians, attributing to the "purer" nordic Scandinavians an even higher position on the racial scale than to the Germans themselves.[10] The Nazis also had great appreciation for the English Germanic sister nation and were full of admiration for British imperialism with which they would have liked to divide the world up peacefully. Fortunately for the rest of the world this love was not reciprocated. Otherwise we would have got a racial hierarchy as the new world order and imperialism would have had a new lease of life.[11]

Irrespective of their occurrence in combination with exclusivist ideologies and irrespective of their divisive effects when they cross-cut other identifications, the identity discourses of empire builders and macro-nationalists (all "pan"-movements) need

---

[10] Sexual contacts with Scandinavian women were encouraged and their offspring highly valued. Such contacts with French women were tolerated while sexual relationships with Slavs or Jews were forbidden.

[11] As it happened, the second world war gave the death blow to three imperialisms: it prevented the German imperialism from reemerging and it sped up the dissolution of the British and French empires by decades at least.

strong inclusive elements.[12] Their strategies might be called expansive and the wars they fight are wars of conquest. Lands and the people that inhabit them are incorporated into one's own sphere of power. (Wars of extermination where the conquerors want to have the land alone are comparatively rare.) Even colonial subjects whom one would never fully acknowledge as equals are described as having some characteristics for which it is worth appropriating them. Some are even *romanticised* like the "warlike races" of the British empire. Never are they completely de-humanised or described in entirely negative terms. The worst which can happen to them is to be described as immature and requiring the care of a guardian for the time being.

In many of the cases described in this book, on the contrary, the exclusivist element has taken over completely. Kaiser describes how Algerians deny each other's Algerianness. In Yugoslavia a common identity has been dismantled. On the local level some groups have gained some territory. Such gains are often offset by losses elsewhere. On the whole, however, the wars have not been about conquest but about separating oneself from one's neighbours, getting a smaller, ethnically more homogeneous territory. At an early stage in Somalia the fight might have been for the presidency of the whole country, but in practice for years now war-lords and local leaders have been content with holding their own little separate territories. Political units and the offices associated with them are multiplied. It sometimes appears as if one of the causes of these widespread fragmentation processes is that there are too many "political elites" and too few countries for them to rule. Thus one forms xenophobic microunits. This may be called negative conquest (Schlee 2000 a, Simons 1999). A cause in which zero-sum games about diminishing state resources in the form of violent conflict has led to the fragmentation of a country is discussed at the very end of this volume in my own contribution about Somalia.

Mary Kenney in her paper about Northern Ireland quotes the typical comment by outsiders to the conflict, 'it's really not about religion at all, you know' (meaning: it's about economics in the sense of class conflict), but she avoids reducing the explanation of communal violence to the economic dimension. The economic interpretation, she suggests, is motivated by the persuasion that "religion is not supposed to be a major political issue at the close of the Twentieth century". But Kenney does not talk much about religion either. Rather than elaborating a hierarchy of identifications, she talks about the past that cannot be forgotten and is commemorated by communal marches with often violent outcome, of secret and semi-secret organisations and the process of socialisation into them: about the reenactment of history and the reproduction of differences and their violent expressions. More frequently than some other contributors she uses the term 'hatred' and with that we arrive at the last of the concepts of our title which this introduction tries to clarify.

---

[12] For a more theoretical treatment of inclusion and exclusion as identification strategies cf. Schlee 2000 c.

'Hatred', the working of symbols, and emotion management

Personally, I regard 'hatred' as the most difficult concept in the title of this book, although in comparison to the other key words, 'construction' and 'identity', it sounds less pretentious, being a common word used in everyday language and derived from an Anglo-Saxon root.

'Construction' can be observed through discourse analysis, 'identity' can be defined by the set of symbols (emblems, features...[13]) which circumscribes it, but what is the empirical dimension of hatred? We all know how it feels if we feel it ourselves and we all know how to enact it theatrically, but we are also aware that such expressions (and their absense) are often deceptive. I best explain what I mean by another case history. It is about a young Somali boy.

> The Somali boy. 21.6.1990. In search of a nomadic hamlet which is one of the localities of my field research - and which is always difficult to locate again after a temporary absence of the ethnographer because of its extreme mobility - we drive about the plains in the northern part of Wajir District in the North-East of Kenya, as night falls. Some camel herders direct us to their settlement which is not far from the track so that we have no difficulties in taking our Landrover there. We make a fire at some distance from the line of semispherical tents covered with mats and busy ourselves preparing dinner and making sleeping arrangements.
>
> A young boy of no more than ten years joins us. He answers our questions and explains where we are. The twenty houses belong to the sons and sons' sons of a single man of the clan Degodia or rather - in many cases - to the widows of these sons and grandsons. The boy's own father, two of his father's brothers and three patrilateral parallel cousins of his father (FFBSs) have all been killed in the Wagalla massacres.
>
> So far the boy. We need some background information about these massacres. Wagalla is an air strip near Wajir, the district capital. "In February 1984, 5,000 male members of the Degodia Somali were corralled and tortured, beaten or shot at [...on this air strip] in what was described by the authorities as an operation to end hostilities between the Degodia and Ajuran Somali clans. The Degodia had previously been given an ultimatum and required to surrender their weapons. According to the authorities they failed to do so on time (they deny this), whereupon they were rounded up by the military. Estimates on the number of dead vary. The

---

[13] Cf. Schlee (1987) about the various kinds of identity markers and their interrelationships.

official government figure is 57[14]; local witnesses however put it at least at 1,000.

Europeans present in the area set it at over 3,000. A recent report quotes 'sources close to the Presidency' giving the total as 2,169 (Africa Confidential Feb. 1989). A source in Kenya lists 363 named persons as among the victims [...]. As yet no compensation has been distributed". (Survival International, ca. 1990)

Whatever the number of dead, the most frequent cause of death is not difficult to imagine. With five thousand people without cover on a fenced airstrip for several days, exposure to the sun and dehydration took their toll. This was the culmination in a tribal war aggravated by incompetent, one-sided and unrestrained intervention by government forces. It had escalated over the preceding months through mutual raids and real or rumored atrocities - herd-girls who had been found raped and with ripped bellies - from a yet earlier state in which Degodia and Ajuran lived together peacefully in mixed hamlets, a period, in the 70s, from which I had friends on both sides. Now some of my friends told me stories about how they had stolen the camels of some other friends of mine.

What strikes us in the manner in which the boy tells about the losses his immediate family and his descent group suffered, is his matter-of-factness. There is no adjective or other verbal or non-verbal element in his account which implies any sort of moral evaluation or betrays any emotion. He just enumerates losses like an accountant. Does this boy hate the Ajuran or their helpers?

After enumerating the dead he explains what happened to their widows. All but two were married by their husbands' surviving brothers (*dumaal*) [or close agnatic relatives, FBSs in this case, of their husbands who fit into this emic category. This type of marriage is likewise referred to as *dumaal*, 'widow inheritance'.] One of the exceptions was a young bride who did not yet have any children and went back to her parents, the other one is a woman beyond childbearing age who continues to live in the hamlet of her husband's brothers and is taken care of by them without being married to any of them. He knows the facts, he knows the rules, he knows the reasons, and there is nothing which betrays any emotion.

A Somali in my company says that the boy certainly also knows what he has to do when he grows up. He will take revenge. But again, does this imply hatred? He has a clear-cut picture of how to behave as a man and may be confident enough to have the opportunity to live up to this ideal

---

[14] This number of 57 is believed to refer to the number of Degodia who had been on the Government payroll. The fact that most Degodia are self-employed as pastoralists explains why this number is so low.

one day. There might be no role inconsistencies. What others expect of him, what he expects of himself and the options life offers him once he is old enough to carry a gun, may all harmonise with each other. He might have a well-balanced emotional household and not suffer from any passions, hatred or otherwise. But who knows? What if he just hides his hatred? This question seems to be beyond the access of empirical research methods. Neither observation nor questions might yield a reliable answer.

The problem addressed by this case history is that to which behaviourism, cybernetics and system theory refer as the 'black box'. In many systems we can observe the input and the output, compare the two and form theories about how one is transformed into the other, but we cannot directly observe what happens inside. The human head is a classical example of a black box. We just do not know what goes on inside the boy.

The observation of behaviour is as close as we can get to the emotions and among all forms of behaviour it is linguistic behaviour which has played the most prominent role in this context. The language in which emotions are categorised and shaped to be made communicable to others in a given cultural context might not tell us much about how people feel but at least about how they socially construct 'feelings'. The first observation we can make in this field is that some cultures make emotions a theme while others restrict the types of situations in which emotions are talked about and the vocabulary used for that purpose. The question "how do you feel?", not just in the polite sense, but also phrased insistently, "how did you really feel in such-and-such a situation?" is very frequent in the psychologising personal discourses of the West.[15] In the other cultures it is hardly legitimate in most contexts. Our Somali boy might not like such questions at all because they interfere with the manliness he strives for.

---

[15] Lila Abu-Lughod introduces one of her papers with a very descriptive episode. She listens to a therapy show on radio in New York in which the psychologist asks the caller, a housewife, who has eating problems related to marital ones, again and again how she felt in this or that situation. She concludes "that the poor caller, had she later gone into therapy" might have "learned to populate her narratives... with a legion of emotions. She would have learned to practice on herself and others, to adapt a notion from Foucault (1985: 5), a hermeneutics of feeling" (Abu Lughod 1990: 24). The Bedouin among whom she lived and worked in Egypt, Abu-Lughod goes on to explain, would find the command to confess one's feeling strange, improper, undignified and nonsensical. And so would, I suspect, the "Bedouin" (in Swahili *watu wa badia*) among whom I worked, the non-Arabic Rendille, Oromo and Somali. Pastoral nomads often correspond to this image. For obvious reasons, toughness is fairly generally highly valued among them while listening too much to one's emotions is not. Epstein (1992: 57) cites LeVine (1984: 82) about the Gusii of Kenya on this issue among whom, in an otherwise rich vocabulary, he found only a small lexicon of distinctively mental phenomena, particularly their subjective aspects. He relates this to the observation that Gusii avoid "psychologising" and prefer to talk about the overt behaviour of people.

But not only pastoralists are reluctant to talk about emotions. In the same place we find a reference to Howell's (1981) description of the Chewong, hunter-gatherers and shifting cultivators of Malakka, where she found a very limited vocabulary relating to inner states.

What if he had verbally elaborated on the 'hatred' which he has not even betrayed by a gesture? He would have used the word *diid*, which as a shared lexeme, in Somali, Oromo and Rendille means 'to reject' and 'to hate'.[16] So is that emotion, 'hatred' shared by speakers of Indoeuropean and Cushitic languages? Or is it even universal? The translatability of 'I hate' as *'wan diidaya'* seems to suggest something along these lines. But the matter is not that simple. If we look for synonyms of 'to hate' in English in Collins Thesaurus, we find 'abhor', 'abominate', 'be hostile to', 'be repelled by', 'be sick of', 'despise', 'detest', 'dislike', 'execrate', 'have an aversion to', 'loathe', 'recoil from' etc. All these can serve as translation of *diid* in one or the other context. Even beyond the reach of the semantic domain of 'to hate' plus all its synonyms, we can find potential English equivalents of *diid*. It can also mean 'reject', 'deny', 'decline'. On the other hand there are other Somali words which can mean 'hatred', like *ne'eb (neceb)*[17] (which may derive from Abarabic *na^{c}b* - violent?[18] and others[19] and, of course, there are other ways, namely metaphors, circumlocutions etc. to express hostile feelings in Somali.

So, we do not find neat equivalences, and nobody would have expected 1:1 correspondences anyhow, but we do find ways to express 'hatred' or closely related emotions in Somali. What if we didn't? A vocabulary "gap" (Epstein 1992: 58) may be due to suppression of the affect for which there is no name, or simply to the complicated nature of the feelings involved which defy the attempt to "find the right words for them". When our search for a word which we can regard as (to a greater or lesser degree) equivalent to the name of an emotion in our own language remains futile, this does not allow us to conclude that the absence of such a word indicates the absence of the emotion. A certain type of analysis, the approach of *Belief, Language and Experience* (Needham 1972), would not be possible in such a case, but we cannot equate non-availability as a research tool with non-existence of the phenomenon.

In spite of these difficulties, some of the best anthropological studies of emotions have started with the meticulous description of words and the semantic fields which are structured by them. Anyone working with lists of words soon finds that the whole sentence is needed to determine the precise meaning of any of these words and that, for the context analysis of the sentence, it is better to have the whole story. And the story, of course, has a social setting with a history. In other words: from language such analyses tend to expand rapidly to the other subsystems of culture, anthropological linguistics soon incorporate the rest of anthropology as well. (Models for such ap-

---

[16] Oromo also has *jib* for 'to hate' and Rendille has *nibhade* - 'I am sick of, strongly dislike'.

[17] Abraham, Major R.C. 1961: *Somali-English Dictionary*, University of London Press

[18] Steingass 1972: A Learner's Arabic-English Dictionary. Librarie du Liban

[19] Mohamed Ali Farah's *Somali Wörterbuch*, Hamburg: Buske 1990 has *nicid* and *karhid* for 'hassen'.

proaches which take language as a starting point include Epstein 1992, contributions to Lutz and Abu-Lughods (eds.) 1990, and to Harré (ed.) 1986.)[20]

It is the view on longer narratives and with a fuller incorporation of context which is characteristic of the contributions to this volume. The one on Java by Quarles van Ufford is a case history covering years. The contributions by Hobart on theatre in Bali and by Rieger on Indonesian novels deal with texts and their performances and go back and forth between the language(s) described and the meta-language of literary criticism/anthropological analysis. Emotions are embedded in and partly hidden by their contexts.

Hatred and other emotions - the pride of belonging, deep feelings of allegiance, the emotional elements of solidarity, love - do not combine very well with the way we have defined 'identity' above. We have described 'identity' as something which takes place at 'the surface, the interface with others' and we have stressed its pragmatic and situational aspects.

This view of identity fits into one school of thought which has been described as instrumentalist[21], mainly in connection with a particular form of identity, ethnicity, as 'the instrumentalist view of ethnicity'. Bentley (1987: 25) discusses this instrumentalism as one part of a dichotomy which he calls 'primordialist - instrumentalist'. Starting with the observation that there seem to be stronger arguments for the statement that societal boundaries cannot be predicted from the distribution of cultural ones[22] than for the opposite view that "analytically useful units can be inferred from observed distributions of culture traits", Bentley discusses the problem whether the claims to common ethnicity, which are evidently 'subjective' since they lack an 'objective' cultural basis, are founded on the 'affective potency of primordial attachments' or 'the instru-

---

[20] If we trace the ancestry of some ideas which are important in this type of anthropological/psychological/linguistic constructionism, we are, among others, led to Wittgenstein. Needham (1972) cites Wittgenstein explicitly and at great length, and Harré speaks of 'language games' (1986: 7). Chomsky is another large figure in the background. Harré's terminology is obviously inspired by Generative Transformation Grammar: "many emotions are manifested in typical behaviour displays. Such displays [...] are together with the utterance of emotion words, among the very forms of expressive display, and such share the deep grammar of emotion words themselves." (1986: 8)

[21] 'Instrumentalism' here is not quite identical with the same term in Dench's usage (cf. above, footnote) where it is part of a different set of contrasts (rational and goal oriented = instrumentalist mobilisation of group consciousness through ethnicity versus the universalist values attached to class).

[22] Bentley's brief allusion to Leach (1954), (to whom he traces this position which was later corroborated by Barth (1969)) somehow undervalues the role of observable cultural features in Leach's analysis of the culturally heterogeneous Kachin / Shan societies of Highland Burma. 'Societies' here comprise a plurality of cultural units and thus 'cultures' and 'societies' are not coterminous. But the constituent parts of these societies articulate with each other through their specialisations and the cultural differences which symbolise them. It is integration t h r o u g h differences, not integration i n s p i t e o f differences. The importance of 'objective' cultural traits for this symbolic interaction can hardly be overstressed. For my reading of Leach see Schlee 1994 b). On Bentley (1987) cf. als Yelvington (1991).

mental manipulation of culture in service of collective political and economic interests'. For each position he cites a number of authors, thus suggesting the existence of a 'primordialist' and an 'instrumentalist' school.

'Instrumentalism' here implies taking advantage of the effect that "robing interest groups in ethnic (cultural) garb takes advantage of the legitimating nationalist ideologies of modern states and/or renders such groups less vulnerable in the face of numerical or political inferiority" (ibid.), a strategy which - as we have seen above in our discussion of Dench vs. Roosens - may work better in America than elsewhere. One can, of course, widen this concept of 'instrumentalism' to include individual strategies like situational affiliation (to "pass" as Belgian in the street, being Italian at home, as second generation Italian migrants in Belgium do, cf. Roosens 1989: 141) or the instrumental use of ethnicity and clanship among northern Kenyan pastoralists to get access to water and pasture.

Among various Cushitic speaking groups of camel herders of this area, who differ quite markedly along linguistic and cultural lines, we find the same clans. Obviously ethno-genetic processes here have cut across clans, so that in the case of many clans one fragment has ended up in one ethnic group and another fragment in another. A socially skilful herder, who normally relies on his ethnic group for pasture, water, and defence against enemies, may, in the case of a local drought or some other distress befalling his own people, address members of another ethnic group and appeal to the common roots of his clan and theirs to get grazing or watering rights or protection or even gifts of livestock from them if he has lost his own. No doubt, this is an instrumental use of social identifications (Schlee 1989).

The primordialist view, on the other hand, stresses the fundamental, one might say pseudo-natural aspect of ethnicity (more generally: identity) and the emotions it involves. A rationalist, instrumentalist perspective which compares the costs and benefits of different identifications somehow does not explain why people cry when they hear their national anthem, die for their fatherland or react with hostility to people who exhibit symbols of "the Other". It does not explain sensations. "...ethnic-identity claims involve symbolic construal of sensations of likeness and difference, and these sensations must somehow be accounted for" (Bentley 1987: 27).[23]

---

[23] Bentley (1987: 26) criticises both the instrumentalist and the primordialist perspective, because "neither addresses the question of how people recognise the commonalities (of interest and sentiment) underlying claims to common identity. Primordialist models point to an array of potent symbols but fail to explain what elements of commonality are embodied in particular symbols (name, descent, language, religion, etc.) in particular settings. Instrumentalists variously view ethnicity as a conscious expression of short-term economic interests ... as a fiction constructed by leaders ... or as the product of some ... process of interest aggregation".

Some of the papers in the present collection at least partly do what Bentley is looking for in vain. How in one setting religion becomes important and in another ethnicity or language, is discussed by various contributors.

To account for these emotions, Bentley takes recourse to Bourdieu's "theory of practice" (Bourdieu 1977). According to this theory, a given social environment produces a habitus which is a system of durable, transportable dispositions, not just transient identifications.

This implies that in order to understand the emotions attached to one or the other social identification we have to look at the process of how this identity is implanted into its bearer through socialisation.

We have seen that the materials of which "imagined differences" are constructed often are real enough. Nobody would deny the observable and describable differences in belief, language and life style between Hindu Balinese, Muslim Javanese administrators and American tourists (Hobart), or other collectivities marked by similar levels of difference which figure in the other contributions. It is, however, difficult to deduce from such data about culture   w h i c h   cultural elements are used to form which "image" of a collectivity, one's own or the "other", and it is in this process of cultural ascription of meaning to cultural materials that an element of "imagination", of coining images, comes in, in spite of the reality of some of the elements used (others may be faked or freely invented) and in spite of the reality (and often cruelty) of the consequences of such processes.

Love sometimes bridges ethnic divides. Even among the religiously distinct and ethnically largely endogamous Uighur there is a certain amount of intermarriage with Han Chinese. But Bellér-Hann also reports the tragic case of a wife who had hidden the fact that her father was Han from her Uighur husband and who was immediately divorced after her husband found out that she was half-Han. She had been brought up as a Muslim and Uighur but now the hard, the "real" aspect of imagined differences caught up with her. In other cases, like young Moroccans who categorise themselves in class terms rather than ethnic terms, ethnic constructs might get de-constructed again. One could have turned the key concepts of the title of this book into their opposites and spoken of real differences, deconstruction, and love, rather than imagined differences, construction and hatred. One might have got an interesting view of the same phenomena, looking the other way.

Love, of course, is not the opposite of hatred but its complement and often accompaniment, and deconstruction is the pre-condition of construction of identity, because, if identities were only constructed and not dismantled, one would have to postulate a steady increase in the number of such constructs at all times in all places. There is no evidence to support such a hypothesis.

Also Schlee (1985, 1989), discusses name, descent, language and religion and their potential for inclusion and exclusion as well as their potential to justify a variety of affiliations. Obviously some such identifiers are strong enough to modify others. One may be led, for example, by one's religious identification as a Muslim to develop an ideology of Arab descent, and turn out to be an ardent believer in one's own constructs.

Aspects of the problems of emotion and habitualised attitudes which accompany social identification can be discerned in all the contributions to the section on "Hatred and the boundaries of social identities" in this volume. We have discussed these contributions above from the different angle of "identity". Emotions and emotion management are even more in the foreground of the papers combined under the heading "The politics of difference: escalating violence, shifting boundaries and the fragmentation of states."

Birgit Mara Kaiser, in her contribution about the periodicals of Algerian political movements finds 'hatred' invariably attributed to the other side. A pun describes the FIS (Front Islamique du Salut) as 'FIS de la haine' – 'sons (*fils*) of hatred'. The FIS, in their turn, describe their opponents as *éradicateurs*. Thus one mobilizes one's own people by describing to them how much their opponents hate them.

Another figure of speech is to describe the opponent as pathological. Unless one is a doctor, one does not need to know about pathology. Describing the adversary's frame of mind as pathological is a good excuse for not trying to understand it. We have come across this form of systemic ignorance above, when discussing why social sciences have worked rather little on violence in comparison to other subjects.

The contribution by Purnaka L. de Silva, "Combat modes, mimesis and the cultivation of hatred: revenge/counter revenge killings in Sri Lanka" focusses on emotions in the context of the course taken by conflicts, especially 'hatred' in its connection with revenge killings. His study of violent political movements in Sri Lanka deals also with internal strife which is often more bitter than the struggle for the revolutionary or national causes around which these movements have formed. His paper reminds us that conflicts are not fully explained by their causes. In addition to their causes one needs to take into account their courses. Violence may mimic earlier violence and revenge generates counter revenge The conflict itself is the ground on which hatred is cultivated.

P. L. de Silva draws some comparisons between the two islands, Sri Lanka and Ireland, and Mary Kenney explores the Northern Ireland case more fully. She places emphasis on socialisation into a world of armed groups who habitualise a violent history by celebrating and re-enacting it. All authors write about the point where emotions enter the social scene and shape social processes and where the latter shape the former.

Those who want to address the problems of our time may not find a new theory of social identity and the dynamics of solidarity and hostility in this volume, but they are guaranteed to find plenty of food for thought and quite a number of components of such a theory in a variety of combinations. What more can one expect in a field of knowledge where all attempts at a unified and all-embracing theory so far have been accused of one-sidedness and simplification and ultimately abandoned?

References

Abu-Lughod, Lila 1990. Shifting politics in Bedouin love poetry. In: Catherine A. Lutz and Lila Abu-Lughod 1990: 24 - 25

Abun-Nasr, Jamil M. 1965. *The Tijaniyya: a Sufi order in the modern world.* London: Oxford University Press

Anderson, Benjamin 1983. *Imagined communities: reflections on the origin and spread of nationalism.* London: Verso

Armon-Jones, Claire 1986. The social functions of emotions. In: Harré, Rom 1986: 57 - 82

Barth, Fredrik (ed.) 1969. *Ethnic groups and boundaries,* Boston: Little, Brown

Bentley, G. Carter 1987. Ethnicity and practice. In: *Comparative Studies in Society and History,* Vol. 29, No. 1: 24 - 55

Bourdieu, Pierre 1977. *Outline of a Theory of Practice.* Cambridge: Cambridge University Press

Cohen, Anthony 1985. *The social construction of community.* London and New York: Tavistock

Cohen, Anthony (ed.) 1986. *Symbolising boundaries: identity and diversity in British cultures.* Manchester University Press

Cronin, Richard 1989. *Imagining India.* Houndmills etc.: Macmillan

Dench, Geoff 1986. *Minorities in the open society,* London and New York: Routledge

Elias, Norbert 1969. *Über den Prozeß der Zivilisation,* Bern: Francke

Elwert, Georg 1989. Nationalismus und Ethnizität: über die Bildung von Wir-Gruppen. *Kölner Zeitschrift für Soziologie und Sozialpsychologie* (3): 440 - 464

Epstein, A.L. 1992. *In the midst of life: affect and ideation in the world of the Tolai.* Berkeley etc.: University of California Press

Eriksen, Thomas Hylland 1993. *Ethnicity and Nationalism: Anthropological Perspectives.* London: Pluto

Eriksen, Thomas Hylland 1995. *Small Places, Large Issues: an Introduction to Social and Cultural Anthropology.* London: Pluto

Firat, Gülsün 1997. *Sozioökonomischer Wandel und ethnische Identität in der kurdisch-alevitischen Region Dersim.* Saarbrücken: Verlag für Entwicklungspolitik

Foucault, Michel 1985. *The Use of Pleasure.* Vol.2 of *The History of Sexuality.* New York: Pantheon

Fox, Richard G. 1985. *Lions of the Punjab: culture in the making.* Berkeley and Los Angeles: University of California Press

Gellner, Ernest 1981. *Muslim Society.* Cambridge: Cambridge University Press

Gellner, Ernest 1983. *Nations and Nationalism.* Oxford: Blackwell

Giddens, Anthony 1987. *The Nation state and violence* (Vol.II of *A contemporary critique of Historical Materialism*). Berkeley Los Angeles: Univerity of California Press

Hann, Christopher M. 1996. Ethnic cleansing in Eastern Europe: Poles and Ukrainians beside the Curzon line. *Nations and Nationalism* 2: 389 - 406

Hann, Christopher M. 1998. Postsocialist nationalism: rediscovering the past in Southeast Poland. *Slavic Review* 57, 4: 840 - 863

Harré, Rom (ed.) 1986. *The social construction of emotions.* Oxford: Blackwell

Howell, S. 1981. Rules not words. In: Heelas, P. and Lock, A. (eds.): *Indigenous psychologies: the anthropology of the Self.* London: Academic Press

Inden, Ronald 1990. *Imagining India.* Oxford: Blackwell

Kimmerle, Heinz 1992. *Derrida zur Einführung,* Hamburg: Junius

Leach, E.R. 1954. *Political systems of Highland Burma.* London: Athlone

LeVine, R.A. 1984. Properties of culture: an ethnographic view. In: Shweder, R.A. and R.A. LeVine (eds.)

Lutz, Catherine and Abu-Lughod, Lila (eds.) 1990. *Language and the politics of emotion.* Cambridge, New York etc.: Cambridge University Press

Marcus, George and Michael J. Fischer 1986. *Anthropology as cultural critique: and experimental moment in the human sciences.* Chicago: University of Chicago Press

Martin, B. G. 1967. Unbelief in the Western Sudan: ʿUthman dan Fodio's "Taʿlim al-ikhwan". In: *Middle Eastern Studies* 4, 1: 50 - 97

Merera Gudina 1994. The new directions of Ethiopian politics. In: Marcus, Harold G. (ed.). *New trends in Ethiopian Studies. Papers of the 12ᵗʰ International Conference of Ethiopian Studies.* Vol II: 913 – 932, Lawrencevill NJ: The red Sea Press.

Needham, Rodney 1972. *Belief, language and experience*. Chicago: University of Chicago Press

Parkin, David (ed.) 1985: *The Anthropology of Evil*. Oxford: Basil Blackwell

Rattray, Robert S. 1992. *The tribes of Ashanti hinterlands*. 2 Vols, Oxford

Riches, David (ed.) 1986. *The Anthropology of Violence*. Oxford: Basil Blackwell

Roosens, Eugeen E. 1989: *Creating ethnicity: the process of ethnogenesis*. London etc.: Sage

Ruf, Urs Peter 1994. *Mobile Seßhafte: Die Sedentarisierung von Nomaden in Mauretanien*. Saarbrücken: Breitenbach

Ruf, Urs Peter. 1999. *Ending slavery: hierarchy, dependency and gender in central Mauritania*. Bielefeld: transcript

Schlee, Günther 1985. Interethnic clan identities among Cushitic-speaking pastoralists. *Africa*, 55 (1): *17 – 38*

Schlee, Günther 1987. Rendille Ornaments as Identity Markers. In: *Kenya Past and Present*, 20: 31-37

Schlee, Günther 1989. *Identities on the move: Clanship and pastoralism in Northern Kenya*. Manchester University Press and New York: St. Martin's Press (paperback Nairobi: Gideon S. Were; Hamburg, Münster: Lit-Verlag)

Schlee, Günther 1994 a. Loanwords in Oromo and Rendille as a mirror of past interethnic relations. In: Fardon Richard and Graham Furniss: *African languages, development and the state*. London: Routledge: 191 - 212

Schlee, Günther 1994 b. Ethnicity emblems, diacritical features, identity markers: Some East African examples: In: Brokensha, David: *A River of Blessings. Essay in Honor of Paul Baxter*. New York: Maxwell School of Citizenship and Public Affairs, Syracuse University (Foreign and comparative studies. African series; 44), Syracuse University: 129 - 143 (also Bielefeld, SDRC, WP No.160, 1991)

Schlee, Günther 2000 a. Die soziale Konstruktion von Feindschaft. *Working papers of the Max Planck Institute for Social Anthropology*. No.05, Halle/Saale

Schlee, Günther 2000 b. *Redrawing the map of the Horn: the politics of difference*. Contribution to the biennal conference of the German African Studies Association (VAD), Leipzig, 30.03.–1.04.2000. Conference Proceedings available on CD

Schlee, Günther 2000 c. Identitätskonstruktionen und Parteinahme. *Sociologus* 50, 1: 64 - 89

Schlee, Günther and Abdullahi A. Shongolo 1995. local war and its impact on ethnic and religious identification in Southern Ethiopia. *GeoJournal*, 36 (1): 7 - 17

Shweder, R.A. and LeVine, R.A. (eds.) 1984. *Culture theory: essays on mind, self and emotion*. Cambridge: Cambridge University Press

Simons, Anna 1999. Making sense of ethnic cleansing. *Studies in Conflict and Terrorism* 22: 1 - 20

Survival International, n.d. [c. early 1990]. *Unquiet pastures: The nomadic people of North East Kenya today. Information document*. London

Yelvington, Kevin A. 1991. Ethnicity as practice? A comment on Bentley. *Comparative Studies in Society and History* 33: 158-168

SWITCHING IDENTITY DISCOURSES:

PRIMORDIAL EMOTIONS AND THE SOCIAL CONSTRUCTION OF WE-GROUPS

Georg Elwert

"There is a deep-rooted hatred". Few commonplace formula sound as suggestive as this when it comes to explaining ethnic or national conflict. Hate is not the only primordial sentiment which is cited when ethnic or national mobilisation are the subject. The uneasiness when speaking another language or following foreign customs and the feeling at home in one's own language and customs are similar references. It is seductive to draw analogies between individual motives of behaviour and organisational goals. This creates the feeling that our empathy as individuals is sufficient to "understand" the working of social structure. This is an illusion.

Often, historical work on nationalism and ethnicity walks into the trap set by the self-images of the movements. The reference which should stand for an explanation is rather vague. "History", "culture" and "tradition" implicitly orient our attention to emotionally co-notated complexes which are rarely detailed. The protagonists are only too happy to postulate "historical and cultural roots" even more vaguely. As the movement propagates a history, it is believed that it has one. It is believed that the homogeneity of the movement is to be traced back to a very old common heritage, perhaps indeed to a common ancestry. It is often overlooked that this history can be at one and the same time false **and** productive. It is false or flawed as a historical report. It is innovative as a model projected onto the past of what societal relationships should be. We easily fail to see the skill in political engineering which went into welding the movement together. The historical discourse is the matrix for a normative model.

Nationalism and ethnicity are explicit on those points where they want to attach a consciousness of place and borders, belonging and enemies, to history. They are much less explicit on the points where the decisive forces which drive them actually lie, in the striving after resources and in the construction of networks of trust and mutual support. Economic motives are linked also to internal competition whereas transcendental, historical and moral postulates are possessed of a unifying vagueness. Indistinct goals are the best putty for social coherence.

It is imperative for an analysis of nationalism and ethnicity which wants to catch the ongoing processes and which should have a prognostic power, not to start from the level of self-presenting discourses. We have to study action and structure - iterative and expected action is structure. This study requires comparison. From this level we can and have to analyse strategic action - the contingent and unexpected element which might change structures. Insofar as strategic action is geared towards the creation of emotions we have then to deal with these. Strategic action cannot, however, be built solely upon emotions. Strategic action, be it military or peaceful, requires cool-blooded foresight and reliable logistics; it cannot be dissociated from social structure.

Research on nationalism, ethnicity and fundamentalism has become - as it seems - an easy task. There are authors we all cite, and there are the objects of our study, which delineate themselves so clearly. However, as this paper shall argue, this self-delineation causes problems to social science, because it induces us to overlook

1. processes of switching between different frames of reference, 2. processes of (physical) reproduction (namely the link to families), which do not go without saying, 3. the fuzziness of the limits, which may fulfil specific social functions. The first issue - the process of switching - is rarely used as a reference point in the study of we-groups, since the actors themselves insist on the eternality and stability of their group. It seems to me however that precisely this odd phenomenon can provide us with new insights. We may use it as a plough to work through the garden of ethnicity theory.

So-called ethnic violence in Bosnia, Somalia and Turkey is explained by reference to emotions and traditions. This sounds plausible to us, because the suffering of the victims is expressed in emotions and creates strong emotions in us. But this is only a link of connotations, not a logical one. Violence of the type reported from these countries, social (=organised) violence, with weapons, transport of actors to the field, the premeditation of ambushes etc. needs logistics and the cooly planning mind, not spontaneous emotions (or the vagueness of historical references to traditions). There are central actors like warlords or political entrepreneurs to be studied, and we have to see the role of conflict-channelling institutions, of economic solidarity and of communication in order to understand the stabilisation of we-groups. Switching becomes an important focus in this field of study not only insofar as it helps to understand from cases of failed stabilisation, what the conditions of stability are, but also because it is a flagrant falsification of assumptions about "deep-rooted traditions" which might condition a given we-group.

Less stable than they appear: we-groups

It is a common assumption that ethnicity belongs to the domain of anthropologists, nationalism to that of political scientists, and fundamentalism to that of religious studies. This division of labour produces a problematic division of knowledge. These phenomena share with other we-group processes, namely class movements and religious movements, the same driving forces and systemic patterns. Thus, there are no separate tools for their analysis. Ethnicity, nationalism and other we-group processes share some motives, namely mega-identities, clientelism and moral ethnicity.

We observe mega-identities when migrants, losing their frame of reference which gave them prestige, are attracted by collective references, which compensate for the lost individual one, like Pan-Germany (Großdeutschland), Pan-Turkism, world revolution etc. In competition over new ressources it may be of advantage to create a clientelist network designed as a "we-group". Moral ethnicity appears if behaviour seen as antisocial is felt as a personal threat. Then, one option is to create a social form imagined as a community but framed as an organisation which excludes the immoral ones and unites the moral ones[24].

To analyse processes of social construction is, to my mind, necessary for two reasons: 1. Neither ethnic groups nor nations constitute a "natural" order. They compete in human history with other types of social organisation for the place of the central organising structure. We can even find social structures where there is no we-group of the ethnic type (Elwert 1989). 2. Nations and ethnic groups are social structures which have to be reproduced. That means, they have to be recreated by each succsessive generation. They may have to fulfil new functions and may use old plausibilities. But the transmission of plausibilities works only if the functions are satisfied.

Switching, the overlooked process

One remarkable feature of we-groups is the process we call **switching**. That means a rapid change from one frame of reference to the other. A class movement may become a nationalist one, a nationalist movement transforms itself into religious mobilisation, or a religious network redefines itself as a class movement. Switching processes easily escape scientific treatment because they "change the department" - from religious to social, to political studies and vice versa.

It is surprising that references to stable traditions are quoted much more than examples of such switching. In 1964 Edmund Leach already described a group of people in Highland Burma which sometimes was able to identify itself as an ethnic group, but sometimes was perceived and presented itself as an underclass of their dominant neighbours. In 1973 Canfield already described patrilineal descent groups in the field of tensions that was Afghanistan which were under pressure from religiously defined powers. They reacted with identification or by stating difference and thus turned into religious "sects".

Some years later Sri Lanka's Trotskytes turned their class movement into an ultra-nationalist militant organisation. In the 1990s Iraq's secularist, nationalist Baath party redefined itself under Sadam Hussein as Islamic - and won international support. These days the Palestinian religious movement Hamas may gain political supremacy by restating the (beforehand secular nationalist) Palestinian cause as an Islamic one.

We (Kristina Kehl / Georg Elwert) studied Alevites in Turkey[25]. The first thing we know with some historical certainty about the Alevites, is that they were endoga-

---

[24] See Lonsdale (1993) and on the concept of imagined communities - essential for this paper's argument - Anderson (1988).

[25] Financed by the Deutsche Forschungs-Gemeinschaft, see Kehl-Bodrogi et al. 1997

mous groups who wanted to mark a distance to the Sunnite Ottoman rule. In fact the Shiite façade and the rule of secrecy covered a wide range of beliefs. Under Atatürk's Republic they became fervent republicans, were over-represented on the left of centre republican and in socialist organisations. The installation of the holy men (*"dedeler"*) who kept the oral traditions was discontinued. The holy books (*"buyruk"*) were given away. But since the Alevites' identity was also ascribed to them from the outside and was maintained by their social environment, they were forced to continue living endogamously .

Now, the new conjuncture of religious prestige symbols and boundary definitions, and the self declared moral rearmament of fundamentalism, induces the Alevites to re-create a religious "identity". They are very active in retrieving - with the help of foreign anthropologists - old religious folklore, copying religious books; they confront the painful task of harmonising the incompatible and some move forward directly to the sheer invention of "forgotten" beliefs (with some Iranian help). None of these transformations could alleviate violence against this group. The readiness to hit - wrongly called "hatred" - is conditioned by the internal dynamism of the dominant "community", which, precisely in order to regain its self-image as a community, longs for the symbolic affirmation of difference. Because of the heterogeneity of the dominant ones the easiest option for the definition of the "we" is the creation of foes represented as a negative print of the morality which one would like to have as a self-description. The Alevites are easy targets for this, just because they happen to be there, not because of this or that feature. The remarkable dynamism of a syncretistic group combining an overt and a hidden connotative identity may be caught in a trap if confronted with the rigidity of a modern state's structure. Double façades and integrative dynamism in the transformations of ritual and beliefs can be seen from the outside as falseness and confusion. The accusation is - in systemic terms - that of blurring boundaries and escaping clear categorisation. The showing of unequivocal markers is imposed upon the community, flexibility has to be given up in favour of containment in restrictively conceived limits. This normalisation into an ethnic or religious form, portrayed as modernisation by the internal protagonists, may be seen in systemic terms - without any value judgement - as a "trap".

That anthropologists observe switching as a common process unfortunately does not mean that modern states consider it as a regular process.

The concept of switching refers a) to alternations between reference frames and b) to moves between different more-or-less inclusive conceptions of the group's boundary. The switching may imply a redefinition of the group's boundaries, or these boundaries may be kept and reinterpreted.

Redefinition of boundaries: a segment of a larger group may discover their "real" identity or several groups may "re"-unite under one umbrella. A strategically important minority may be included or an "annoying" group of actors excluded. (Thus

Nazi Germany forged a concept of *"Volksdeutsche"*/ethnic Germans, which included the originally Austrian *"Sudeten-Deutsche"* and the originally Dutch Mennonites of Russia and Ukraine and excluded the Jewish population of East Europe, which had been the main organiser of German schools and other cultural organisations in these countries and whose German ethnicity was hailed and instrumentalised by the German army's high command (*Oberkommando der Wehrmacht*) in the First World War).

Redefinition of content with boundaries maintained: in the case where the boundaries are kept, the change of reference level brings other actors or ressources into play or pushes them to the background where they risk being forgotten. Sensible (or shrewd) political actors preempt changes, they take the lead.

Among the groups marginalised by dominating Christian and Islamic groups in the Horn of Africa the label "Galla" or "Oromo" emerged which was linked to a specific mode of cohesion[26]. A generation and age class system allowed for the integration of neighbours. The expansion of the militant Oromo groups along with and against the Ethiopian empire was a constant undercurrent of history in the Horn of Africa - until they became, in the 20th century, the most widely spread ethnic label in Abyssinia. Modern civil war put them under a different stress. Though one can still observe "Oromisation" (Zitelmann 1994) in refugee camps, in other situations the "identity" (belongingness) is redefined by using some (patrilineal) kinship links, (Cushitic) multilingualism, laicism tainted by Islam or Christianity as a reference in order to become part of a Tigre kindred, a Somali clan, the spearhead of an Islamic movement or an Ethiopian nationalist.

The dynamics of maintaining or reshaping boundaries, of defining values and institutions as core ones is the product of tensions within the socio-political context. This is valid whether the "identity" sought for is the ideologised sentiment of value ascription or the definable characteristics of real or invented cultural traits. Similar contexts of tension will reproduce similar configurations of we-groups (see also Wimmer 1995). When the crucial political categories are religious, the marginal populations tend to become "heretics" (cf. Canfield 1973). When the crucial political categories are national or ethnic, those marginal populations which can only escape the dynamics of peripherisation by marking their difference, show ethnic distinction.

In order to create difference or to reach incorporation, switching may be necessary. This follows a pattern which might be called the "clarity imperative": there is a need for both: an accepted code and clear markers. The code may be: religion, ethnicity, local group, kinship. The code may even narrow down to a sub-code or may widen. So "religion" may be narrowed to book religion, or book religion to Islam. So those Pashtoo nomads who until the last century were Jews then had to mark their dif-

---

[26] Here I refer to a research project led by Thomas Zitelmann and myself; financed by the Deutsche Forschungs-Gemeinschaft too.

ference within the Islamic code, when only this became accepted[27]. Inversely the Christian Bogumil heresy on the Balkan increased the clarity of difference in reference to their Serb and Croat neighbours by switching to Islam, when conquered by the Ottomans - which made the Bosnians.

The codes of "locality" and "kinship", which now are presented as remnants from a past when human beings lived in accordance with nature, are neither natural nor banal at all. Like age, generation, gender and physical features, locality and kinship are means of giving social order a natural appearance, "to naturalise" it[28]. But there is no natural law that made any of these references a strictly observed organising principle to be found in every human group. "Kinship" may be an idiom also expressing ties of neighbourship, "age" may rather mean generation etc. The code of locality in the definition of we-groups may be a means of defining land rights - among the Mapuche in South America as among the Gur-speaking groups of northern Ghana, Togo and Bénin "people of the earth" or "people from here" are common self-given names. In other social environments marriage rights and inheritance are the crucial issues; there kinship (especially unilateral kinship) is the reference code to define the dominant we-group structure (not excluding locality etc. as a secondary reference, to which one may switch).

Changes of shape or parameters of reference can occur with we-groups at an amazing pace (which is conditioned by the volatility of power) (Wallerstein 1980). This does not exclude the continuity of "ethnic" names, which is instrumental for any claims of political inheritance rights.

Ethnic names, a specific type of music (see During 1993 on Uzbekistan), traditional norms and so forth constitute the **inventory** upon which a given group may draw in order to design its limits and its "identity". This inventory may be limited or it may be broad. It will be broad in situations of enhanced interregional communication. This inventory should be distinguished from a closet where one hangs a selection of one's coats, because these symbols are **not owned**. Some salient marker of distinction seen somewhere else may as well be adopted as a sign familiar from childhood. Inventories are shared with other collective actors. Thus symbol use may overlap or may even alternate between enemy groups. The grasp on symbols is, however, not random, it is conditioned by a) the plausibility in respect of other markers of order and b) by the communicative need to create salience and difference. An example for the first is the importance of all references which suggest collective rights of past generations in an

---

[27] The late Eugen Ludwig Rapp informed me of his work on Afghan tombstones. Similarly some Black Sea Christians in Turkey switched to Islam in the situation of 20th century dominated by "ethnic exchanges" but maintained their difference by declaring themselves to be Alevites.

[28] It is in **this** respect, that Clifford Geertz (1973) wrote about primordial structures (cf. also Lentz 1995). In a chain of misrepresenting quotations he is now made responsible for "primordialism" as a variant of essentialism.

environment where **inheritance** is a strong argument for claims. Examples for the second need are national dress, orthographic reforms and racial ideologies.

The phenomenon of switching is uncomfortable for any essentialist theory. Because those "primordial values", which presumably constitute by their very "nature" the boundaries of ethnic groups, suddenly lose relevance. At this point an excursion on the recurrence of essentialism might be appropriate. Since Max Weber's time it has been shown that those groups which call themselves "ethnic" or "national" use the form of boundaries in respect of criteria of functionality of the social structure they aimed at, on the one hand, and criteria of plausibility, which "went without saying" in their respective context, on the other hand. It is **society dressed as community**, which produces the emotional cohesion of these we-groups.

Those who argued against Weber 1922 (or later against R. Thurnwald 1953, W. Mühlmann 1962, F. Barth 1969 etc., who took up his ideas) that there were "natural" forces binding all ethnic groups together - namely language, religion and culture - could be confronted by empirical examples of ethnic groups, recognised as such by all their neighbours, which lacked at least one of these criteria (see the demonstration by Thomas Höllmann (1992) on Southeast Asian examples, and for the history of ideas Ernst W. Müller 1990). The reason why nevertheless, in spite of all these proofs for the formalist perspective, some authors come back to an essentialist view or try to "harmonise" these logically incompatible concepts, may be due to the fact that we all are working in the environment of common popular ideas. Most ethnic groups try to present themselves as "natural"; this induces a continuous stream of "immigration of protoscientific ideas" into social science.

Polytaxis - the latent multiplicity of order and identity

Groups and individuals may belong to different reference groups simultaneously; according to the opportunity of situations they may stress one or an other of these affiliations as their "real" one (see Geertz 1973, Goody 1956, Schlee 1994, Zitelmann 1994). The switching process uses a characteristic of human society, which animal social structures, so popular in theories of in-group behaviour, do not share: the capacity to preserve, in latency, different orders. We are all multilingual, at least in respect of language registers, we master different roles which we put into practice according to the situation and we make use consecutively of several affiliations (several modes of belonging, or identities in the strict systemic sense). We may call this phenomenon **polytaxis** or polytactic potential (from the greek πολυς many and ταξις order).

At this point we need to make an excursion into the concept of identity. At present there is a wealth of essays on this concept. It is not by accident that it is almost never operationalised. Most common is a use whereby identity means, under the appearance of a scientific concept, rather an ideologised sentiment. A closer look reveals three different meanings which sometimes are brought together: a) Belongingness (membership, the binding together of different people, this stems from the old philosophical meaning; I refer to identity in this sense, if not mentioned otherwise.). There is logically no problem to be part of several categories. b) Self -information (what do people think characterises themselves). c) Self-valuation/attribution of prestige (what are parameters of esteem and where does one place one's own group in relation to others). This is a central field of research – as is the foregoing one - which should not be confused with identity in the strict sense. It should, however, be seen in correlation to it.

There is, however, a difference between the working of polytactic identities with closed and with open structures (in most cases identical with the opposition of ethnic groups and nations). For African ethnic structures it is the common case that individuals can claim several affiliations. There we find situational switching (or: ethnic conversion) as an individual process. It is quite rare that there is only one "ethnic identity". (In a famine a Fulani herder in the West African Borgu might opt for the sedentary way of life of a Gando, if he were poor, or might become a Dendi trader, if he had some wealth).

This remarkable freedom of option, we can observe, should, however, not induce us to anthropological romanticism. The multiple opportunities of polytaxis allow also for an involuntary situational switching. A person may be excluded, e. g., if it is "discovered" by oracle that he or she belongs "in reality" not to our we-group, but to the secret order of witches.

There are some configurations where individual switching is a common answer to conjunctural ups and downs (Horn of Africa, the interior delta of the Niger). There are many others where this is uncommon and may be ultimately achieved only with burial after living as the "foreign" married wife or husband for a long period in the new community. The difference between these configurations seems to me to be created by the different (especially more or less elaborated) structure of the boundary zone and its "import procedures", the liminality of social systems (see below).

Once open (ethnic) groups get transformed into "para-national" bodies with established rights in respect of a state, there starts a painful process of opting between this - quite convenient - multiplicity of options and to negate all but one of them by pseudo-historical text production. With nationalities it is rather the exception (and tolerated only for a transition) that there are multiple affiliations. Within the nation-state ethnic options are rigidly welded on to the state structure and its formal procedures. Nationality and subnational entities with only singular options of belonging are such a case. Some countries even insist in a symbolically very prominent way on this singular subnationality by printing it into the identity cards (in Rwanda these were instrumental for the organised genocide of Tutsis (cf. Neubert 1999).

This rigid coupling constitutes a major difference between identities in an ethnic or an national field of reference. Individual switching in the national field tends to become the form of "cheating". Potential multiple belongings (identities) become something dangerous, if agitators label them as disloyality potential. Ethnic cleansing is then some nation states' ultimate answer to polytaxis.

Catalysts of collective switching: political entrepreneurs

Switching is a rather common - although rarely noticed[29] - process. Thus, we need a theory for collective switching. It operates differently from individual situational switching or opportunistic switching in the descriptive sense. In collective, co-ordinated and synchronised switching motives have to be redefined, new labels become the markers of connection, old labels have to be declared invalid currency and boundaries have to be redefined. Therefore a minimal consensus has to be sought. However, in general, the social structure provides no routines or institutions for such negotiation processes. This requires a very specific type of social actor: political entrepreneurs or central persons.

Switching processes, so my hypothesis, are linked to the emergence of leadership in a specific way: while the number of subjectively active actors in a given field (politics) is increased, paradoxically, in the same process the number of actors providing interpretation - especially of new phenomena - and implied in structurally relevant decisions, declines. The subjective impression is that "we are all getting politicised" - more people are entering the political arena. But after an initial ("chaotic") phase, the number of those who indicate (virtual) directions, leaders in the strict sense, decreases. If, subjectively, the chaos of future becomes a problem, if the "creation of a future", the selection of paths for future events becames the *desideratum*, then the moment for a specific type of actor has come. These are people who can produce a restriction of future options while appearing to be opening ways through a thicket. In other words, they can create power "from nothing"; it is a power which emerges from beyond the established decision-making procedures. The ones who can produce this "miracle" shall be called central persons. They are big men, warlords or adopted leaders (from the outside).

Big men and warlords can both convert prestige into power (= big men) or wealth into power (= warlords). They act in the ressource triangle of

---

[29] Leaders long for continuity and "historical roots" and anthropologists are the natural prey of ideological leaders.

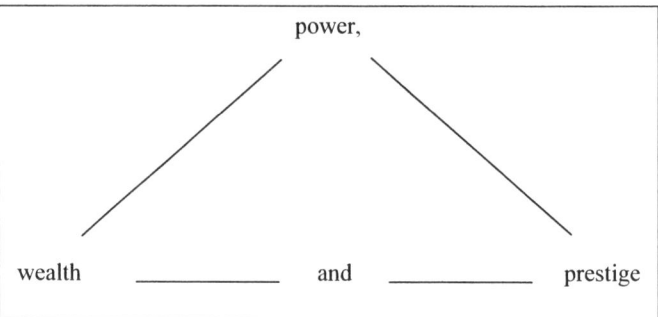

Warlords turn the wheel clockwise. They create power with money for weapons and mercenaries, and win prestige from power, which gives them credit for the acquisition of new wealth. Big men turn it the other way round. They transform prestige into power. Power may create wealth, but wealth and labour power has to be "devoted" to the people in order to create prestige.

Power can also have its origin outside the we-group. Then we call these central persons "adopted leaders". One such case seems to me to be Kemal Atatürk for the Alevi-community. Another more recent example is the role chancellor Kohl played in the East-German transformation process 1989/90. He took over after the Protestant leaders of the civil rights movement reached the limits of their mobilisation capacity. Similar to Melanesian big men those East German leaders had brought their prestige into play (cf. Godelier 1982). But unlike "big men" and unlike Chancellor Kohl, they had no means of regenerating it through economic exchange.

The formal mechanism of importing power from the outside or of creating power from prestige or wealth is not sufficient for giving a movement a twist. For their success, central persons need a very specific personal quality: a capacity to interpret (Deutungsmacht) which links them in a feed-back loop to the polytactic reference schemes of those they want to lead. Interpretation and orientation relieve one of the strain of complexity. The capacity to produce interpretation with seeming clarity and to reduce the complexity of the future is the personal attribute which is sought.

Political entrepreneurs may also switch individually from separatism to nationalism or vice-versa. Thus the former separatist Konrad Adenauer became, as the chancellor of West Germany, a symbol of moderate national feelings in Germany. Silvio Magnano left the Italian fascist student movement to become a successful leader of the (separatist) South-Tyrolians. One is tempted to say that in the environment of nation states one has to be a political entrepreneur in order to switch, since individual switching in these situations is rather prohibited.

Ideologies as a necessary element

Switching is not a random process. It is not even "normal". For social scientists the phenomenon of switching should of course be normal, but for the individual in most situations routine and continuity are the easier options. Switching has to refer, as formulated above, to established symbolic inventories and is limited by these; if for example religious we-groups have no historic precedence and if they do not constitute networks of communication or exchange nor provide institutions for conflict arbitrations, then there is no switching possible in the direction of this religious reference.

Central persons may have to add to the inventory and they have to alter the structure of relevances[30] (new goals have to become more important than those stabilising the routine) before they can operate the switching. To alter the structure of relevance new fears and new hopes have to be conceived. Changes in the field of symbols which concretise and order perception have a peculiar algorithm. They should be close to the routine ways of thinking and simultaneously they should appear to be innovations. "99 % accustomed concepts plus 99 % innovations" would be an appropriate formula. That means: the best solution is travesty! The innovations are presented as traditions (see Papstein 1978 and Hobsbawm & Ranger 1983 on the invention of tradition) and/or conceptual limits keep their place and the appearance is altered[31] (see Papstein 1978 and Hobsbawm & Ranger 1983 on the invention of tradition).

If deeper changes in the social structure are sought for or if marginal persons want to occupy centre stage, then another algorithm might be more appropriate or be used in combination: the creation of a co-ordinate system. Something is defined as a core norm and all behaviour is judged in terms of distance to this zero point. Belonging to a specific "race" or belief in some values or rather practice of some rituals are defined as "the fundamentals" from which any other condition of well-being can be deduced. It seems unconvincing to me to accept the self-made definition of the protagonists that the "fundamentals" are the doctrinal core of their religion. Whether the 'shador' or trinitarianism, these beliefs are seldom those found in the holy books. Symbols are chosen which react to other symbols in the time of present action. Even a non-doctrinal religion such as Hinduism gets attributed some "fundamentals" (see Randeria 1995). The leaders define their own place as "zero"; that is the irony of fundamentalism.

---

[30] This necessary change in the structure of relevance assimilates switching we-groups to processes of individual conversion as described by Berger and Luckmann (1980).

[31] This solution of changing the symbols and keeping the content can even be found among "new" theories in the humanities.

People driven into otherness

It should not be forgotten that beyond ideologies used for active switching people might be driven into another self-definition. Most of the Jews expatriated by Nazi-Germany gave up the self-definition "German" and kept the new American, Israeli etc. identity even after the war, when they could opt back.

A paradigmatic case is that of the Alsatians (and Lorrainians[32]), the inhabitants of the former German province Elsass-Lothringen (1872 – 1918) on the left bank of the river Rhine (following Jahr 1998). In 1914, when the First World War started, they were as engaged for the nationalist case as any other German "tribe" ("Stamm"). But since their "Germanness" dated only from 1872 (when Germany annexed this part of France without asking its inhabitants, based only upon the linguistic fact that they spoke German) the military hierarchy was distrustful. Thus they treated this territory, once the war started, as occupied land. When German troops accidentally fired at each other, it was suspected that these were shots from a guerrilla group, though this never existed. Censorship was imposed upon newspapers and letters. If an Alsatian soldier did not return from the battlefield, it was immediately suspected that he was a deserter, whereas with others it was assumed that they were killed or taken prisoner. In spite of no statistical support for this prejudice, the Alsatian recruites were given special treatment. Civilians who called each other names by making reference to the others' home region faced imprisonment, if the verbal aggressor was Alsatian and the other not - but not vice versa[33]. People felt abandoned by Germany. Without any underground pro-French movement the opinion changed completely till 1918. When the French entered the territory after the peace agreement, they were hailed and everyone declared her - or himself to be French, although the majority of the population had given up bilingualism during the German period and although for most people "French" was only their parents' or grandparents' identity. The same procedure seems to be used by the Turkish army "in order to" drive any Turkish identity out of the Kurdish-speaking populations of its East. The Russian government probably "succeeded" between 1996 and 2000 in driving out any remnant of Russian identity from among the population of its province Chechnya (cf. Tishkov 2000).

Populations deprived of equal access to the social and material goods relevant to them tend to opt for an other identity. The German proletariat of the 19th century which opted for the internationalist we-group of "the working class" is, to my mind, such a case. This phenomenon is strengthened, if these people get ascribed a different identity by the majority - under this condition labelling and insult can become a material force. Some movements of American Blacks seem to me to be such a case (cf. Irek

---

[32] In German "Elsass-Lothringer" or simplified "Elsässer", though this means only the southern, Allemanian part of the population.

[33] The Suebian could call the Alsatian from the Vogese mountains "Du Wackes!" but not the Alsatian the Suebian "Du Schwob!" (the penalty being one year prison).

1994). A more prestigious status and the hope for a better material status associated with it make switching the best and easiest option.

Family structures as a core element of ethnicity and national identity

Switching is more commonly linked to daily behaviour than anthropological or political writings suggest: the definition of belonging to some group is directly linked to the field of kinship and alliance structures. It depends upon the kinship structure taking into account whether a person belongs to her/his father's, mother's, mother's brother's or spouse's ethnic group. Once ethnic groups or nations get established, the production of kinship laws is one of their first preoccupations.

This brings us back to the classic definition of an ethnic group. Frederik Barth's (1969) definition, referring to ascription and self-ascription of boundaries, is too broad. This remained unnoticed for some time, since every reader had some preconception of what was meant. The definition implies also, if we read it carefully, political milieus and other subcultures. What was implicitly thought, but not written, as a defining characteristic, is that these groups are a sub-set of those groups which transcend families and which integrate families as the central reproductive structures. Thus we have to amend the definition:

> Ethnic groups are family-comprehending social categories, which ascribe themselves (or get ascribed by others) an (exclusive or multiple) identity,

To be born into a family identified with a given group produces the right to belong to this group according to the membership definition attached to the family. Switching implies the negotiation of identities, legal conflicts over the question to whom someone belongs and the "underliving" ("cheating") present in all human behaviour towards norms. All this is exposed in individual strategies dealing with ethnicity via kinship and alliance. People may be included by an initiation ritual which is required for marriage. They may opt for matrilineality instead of patrilineality. They may, in an virilocal environment, use uxorilocality as a means of integration. Endogamy as a group norm is no accident, it may be a strategically necessary element.

States are conscious of this. It is remarkable that even countries which claim - in simplification - that their citizenship is defined according to locality ("*ius soli*") and not according to descent ("*ius sanguinis*") like France and the US, devote much attention to the difference between marriage and "sham marriage" or to the marital status of their citizens' children born abroad.

This link between the dynamics of we-groups and reproduction has impacts upon demography, in the case where we want to break down statistics to the level of groups differentiated by social structure or culture. The mode of inclusion affects demographic growth or shrinkage on different levels. That migration is linked to individual switching, is obvious. Whether migrants who marry in, are counted as locals or not, depends upon the specific mode of inclusion. Neither the modes of inclusion nor the groups' limits are stable. The limits may meander around within a generation.

In some groups (e.g. the Byalebe or Berba of northern Bénin) women have no ethnic status at all. Their social integration is achieved through sons, who undergo the initiation ritual. To bear children is a primary social necessity for women in these or similar social conditions.

Stabilisation of we-group identities

Once we see switching as a normal process which reveals to us the universal polytactic potential, then we can take a fresh look at those groups which do not switch or do at least keep their boundaries. What stabilises ethnic groups and other we-groups? Current theory is mostly concerned with processes of splitting, of re-drawing boundaries and the creation (invention) of legitimating ideology.

Not one language directly, but one network of communication combined with shared social norms seems to be at the basis of all processes of we-group formation. Even in situations of seeming powerlessness this combination allows for the attribution of honour and shame (the "reputation sanction") as a means of social control.

Those features of community which strike us most - a common habitus (similarities in style and routines) - have been studied by Ralph Bohnsack and his group (1995) in their analysis of group formation among German youths. It turned out that habitual community is a later development. The start is a mutual articulation of individual plans for activities, creating an interdependence, which one may call a community of fate (Schicksalsgemeinschaft). Norm-breaking or violence which provoke revenge are powerful but risky means of creating a community of fate in the emphatic sense; the weaker the groups' capacity to create a common code or habitus, the stronger is the inclination to produce collective risk or foes if necessary by means of violence .

We can go further: "hatred" among German skinheads and rightwing radicals is not a sentiment against the "enemies" invented by them but a shorthand symbol for the community-feeling generated by the self-initiated violence. The emotion is thus not the origin of the violence, but is a semantic element, a sememe, coming to work in the process of group creation or confirmation through violent confrontation. This can be generalised: violent confrontation is one of the most powerful means of creating or recreating ethnic or national identification (see Schlee / Shongolo 1995 on Southern Ethiopia).

Two processes are central: moral economy and instiutions of conflict resolution.

a) Moral economy/practical solidarity is a distribution process of goods and services which, by many actors, is not seen as (market-)economy. The principles of distribution are rather those which economic anthropology calls generalised reciprocity or redistribution. This extends from help for anonymous persons belonging to the same we-group to redistribution through welfare and pension schemes (see Elwert 1987, Kohli 1987).

b) Institutions of conflict resolution increase the conflict processing capacities (Konfliktfähigkeit). This may be achieved by the creation of institutions for arbitration or by the implementation of a normative system equally relevant for all the members of the we-group (see Albert Hirschman 1994). It was not "common values" but the new *"Bürgerliche Gesetzbuch"* (common law) which, at the end of last century, made national Germans out of citizens of German states (Elwert 1998). It is often stated, that common values - at least a minimal core - are needed to create a we-group. Empirically we have difficulty finding cases to illustrate this point; what we rather find, are conflict regulating institutions and mutually accepted procedures which forego the creation of common values.

German authors are supposed to bring language into play following Herder, who "naturalised" nations by reference to language[34]. There are, however, sufficient we-groups of ethnic form without a common language, to keep a distance to this discourse (cf. Höllmann 1992). We should rather draw attention to the fact that communities of discourse can also be interpreted or seen in relation to arbitration of conflict and economics of reciprocity. Arbitration requires a code and this code has to have a linguistic form (a given language or two corresponding isomorphic registers of two languages). The cohesion of "the Slovenes" in the Austrian Province of Krain is at first sight a surprising fact. Its endurance over 800 years under German speaking administration was due to the fact that the most important legal code for their mode of life, the forest code, was written in Slovenian. Slovenes in Italy who never shared this reference were never able to create a political entity or at least a majority movement in any regional unit.

Social systems do not only exist within the self-limiting status of ethnic groups, although the mode of information storage in anthropology (arranged according to ethnic groups) may suggest this. There are two modes: one is characterised by opening up and networking with the imperative to include an optimal number of persons, who beforehand were strangers, into one's own network of reciprocal relations. The other is the restrictive closing up of we-group formation that this paper dealt with.

---

[34] See Diericks 1989 for a discussion of Herder and its followers.

Violent confrontation or its threat can also be used in order to win in a competition within a given ethnic or national entity. If an elite opts for the networking mode described above, another strategic group may opt for closing up. In order to win the competition this second group has to create a confrontation at the group's frontiers. This confrontation - portrayed in the discourse as defense of honour or welfare - hides the motive of internal competition. We call it endostrategic mobilisation (*Binnenmobilisierung*), because the main strategic goal is an interior one (Eckert / Elwert / Gosztonyi / Zitelmann 1999).

It is both forms, the bimodality[35] of networking and group closure, which make for the dynamism of mankind. Though we may conceive some historical processes as an alternation of both modes, I want rather to draw attention to social arrangements, which combine both - the definition of people as strangers and their inclusion.

The self-description of those features of we-groups which make for their stability rarely mention the fact that all these arrangements seldom produce unambiguous borderlines. Yet the multiplicity of social subsystems produces rather complicated legal arrangements: e.g. differentiation between political and economic citizenship or civic rights for strangers as social or economic actors. Each of these boundaries can be subject to a tidal movement whereby some actors are for some time in or out. This causes the social boundary - mostly unnoticed by the majority of the population - to become a broad "liminal zone"[36]. This liminal zone fulfills important social functions. Here is a field where new ideas and arrangements are tested out before they become adopted as "ours". This very adoption as "ours", the "nostrification", requires social arrangements or institutions for some items.

In order to find out what can pass and what needs to be scrutinised, this liminal zone functions as a filter. Because of their precarious positions persons in this field are highly sensibilised. They may perceive sooner the usefulness of a new arrangement (because they saw its functioning outside the system or in the liminal zone sooner) and they may react more vigorously to something as "strange" (because they want to be "in").

The 'modernity' of nationalism

The strength of the human race in respect of other animals is its high flexibility. Multiple identities and switching processes contribute considerably to this. The creation of nation states, in some sense, certainly was an "evolutionary success", or, to say it more precisely, it produced a pattern which proved to be instrumental for pattern

---

[35] Achim von Oppen (1993) gave a remarkable description of groups on the upper Zambezi and Kasai in Central Africa alternating between closure and networking.

[36] This was developed in the paper by Elwert et al. (1993). We originally owe the concept to Victor Turner (1969), who used it for the description of an element of initiation rituals. Ayse Çaglar (1993) yet earlier transferred it to a similar meaning as I did later.

expansion in other fields. However, this very same creation produced a set-back in respect of flexibility for an individual's polytactic social behaviour. Rather complicated legal arrangements try to cope this draw-back (e.g. differentiation between political and economic citizenship, civic rights for strangers as social or economic actors). Thus they contribute to the process whereby social boundaries change their character. Although still perceived as a dividing line, they get broadened to liminal zones of transition. These blurred zones of ambivalent membership work as surrogates for the polytactic ethnic flexibility – the normality of multiple membership – characteristic for many stateless societies.

From the perspective of an individual actor who makes opportunistic use of his multiple affiliations in an ethnically defined environment, a national structure still looks "underdeveloped". There is still a long way before we reach the flexibility of we-group identity, which is the strength of ethnic systems.

Nationalism and other we-group mobilisations are, however, a product of "modernisation" in a restricted sense. If we conceive the concomitance of expanding market economies with expanding communications systems linked by a positive feedback as "formal modernisation", then nationalism and fundamentalism clearly are aspects of this. We should, however, keep in mind that this definition of modernisation does **not** imply any reference to (civic) values or to social differentiation through institution-building.

Warlord systems and genocides are part of modernisation in this perspective. Insofar as modernisation increasingly creates links to anomymous persons, and, as these links increasingly dominate the life world as "societal" (gesellschaftliche) relations, there emerge **undercurrents** which reinterpret and reconstruct social links as something built upon emotions and or face-to-face relations (cf. Frühwald 1992). If, for example, marriage is less an affair to be regulated by lineages, and if selection of mating partners is opened to persons unknown to the heads of families, while the formal guarantees and rituals are handled more and more by state authorities, then **"love"** becomes an attractive code for the interpretation of decisions leading to marriage (cf. Luhmann 1982). I put this example into the foreground in order to underline the fact that nationalism is not the only "undercurrent". But it is a rather obvious case. Societal links are reinterpreted as community (Max Weber 1922). The real process may be one of building institutions which link persons, who are, in most cases, anonymous to each other. The façade of self-descriptions dwells upon images of community, using metaphors of face-to-face groups and invoking emotions. Emotions such as love, hatred and fear which were for a long time in the domain of intimate communication are now being transported through mass media. The Rwandan genocide of 1994 has shown how powerful this instrument can be (Neubert 1999: 162).

Nationalism and its concept of "Nation" also contributed to our image of a modern world. It contributed many ideological elements which today go without saying, such as the "Hero" and "Freedom". Modern politics is in one important aspect a symbolic process, motivated and limited by sociohistorical dynamics. That modern nationalism is so intimately linked with war is not an obvious or even natural combination. For the masses, who had to be integrated as soldiers, war was a costly and risky enterprise. A reconstruction of the prestige system was necessary in order to alter this attitude. The "Hero", and especially the dead one, had to be constructed as peak element of the prestige pyramid and even as an object of secular quasi-religious devotion. This took the image of ridicoulousness away from soldiers, as it was exemplified in Plautus' much read "*miles gloriosus*".This ideologem was then artfully intertwined with oscillating metaphors of "Freedom". Freedom was seen on the one side as a controlled realm conceived as "own" - the own farm or workshop or family - and on the other side as an accessible realm - the freedom of movements for migrant traders and access to commodities. The oscillation between both aspects was the strength of the concept.

The more politics were associated with communication, the more it was plausible to link we-groups to languages. Thus the idea that one nation should have one language - and later - that one language makes a nation, incrementally is gaining acceptance though during the period when nationalism was formulated, the social reality was still that of multilingualism.

In its beginnings nationalism was far from a plausible concept. Now the combination of an "obvious reality" - language - with strong sentiments of prestige - heroes - interwoven with equally strong sentiments of fear and hope - namely freedom - , looks almost unchallenged and contributes to our image of the modern world. This combination however had to be acquired in a two-century long process of variation and selection. But this is not the end of we-group history; competing concepts may yet be in their process of evolution.

National boundaries will only be given up if the wider space created implies a stable frame for action, a realm of foreseeability. The contingency of human action needs to be controlled - not suppressed - by conflict regulating institutions. The reference to new realms of action has to be validated by an emotional experience. The fear of violence would be antinomic to this.

Thanks

For useful suggestions I have to thank Erdmute Alber, Alexandra Billod, Artur Bogner, Ayse Çaglar, Chris Gregory, Krisztina Kehl, Ute Luig, Rainer Münz, Günther Schlee, Andreas Wimmer and Thomas Zitelmann.

References

Anderson, Benedict 1988. *Die Erfindung der Nation - Zur Karriere eines folgenreichen Konzepts.* Frankfurt a. M.: Campus (original: *Imagined Communities.* London: Verso 1983)

Aronson, Dan 1976. Ethnicity as a cultural system. In: Henry Frances (ed.). *Ethnicity in the Americas.* Den Haag: Mouton

Barth, Frederik 1969. Preface. In: Frederik Barth (ed.). *Ethnic groups and boundaries.* Bergen: Universitets Forlaget: 9 - 38

Berger, Peter and Luckmann, Thomas 1980 (1977*). Die gesellschaftliche Konstruktion der Wirklichkeit.* Frankfurt: Fischer

Bohnsack, Ralf, Loos, Peter, Schäffer, Burkhard, Städtler, Klaus and Wild, Bodo 1995. *Die Suche nach Gemeinsamkeit und die Gewalt der Gruppe - Hooligans, Musikgruppen und andere Jugendcliquen.* Opladen: Leske und Budrich

Çaglar, Ayse 1993. The Prison House of Culture in the Study of Turks in Germany. *Sozialanthropologisches Arbeitspapier Nr. 31.* Berlin: das arabische buch

Canfield, Robert Leroy 1973. Faction and conversion in a plural society. Religious alignments in the Hindu Kush. *Anthropological Paper No. 50.* Ann Arbor: University of Michigan

Cohen, Abner 1974. The Lesson of Ethnicity. In: Abner Cohen (ed.). *Urban Ethnicity.* London, New York: Tavistock Publication

Diericks, Ludo 1989. *De Groene Idee, Mens en Natie.* Gent: Kritiek

During, Jean 1993. Nation et territoire en Asie Intérieure. In: *Yearbook for traditional music* 25: 29 - 42

Eckert, Julia, Elwert, Georg, Gosztonyi, Kristòf, Zitelmann, Thomas 1999. Konflikttreiber - Konfliktschlichter. Erste theoretische Erkenntnisse einer vergleichenden Untersuchung in Bosnien, Bombay und Oromiya Regional State (Äthiopien). *Sozialanthropologisches Arbeitspapier 75.* Berlin: das arabische buch

Elwert, Georg 1987. Ausdehnung der Käuflichkeit und Einbettung der Wirtschaft - Markt und Moralökonomie. In: Klaus Heinemann (ed.). Soziologie wirtschaftlichen Handelns. *Sonderheft der Kölner Zeitschrift für Soziologie und Sozialpsychologie:* 300 - 321

Elwert, Georg 1989. Nationalismus und Ethnizität - Über die Bildung von Wir-Gruppen. In: *Kölner Zeitschrift für Soziologie und Sozialpsychologie Nr. 3:* 440 - 464

Elwert et al. 1993. Die Herausforderung durch das Fremde. *Outline for a project group of the Berlin-Brandenburg Academy of Science.* Berlin

Elwert, Georg 1998. Deutsche Nation. In: Bernhard Schäfers and Wolfgang Zapf (eds.). *Handwörterbuch zur deutschen Gesellschaft:* 123 - 134. Opladen. Leske and Budrich

Frühwald, Wolfgang 1992: Romantik. In: Erwin Fahlbusch et al. (eds.) *Evangelisches Kirchenlexikon.* Göttingen:Vandenhoeck and Ruprecht: 1667 - 1675

Geertz, Clifford 1973. *The Interpretation of Cultures.* Chapter: The integrative revolution. Primordial sentiments and civil politics in the new states. First 1963. New York:Harper

Godelier, Maurice 1982. *La production des Grands Hommes. Pouvoir et domination masculine chez les Baruya de Nouvelle-Guinée.* Paris: Librairie Arthème Fayard

Goody, Jack 1956. *The social organisation of the LoWiili.* London: H.M. Stationary Office

Haarmann, Ulrich 1991. Affen hoch zu Ross. Die Resistenz innerislamischer Feindbilder zwischen Arabern und Türken. In: *Frankfurter Allgemeine Zeitung* 13. 2: N 3

Hirschman, Albert 1994. Social conflicts as pillars of democratic market society. In: *Political Theory* 22, 2: 203 - 216

Hobsbawm, Eric J. and Ranger, Terence (eds.) 1983. *The Invention of Tradition.* Cambridge [Cambridgeshire], New York : Cambridge University Press

Höllmann, Thomas 1992. Kritische Gedanken zum Ethnos-Begriff in der Völkerkunde - am Beispiel festländisch-südostasiatischer Bevölkerungsgruppen. In: *Tribus Nr. 41:* 177 - 186

Irek, Matgorzata 1994. *The European roots of the Harlem Renaissance. Berliner Beiträge zur Amerikanistik 1.* Berlin: Freie Universität

Jahr, Christoph 1998. *Gewöhnliche Soldaten. Desertion und Deserteure im deutschen und britischen Heer 1914 - 1918.* Göttingen: Vandenhoeck and Ruprecht

Kehl, Krisztina 1992. Vom revolutionären Klassenkampf zum wahren Islam. Transformationsprozesse im Alevitum der Türkei nach 1980. *Sozialanthropologisches Arbeitspapier Nr. 49.* Berlin: das arabische buch

Kehl-Bodrogi, Krisztina et al. 1997. *Syncretistic Religious Communities in the Near East.* Leiden, New York: E. J. Brill

Kohli, Martin 1987. Ruhestand und Moralökonomie. Eine historische Skizze. In: Klaus Heinemann (ed.). Soziologie wirtschaftlichen Handelns. *Sonderheft 28 der Kölner Zeitschrift für Soziologie und Sozialpsychologie*: 393 - 416

Leach, Edmund (1964) 1993. *Political Systems of Highland Burma*. London: Athlone

Lentz, Carola 1995. Ethnizität und "Tribalismus" in Afrika. Ein Forschungsüberblick. In: *Leviathan* 23,1: 115 - 145

Lonsdale, John 1993. Staatsgewalt und moralische Ordnung. Die Erfindung des Tribalismus in Africa. In: *Der Überblick* 29,3: 5 - 10

Luhmann, Niklas 1982. *Liebe als Passion*. Frankfurt/M.: Suhrkamp

Mühlmann, Wilhelm E. 1961. *Chiliasmus und Nativismus. Studien zur Psychologie, Soziologie und historischen Kasuistik der Umsturzbewegungen*. Berlin: Reimer

Mühlmann, Wilhelm E. 1962. *Homo Creator. Abhandlungen zur Soziologie, Anthropologie und Ethnologie*. Wiesbaden: Harrassowitz

Müller, Ernst W. 1980. Der Begriff "Volk" in der Ethnologie. In: *Saeculum Nr. 40:* 237 - 252

Neubert, Dieter 1999. Dynamics of Escalating Violence. In: Georg Elwert and Stefan Feuchtwang and Dieter Neubert, (eds.). *Dynamics of Violence:* 151 - 174. Berlin: Dunker and Humblot

Oppen, Achim von 1993. *Terms of Trade and Terms of Trust*. Münster: Lit

Papstein, Robert 1978. *The Upper Zambezi: A History of the Luvale Peoples*. Ph.D thesis, University of California, Los Angeles

Randeria, Shalini 1995. "Hindu-Fundamentalismus": Zum Verhältnis von Religion, Politik und Geschichte im modernen Indien. *Sozialanthropologisches Arbeitspapier Nr. 67*. Berlin: das arabische buch

Schlee, Günther 1994. *Identities on the move. Clanship and pastoralism in Northern Kenya*. Nairobi, Kenya: Gideon S. Were Press (first published 1989: Manchester University Press)

Schlee, Günther and Abdullahi Shongolo 1995. Local War and its Impact on Ethnic and Religious Identification in Southern Ethiopia. In: *Geo-Journal* 36, 1: 7 - 17

Thurnwald, Richard 1953. Sippe und Stamm. In Erwin von Beckenrath (ed.). *Handwörterbuch der Sozialwissenschaften*. Vol. 1: 272-277. Stuttgart: G. Fischer

Tishkov, Valery 2000. *Understanding violence for post-conflict reconstruction in Chechnya*. Paper presented to the 4th International Security Forum, Geneva

Turner, Victor 1969. *The ritual process*. London: Routledge and Kegan Paul

Wallerstein, Immanuel 1980. *The capitalist world-economy*. Chapter 11: The two modes of ethnic consciousness: Soviet Central Asia in transition: 184 - 192. Cambridge. Cambridge University Press

Weber, Max 1922. *Wirtschaft und Gesellschaft*. Tübingen: Mohr

Wimmer, Andreas 1995. Stämme für den Staat - Tribale Politik und die kurdische Nationalbewegung im Irak. In: *Kölner Zeitschrift für Soziologie und Sozialpsychologie* 47,1: 95 - 113

Zitelmann, Thomas 1994. *Nation der Oromo. Kollektive Identitäten, nationale Konflikte und Wir-Gruppenbildungen*. Berlin: das arabische buch

ABSTRACT

The strength of the human race in respect of other animals is its high flexibility. Multiple identities and switching processes contribute considerably to that. The creation of nation states (which was an "evolutionary success", or to say it more precisely, which proved to be instrumental for pattern expansion in other fields) produced, however, a set-back in respect of flexibility in individuals' polytactic social behaviour.

Rather complicated legal arrangements try to cope with this draw-back (e.g. differentiation between political and economic citizenship, civic rights for strangers as social or economic actors). They contribute thus to the process of social boundaries becoming broadened liminal zones as surrogates for polytactic ethnic flexibility.

From the perpective of an individual actor who makes an opportunistic use of his multiple belongings in an ethnically defined environment, a national structure still looks "underdeveloped". It is still a long way till we will reach the flexibility of we-group identity, which makes the strength of ethnic systems.

Nationalism and other we-group mobilisations are, however, a product of "modernisation" in a restricted sense. If we conceive as "formal modernisation" the concomitance of expanding market economies with expanding communications systems linked by a positive feed-back, then nationalism and fundamentalism clearly are aspects of this. We should, however, keep in mind that this definition of modernisation does **not** imply any reference to (civic) values or to social differentiation through institution building. Warlord systems and genocides are part of modernisation this perspective.

These processes are illustrated by the re-definition processes of the Alevi identity in Turkey which responded to the opportunities of secularism and the hostility of Sumi "fundamentalism", and by the ethnicisation of religion in former Yugoslavia.

Part II

Unravelling conflicting emotions

TEMPERAMENTAL NEIGHBOURS:
UIGHUR-HAN RELATIONS IN XINJIANG, NORTHWEST CHINA
Ildikó Bellér-Hann

Introduction

The geographical focus of this chapter is the northwestern province of the People's Republic of China (PRC), nowadays known as Xinjiang, where, behind a façade of socialist multiculturalism, Han Chinese in effect still rule over non-Han minorities. The region, which incorporates a long stretch of the ancient Silk Road has had a long history of Chinese presence, going back to the times of the Han dynasty. It has been officially part of China since 1884, although the effective incorporation of the area into the Qing Empire dates back to the second half of the eighteenth century. The largest administrative unit of the PRC, the Xinjiang Uighur Autonomous Region (XUAR) is home to thirteen officially recognised nationalities, six of whom are Muslim and speak Turkic languages.[37] The largest of these groups, the Uighur, have been the titular majority of the region since the foundation of the XUAR in 1955. There has been ethnic tension in the province throughout this period, and preceding generations are also often presented by the Uighur in terms of ethnic conflict and violence.

This chapter is largely based on a stay of two months in the oasis town of Ürükzar in Southern Xinjiang in 1995.[38] Ürükzar is the administrative centre of a

---

[37] This figure is based on a Xinjiang source, see Dowamat 1993: 78. For data on the officially recognised minorities in China see Gladney 1994 b: 172-3.

[38] Ürükzar is a pseudonym. I originally planned three research trips in consecutive years. In 1995 I was able to stay in Ürükzar with the tacit approval of the local authorities, the first foreigner to be able to do so for half a century. As I had a tourist visa, I could not do research but was nonetheless able to make many contacts among the Uighur residents. At the end of my stay in 1995 a research permit was approved by the authorities of the XUAR for a five months' stay in 1996, followed by a period of two months in 1997, within the framework of a joint research programme with Han Chinese partners at Xinjiang Normal University, Urumqi. Fieldwork in 1996 was relocated to Kashgar, which displays broadly similar patterns. The last period of research in 1997 was eventually completed outside the Peoples' Republic of China altogether, among the Uighur living in Kazakstan. In spite of its ancient history and prominence throughout the later, Islamic centuries as a religious and trading centre, Ürükzar has received little attention in works of modern political history (dominated by Kashgar, Ili and the provincial capital, Urumqi). Unlike some of the other oasis towns of the region, it has little prominence in foreign travel writing, except for descriptions of its ancient, pre-Islamic sites. In contrast to other locations, western missionary presence in the twentieth century has been negligible. Since the town was opened to foreign visitors only in the early 1990s, in 1995 individual tourists were still a novelty. As the town boasts no institution of higher education, foreign missionaries, who elsewhere register as students or work as English teachers, had not established themselves by 1995.

The perspective of this paper is one-sided: it focuses on inter-ethnic relations from the point of view of Uighur identity. My data come primarily from direct conversations with Uighur people in their mother tongue. My command of Uighur and lack of Chinese occasionally led to suspicious reactions from

county (*nahiyä*) of 400.000 people, 92 % of whom are Uighur. The townships (*yeza*) it governs have an almost exclusively Uighur settled agricultural population, but the town, with a population of 50 000, has a nearly 40 % Han Chinese presence, and their numbers are rapidly growing here. Few of the Han speak even basic Uighur, while few Uighur have more than a rudimentary knowledge of Chinese. The choice of this particular town was not mine: it was suggested by Han Chinese partners in the provincial capital Urumqi, who thought that the oasis I had originally suggested was not a feasible choice: it was too poor, and it had a reputation for being a stronghold of Islamic mysticism always closely associated with anti-Han sentiments. Ürükzar, on the other hand, had appeared prosperous and stable, hence the suggestion that it would be a suitable fieldsite. In fact this oasis too can look back on a history chequered with protests and uprisings, but the approval of the authorities for an extended stay led me to expect stability, equilibrium and peaceful co-existence rather than conflict, hatred and violence.[39]

The emergence of the Uighur as a modern ethnic group is essentially a twentieth century phenomenon, comparable to developments among the Uzbek and other Turkic groups in the former Soviet Union. After 1949 China followed the Soviet model in many respects, including collectivisation and the economic exploitation of its peripheral regions. Policies towards 'national minorities' comprised an attempt to *control* rather than to *integrate* them. (Bergère 1979; Gladney 1991: 66). Rudelson has studied the dynamics of ethnic consciousness among Uighur intellectuals (1997). He has shown how competing self-definitions among Uighur intellectuals of different oasis backgrounds combine with class differentiations to work against the emergence of a unified Uighur ethnic group. Through a detailed study of the Chinese Muslims Gladney has shown how the intricate, dynamic interplay between self-perception and state interference shapes ethnic identity in the PRC (1991). He has addressed both general aspects of ethnicity within the PRC (1991; 1994 b) and the case of the Uighur of Xinjiang in particular, including their ethnogenesis and the role adopted by the state in the process (1990; 1991; 1994 a). In a recent article he addresses ethnic identities in a transnational perspective and, developing a model of 'relational alterity', argues that essentialised attempts at final definitions of the meanings of identities (such as a Uighur, Muslim, Turk, or dweller in a particular oasis, citizen of the PRC etc.) should give way to an examination of the circumstances which temporarily foreground some identities and background others (1996).[40]

Han residents, and prevented me from studying Han perceptions of the Uighur and indeed their self-perceptions.

[39] For an introduction to the Uighur and Chinese in Xinjiang see Hoppe 1998, esp. Pp. 56-170, and 308-349.

[40] I became aware of Joanne Smith's forthcoming article (Smith 2002) only after my completed article had been submitted and accepted for publication. We carried out fieldwork at the same time in Xinjiang independently for one another, and wrote our respective pieces on the subject of ethnic relations unaware of each other's work. I consider similarities between our approach as mutual confirmation of

In contrast to Gladney's focus, in this chapter I shall examine lower levels of identity in a town that qualifies as one of the more remote ones of the Silk Road. I shall consider the different strategies employed by the Uighur of Xinjiang to reproduce and reinforce ethnic boundaries vis-a-vis the Han Chinese, efforts which are also instrumental in promoting the 'amorphous, invented' identity of the Han, both nationally and within Xinjiang (Gladney 1994 a: 112; cf. Grobe-Hagel 1991: 14). It may appear paradoxical that, in spite of the existence of clear-cut rules, ethnic boundaries are sometimes crossed. In spite of the dominance of the Han in what can be characterised as a 'ranked' hierarchical relationship between the two groups (Horowitz 1985: 22), in some aspects of daily interaction the rules are sometimes dictated by the lower-ranking group, the Uighur.[41] Such interaction may take a variety of forms. The markers of difference most often discussed are language and religion, but a host of other distinguishing features augment the repertoire of boundary markers to emphasise real or imagined differences. I am especially interested in how various traits that are evoked as ethnic boundary markers serve also as intra-group markers of difference. Ideas concerning the body, diet, temperament and other, more visible symbols, some of which are easily overlooked or dismissed as 'trivial', such as women's fashion sense, may all become subtle expressions of ethnic identity while remaining markers of intra-group difference between the generations, the sexes, the sophisticated city dweller and the uneducated peasant, or other, hierarchically ordered groups within Uighur society. They become markers of ethnicity only in the close physical or symbolic presence of another group. Hence an oasis town in which Uighur and Han coexist and have to interact regularly is a good location for observing how such symbols double up and operate as markers of ethnicity.

Some of these symbols and ideas which in the context of the oasis town may acquire the force of ethnic boundary markers also develop this second meaning within villages where the population is virtually exclusively Uighur. Here the presence of the other group may be restricted to a few Han Chinese government officials working in the township leadership, or a handful of recent settlers, but the force of this presence is still considerable. Even in 'pure' Uighur villages, nowadays increasingly rare, Han Chinese hegemony over what is perceived as Uighur land has been imprinted on people's minds by past experience; and it is constantly renewed in the representations of the media, through continuous rumours of ethnic violence and anti-Han protests throughout the province, and through the direct impact of policies associated with the Han, such as birth control or religious policies. In these conditions, no aspect of culture is innocent of ethnic implications: a change in female fashion may be an expression of a desire to mark social distance between peasants and cadres, but such a decla-

---

our evaluation of the ethnic situation in Xinjiang, and consider the two articles complementary, since Smith's ethnographic material is based on fieldwork in Urumqi, and mine in a smaller oasis centre in southern Xinjiang.

[41] A similar observation was made by Gladney concerning asymmetrical hospitality patterns between Han Chinese and Chinese Muslims (1991: 120-122).

ration remains within certain parameters which make it plain that the wearer is Uighur rather than Chinese. Thus various expressions of intra-group indentities may simultaneously acquire meanings as markers of religious, regional or ethnic belonging. The multiplicity of meanings may not be obvious to all observers: a particular dress may reveal to a Han Chinese only that the wearer is an Uighur, but Uighur women may recognise a particular cut and know that the material of the dress is of the most expensive sort which only cadres or the wives of rich merchants can afford. External identity markers which are also at the same time internal shapers of identity, are neither uniform nor unchangable. Actors themselves usually consciously insist on uniformity and continuity through time and emphasise external aspects as establishing and confirming their group identity. However, they may also acknowledge, albeit implicitly, that components of identity, such as a person's temperament (*mijäz*), are susceptible not only to personal variation within the group but also to social construction and therefore to change in the course of further social interaction.

Time and space

One of the most fundamental dichotomies between the two major ethnic groups in Ürükzar lies in the keeping of time. The Han observe the official time known throughout the PRC as Beijing time. This is the time displayed on clocks in public places, including all government offices. Beijing time determines bus and flight arrivals and departures. However, the Uighur live by local, 'Xinjiang time' which is two hours behind Beijing time. If a foreign visitor fails to identify a person's ethnic affiliation from physical features and other attributes, a glance at the person's watch can usually provide a decisive clue.

Yet it would be a mistake to imagine that Han and Uighur maintain rigid temporal apartheid. In reality, many accommodations are reached. Office workers who in eastern China would begin work at 8.00 am turn up for 10.00 am in Ürükzar: the rhythm of their day is basically in harmony with that of the sun and of the Uighur. Uighur who work alongside Han may have to use Beijing time for some formal purposes. Such people may as a matter of course add the phrase 'Xinjiang time'or 'Beijing time' to every time specification they have to make, but in most social interaction it will be obvious from the context which is being used.

Like many other Central Asian urban settlements, Ürükzar gives a first impression of sharp spatial segregation. The new colonial town sharply contrasts with the old Muslim town situated by the river. This segregation has antecedents which pre-date communism. In a historical study of Qing policies in Xinjiang Millward points out that the cautious policies of the Qing to segregate the Han from the local Muslim population, aimed at preventing conflict and violence, were seldom rigidly imposed. Segregated communities developed only following the first wave of Muslim rebellions in the early nineteenth century. In Ürükzar the spatial segregation is well documented from the late nineteenth century, by which time there existed a separate Chinese and

Muslim garrison (Millward 1998: 140). The visible sense of apartheid is confirmed by the local Uighur guide, who tells western visitors that the Old Town is 'pure' Uighur, while the New Town is overwhelmingly Han. Such seperation of new and old towns is a common feature of cities in Xinjiang. Although today there is no specific boundary marker between the two, Uighur cart-drivers point to a stretch of a major road which they regard as the border. The physical appearance of the two parts presents sharp contrasts: the Old Town with its adobe houses has a Middle Eastern atmosphere that contrasts sharply with the wide, geometrically designed asphalt roads and modern blocks of the New Town. All the major government buildings, the main post office, the central bus and taxi stations, the court, the prison, the Communist Party and police headquarters, the western style hospital, some small factories, the main library, banks and larger shops are located in the New Town. So too are the major sites of entertainment, the two dance halls and the theatre. The Old Town has most of the characteristics of a Muslim city: inward looking houses protected with walls from curious passers-by, the Friday mosque, a central square around which the weekly Friday bazaar is held, and a permanent covered bazaar. Most of the roads here are dirt roads where carts pulled by donkeys, mules or horses compete chaotically with pedestrians, buses and bicycles.[42] Street peddlars and beggars are numerous. The Old Town boasts a number of schools, a local history museum, a small library and some banks. It also has a large hospital, but this is a 'minority national' hospital where traditional Uighur medicine is practised. Cheap private hotels catering for Muslim traders still bear more resemblance to old style caravansarais than to modern hotels. In the heart of the Old Town, where the major bridge runs into the central square, unemployed unskilled labourers and potential employers meet at dawn every day (*medikar baziri*).

But the sense of apartheid is deceptive. Although the modern buildings and asphalt streets of the New Town present a façade of Han rule, behind them we find the landmarks of Muslim quarters. These neighbourhoods in the New Town may remain undetected by the short term visitor. They are tight-knit communities with most of the attributes of the Muslim quarters of the Old Town. Their small mosques are invisible to the passers-by on the main streets. The call to prayer is recited without a loudspeaker, and so is unheard outside the immediate neighbourhood. This is a reminder of the limits within which Islam is tolerated: it must remain invisible and muted to the outside world.[43] In contrast, loudspeakers remain in use along the major roads of the New Town, transmitting Chinese language news, music and announcements. Although the major mosque, a cultural monument, and another important Friday mosque are both located in the Old Town, the town's most important shrine is only five minutes' walk from the intersection of the main asphalt roads of the New Town. In the Old Town there is a Chinese school, surrounded by Muslim neighbourhoods.

---

[42] On the juxtaposition of the traditional, old town and the colonial town see Brown (1984) and Eickelman (1981: 273-277). On the Muslim city see Eickelman (1981: 266-273).

[43] On the religious policies of the Chinese state see Dillon 1995: 17-26 and Grobe-Hagel 1991: 31-67.

Thus the spatial organisation of the town exhibits both segregation and subtle patterns of intermingling. While whole neighbourhoods appear at first sight to be ethnically homogenous communities, and are somtimes presented as such by local residents, behind the apparent spatial segregation lies a more complex reality of shared spheres and interaction. Han in government employment occupy modern blocks in the New Town, but these work units are shared with Uighur employees and their families. Shared public spaces, particularly in the marketplace and street stalls, are frequently the scenes of open conflict. When the arguing parties involve a Han and an Uighur, differences in opinion over faulty merchandise, high prices, mistaken calculations or wrong change will invariably be expressed in ethnic terms. Such scenes may quickly become a source of violence as more people join in on both sides.

Ethnic boundaries are occasionally straddled in leisure activities. In theory the clientèles of the two dance halls, situated along the same main road in the New Town, are separated along ethnic lines, and the Uighur dance hall is indeed frequented by Uighur only. Yet the Chinese dance hall has a mixed group of customers. Educated young Uighur sometimes take their female partners there because it is said to be a clean, safe and civilised place in contrast to the Uighur dance hall, which is known for heavy drinking, brawls and prostitution. In this context the Han are clearly marked as the bearers of civilisation.[44] Although Han men are said to be keen on establishing contact with Uighur women, they avoid the Uighur dance hall since it is perceived as highly dangerous, in part due to excessive alcohol consumption. Educated Uighur may also criticise the culture of the dance hall, but they may suggest that its abuses are the fault of the Han, who have made cheap alcohol widely available. This is consistent with the more general tendency to attribute social evils to Han influence (e.g. various forms of gambling). Their presence there would imply sexual interest in Uighur women, an area of interaction between the groups which is most likely to provoke extreme reactions.

Occupation and education

Occupational segregation in Ürükzar mirrors both basic ethnic dichotomy and the fuzziness of boundaries in the town. Uighur catering is primarily based on the dietary observances of the Muslims, who meticulously avoid eating pork, a prime ingredient in Han cuisine. Other services too, such as tailoring, hairdressing, certain branches of trading and local education, reflect duality, Uighur traders attract Uighur

---

[44] Civilised or cultured (mädäniy) behaviour appear as key concepts in Uighur language journals and magazines, which condemn the backwardness of some Uighur practices. Instead of explicitly holding up the Han as a positive model to emulate, 'bad' habits are condemned as recent deviations from the old national norms of Uighur culture. For examples see Hüsäyin 1995 a, 1995 b, 1995c; Toxti 1995; Tahir 1995.

customers, Han cater for Han Chinese customers.[45] The ethnic division of labour has a strong symbolic colouring: the drivers of carts drawn by draught animals, primarily associated with the Old Town, traditionalism and backwardness, are exclusively Uighur, while rickshaws in the New Town are operated exclusively by Han Chinese. Blacksmiths, goldsmiths and other indigenous craft workers are all Uighur, while street-peddlers selling ice-cream and yoghurt tend to be Han Chinese or Chinese Muslims.

However, the divisions are far from complete. For example, the permanent marketplace in the New Town is divided into an Uighur and a Chinese section, each of which sells clothing, shoes, vegetables and meat and generally their customers do tend to line up according to ethnic affiliation. But some customers straddle this line, especially in the clothes market. Typical Uighur products such as flat bread or dried apricots are normally sold by Uighur, but their customers may include Han, keen consumers of most Uighur delicacies. Employment in areas such as construction work may also be multi-national, though in practice specific gangs of labourers may remain ethnically homogenous. A higher degree of mixing can be observed in government offices because of regulations which require the presence of a certain percentage of minority cadres. The duties (and the boredom) are shared by members of the two groups, and this common experience may foster a certain degree of comradeship, usually along gender lines. Han and Uighur male colleagues occasionally take a drink together at street stalls. This apparent comradeship can easily give way to ethnic stereotyping. On one such occasion two Han members of the party fell off their chairs and lay on the pavement unconscious for a few minutes. After the fall of the third and last Han one Uighur, himself on the verge of collapsing, said repeatedly: 'look at the Han! They do not even know how to drink properly! We Uighur manage better than them!' This was a relatively rare scene in which members of the two groups displayed a high degree of physical proximity, sharing the same table in the street and even drinking from the same glass. Yet it is precisely this kind of contact which has a high potential for conflict. In other examples of friendly inter-ethnic socialisation, e.g. the participation of Han guests at an Uighur wedding, interaction remains on a more formal level and a relatively high degree of physical distance is consciously maintained.[46]

Occupational segregation and mixing are both encouraged by the state. On the one hand certain types of jobs are filled exclusively by Han. On the other hand, by law government offices must employ a certain percentage of minorities (the exact figure varies at different levels of administration). However, the appointment of an Uighur to a relatively senior position may still in practice prove to be nominal, if real power is

---

[45] The Chinese Muslims, like elsewhere, occupy a somewhat ambiguous position between the two major groups. Their groceries and hairdressing salons may be frequented by members of both groups. On the complex interplay between food and ethnicity see Cesaro's recent article (2000).

[46] A further example of ethnically mixed socialisation is birthday parties, a recent fashion among small town youth.

exercised by a Han deputy.[47] This appeared to be the situation with the county leadership, where the chief party boss was an Uighur but power was clearly concentrated in the hands of his Han deputy, with superior education. This was also the case with the leadership of a women's organisation, in practice under the tight control of the Communist Party.[48] All township representatives of this organisation were Uighur, and the county level leadership, too, was headed by an Uighur lady. She had been an ordinary peasant woman before becoming a cadre and receiving training at short party courses. Literate in her mother tongue and highly intelligent, she had no knowledge of the Chinese language, and constantly looked for the approval of her Han deputy at a conference. Although at the county level government organisations all employ official interpreters whose job is to translate between Uighur and Chinese, in this case there was no need for such mediation. Unusually, the deputy leader, born and brought up in Ürükzar, spoke fluent Uighur and so the communication around the conference table was entirely in that language. When my Han research partners came to visit me briefly, and met this woman, they were convinced that she was a Chinese Muslim rather than a Han. Their assumption rested on the widely known phenomenon that among Chinese Muslims in Xinjiang it is quite common to be bilingual in Chinese and Uighur, while bilinguilism is rare among Han.[49]

Other leading Uighur cadres in the leadership of Ürükzar are well-educated and have enough knowledge of at least spoken Chinese to be promoted to the highest levels of government organs in the provincial capital. Minority nationals receive favourable treatment at the university entrance examination, one of the many privileges granted to urban residents of recognised minority groups by the state, which makes claiming minority status desirable (Gladney 1991: 219 - 220). Nevertheless, few young people can ever hope to gain admittance to higher education establishments from a smaller town, especially one such as Ürükzar, if they have a history of exclusively Uighur primary and secondary education, which does not equip them with sufficient knowledge of Chinese necessary for what is basically a Chinese higher education programme. Many secondary school graduates from minority schools in Ürükzar were facing unemployment in 1995. Some opted for the local equivalent of the Open University, which they could pursue through correspondence courses, but others were bit-

---

[47] Gladney confirms that this tends to be the general pattern in minority areas all over China (1994 b: 185).

[48] The All-China Women's Federation.

[49] The bilinguilism of the Chinese Muslims is not met with universal approval among the Uighur. They are surrounded by suspicion and mistrust. This has much to do with memories of bloody conflicts between the Uighur and Chinese Muslims. The Chinese Muslims occupy an anomalous position between the two major groups. As one Uighur summed it up: 'The Chinese Muslims are worse than the Han. They share their language with the Han and religion with us. They belong to neither group.'

ter and complained of pro-Han discrimination in certain prestigious public sector jobs, e.g. in banks and in the army.[50]

The Uighur resent the well-known fact that the developing oil industry of the province tends to employ only Han brought in from the overpopulated areas of China proper. Not only are there no skilled Uighur in higher level jobs, but even unskilled jobs are offered to Han migrant labourers, some of whom occasionally visited Ürükzar to attend the dance halls and relax. Such apartheid in certain employment sectors is particularly resented by the Uighur and is among one of the most frequently mentioned reasons for hostile feelings against the Han.

For most office jobs a good command of at least spoken Chinese is usually a precondition. It is Chinese education which paves the way to such jobs and Rudelson's analysis of the dilemma faced by Uighur intellectuals concerning the education of their children is also valid for small town parents in virtually all occupations (1997: 115). Uighur housewives, cleaning ladies, traders and primary school teachers with young children may all consider the possibility of sending their children to the Chinese schools rather than to the Uighur speaking minority schools. The majority of Uighur children attend the latter but some Uighur families do choose to educate their children in Han schools to give them better career opportunities. Such children, although fluent in Uighur, speak very good Chinese and tend to consume more of the products of Han culture. Their ability to read and write Uighur is limited. They belong to a group of their own, sarcastically referred to as the fourteenth nationality of Xinjiang *(on tötinçi millät)* (Rudelson 1997: 128). They are singled out by their Uighur peers on the basis of their different education, and are treated as Uighur with a 'Chinese temperament' *(mijäzi xänzu)*. Entrance to this dubious category can be gained not only through formal education but also through informal socialisation. Some local Uighur officials sharing residential quarters with their Han colleagues discourage their children from playing with their Han peers. They too say that this would result in Uighur children becoming sinicised in 'temperament' *(mijäz)*. Such attitudes lead to a conscious reproduction of social distance between families living in the closest proximity.

The emergence of this group within the younger generation has provided conflicting sentiments among the Uighur themselves. Resentment stems from their having become a little less than 'real, true' Uighur. They are seen as only 'half' *(çala)* Uighur, and as such they constitute an anomaly.[51] But their good command of Chinese and

---

[50] By 1997 unemployment of young Uighur secondary school graduates in the town became a source of general concern, and the local government made a conscious effort to create employment opportunities for them in the two libraries, at hotel receptions and other 'white collar' jobs.

[51] The 'half' or 'tame' Uighur is not a new phenomenon in Xinjiang. Using the local elite for governing multi-ethnic Xinjiang is an old device inherited from imperial China, as is well-documented in Grenard's description at the end of the nineteenth century when the term *çala* was already in use to describe indigenous people with a Chinese education (Grenard 1898: 273-4). For modern Chinese usage see Rudelson (1997: 127).

their familiarity with the ways of the dominant group gives them enviable resources. Their education may become their most significant asset among the peer group even at an early age. Chinese-educated Uighur do not become socially isolated. They seem to be desirable marriage partners for the Uighur educated in minority schools. As in the provincial capital, in Ürükzar too, young Uighur men with an Uighur education are said to be particularly keen on marrying Chinese-educated Uighur women, clearly seeing such an alliance as 'marrying up'. The rationalisation for such a preference is that, owing to their Chinese ways, these girls are more easy-going, straightforward and 'less complicated' than Uighur girls educated in minority schools. This means that they are more modern but also that they are more likely to ignore Uighur traditions. However, there is general consensus that there are frequent arguments between marriage partners and that many such marriages end in divorce. Such arguments are potentially explosive and may turn particularly bitter when the partner with an Uighur education accuses the other with a Chinese schooling of having become a Han. One of the explanations for this is that traditional gender relations cannot countenance the wife enjoying much better career prospects than her husband. An ideal marriage partner for such a 'half' Uighur girl would be a Chinese educated Uighur husband. That they do marry Uighur men with Uighur education can be explained by their (or their families') wish to reinforce ties with their own people that have been seriously loosened. The children of such marriages are often sent to Chinese schools themselves, although the parents may try to counterbalance this by sending their child to an after-school club where she/he can learn traditional Uighur dance or music. In Ürükzar such courses for schoolchildren were typically available during the summer holidays over a three week period. The Uighur dance course, attended exclusively by girls, was hugely popular among Uighur families, regardless of educational background.[52]

A young Uighur housewife who had finished a Chinese secondary school looked down upon her primary school teacher husband, a graduate of a minority school. The husband humbly accepted and often joked about his inferiority. Although she seemed to be habitually bad-tempered with her neighbours, she could always be relied on to help Uighur school children with their Chinese homework (Chinese is compulsory in all minority schools), and therefore people tried to humour her and good relations were maintained in spite of her arrogance.

The anomalous position of the small town Chinese-educated Uighur is shared by many Uighur government officials, township and party leaders, regardless of their educational background. They have close working relationships with Han officials and the policies they have to execute are often met with disapproval by local residents. Any suspicion of pro-Han sympathies may also provoke angry reactions against Mus-

---

[52] The fact that many young girls hope to pursue careers as folk dancers is perhaps another indication that the stereotype promoted by the Chinese authorities of the colourful, exotic minorities who dance and sing is not a pure Chinese invention: the Uighur themselves regard this as an important expression of their identity.

lim religious leaders.[53] When anger is turned directly against other Uighur, the incidents are classified by the authorities as criminal cases rather than ethnic conflict. The Uighur, however, invariably classify such conflicts in terms of ethnic antagonism.

Many urban Uighur do have a basic knowledge of spoken and a more limited knowledge of written Chinese. The Han residents, though perceived as monolingual Mandarin speakers, may in practice understand more of everyday Uighur conversation than they like to admit, but many remain completely ignorant. Linguistically, it would seem that many urban Uighur have penetrated the Chinese arena in line with the wishes of the authorities: the acquisition of the language of the dominant group is an important step towards acculturation. However Uighur may rationalise this imbalance in the linguistic situation in terms of favourable self-stereotyping. They interpret it as proof of the Uighur's higher intelligence. As one Uighur street peddlar with only a limited knowledge of Chinese summed it up: 'we Uighur all know some Chinese, look at the Han, they have been living among us for a long time and are still incapable of learning our language - surely a sign of their stupidity!' Uighur informants in Ürükzar were sure that the linguistic situation in some other oases was different. Some people were convinced that in Kashgar more Han could speak Uighur, but even this assumption was explained in unfavourable terms for the Han: there the Han were said to be under more pressure to learn Uighur, and to do it out of fear and necessity. Lack of knowledge of the majority language in Kashgar, a traditional stronghold of Uighur culture as well as anti-Han sentiments, could result in difficulties with shopkeepers, a potential source of violent conflict. In Ürükzar the Uighur complain of a reverse situation. They say that they are often ignored by Han shopkeepers if they do not address them in Chinese.

Just as the Uighur must be seen as a socially and regionally heterogeneous group whose ethnic identity has been shaped by a subtle interplay of official policies and self-perception (Gladney 1990), it would be equally mistaken to consider the Han Chinese living in Xinjiang as a homogenous group with a static group identity. In fact they have arrived in Xinjiang at different times and in very different circumstances (Lattimore 1950: 140; Dillon 1995: 31). They too are socially divided. Recent economic trends have further encouraged Chinese labour migration into Xinjiang. Many of these newcomers consitute part of the enormous floating population of China, on the move in order to find employment and escape residence registration and thereby family planning restrictions.[54] While officially registered Han Chinese government employees, traders and workers tend to be concentrated in the New Town, unregistered migrant Han families from the most overpopulated provinces of the interior often set

---

[53] In the late spring of 1996 the *damollah* or main religious leader of Kashgar was the victim of an assassination attempt. Rumours were circulating in 1996 of the successful assassination of a village *imam* near Ürükzar.

[54] On the increase of this floating population brought about by the economic reforms see Kane 1995: 199, and Hoppe 1998: 308.

up temporary accommodation in the Old Town in the Muslim quarters. These men do construction work and other temporary jobs. Their very presence here is a form of rebellion against the state, they often live in extreme poverty with numerous children in makeshift accommodation and take on work the Uighur would not be happy to perform. In these circumstances the Uighur do not feel threatened by them, and make no attempt to increase social distance. Han migrant families are accepted as temporary residents in the Muslim neighbourhoods and inter-ethnic relations seem to be good. Their children mix freely with local Uighur children on the streets and, unlike Uighur government officials in the New Town, here Uighur parents do not worry about the 'contaminating' effects of such contacts which might result in a sinicised temperament in their own children. On the contrary, Uighur adults may comment favourably on the ability of the migrants' children to pick up Uighur very quickly.

Dress code and fashion

Stereotypes continue to be formulated on the basis of more formalised, hierarchical power relations between the Uighur and their Han overlords. Since some mixing within the urban context is inevitable, physical distance may prove to be ineffective as boundary marker and symbols connected to the body may take on particular relevance. Both Uighur and Han Chinese are usually confident in being able to tell an Uighur from a Han. However, it is not just bodily features which facilitate distinction: the observer has a whole set of other clues simultaneously available (cf. Horowitz 1985: 46 - 47). These include preferences concerning styles of body decoration and clothing, which are instrumental in drawing the boundary of the self. In both men's and women's worlds the Uighur have symbols which distinguish them from their Han neighbours. Skin colour is viewed as a continuous scale with white/European at one extreme and yellow/Asiatic at the other. Uighur children at school are taught that, like the Han, they are 'yellow'. Following this classification many Uighur describe themselves as yellow-skinned and therefore members of 'the Asiatic race' as they put it, but they also notice the numerous deviations from the constructed stereotype. They say about other Uighur with a paler countenance that they 'look as if they could not possibly be Uighur'. This is, however, a positive feature. That the *ideal* skin colour for the Uighur is the one which contrasts most sharply with the colour associated with the Han is best illustrated by the trouble that some young Uighur townswomen take in applying white powder thickly to their faces. This fashion is almost always followed by the bride at Uighur weddings.

Dress code also provides a set of clues for both stating and recognising ethnic affiliation. Uighur standard male attire nowadays is more 'modern' and therefore close to the Chinese pattern, in both villages and towns. Yet they are quick to point out that Han office workers wear differently cut suits. The most important difference in male attire is the headgear. Uighur men usually cover their heads, either with a 'traditional' Islamic skullcap, the *doppa*, a cap (*şäpkä*) or a straw hat decorated with a ribbon with the inscription 'World Cup' (*şiläpä*), which has become fashionable among cadres since 1994. A few peasants still wear their *tumaq* or furcap, even in the summer. In relation to the Han, these various items of headgear are important symbols of ethnic affiliation, but the same items also serve to separate generations of Uighur and some versions of the skullcap are indicative of regional belonging. Changing fashions in skullcap also appear to mark class membership among Uighur: in the 1950s poorer peasants adopted the skullcap previously exclusively worn by rich peasants, while the emerging new style of government cadres in the1980s is being appropriated and imitated by peasants in the 1990s. Uighur male headgear is thus loaded with meaning. Although the skullcap is more or less obligatory in the mosque and a white turban complemented with a white belt over black clothes constitutes Uighur male funerary costume, these markers of religious affiliation do not blur the difference between the co-religionist Uighur and the Hui or Chinese Muslims: the many varieties of skullcaps worn by Uighur men are all easily distinguishable from the Hui skullcap. The Chinese authorities, who like to distinguish between a minority group's 'religion' and 'local customs', classified items of Uighur male headgear into the more dangerous and controversial 'religious' category during the 'Cultural Revolution', when both the skullcap and the turban were banned (Rudelson 1997: 104).

As Uighur men themselves point out, in addition to headgear a number of other obvious clues contribute to ethnic recognition. Many Uighur men over forty sport a beard, which contrasts them both with the Chinese, who have less facial hair, and also with younger Uighur. Young Uighur males in town tend to grow their hair longer and to wear a cap. At least in the summer they leave their shirts half open, and many go around with a a big knife sticking out of their back pocket. The carrying of a knife, a symbol of potential violence, is viewed by many Uighur as uncivilised and confirms Han stereotypes of 'uncultured' minorities. But for young Uighur men, especially those of peasant origin, who are for the most part of the year without employment, a knife is both a symbol of masculinity and a resource which may come handy in case of conflict.

Fashion and body decoration are also prominent in women's self-presentation. Many urban women are angry when they recall the days of the Cultural Revolution, when they had to wear the unfeminine Maoist uniforms. Nowadays Uighur women use many items which the Han do not (headscarf, henna on nails, earrings of a characteristic, recognisably 'native' design, and further items of golden jewellery). Among the Han items of clothing are highly varied and may reflect differences in seniority, occupation and social class: fashion-conscious, young Han Chinese women tend to dress in pastel or plain colours, wear western-style clothes, including tailored trousers or even jeans. Elderly ladies put on navy blue trouser suits reminiscent of the Maoist period. In contrast, as a general rule Uighur women tend to don bright colours and their clothes follow different patterns of tailoring. Women's fashion reveals much variation, but these variations remain within certain parameters circumscribed by unwritten rules which allow for little overlapping between the two groups. Uighur peasant women, who often appear in town from nearby villages on market days, wear a baggy dress over bare feet in the summer and thick nylon stockings in the winter. These latter have become available and fashionable over the last twenty years and are fast replacing the traditional baggy trousers even in the countryside. More sophisticated, urban women wear a more transparent and thinner version than peasant and lower class women. Waistless dresses meet the requirements of the Islamic modesty code, and even though Uighur female cadres' clothes are often designed to display a waistline, most avoid wearing a belt. The sporting of belts and especially trousers by Chinese women are features which Uighur cite as significant differences between the two groups.

As elsewhere, among the Uighur, too, clothes are invested with numerous symbolic meanings. Implicitly they are regarded as an extension of the body, which can influence essential bodily features. Uighur women told me that a characteristic bodily feature of the Han, the flat nose, (which the Uighur consider unattractive and even ugly) is the result of Han women's habit of wearing a belt or trousers at least during the first months of their pregnancy which flattens the baby's nose. I was also told that in Shanghai, where such customs are being abandoned by the Han, their children are growing up more handsome, with 'natural' facial features resembling those of the Uighur. Uighur women's clothes are not merely markers of ethnic affiliation: like male headgear, they too mark numerous intra-ethnic alliances as well as boundaries. Young girls who wear similar dresses are very often close friends, for whom identical dress is a symbolic expression of a specially close friendship. Material, cut and the number of dresses a woman possesses are all indicative of her and her family's social prestige. Female cadres, who stand at the top of modern Uighur urban society, are constantly introducing new ideas to distinguish themselves from the lower groups. The latter, like their male counterparts, continue to subvert these efforts at differentiation by imitating their style as fast as they can. It may seem ironic that new types of material and other fashion ideas taken up by the Uighur elite are said to originate mostly in the interior of China, especially in Shanghai. Long distant traders, often Uighur, choose colourful prints which are then further adjusted to local requirements by refined ways of tailoring and accepted as typically Uighur. Some of the meanings expressed in clothes are decipherable only to other close female relatives, neighbours and friends: an Uighur housewife's wardrobe is perceived by some as a reflection of her marital relations with her husband, since one of the husband's conjugal obligations consists of presenting his wife with clothes at regular intervals.[55] The distinctive style of Uighur women's clothes, perceived by most as more feminine than Han styles, contributes to the representation of them as a colourful minority, distinctive from the Han, and against whom the Han can then define themselves (cf. Gladney 1994 a).

---

[55] Alongside home-made bread, cloth has for a long time been the most important gift presented at life cycle rituals, religious festivals and rituals connected to apprenticeship. Like bread, such gifts are usually presented by women. Cloth has also remained the usual medium for payment to religious specialists for their various services.

Traditional Uighur female headgear had as many varieties as male headgear. Nowadays only elderly women wear a fur hat on top of a long white scarf. The white scarf is worn by others, but only at mourning and other Islamic rituals. The numerous female versions of the skullcap are rarely worn today, except by young girls and children. Instead, at about the same time as nylon stockings appeared, bright-coloured synthetic headscarves were introduced from Russia and these have had a major impact on Uighur female headgear. In line with Islamic traditions, hair must not be shown to strange men and village etiquette requires the wearing of the headscarf from puberty onwards. The custom is less diligently observed by township cadres but in Ürükzar overall the headscarf is more ubiquitous than the main alternative, a brown veil *(çüm-bäl)* covering the whole head, including the face. This is only worn by women from conservative families often labelled as fanatics.

Uighur informants often told me of the great esteem they hold for the upper part of the human body, the head in particular. This is why they place so much emphasis upon headgear. Headgear preserves its symbolic function as a marker of gender until the very last ritual: a white skullcap placed on the coffin when it is carried to the cemetery shows that the deceased was a man, while women's coffins are decorated with a white scarf covered by a colourful female skullcap. Informants claim that even poorer people try to avoid second-hand caps and hats. In contrast, all town and village markets have an extensive and thriving second-hand shoe section. Uighur merchants bring cheap second-hand shoes from the interior of China, which are then repaired and cleaned by Uighur craftsmen and resold on the local market, mostly to Uighur customers. The great care with which headgear is chosen[56] and the insistence that it must never be worn by anyone else before, contrasts conspicuously with the free association of Chinese shoes with the inferior, lower parts of the body. Nevertheless, shoe styles also reflect ethnic affiliation. Uighur townswomen insist on wearing colourful high heels, and even village women do the same when attending weddings or visiting town. Fashion-conscious Han women tend to wear similar types or what Europeans might call more 'sensible' shoes, but no Uighur woman would be seen in the black, flat Chinese espadrilles typically worn by elderly Chinese ladies.

In Uighur society hair, too is loaded with symbolic meanings. Ideally an Uighur woman should grow her hair as long as possible. Long hair symbolising femininity is traditionally associated with good luck. In the past women often used artificial or natural extensions to make their hair look longer. The most important ritual in women's life in pre-modern Uighur society was the 'the hair-tying ritual' *(çaçwaq toyi)*[57] usu-

---

[56] Cf. the ritual presentation of headscarves observed among Uighur refugee women in Kazakstan at weddings and other life-cycle rituals.

[57] This is the term used in Ürükzar, but alternative terms such as *juwan toyi* and *çaç qoşaq toyi* are used in other oases. On the ritual see Bellér-Hann forthcoming.

ally performed during the last stages of a first pregnancy or shortly after birth.[58] Regional variations exist as to the exact timing of the ritual, (in some locations it was only performed after the birth of the third or fourth baby), but it is certain that it was a significant rite of passage for a woman, more important than a wedding. The new status of the woman was marked by the adoption of a different number of braids, the cutting of the hair at the temples, and a minor change in the pattern of the front of her clothing. Today most Uighur townswomen continue to have long hair usually worn in a bun, regardless of their age. Although the Uighur, like the Han, mostly have black hair, Uighur townswomen who frequent hairdressers tend to insist on waves which they say are unpopular among the Han Chinese. Short haircuts are also associated with the Han. In Ürükzar only a handful of young unmarried Uighur girls were brave enough to experiment with short hairstyles and also with trousers. Although in some cases their families tolerated such 'deviations', these girls were often the butt of jokes and even hostile reprimands from strangers and friends alike for 'their Chinese ways'. On one occasion a young Uighur man started teasing an Uighur girl because of her new, 'Chinese' haircut. This took place on a street corner among other young people, and what started as mild teasing ended with the boy trying to hit the girl after she defended her right to keep up with fashions. At home, however, she took to wearing a headscarf for several days because she feared the reaction of her father and brothers. These young girls who deviated from the accepted dress code found it particularly hurtful when their appearance caused them to be addressed in Chinese by Uighur shopkeepers, who had genuinely mistaken them for Han in spite of their 'typical' Uighur bodily features. Comparing an Uighur to the Han may be used as a serious allegation (when an Uighur-educated husband accuses his Chinese-educated wife), or a relatively mild form of disapproval (when an Uighur mother says that her daughter is as stubborn as a Han). Behavioural stereotypes which project the Han negatively are paralleled by unflattering assumptions about what is perceived as 'typically Chinese' facial features: one Uighur woman commented that her young nephew unfortunately looked 'as unattractive as a Han'.

'Temperament' and diet

As mentioned in the preceding section, items of clothing such as a belt may be seen as influencing bodily features and perceived as indications of an individual's change of 'temperament'. I now wish to explore this idea further. I have indicated the common Uighur belief that a Han temperament may be acquired either through formal education or through informal socialisation. The latter possibility is only considered where stereotypical power hierarchies dominate (among children of Han and Uighur officials in the New Town where the former are dominant) and ignored in a reverse situation (the Han 'floating' population in Muslim neighbourhoods). *Mijäz* or 'temperament' is a central component of Uighur personhood and identity. It has a strong

---

[58] For native descriptions of traditional Uighur clothes with special reference to the hair-tying ritual see Jarring 1992 and Raxman, Hämdulla / Xuştar 1996: 131-2.

material, bodily aspect. Each person, male or female, is said to be born with a fundamental hot (*issiq*) or cold (*soğaq*) temperament. Cold temperament is associated with
pale ('white') skin while darker people are said to have a hot disposition. According to
some informants, more women tend to be white skinned and therefore of a cold disposition, while more men fall into the dark skinned, hot disposition category. Some argue
that an excessive consumption of 'cold' foods before conception and during pregnancy
is conducive to the birth of a girl, while lots of 'hot' food leads to the birth of a boy.
Although babies are believed to be born with a specific disposition, either hot or cold,
this basic nature may be modified and transformed by lifestyle. A written source from
pre-1949 describes beliefs about the long term nature of a craftsman's temperament: if
his job involves constant exposure to heat, as is the case of a blacksmith or a baker, he
will develop a cold disposition, while exposure the materials associated with cold,
such as water, will result in a hot disposition (Muhammad Ali Damolla 1905 - 1910:
25).[59] Modern informants confirm older written sources that most foods have an essentially hot or cold nature. To have a well-balanced, healthy body is to be neither cold
nor hot, but to maintain a moderate temperature (*mötidil*). For this one needs to eat
foods which counterbalance one's original disposition. Hot or cold disposition is said
to determine a person's reactions to different foods and sleeping pattern, which in turn
may affect general well-being as well as character: people with a hot disposition are
considered hot tempered, while those with a cold disposition are said to be of a calm
nature.

The diet of the Han is viewed with considerable suspicion by the Uighur, not
only because of their inclusion of pork but also because of their complete ignorance of
this required balance. The main rationalisation for the pronounced asymmetry of
Uighur-Han hospitality, (the Uighur dictate the rules, entertaining Han colleagues
when they wish to but denying them the right to reciprocate) remains focused on the
issue of pork consumption and its contaminating effects on other foodstuffs. But there
are other, more complex, hidden dimensions in the suspicion surrounding the Han,
whose disregard of the rules governing hot and cold temperament produces people
with uncontrolled dispositions. Han *mijäz* can appear as the sum of out-of-control bodily processes. Fear of pollution may focus on pork consumption and on the consumption of foods which may possibly have been in contact with pork, but beneath this rationalisation for shunning Han hospitality lies a more general anxiety of contamination
of organisms which are not controlled according to the main organising principles of
hot and cold.[60]

---

[59] Ideas concerning temperament among the Uighur are based upon informants' accounts. For further
references see Grenard (1898: 111).

[60] Similar ideas of 'hot' and 'cold' can be found elsewhere in Asia, for example in Pakistan and Afghanistan. For a good elaboration of such ideas in the context of medical anthropology in Afghanistan
see Penkala 1980, who discusses possible historical antecedents.

One extreme illustration of this point was provided by an elderly lady whom I visited in her village with her grandchild. As a small gift I gave her a packet of tea which I had bought in a local shop. It was brick tea, widely consumed by the Uighur, but the lady refused to accept it, saying with evident disgust that it was only suitable for the Han. Since she was illiterate, she could not read the Uighur text (in Arabic script) on the packet which assured the consumer that it was suitable for Muslim consumption. It was clear that it was my own anomalous position, neither Uighur nor Han, but definitely a stranger (and the first foreigner she had ever met) which bothered her, but she articulated her anxiety in the more familiar terms of anti-Han sentiments. Her granddaughter's efforts to convince her of the appropriateness of my gift failed to persuade her, and she insisted that the tea was likely to be contaminated by the touch of the Han Chinese harvesters. Back in town my young Uighur friends were very pleased to take the tea home to their families. Fear of contamination and also of potential hostilities, not just between patients but also their visitors, lie behind Uighur informants' disapproval of the juxtaposition of Han and Uighur patients in the wards of the town's 'western' hospital. Similar ideas may also lurk behind references to Uighur villages or neighbourhoods without any Han residents as 'clean' (pakiz).

Uighur avoidance of food touched by Han does not prevent them from taking considerable pride in the hospitality they may offer to the latter. Although ethnically mixed parties are rare, Han guests are occasionally invited to Uighur weddings. On one occasion which I witnessed the groom, a hospital doctor, invited his Han colleague together with his family. They were given a prominent place among the wedding guests, although they had their separate table and their own plates.[61] Their partaking in the meal pleased the hosts. The symbolic incorporation of the Han into the wedding party through consumption of their food temporarily reduced the differences between them.[62] Han enthusiasm for Uighur foods serves to increase the Uighur's self-esteem.[63] Some Uighur go as far as to say that as a result of close contacts and the adoption of a few Uighur dishes, the Han of Xinjiang are different and 'better' than other Chinese of the interior.[64]

---

[61] At weddings two or more guests share trays of food from which they eat with chopsticks and by hand.

[62] However, Uighur hospitality to the Han is limited. They are not welcome at religious festivals, the two major Muslims holidays, which are marked by the slaughtering of a sacrificial sheep and extensive entertaining.

[63] Rudelson emphasises how pejorative Han views of the Uighurs can lead to a considerable loss of self-esteem among Uighur intellectuals (1997: 125). Although I too came across such views, many of my informants, who were not intellectuals by occupation, managed to find grounds for increased self-esteem in day-to-day interaction with the Han.

[64] In this connection it must be noted that a number of dishes which today are considered 'typically' Uighur are most likely of Chinese origin, as their Chinese names imply, the best example being the popular noodle dish known as läğmän.

Nevertheless such views are not shared by all and Uighur are eager to exploit differences in Han tastes. Dried apricots in the orchards of the suburbs and townships are produced exclusively by indigenous farmers. Orange coloured dried apricots which look appetising but have been chemically treated by the producer are marketed at higher prices for Han consumers, who believe them to be cleaner than the naturally sun-dried brown coloured ones consumed by the native producers. The Uighur are aware that the latter are more natural, being free of chemicals and fully sun-dried, and laugh at the Han for this misguided preference.

Boundary crossing and intermarriage

Adopting the food habits of the other group can be considered as an example of ethnic boundary crossing by the Han which results in a more general reinforcement of Uighur self-esteem. Other adaptations have the same effect. Some Uighur women related with unconcealed pride that nowadays there are local Han families who have their sons circumcised in the hospital, because they have realised the health benefits of this Muslim custom. Another Uighur woman made positive comments about a Han child in a predominantly Uighur village, who looked charming when dressed up in Uighur clothes. In another oasis I came across cases of Uighur couples adopting Han children from an orphanage. The parents insisted that this was a meritorious deed (*sawap*) and they were determined to raise the children as Uighur. Such situations were regarded as straightforward, since socialisation in these instances was believed to be determinant.[65]

Day-to-day interaction between the two groups inevitably raises issues of the degree to which ethnic mixing is acceptable, and how far it is possible to tolerate departures from the ideals which are supposed to ensure group cohesion (Banton 1994: 11). Intermarriage constitutes one extreme of group interaction (Smith 1981: 37). In Xinjiang it is said to be more common in the bigger cities, but in smaller oasis towns such as Ürükzar it is said to be virtually non-existent because of the sanctions the Uighur community imposes on the parties involved. People explain these by telling stories of deviations from the articulated value system. Such stories fall into two main categories. One type is the hopeless love between a Han Chinese youth and an Uighur girl, and it is told mainly within the context of the provincial capital. The other type involves tales of mixed marriages. I personally knew of one such case which involved an Uighur man married to a half-Han half-Uighur lady, born and raised in Ürükzar. This case illustrates to what an extent deviation from the ideal may occur and become accepted. She appears to have been fully integrated into local Uighur society in spite

---

[65] Direct contact between the members of the two groups outside well-established office situations is always potentially ambiguous, as has been mentioned above. One day an elderly man came back from the fields where he had been working and asked his wife to go quickly because a strange young woman was in labour among the trees nearby. As she explained, her immediate reaction was to ask if the woman in need of help was Han or Uighur. Following her husband's reprimands she felt ashamed and hurried out to assist with the birth.

of her mixed parentage. Although she was educated in a Chinese secondary school, from a very young age she was brought up and socialised as an Uighur and thereafter married a former Uighur classmate, also a local man. Since she was raised as an Uighur at home, she observed the Uighur dress code in every detail. She also spoke fluent Uighur, she was seen as no different from other local Chinese-educated Uighur; she was a popular member of Uighur town society, took part in Uighur women's social visiting and was better liked by many than her husband, widely perceived as a dishonest businessman as well as a womaniser. Their only child, a lively six year old girl, spoke Uighur as her mother tongue, mixed with Uighur children and every detail of her appearance was typically Uighur. Her mother received a great deal of sympathy and was visited by Uighur friends when she was admitted to hospital with a tumour. Her temperament (*mijäz*) was not regarded by anybody as 'Han', confirmation that temperament is implicitly viewed as a social construct rather than determined by descent.

Another example of intermarriage between a half-Han and an Uighur ended in violence and divorce. In this case an Uighur man married a woman he believed to be 'pure' Uighur. Since she was from a different oasis, she was able to persuade her fiancé that because her mother had died and her father was in prison it was impossible for her family to attend the wedding. Only half of her story turned out to be true. Apparently when one day the husband returned home, he found a strange man eating at his table. He understood this to be his father-in-law, who had just left prison. My Uighur informants emphasised that what made the husband realise that this man was a Han rather than an Uighur was not his physical appearance but his *way of eating*: the Uighur have been using chopsticks for eating most dishes for several decades, one of many adaptations of Han culture. However, there is a small but rigorously observed difference between the way members of the two groups serve the favourite food of modern Uighurs, *läğmän*, a noodle dish with a meat and vegetable sauce, also well liked by the Han. Whereas the Uighur have the sauce poured over the noodles, Han have the two parts of the dish served on separate plates. This clue revealed the father-in-law to be a Han, before he even said a word. Divorce followed virtually immediately. This case illustrates that finding an Uighur marriage partner for a woman of mixed parentage may be problematic, hence the woman's attempt to deceive. According to informants, born and brought up in an Uighur environment, she had been socialised entirely into Uighur-Muslim culture which made it 'impossible for her to wish to marry a Han'.

Stereotypical representations in both groups focus on the Han male from the point of view of an Uighur woman. Han men are said to make more desirable husbands because they help more with children and housework and treat their wives more gently and with greater consideration than Uighur males. However, even this 'positive' stereotype has a negative edge, since the traits recognised in the stereotypical Han husband are considered 'unmanly' by most Uighur, including women. I never came across parallel representations comparing the advantages or disadvantages of a Han bride from the point of view of an Uighur man. These lopsided stereotypes point to a general tendency for Han men to wish to marry Uighur women rather than the other way around. This is consistent with the Uighur's emphasis on exercising control over women. Like the imbalance in dietary relations, this may therefore be perceived as a one-sided form of ethnic boundary crossing which is primarily regulated by the dominated group.

Conclusion

In this paper I have focused on Uighur attitudes towards the Han in Xinjiang. In the background there a living historical memory of oppression and atrocities suffered by local people during ethnic conflict in the past, which I have not discussed here. To this are added more recent memories of humiliation and worse during the Maoist period, which are again inevitably associated with Chinese rule. Foreground factors include accelerating Han immigration into the region and the better job opportunities which they enjoy, enforced birth control policies, which in recent years have been also extended to minorities, and religious oppression.[66]

The colonial nature of Han rule in Xinjiang, the long history of group conflict and the Uighur's repeated attempts at independence all point to the pattern which Horowitz calls a 'ranked system'(1985: 22). As this model predicts, members of the Uighur élite have ambivalent feelings: both pride in their own superior habits, and resentment over the backwardness of their own people. Chinese presence gives rise to conflicting desires, e.g. distancing as well as close contact and emulation (Horowitz 1985: 166 - 184). A certain degree of cautious, positive stereotyping of the Han may be found among some Uighur intellectuals, who may distance themselves from the less educated and poorer members of their own group and invoke the ideals of more cultured behaviour to be found among the Chinese. But such attitudes remain limited to certain small sections of society and even here they do not preclude a strong commitment to the actor's own group.

Official policies, which recognise minority rights as part of a strategy of control, encourage the fragmentation of minorities and the acculturation of élite groups in larger urban centres and even small town residents with medium level education. I have tried to show how local perceptions dichotomise life in an oasis town, and how boundary maintenance by the Uighur reinforces an official duality imposed by the state. Instead of concentrating on the most obvious manifestations of difference, religion, script and language, I have argued that numerous other, seemingly 'trivial' visible symbols as well as ideas concerning the body and personhood are employed to exaggerate real and imagined differences between the two groups. These ethnic markers largely overlap with strategies which have been employed for centuries to mark inter-

---

[66] For a recent evaluation of the political and economic situation in Xinjiang see Bovingdon and Gladney 2000.

nal status and identity in Uighur society. As Peach observed in another context, 'the language, values, religion, culture and dress of ethnic minorities are not simply badges of degradation imposed by more powerful groups to imprison, confine and divide those whom they dominate. They are elements of group and personal identity, fostered from within the group' (1981: 31). Although actors themselves are sometimes inclined to essentialise these elements of group and personal identity as static and given, constant changes of these components may be discerned. People recognise the dynamic elements. The idea that Uighur children might acquire a 'Han temperament' through interaction; and the idea of the 'fourteenth national minority' consisting of Chinese-educated Uighur are ways in which actors themselves implicitly acknowledge the constructed and therefore shifting nature of the 'given' traits which are supposed to form the core of 'Uighurness'. Components of ethnic identity are closely connected to the varied ways through which personhood, status and other social roles are constructed. They may double as markers of ethnicity in relation to another group but they also retain their multiple meanings as markers of intra-group social relations. Their constant reformulation is dependent on the social relations which they stand for, which they in turn help to shape. This is truly a 'dialogical' relationship in capturing these traits and in their conscious and unconscious applications we see 'constantly shifting relations and multiplicities of perceived identities that mask many levels of social simultaneity' (Gladney 1996: 456).

Most of the materials that I have discussed were collected during a two-months' stay in Ürükzar in 1995. In the following year a projected five months' stay in the same location was interrupted after only two weeks because of violence. It was difficult to ascertain exactly what happened. Local media announcements asserted that nine Uighur died due to 'criminal activity', but informants spoke of revenge taken by Uighur peasants upon corrupt Uighur officials who were perceived as overstepping the boundary of acceptable collaboration with the Han. According to other rumours at the time the incident was followed by the arrest of six hundred Uighur in the county. This incident was one relatively minor episode in the general unrest characteristic of Xinjiang in the mid-1990s, a period during which the authorities were attempting to clamp down on separatists ('splittists') and on religious extremists ('fundamentalists').

The apparent tranquillity of Ürükzar was thus shown to be an illusion, as underlying tensions spilled over into violence. Yet this had little or no impact on daily patterns of interaction in the town, since it merely reconfirmed the fundamental structuring aspects that were partially disguised during the relatively tranquil period of my initial stay.

Acknowledgements

This paper is the outcome of fieldwork supported by a grant from the Economic and Social Research Council of Great Britain (R00023-5709). My thanks are due to the Chinese authorities as well as to a great many individuals in the location of the research. I am also indebted to Ambassador Gunnar Jarring who has generously allowed me access to the manuscript Prov.207.I. housed in the Lund University Library.

References

Banton, Michael 1994. Modelling ethnic and national relations. In: *Ethnic and Racial Studies* Vol.17. No.1. January 1994: 1 - 19

Bauman, Zygmunt 1990. Modernity and Ambivalence. In: M. Featherstone (ed.). *Global Culture. Nationalism, Globalisation and Modernity. A Theory, Culture and Society .(special issue)* London: Sage: 143 – 169

Bellér-Hann, Ildikó forthcoming 2001. 'The hair-braiding ritual' [in Russian] In: *Issledovaniya po Uigurovedeniyu, Materialy konferentsii posviashennoi 50 letiyu Uigurovedeniya w Kazakhstane*. Almaty: Gylym Press

Bergère, Marie-Claire 1979. L'influence du modèle Soviétique sur la politique des minorités nationales en Chine. Le cas du Sinkiang (1949 - 1962). In: *Revue Française de Science Politique* 1979. Vol.29. No.3: 402 - 425

Blecher, Marc 1995. Collectivism, Contractualism and Crisis in the Chinese Countryside. In: R. Benewick and P. Wingrove (ed.). *China in the 1990s*. London: Macmillan: 105 – 119

Bovingdon, Gardner and Dru Gladney (eds.) 2000. *Inner Asia* 2000. Vol.2. No.2 *Special Issue: Xinjiang.*

Brown, Kenneth 1984. The Uses of a Concept: "The Muslim City". In: K. Brown, M. Jolé, P. Sluglett, S. Zubaida (ed.). *Middle Eastern Cities in Comparative Perspective. Points de vue sur les villes du Maghreb et du Machrek. Franco-British Symposium. London 10 - 14 May 1984*. London: Ithaca Press: 73 – 81

Cesaro, M. Cristina 2000. 'Consuming Identities: Food and Resistance among the Uyghur in Contemporary Xinjiang' In: *Inner Asia* Vol.2. No.2: 225 - 238

Dillon, Michael 1995. *Xinjiang: Ethnicity, Separatism and Control in Chinese Central Asia*. Durham East Asian Papers, 1. Durham: Department of East Asian Studies, University of Durham

Dowamat, Tomur 1993. *Xinjiang - My Beloved Home*. Urumqi: Xinjiang People's Publishing House

Eickelman, Dale F. 1981. *The Middle East. An Anthropological Approach.* Englewood Cliffs: Prentice-Hall

Gladney, Dru C. 1990. The Ethnogenesis of the Uighur. In: *Central Asian Survey* Vol.9. No.1: 1 - 28

Gladney, Dru C. 1991. *Muslim Chinese. Ethnic Nationalism in the People's Republic.* Cambridge (Mass.) and London: Council on East Asia Studies, Harvard University

Gladney, Dru C. 1994 a. Representing Nationality in China: Refiguring Majority/Minority Identities. In: *The Journal of Asian Studies* Vol.53. No.1: 92 - 123

Gladney, Dru C. 1994 b. Ethnic Identity in China: The New Politics of Difference. In: William A. Joseph (ed.). *China Briefing, 1994.* Boulder: Westview: 171 - 192

Gladney, Dru C. 1996. Relational Alterity: Constructing Dungan (Hui), Uygur, and Kazakh Identities Across China, Central Asia and Turkey. In: *History and Anthropology* Vol.9. No.4: 445 - 477

Grenard, F. 1898. *Mission scientifique dans la Haute Asie 1890 - 1895.* Paris: Ernest Leroux

Grobe-Hagel, Karl 1991. *Hinter der Grossen Mauer. Religionen und Nationalitäten in China.* Frankfurt am Main: Eichborn Verlag

Hoppe, Thomas [1995] 1998. *Die ethnischen Gruppen Xinjiangs: Kulturunterschiede und interethnische Beziehungen.* Hamburg: Institut für Asienkunde

Horowitz, Donald L. 1985. *Ethnic Groups in Conflict.* Berkeley, Los Angeles, London: University of California Press

Hüsäyin, Nizamidin 1995 a. Bizdiki illätlär. In: *Şinjaŋ Mädäniyiti* 1995. Vol.1: 61 - 79

Hüsäyin, Nizamidin 1995 b. Bizdiki illätlär. In: *Şinjaŋ Mädäniyiti* 1995. Vol.2: 61 - 72

Hüsäyin, Nizamidin 1995 c. Bizdiki xotun - qizlar dişvarçiliqi. In: *Şinjaŋ Mädäniyiti* 1995. Vol.3: 76 - 79

Jarring, Gunnar 1992. Garments from Top to Toe. Eastern Turki texts relating to articles of clothing edited with translation, notes and glossary. *Scripta Minora* 1991 - 2. 2: 1 - 93

Kane, Penny 1995. Population and Family Policies. In: R. Benewick and P. Wingrove (ed.) *China in the 1990s.* London: Macmillan: 193 - 203

Lattimore, Owen 1950. *Pivot of Asia.* Boston: Little, Brown

Millward, James 1998. *Beyond the Pass. Economy, Ethnicity and Empire in Qing Central Asia, 1759 – 1864* Stanford: Stanford University Press

Muhammad Ali Damola ca. 1905 - 1910. *A collection of Eastern Turki folkloristic texts.* Kashgar (unpublished manuscript, Jarring Collection, Lund University Library)

Peach, Ceri 1981. Conflicting interpretations of segregation. In: P. Jackson and Susan J. Smith (eds.). *Social interaction and ethnic segregation.* London: Academic Press: 19 - 33

Penkala, Danuta 1980. "Hot" and "Cold" in the Traditional Medicine of Afghanistan. *Ethnomedizin* VI, 1 - 4: 201 - 228

Raxman, A., R. Hämdulla and Ş. Xuştar 1996. *Uyğur Örp-Adätliri.* Ürümçi: Şinjaŋ Yaşlar - Ösmürlär Näşriyati

Rudelson, Justin 1997. *Oasis Identities. Uyghur Nationalism Along China's Silk Road.* New York: Columbia University Press

Smith, Susan J. 1981. Negative interaction: crime in the inner city. In: P. Jackson and Susan J. Smith (eds.). *Social interaction and ethnic segregation.* London: Academic Press: 35 – 58

Smith, Joanne N. 2002 (forthcoming). "Making Culture Matter": Symbolic, Spatial, and Social Boundaries Between Uyghurs and Han Chinese' In: *Asian Ethnicity* Vol.3, No.2

Tahir, Muhämmät Yusup 1995. "Tuğulğan kün"gä tuğulğan qaraşlirim. In: *Şinjaŋ Ayalliri* 1995. Vol.5: 28 - 31

Toxti, Salamät 1995. Hazirqi dävr Uyğur ayallariniŋ oylişip körüşigä tegişlik bir qančä mäsilä. In: *Şinjaŋ Ayalliri* 1995. Vol.7: 7 - 8

ABSTRACT

The Xinjiang Uighur Autonomous Region situated in northwest China is home to thirteen officially recognised ethnic groups. The chapter focuses on ethnic relations between the two largest groups, the Turkic speaking Muslims known as the Uighur and the Han Chinese. It discusses relations between the two groups competing for resources within the framework of a dichotomy. However, instead of presenting this simply in terms of unequal power relations between ruled and rulers, it attempts to show the complexity of this relationship through forms of interaction and mutual stereotyping, in which the oppressed group may dictate the rules. The chapter also explores subtle expressions of boundary drawing by the Uighur, who, when circumstances require, mobilise existing intra-group identity markers to double as markers of ethnic affiliation.

MURDER IN THE CATHEDRAL

DISRUPTED TIME, BROKEN SPACE: VIOLENCE IN THE REGIONAL HISTORY OF AN INDONESIAN CHURCH

Philip Quarles van Ufford

An Incident

The funeral of the pastor of the main Protestant church in Situardjo was attended by many. After the church service they all moved in slow procession to the nearby graveyard where the ceremony continued. The body was taken to the grave. The crowd settled around the family of the deceased and the hierarchy of the church became visible during these final moments. The mourning family stood at the centre: the widow with her son and two daughters supporting her. They faced the church authorities - high-placed regional representatives - at the opposite end of the grave, a great number of priests from the parishes and other local church officials surrounding them. A large flock of faithful from various congregations made up the outer ring of the Christian church community escorting the deceased Reverend to his grave.

Clearly the deceased had been a man of great eminence in the church. He had occupied many important positions and shaped some of the major ecclesiastical transformations in the region. He had been one of the most influential church officials for a long time. The sheer number of people present at the grave, with all the offices of the regional church bodies visibly represented, made it very clear: this constituted an important public event in the church as much as it was a tragic moment for his closest relatives.

When the officiating pastor had performed the last recitations from the Bible and the death rites, there was a moment of silence as the bearers prepared for their last task. They lifted the body and slowly, carefully, lowered it into the grave. The *rite de passage* now approached its climax. Suddenly, loud, and clearly uncontrolled sobs and shrieks shattered the moment of stillness. The youngest daughter of the deceased was shivering all over her body. She stood very erect at the graveside, looking not at her father's corpse but at the men standing at the opposite side of the grave: the high officials of the church. She shouted: "You, there, you have killed my father, you murdered him. Don't stand there pretending that you are grieving for him, hiding your pleasure at his death. I cannot stand it anymore. You are murderers!"

Then she ran away, sobbing uncontrollably, followed by her brother. Shortly afterwards everybody went their way as quickly and silently as possible. Ritualised stillness had exploded and everybody was afraid of the consequences. Terror and uncontrolled emotions had shattered the funeral rite. The burial of the father and church leader had collapsed. Those who had seen and heard the explosion slunk away. Public order and private decorum had been shaken. The uncertain dynamics of violence - 'murderers' had been publicly fingered - had manifested itself and more was to follow.

For the daughter the accusation of murder was the beginning of a process of increasing seclusion and self-ostracism. For many years she did not leave her parents' house except for the most urgent personal business. Together with her mother she barricaded herself in the large and beautiful house cum regional office that had been the proud centre of the family's and of the church's life for so many years. The new church leaders made no use of the official quarters, but neither were they vacated. Its contents, books, papers, reception hall, archives, furniture - all the material paraphernalia representing the last thirty years of church history acquired layers of dust. The official past became barren, no longer related to the church's further developments. It just withered away. The house became an unfinished tomb. It was not even a museum, for few were permitted to enter.

While the accusation at the graveyard led to tragic personal consequences, church life was also affected. Clearly a new church leadership had replaced the old. The new leaders' protestations of good will and their politeness towards the family were ambivalent at best. These were rejected and only deepened the conflict. Some of the new officials quietly made it understood that they deplored the incident. They would not require the family to move out, at least not at short notice. Yet they made it absolutely clear that in their view the residence was indeed theirs. The widow took a different view.

The spacious house became a kind of sepulchre, its splendour slowly dissolving in the midst of a large and busy church compound where the (other) central offices of the church in the area were also located. The church's past and its present were increasingly divorced from one another. Interrupted time also manifested itself in spatial ways at the central premises of the church.

The tragic events at the centre of the church marked the beginning of a series of violent clashes on the periphery. Incisive, bitter and sometimes even violent transformations of the institutional landscape followed shortly after the burial of the high official. Only two out of a total of twenty-five local congregations remained unaffected. In the next few years the great majority of the local priests left their parishes. Some were literally chased out of their houses by their own parishioners. In some cases new local church boards appropriated the houses the priests lived in. Sometimes the priests lost access to the *sawah benkok*, the 'communal' land owned by the local church. Much of their income derived from these lands. Moreover, local pastors lost their *arta dahar*, a 'salary' from the offerings of the local constituency. Any chance of gaining support and patronage from the centre had clearly disappeared after the 'violent death' of their former patron. Of all local priests in the whole region only two were able to continue their work.

A great bitterness manifested itself in the area. The old order collapsed. The possibility of any kind of meaningful relationship with the new order broke down. There was a vacuum for some time. All sorts of 'accidents' occurred. Church life acquired violent dimensions. It was as if a volcano exploded, with its eruptions uncontrollably destroying whatever stood in its way. Suddenly opponents in church politics transformed into hunters and their prey. The cry of murder at the burial had as it were conjured up struggles in the periphery. Political differences were now settled once and for all. The question who were the winners and who the losers had been unequivocally answered. Now was the time for the settlement of old scores, the payment of old debts. And unpaid debts were found everywhere. Any common ground on which settlements could be based had disappeared. The normal routines of church politics had as it were evaporated. The murder of the highest church official clearly had destroyed any common space which still might have been there for bridgeing the differences. A time of reckoning had begun.

Violence in a context of political and religious transformation; Some elements for an interpretation

'One makes war to win, not because it is just' (Foucault)[67]

The incidents are violent and tragic manifestations of a deep crisis in longer-term processes of transformation in the Javanese church. I have been studying these over a relatively long period of time. So far, however, I refrained from including them in my analyses of the churches in Java (Quarles 1980, 1987, 1988, 1996). I wasn't sure what to make of them. Weren't these events too idiosyncratic, too personal? What to make of this case of 'murder', what of the self-imposed ostracism, of the sudden uncontrolled outbursts of anger and inflicted havoc? These affairs had so far seemed too much out of the ordinary. Weren't these an exception to the normal rules of the game of settling conflicts in church politics? Did perhaps some personal characteristics of the actors involved play a major role? Still, daughters do not habitually accuse bystanders at their father's funeral of murder, or do they?

---

[67] Foucault biographer, James Miller, recounts a dialogue between Chomsky and Foucault that is paradigmatic of the two modes of theorising concerning power and violence: the 'humanistic' and the 'sceptical' (Miller 1993: 202-203). The first conceives of social transformation primarily as the outcome of conscious efforts, ideals, models and interventions, notions of an ideal order, basic human needs and aspirations. This is the constructivistic perspective, leading to a range of theories. The second mode conceives of human interaction basically as a struggle for power. But human aspirations and ideals only play a very limited role here. It seems as if the process of transformation consists of complex sets of intended and unintended consequences. It is manageable to some extent only, but governed by no one. Bax has extensively analysed the interactions between religious transformation and violence (Bax 1995, Goudsblom 1997). Religious practices and routines are now seen as modes of coping with violence; controlling, allowing and engendering violence at the same time (see also Fletcher 1997).

Broader institutional and political conflicts had manifested themselves on a much wider scale than just in the Situarjo region. Conflicts had erupted throughout the whole church. Yet, in most cases the conflicts lacked the violent nature which became characteristic of Situardjo after the 'violent burial' . Of course there were winners and losers everywhere. But why such violence here while similar battles between the various factions in the Javanese church were settled in more peaceful ways elsewhere? Why was there compromise or transfer of power in other places and why ruthless reckoning here?

In this essay I look at these - sporadic - cases of murder and violence in the churches of Central Java *not* as an exception to the daily routines of establishing order. Violence does not belong to a domain from which the practices of the religious and political order in the church can be kept aloof. On the contrary: violence must be seen as being at the core of religious and political practices. The various religious, political and administrative routines must be interpreted as ways of dealing with a core problem: the basically violent and erratic nature of human interactions. Religious political and administrative ordering derives its vital role from the fact that it deals with the violent nature of human interactions and institutions.[68]

I thus conceive of violence and the administrative and religious routines in the churches as not separated but interrelated practices. The violent nature of the events is not an aberration, a metastasis of the peaceful ways in which the daily life of the churches is handled and in which conflicts are normally settled. Violence is always there. However, it comes to the fore when the daily practices of dealing with it crumble. Thus coping with violence is the 'normal' everyday dimension of religious and political routines and the settlement of conflicts. Violence may manifest itself if these routines break down totally. The violent nature of our human affairs constitutes the core of processes of identity construction, getting to know who 'we' are as opposed to 'them', and going about daily institutional routines.[69] For our understanding of the violent behaviour which I presented above, this change of perspective is significant. What must be explained is how the occurrence of violence and the breakdown of the mechanisms of dealing with it are interrelated.

---

[68] This implies, first, recognition of the basic failures of constructivistic perspectives. They cannot cope with the notion of unintended and unconstructed consequences and violence (Timur Kuran 1995: 289ff). Secondly, the notions put forward by Ben Anderson (1972, 1990) and Clifford Geertz (1980) concerning the 'emic' Javanese and Balinese conceptions of power merit serious reconsideration. Their so-called emic models have a much more general applicability, also in the matter of understanding politics and violence. Foucault, 'the' Javanese and Balinese have a lot in common when allowing for manifestations of power and violence as (almost) metaphysical phenomena. The distinction between the various conceptions is 'constructivist' versus 'tragic or sceptic' rather than etic versus emic.

[69] The study of linkages between violence and processes of civilisation, identity-formation and the daily routines of political communities has been at the core of a range of studies following Norbert Elias. For some recent developments in this line of research see Bax (1995) and Fletcher (1997).

When I take the view that processes of ordering and their loss (possibly result-ing in violence) take place at the same time, the question is to what kind of historical analysis this may lead. Put differently: How can we study intended and unintended consequences in an interrelated way over time? In my view the concept of cycles pro-vides an important analytical tool. The notion of cycles sensitises to the fact that bal-ances between processes of ordering and their loss may shift. So we need to study how processes of civilisation and decivilisation are interrelated. The notion of cycles makes us aware of the fact that extrapolation of linear developments cannot be taken for granted. The quest for order, ie coping with violence successfully, may simultaneously involve loss of control and declining effectiveness. Yet, like in spring or winter, one process is predominant for some time (for an earlier attempt to study cycles in this church's history see: Quarles van Ufford 1988). The notion of cycles allows us to ana-lyse not only quite different and sometimes contrasting processes. The notion of cycles also provides us with a view on shifting balances over time that cannot be explained as intended outcomes or as part of a process of constructing order. On the contrary, it seems that these changes 'just' happen, almost irrespective of all our efforts. The no-tion of cycles helps us to do away with the preoccupation with studying power as pri-marily a dimension of ordering, constructing and controlling.

Ben Anderson (1972: 20 - 21; 1990) has called attention to this view when de-scribing what he (then) conceived of as the 'emic' Javanese notions of power: 'The typical historical sequence of concentration-diffusion-concentration-diffusion without any ultimate resting point.'[70] I take the view that his sensitive analysis of the 'Java-nese' idea of power does not apply to Javanese culture alone but is relevant much more generally. Accordingly, I will analyse the 'murder in the cathedral' as a particu-lar event in a transformation from one cycle to another.[71] The murder may become meaningful only when viewed as a specific incident in longer-term processes.[72] The incidents in Situardjo were an exception, not the rule in these crucial moments of transformation of the church. Similar conflicts in other areas were sometimes of a similar nature, yet not violent. We must try to explain the difference.

---

[70] Huesken (1989) argues that almost all modern theories of rural change in Southeast Asia suffer from 'hodiecentric tendencies', ie the assumption that changes occurring over a relatively brief span of time analysed warrant generalised linear perspectives in the historical study of peasant societies. His analysis also leads to a notion of cyclical development.

[71] It is beyond the scope of this paper to go into greater detail. Yet I wish to make clear that, as the title of this essay reveals, I am deeply indebted to T.S. Eliot's view of time. My wife made me appre-ciate his admirable treatment of the extremely elusive and slippery notion of the 'now', its basically contradictory nature as lying somewhere between 'time past' and 'to come' and historical transforma-tion. In his Murder in the Cathedral Eliot writes of history in a way that comes very close to the 'Java-nese' view. See, for example, George Williamson (1955: 205ff). not in bibliography!

[72] Compare Goudsblom (1977: 186) on the only reliable starting point sociologists of history have at their disposal: the 'now': "the only point of departure that we have to accept is the following: the world has come to be what it is and not to something different" (transl. mine). In my view there is no such common ground. The notion of the 'now' is too slippery if left to itself (cf Quarles 1996).

I focus on two sets of events and lines of argumentation: the dramatics of a sudden and incisive transformation in a short period; and the shifting balances of intended and unintended outcomes over a longer period of time.

a) The rules of the game pertinent to the institutions of the church suddenly evaporated. The actors who had established them started to betray their own clients. The pastor, the powerful 'big man' in the region had been betrayed by the very missionary mentors who before had elevated him to his position of power. Like the Archbishop of Canterbury, he was stabbed to death in his own cathedral by his own kind. Violence could burst out as the domains of trust broke down in a totally unexpected and sudden way. The actors who had been opponents for quite some time now had no common space anymore. The distinctions between friend and foe had broken down.

b) The violent outbursts constituted the final demise of an intensive, coherent and prolonged effort to incorporate the Javanese churches into the parameters of Dutch missionary orthodoxy. Violence did not strike the mission's opponents. On the contrary, it overwhelmed the archbishop and those actors who had become the most impeccable executors of the earlier mission. Those who in good faith had implemented, supported and strongly defended the religious orthodoxy and political and administrative rationality of the missionary movement were hit. I shall argue that extreme loyalty had estranged the clergy from its own changing context. This may help us see how the unintended and intended outcome of long term missionary strategies are interrelated.

Transformation of the missionary landscape in Situardjo

The incidents described above took place between 1969 and 1974. For the church and missionary landscape in Central Java these years meant a major historical turning point. But the events had been in the making a long time before; in fact, we must go back to the decades immediately following World War II. This period of the church of Central Java was a time of missionary restoration, primarily emphasising the need for continuity with a (colonial) Dutch ecclesiastical and missionary past.

After 1945 most of the Christian churches in Indonesia had changed their relations with the Dutch missionary institutions as a result of the political struggles against the Dutch. While in a formal sense most churches, also the church of Central Java, had already become independent long before the World War II, these churches now emphasised some of the consequences of political independence. At the end of the Japanese occupation an Indonesian nationalist movement against Dutch predomination had started to manifest itself among the Indonesian Christians. This movement set the goals for the years to come on the national scene. The church of Central Java was in a way one of a few exceptions however. It re-established intensive links with its former Dutch partners. For the church in Central Java the period between 1945 and 1970 was a time of restoration, not of transformation. The efforts to carry out grand (colonial) missionary schemes of christianising and modernising in Central Java were taken up again. In a way the church of Central Java became an anachronism in the newly emerging independent Indonesian context. The leadership chose to look backwards. The tragic events that took place later must surely be placed in this wider context. But there was more than an intensive effort to restore the old order.

Erosion started to affect the institutional foundations of the church. The very centre of official missionary orthodoxy was increasingly being divorced from the daily practices of administering the churches. This can be seen most clearly at the core of the new relationships which were established after the War. New nodal points of religious and administrative authority were established. The most powerful and prestigious actors were 'pairs of pastors' - a Javanese church leader and a Dutch missionary. Such pairs were the centre of both the theological and the administrative domain of a regional church community. Situardjo was one of these. The two churches - in the Netherlands and in Indonesia - officially shared responsibility for missionary tasks in each region. These pairs of pastors symbolised this close partnership and cooperation.

The agenda of the church remained unambiguous, deriving its inspiration from Dutch missionary views. In this missionary discourse the religious and the secular dimensions of the collaboration fused. While the propagation of the gospel constituted the core, modernisation of Javanese society was seen to be equally important. Large networks of medical facilities such as hospitals, clinics, paramedical institutions, educational facilities - from hundreds of primary schools to a Christian university - were set up. The church was responsible for a great number of institutions in a growing number of activities: credit facilities; transmigration offices; agricultural extension; orphanages, old people homes etc. There were no sharp boundaries between these secular institutions and the church. On the contrary, according to church doctrine the secular activities constituted a crucial part of its responsibilities. The transformation and modernisation of society was seen as an important task. It was thought that modernisation of society would open the people's hearts to the word of God. Thus all 'secular' Christian activities were placed under the umbrella of church leadership, i. e. the priests and theologians.

In the various regions of central Java, the *pendeta utusan*, the Javanese and Dutch 'paired pastors', shared responsibility. They supervised the various activities mentioned above. Almost from the start, actual administrative practice changed. In the 1950s and 1960s the model slowly disintegrated. The Dutch pastors could not remain in their regional positions because of political problems between the two countries. They all had to leave Indonesia. This had serious consequences. The departure of the Dutch missionaries struck the collaboration at the heart. The official discourse of missionary cooperation was still officially upheld, but the religious and administrative practices of the Javanese *pendeta utusan* changed considerably. Now the collaboration between the two churches was in fact symbolised by one man only. The result was that the Javanese priests became religious and administrative monopolists. Midway into the

1960s they had acquired a position of almost unchecked power. They had gained exclusive access to various sources of missionary power, religious, administrative and financial. The growth of the church was their doing. Meanwhile, the institutional landscape which, from 1945 onwards, had allowed their monopoly to emerge in the first place was breaking down.

The official words and concepts chosen by the two - Dutch and Javanese - churches to describe the relationship indicated that the bonds were regarded as unshakeable. The two were 'natural' partners, their relationship willed by God. Official imagery spoke of the bond between an elder and a younger brother, between father and son. The cooperation was a good match for practical reasons as well: Dutch religious expertise complemented Javanese local knowledge and practical skills. The 'pairing of the two pastors' symbolised the unshakeable bond between the two churches. Until the early 1970s this official discourse was upheld. There was an almost obsessive preoccupation with the concepts describing the bonds between the two partners. Especially the Javanese officials for whom so much was at stake became experts in this sacred imagery. If this was indeed a 'natural' bond, then - God willing - no man could undo it. These words were reiterated time and again. The missionary orthodoxy, the speech of intimate relations at the centre, of the daily bonds of loyalty and friendship provided a strong ideological basis. The relatively generous subsidies from the mission only strengthened this seemingly unbreakable union. Collaboration became an ideological obsession precisely as its institutional foundations had inexorably been disintegrating almost from the beginning.

Now the most important aspects of transformation of the missionary landscape in Central Java can be indicated. Church leadership became increasingly preoccupied with upholding the official doctrine of collaboration. Church leaders emphasised and clung to a missionary orthodoxy of a fading, all but obliterated past. By doing so they divorced themselves from their own context and became as it were the prisoners of their own convictions. Their collaboration at the international level became segmented from the aspirations of the Christian communities they were officially guiding. As brokers, the leaders of the Javanese church emphasised that they were building and maintaining bridges between the churches. And indeed they did. They cemented the bridges of collaboration and were so busy doing this that they failed to notice that almost all traffic on them had ceased. They also failed to notice that other people were placing mines under them.

The making of violence and tragedy at the local scene: Situardjo

Reverend Suprapto, whose life ended in such a tragic way, started his working life as a teacher at a secondary Christian school until 1949. He was a third-generation Protestant. His youth and education was stamped by the Dutch mission, he had established good personal relations with missionaries, received an intensive education at various Christian schools and acquired a teaching job. His wife had also been thoroughly prepared by a Dutch missionary family for her future role as a Christian housewife. As a girl she had been groomed for this. She was taken into the home of a Dutch missionary family for three years, and it was hoped that she would become wife to a Javanese pastor and mother of a Christian family.

In 1949, after the two wars in Java, the Dutch missionary returned to Situardjo and hand-picked the Reverend Suprapto for two more years of higher theological education. This training would prepare him for even greater responsibilities. The course of his life was shaped to a very large extent by these various forms of Dutch missionary guidance and support. The mission not only shaped his aspirations but also enabled him to fulfil these. His outlook on the public domain of the church as well as in his private life as husband and father derived from this training. When he was asked to become the missionary pastor of the Situardjo region and to share religious and administrative responsibility with a Dutch missionary, this constituted the apogee of his hopes and aspirations. He became colleague to his guru and spiritual guide.

For twenty years Reverend Suprapto carried out his work to the best of his abilities. His responsibilities had increased considerably when his closest friend, the Dutch missionary, was obliged to leave Indonesia due to the Irian Barat affair. But this departure did not put an end to the official collaboration. Generous financial assistance for all the work that he was doing continued. It even increased. The Suprapto family moved into the beautiful and prestigious home built and long used by Dutch missionaries, the place where the history of the church had begun. His aspirations had been fully blessed; he was a man of great importance and power for more than twenty years. Almost until the end no one opposed him - at least not successfully. He was an able and strong man totally prepared for his job. He continued established missionary policies by creating 'networks of trust and supervision' in much the same way as his Dutch mentor had done before him. He placed personally trusted clients as local pastors in the various congregations. He gave them access to training and higher education and kept close scrutiny. They were paid and supervised by him.

Only in the major city, where two local congregations were financially self-sufficient, did two theologians with an academic background find a place. Together with a slowly growing intelligentsia in the church they started to organise an alternative to the Suprapto rule. From time to time accusations of fraud and of financial irregularities made it clear that his authority was not entirely unopposed. But this had never seriously affected his position, as he was the source of income for most of the local church officials. They were too dependent on him. Moreover, his position was confirmed in a number of official documents signed by the highest authorities. It was established Dutch policy to place their trust in a select few only. To be sure, opponents had contested this power base of personal trust; they frequently tried to provide the relevant Dutch authorities with 'information'. This had happened in Situardjo as well as in many other places. But time and again the Dutch reaffirmed their loyalty to their 'natural' partners, *pendeta utusan* such as Reverend Suprapto. Accordingly, the official structures of the church in Situardjo remained under his control while, underground, opposition was fermenting.

Elsewhere I have analysed in some detail the subtle plot woven by some of Suprapto's contestants in order to undermine his position (Quarles 1980: 185 - 188). I shall not repeat it here. The plot was simple and successful. Some organisational rearrangements were made that transferred Reverend Suprapto to a new committee of which he was a member only. The financial relationship with the Dutch was no longer his private domain. His powers were curtailed. Decisive as this may have been, the sudden loss of power does not explain the violent events which occurred later on. Similar changes took place in the other regions of the church as well. The established authorities were clearly losing their power to a new generation of Indonesian priests and church folk. But in other places the inevitable transfer of power was not as bitter and indeed violent as it was in Situardjo, where Suprapto's former clients often were viciously chased out of their local constituencies. Why the violent settling of scores? For a long time I had not even an inkling .

After my first period of fieldwork I re-visited the area for follow-up research fifteen years later. Reverend Suprapto's widow and daughter still lived in isolation in their house and would not see me. Then I had the unexpected opportunity to discuss the issue of violence explicitly with some of the leaders of the new elite who had successfully plotted against the pastor. Sufficient time had elapsed for a better understanding, it seemed.

The new church leaders told me that they had been seriously shocked by the murder accusation at the funeral. They informed me also that they had not orchestrated the subsequent forced expulsion of the local pastors. While they had nurtured relations with their own clients in the various local churches the eruption of uncontrolled aggression had taken them by surprise. Violence had not been planned, it had 'just' come about, almost as a natural event like a devastating *banjir,* a sudden and unexpected flood, destroying everything on its way.

I tended to believe them, rightly or wrongly. And I still do. These people had not planned the violence. Why then did it happen? We discussed the whole affair again, the administrative calculations and political schemes, the successful inclusion of a Dutch representative in a ploy when he visited the area on a 'mission'. I knew the 'facts' already and had published about it, using pseudonyms. They had even read my analyses, and we discussed these too. As our talk progressed I came to realise the importance of one small point which I had failed to grasp fully before. Reverend Suprapto's murder was not the act of opponents in a winning mood. No, if this was murder, it was his friends who stabbed him in the back.

The logistics of the success of the scheme woven by Suprapto's opponents had depended on a little trick. One of them had driven to a town, fifty kilometres distant, to meet as if 'by chance' a visiting Dutch missionary official en route to Situardjo. They completed the journey together in his car and had an hour of uninterrupted talk. A lot of information was exchanged. The next day Reverend Suprapto took the Dutchman on a tour through the region, doing the regular things, providing reports and information, doing a bit of planning. But never during that day did the Dutchman inform him of the criticisms and new organisational arrangements to which he had been agreeing the day before. The 'elder brother' kept silent. He never even hinted that he was about to sever the unique, almost sacred bond of collaboration with his trusted 'younger brother'. But just a few weeks later the thick ideology of trust and cooperation suddenly proved to be empty. When official letters arrived, sent by his friends in Holland, Reverend Suprapto realised that he had been betrayed. Betrayed in his own house by his closest partner, the representative of a missionary organisation to which he owed the life he had led, his views, tasks and responsibilities. He had not lost a war to opponents, not even a battle. He had been murdered in the cathedral, silently and efficiently, by the very friends he trusted most. It had been done silently and efficiently. Fifteen years later his political opponents made clear to me what had suddenly crushed Reverend Suprapto's heart, broken and killed him. *Et tu Brute.*

The scene at the cemetery with which I started my essay was a logical consequence. Could the daughter or her mother accept this analysis? They too were crushed. The daughter could never admit to an analysis such as I am presenting here. These causes of her father's death she could not name. A public acknowledgement of the betrayal would render meaningless, senseless and irrelevant all Suprapto and the family had stood for. Much as her father had been paralysed into his death, the daughter found herself trapped and totally at loss. When she accused her father's opponents of 'murder' this constituted the last enactment of the values for which he had stood all his life. It was an ultimate and desperate effort to bring back honour and dignity to her father. The desperate accusation might perhaps restore meaning to his life and death and so to her own life as well. To be sure, it tended to confirm that a political struggle had been lost. Yet, it was a desperate effort to validate and rescue at least some meaning and dignity in the life of a father and a priest who had died in the wake of betrayal.

For the church in Situardjo these acts and words however destroyed any possibility of settling regional conflict. The daughter re-enacted in a highly dramatic way the values for which her father had lived. She reconstituted the past only and blew up any bridge that might have been built between past and future. At the funeral the 'now' exploded. Violence had been unbound, all order lost, time shattered. Her desperate effort to restore dignity to her father could only be undertaken at the expense of the new leaders. Any common ground which still may have existed between the competing factions disappeared as a result of the accusation. Her suicidal act broke off the remaining links between winners and losers. Compromise had now become impossible: the future was in contradiction with the past. The subsequent series of explosions in the congregations where the clients of Reverend Suprapto lived were the logical consequence of the first bombshell at the burial. Violence took its own irrevocable course.

Anomaly and accident

Now I shall take a different approach. The first line of argument explored in the previous paragraph has some rather serious flaws. The analysis of the erupting violence in terms of betrayal and a subsequent effort to reconstitute meaning and dignity may well be a bit too straightforward. The roles of the various actors are too tightly differentiated: there is a victim, we seem to know who is the traitor, there are various murderers, maybe some passive and thus guilty bystanders or accomplices. Is my own analysis the work of an impartial policeman, conducting objective investigations in the field and double-checking relevant documentation? Will a judge be convinced by the results of this research? I think not. The roles are too clearly defined and may be too heavily loaded with moral notions such as trust, betrayal and guilt.

In this paragraph I will argue against my first line of argumentation. It implies too clear a differentiation of the roles of characters on the stage and is predicated on the assumption that the various actors acted on the basis of rational planning. The metaphor of murder turns some actors into agents who actually do the deadly deed and tends to deprive the victim of his own agency. After all, how can he be responsible? He was the one who was killed, was he not? But is this distinction between 'agents' and 'targets' warranted?

The death of Reverend Suprapto, his daughter's exile and the forceful eviction of many priests may also be looked at differently: as an accident, something which just happens, unfolding itself, the outcome of a very complex whole of intended and often quite unintended consequences of concrete actions over a long period of time. The violent events may be regarded also as an unfortunate coincidence, unexplainable in terms of any consistent logic or rationality. Violence occurs not as the result of human action, but because the rules and routines which guide the interactions have broken down. Violence may have manifested itself because the notions of self-interest, meaning and rationality have been eroding and breaking down for a very long time. From this perspective everybody, or put differently, *nobody* is 'the' cause of the outbreaks of violence, or guilty of the betrayal or the murder and havoc which occurred in the Situardjo region.

From this perspective the notion of strategies to establish order and legitimacy emphasise only part of the transformations which take place. The notion of cycles may well alert us to the various undercurrents that are also there although they may manifest themselves only after some time. And then we may see the emergence of a new cycle of ordering and structuring. This perspective suggests that events take their course and cannot be fully explained by the doings of the actors. If this is the case, the moral overtones implied in the clearly differentiated roles of hunter and prey, of murderer and victim, of agent and target become somewhat meaningless. At least they must be seen as biased. The death of Reverend Suprapto may equally well be seen as an outcome of his own making! It may be important to try to understand in what way victim, murderer and traitor became interdependent. How can we understand that Reverend Suprapto had also been party to the confluence of occurrences that, *inexorably*, led to his own death?

In a way Suprapto was both willingly and unwillingly involved in this series of tragic events because he upheld an unwarranted belief in a missionary orthodoxy that had become an anachronism. Above I sketched the institutional landscape of the Javanese church after World War II as a period of restoration, a rather desperate attempt of the Dutch mission to cling to a point of view and an orthodoxy which fitted an earlier colonial period. Suprapto became an actor and accomplice because he clung to a belief and a set of practices which increasingly isolated him. The strength and unambiguous nature of his views, their inflexibility, became his 'psychic prison' (to borrow one of the lucid metaphors designed by Gareth Morgan (1986) for understanding our often strange ways of organisation, creating order and controlling violence). In part the events that led to his death can be described as a process of increasing seclusion, self-righteousness and self-imprisonment. In a way he was an agent of his own undoing.

Violence in the church of Situardjo: betrayal and accident

The two lines of argumentation offered above are not parallel. The first focused on the changing nature of the interactions in the church of Situardjo. Conflicts between different elites manifested themselves. The nature of the internal relations in the church had altered. The sources of power to which the religious elites had access changed considerably. Different notions of the Christian identity of the church emerged. In this context the role of the Dutch mission was stressed. Its betrayal of the deceased pastor constituted a key element. The priest had been put aside by his own religious mentors. This indeed can be construed as betrayal.

For the pastor, however, it had been unthinkable to publicly speak out against his religious and ecclesiastical mentors. They had raised, educated and elevated him to his prestigious responsibilities. If he himself had spoken of betrayal he would at the same time have destroyed his own identity and past. He had kept silent and died. The accusation of murder was not made by him but by his daughter. She transformed the betrayal he had endured into murder. Her father had been killed. That she knew. She did not direct her accusation against the traitors, however, but against her father's local and regional opponents and rivals. But they were merely travellers on a road opened up by others.

Secondly, I argued that if indeed betrayal and murder had been the case it may well have been tragically inevitable. Tragic also because Reverend Suprapto was an agent of his own demise. There is more to it than can be said from a murder and victim perspective. The expatriate missionaries, to mention an important aspect, had their own changing religious political interests in the Netherlands. Their actions were quite legitimate in the context of changing missionary perspectives and institutions at that time. They did not lack integrity or ethical awareness. On the contrary, as church leaders they were responsible to their own Dutch context. What can be construed as betrayal in the Javanese scene was quite rational and legitimate behaviour in the other domains. The missionaries had to change their allegiances and rules of collaboration in Central Java. The rules had been defined in and for a former situation. The official discourse of partnership and close collaboration, though officially still upheld, had lost its footing. It had become an anachronism long before a meaningful alternative had become apparent to the Dutch mission. Shall we insist on 'betrayal' here?

The implosion of rules and routines and the sudden proliferation of violence in its various manifestations constituted to the best of my interpretation an accident willed by none. Major transformations just happened simultaneously in various places and in different domains. The breakdown of rules and established practices was no one's deliberate making. Quite the opposite. With the notion of *accident* the outbursts of violence are no longer seen as the product of conscious and deliberate moves or schemes. Rather, it suggests a series of simultaneous collapses of established rules and regulations which rendered order illusory and violence uncontrollable. My final analysis is: Reverend Suprapto met his death in his own cathedral. It just happened.

References

Anderson, B.R. O'G 1972. The Idea of Power in Javanese Culture. In: Claire Holt (ed.). *Culture and Politics in Indonesia.* Ithaca: Cornell university Press: 1 - 71

Bax, M. *Medjugorje; Politics and Violence in Rural Bosnia.* Amsterdam: VU University Press

Cornelis, A. 1993. *Logica van het Gevoel; Stabiliteitslagen in de Cultuur als Nesteling der Emoties,* Amsterdam: Stichting Essence

Fletcher, J. 1997. *Violence and Civilization; An Introduction to the Work of Norbert Elias.* Cambridge: The Polity Press

Foucault, M. 1980. *Power/Knowledge.* New York: Harvester Wheatsheaf

Geertz, C. 1968. *Islam Observed; Religious Development in Morocco and Indonesia.* Chicago: The University of Chicago Press

1980 *The Theater State in Nineteenth Centrury Bali.* Princeton: Princeton University Press

Gilhuis, J. 1955. *Ecclesiocentrische Aspecten Van het Zendingswerk.* Kampen: Kok

Goudsblom, J. 1997. *Het Regime van de Tijd.* Amsterdam: Meulenhof

Huesken, F. 1989. *Een Dorp op Java.* Bloemendaal: Aramith

Holtrop, P.N. (ed.) 1996. *ZGKN; Een Bundel Opstellen over de Zending van de Gereformeerde Kerken in Nederland ter gelegenheid van de Honderjarige Herdenking van de Synode van Middelburg 1896*

Kuran, T. 1995. *Private Truths, Public Lies; The Social Consequences of Preference Falsification.* Cambridge: Harvard University Press

Miller, J. 1993. *The Passion of Foucault.* New York: Simon and Schuster

Morgan, G. 1986. *Images of Organisation.* Beverly Hills: Sage Publications

Mulder, D.C. 1996. Hoofdmomenten uit de Geschiedenis van de Gereformeerde Zending na 1945. In: P.N. Holtrop (ed.). *op.cit.* 1996: 107 - 126

Quarles van Ufford, Ph. 1980. *Grenzen van Internationale Hulpverlening; Een Onderzoek van de Relatie tussen de Aard en de Effecten van de Hulprelatie tussen de Javaanse Kerk van Midden-Java en de Zending van de Gereformeerde kerken in Nederland.* Assen: van Gorcum

1987 Probowinoto, an Exemplary Indonesian Christian. In: Niko Kana and N. Daldjoeni (eds.). *Ikhrar dan Ikhtiar dalam Hidup Pendeta Basuki Probowinoto.* Jakarta: BPK Gunung Mulia: 162 - 182

1988 Cycles of Concern, Dutch Reformed Mission in Central Java 1896 - 1970. In: Ph. Quarles van Ufford and J.M. Schoffeleers (eds.). *Religion and Development: Towards an Integrated Approach.* Amsterdam: Free University Press: 73 - 94

1996 Reality Exists; Acknowledging the Limits of Active and Reflexive Anthropological Knowledge. In: A. van Harskamp (ed.). *Conflicts in Social Science.* London: Routledge: 22 - 44

Reenders, H. 1996. Reformatie van de Zending naar Calvinistisch Model. In: P. N. Holtrop (ed.). *op.cit.* 1996: 12 - 36

Said, E. 1993. *Culture and Imperialism.* London: Vintage

Simons, A. 1990. *Het Groteske van de Taal; Over het Werk van Michail Bachtin.* Amsterdam: SUA

Williamson, G. 1955. *A readers guide to T.S. Elliot.* New York: The Noonday Press

ABSTRACT

Definitions of 'we' vs. 'them', 'past' vs. 'future' pose challenges to people with which they can cope in a variety of ways. They can live with dilemmas like competing demands of loyalty or they can try to solve them by closing the boundaries of identities and organising their defences. The processes of social closure may have violent consequences like bloodshed and murder.

'Murder in the cathedral' is the investigation of the death of a pastor as the logical outcome of a series of events in which ever clearer definitions of the boundaries between 'us' and 'them' and explanations of the past which fitted these have combined into an inescapable web. Death, hatred, fixed identities, loss of ambiguity have come about simultaneously.

Part III

Hatred and the boundaries of social identities

LANCES GREASED WITH PORK FAT:
IMAGINING DIFFERENCE IN BALI
Mark Hobart

In 1635 the ruler of Makassar ordered the king of Gélgél, the then effective ruler of Bali, to convert to Islam or face war. To which the Balinese answer was that they had an army of seventy thousand men ready and waiting 'with lances greased with pork fat' (Wessels 1923: 438 - 39). In the event this measure did not prove necessary. A massive fleet of Muslim forces from different parts of Indonesia had gathered in South Sulawesi to launch a *jihad* against Bali. The concentration of troops was too good an opportunity for the Dutch East India Company to ignore and they attacked and effectively destroyed the invasion force before it could set off. Bali was saved so that it could enjoy its fate as an iconic tourist paradise.

Thereafter Bali became part of the Republic of Indonesia when the latter declared Independence in 1948. And Balinese were among the active fighters for that independence. Economically, for years Bali has been the province with the fastest rate of growth in the archipelago and Gianyar, the district where I worked, the most rapidly growing in Bali. This is partly due to increasing agricultural output, but mostly to the fact that Gianyar has been a driving force behind the 'cultural' end of the tourist economy of Bali. Apart from being the 'traditional' centre for dance and theatre, it has also become the centre of production of art objects, which are exported not just within Indonesia, but world-wide.

In spite of their new-found relative affluence, during the 1990s Balinese privately expressed more serious worries about what was going on than I had heard them do before. Part of their concern was over the effects that tourism was having on the island, not least whether the continued building of hotels, golf courses and the other paraphernalia of tourism was sustainable. Part was over what they felt to be the decline of their way of life, language and culture, due not just to tourism, but to the sundry effects of development, and most especially the impact of television. Part was the fear that, despite the belated recognition of Hinduism as a religion according to the state constitution, they felt threatened by what they considered the incursion of Islam. To what extent though was religion the idiom for, say, ethnic difference? And to what extent are ethnic differences themselves idioms for talking about economic and political differences? In this chapter, I would like to consider certain aspects of how, three hundred and fifty years after the threat from Sulawesi, Balinese represent themselves publicly and their relations with other Indonesian peoples.

It has become commonplace for anthropologists and sociologists to talk about society producing and reproducing itself (e.g. Giddens 1984: 16 - 37). It has become equally common for scholars of Bali to write about how Bali is the complex product of the western imagination (e.g. Boon 1977, 1990; Vickers 1989). It is far from clear though quite how a society sets about reproducing itself. As society is an abstract - indeed an impossible - object (Laclau 1990) it is still less clear in what sense it can do so at all. There is a residual constitutive metaphor at work. If it is not through some mystical act of auto-copulation or phoenix-like regeneration, how does social reproduction happen? Apart from the sorts of structural processes much trumpeted in development studies, an important means, I suggest, is through the activities of people, often as 'complex agents' forming part of public life.[73]

Social reproduction is not unmediated. Again there is a covert transcendentalist tendency in much writing about development, which assumes that the medium through which development is promulgated and argued over, are purely instrumental and so, analytically, incidental and therefore marginal. Against this, I shall argue that it is neither possible, nor desirable, to separate the medium and the message (cf. McLuhan 1964). How people imagine, talk about and rework their understanding of their and others' place in the world cannot be extrapolated from the ways in which, and circumstances under which, they do so without serious misrecognition of that understanding.

There are countless different kinds of occasion on which people are more or less continually reworking their worlds. Certain occasions are particularly important, because what happens is not only public, but may change what is going on in one way or another. In Bali, the frequent meetings of corporate groups are times when groups reconstitute themselves and change their institutional arrangements (see Hobart 1991). Other important occasions include inviting Divinity through spirit-mediums to pronounce on major proposed changes; and when individuals consult such mediums about personal or domestic difficulties. Far from being offered timeless formulae by which tradition is invented, the more popular mediums rework existing institutions in the light of their, and their public's, appreciation of how Bali is changing.

There is another set of activities, as overlooked by scholars of development as it is emphasised by Balinese themselves. This is when Balinese review what is going on around them and comment explicitly on it, namely theatre. I shall concentrate on some of the implications of theatre for the study of development here, both because the extent to which people do comment on their own lives and circumstances is often neglected, and because both actors and audiences consider theatre plays as privileged moments for critical reflection. In fact the leading actor in the extracts which follow talked to me afterwards about how crucial it was for actors to be commentators and critics of what was going on in Indonesia.[74] It was necessary, he said, because the intellectuals who should have been doing this through the media of newspapers and television and in schools through education were too timid to provide the necessary and ap-

---

[73] By a complex agent I mean that decisions and responsibility for action involve more than one party in deliberation or action. These may be households, associations, corporate groups, courts, theatre troupes and so on. The term is from Collingwood 1942; see also Inden 1990; Hobart 1991.

[74] He played the *Panasar,* the anchorman, see below.

propriate critical commentary. So the burden fell on those actors who were still brave enough to speak up. This assessment is shared by at least the more mature members of theatre audiences I spoke to. If we are to move away from a vision of society as per-during imaginary essences towards a more situated analysis of the occasions when people rework their own social and cultural arrangements, then we need to pay closer attention than we have on the whole to what they are doing on such occasions.

In the vogue for self-absorption, which passes for 'reflexivity', scholars have primarily considered how that studiously vague entity 'the West' imagined Bali and have tended to overlook the questions of how Balinese imagined, and imagine, Bali and its differences with other places and peoples.[75] By this I understand not just how Balinese represent themselves on particular occasions, but the ways in which they talk about differences. An unfortunate legacy of Dutch structuralist analyses of Indonesia is that it is often assumed that Indonesians generally structure their thought in terms of dichotomies. Such an approach is not terribly helpful in understanding either how theatre works or how differences may be constituted.

At first sight theatre appears an unlikely means of commenting on, and revising ideas about, the present and near future, because it deals with the past. Theatre is used, however, to re-present the past, to comment on, and review, present practices. In other words, it is a 'scale of forms' in Collingwood's terms (1933: 54 - 91), in which the present is constituted of past acts, but is being continually revised in the light of subse-quent acts of thinking and commentary.[76] The point of such a scale of forms is that dif-ferences are not conceived of as dichotomous (either/or), but as overlapping (both/and). The past (or the future) is both different from the present, and connected with it. One of the problems of writing about ethnicity is not just that it is situational (whether one is from a particular region, is a Balinese or an Indonesian in a particular situation), but that scholars tend to present ethnic differences as dichotomous: Java-nese *versus* Balinese, Balinese *or* Indonesian, Hindu *or* Muslim. As we shall see, in the play I have selected (and much the same goes for other plays I have watched), dif-ferences are not represented so simply.

---

[75] A problem with Ben Anderson's book, *Imagined communities*, which is in one sense the originary text behind this volume is that, whatever his sensibilities to the nation as 'an imagined political com-munity' (1983: 15), both 'imagination' and 'community' are conceived of in very western terms. In fact his image is of the community as consisting in 'face-to-face contact', of common or shared inter-ests, rather than, as Srinivas once remarked, as they actually are 'back-to-back'. Although Anderson writes that 'communities are to be distinguished, not by their falsity/genuineness, but by the style in which they are imagined' (1983: 15), the range of styles he allows is tightly circumscribed. Anderson also presupposes that one can talk of community and imagination prior to a consideration of whether other peoples imagine their social arrangements in commensurable ways.

[76] In a scale of forms 'each lower level or earlier stage is a necessary condition of the next, does not necessitate the emergence of the next level, but yet is seen from the standpoint of that level as leading to it and in fact incorporated in it' (Mink 1969: 134-35).

This is quite enough preamble. Let me turn to the play, which was performed in the village where I work, Tengahpadang in Northern Gianyar, on the night of 11 - 12th. March 1989. The occasion was a festival in one of the best known temples in the region. After the death of his son in a motorcycle accident, the local prince was left without an heir. He had then made a vow to the deity of the temple that, if he had a son, he would pay for a theatre performance, a Prèmbon (a variant on the better known genre of Arja, often called 'romantic operetta', in which some male characters wear masks). The actors were mostly from Gianyar, but worked during the day for Indonesian Radio (R.R.I.).

They took as the plot the promise made by the prince of Nusa Penida, an arid island off the south coast of Bali, to the effect that he would build a temple if he were able to beget a male heir. The play had four important characters, with the actors playing minor walk-on rôles as well. The key figures are the old retainer, *Panasar*, the root is 'base, foundation', ('anchorman' is the nearest English equivalent which comes to mind) and a young retainer, his younger brother, *Wijil*. There are two aristocratic figures: the prince of Nusa Penida, Sri Aji Palaka and his low caste wife, who plays the stock rôle of the *Liku*, a slightly mad and spoiled princess.[77] Of the minor rôles only a wise old villager is relevant here. The plot was simple. It is simply the events on the morning leading up to the completion of the inauguration of the new temple and discussion of how important it is that the prince fulfils his vow. This framework left much room for the characters to comment on current events, while ostensibly talking about events in Nusa Penida in the distant past. It might seem an odd choice of subject matter for a paper about development, ethnicity and imagined differences. We shall see.

The Prince's Promise

Translations from Balinese are in ordinary type.
Words left in the original Balinese are in italics.
Translations from Old Javanese (awi are in bold),
those from Indonesian are underlined.
Words which are in English in the original are bold and italic.

1. The introduction to the play:

(*The old retainer enters alone and sings to himself.*)

Old Retainer   (*He suddenly notices that the audience is there.*) Oh! Good Heavens! May I offer

                          my **apologies** to you all? And thank you for being kind enough to come here to-

---

[77] My analysis of excerpts from the play is based on discussions with four different sources. These were the actress who played the prince; the actor who played the *panasar*; a group of elderly males, of whom two had themselves been actors; and a group of women, including a grandmother, mother and daughter. My interpretation of the dialogue and its significance is that of these Balinese. The theoretical comments are mine.

night. I trust that you will all enjoy good health and happiness. As a Hindu <u>community</u>,[78] we should pray as always that we shall all find peace. On this, the occasion of a religious ceremony, how should we achieve this? Come, let us offer our faithful service together to ask for God's grace. **All of us** living on this island cherish our <u>artistic and cultural life</u>. Oh! I urge you all to share in ensuring that whatever's needed is done when it is time for *barong* processions,[79] so that we can guarantee that our artistic life continues to flourish.

How do we do it? How do we bring it about? For example, Ladies and Gentlemen it's gracious of you to put on this play and to come and watch, **because** if we aren't going to appreciate and look after the arts, who else are we to tell to do so? That's the reason that <u>guests</u> now come, that <u>tourists</u> come from all over the world. What are they really looking for? Is it not **solely because of** your arts, your <u>skill</u> at crafts, your wisdom and knowledge of **all sorts of** art objects?

That's the reason then that <u>tourists</u> come - what's this? Two of them have turned up. '*Welcome, good afternoon, thank you. I hope you glad see here.*' I know a couple of words to use to start up a conversation. Well, now people from overseas enjoy watching, but we've all grown indifferent. Don't let it be like that. If it can be as it is here, I can feel happy and proud to address you, can't I? I hope that we can manage to treasure what we have for ever and make it still better than it is now.

---

[78] Significantly he used the word <u>umat</u>, which is of Arabic origin and usually used by Muslims to refer to the congregation of the faithful. The significance of this usage will be discussed later.

[79] *Barong* are the large puppets, often compared to Chinese lions, which are danced by two people on special religious occasions. They also used to process through the countryside during one month of the year at the Balinese New Year. This is now rare because people prefer to spend the time making money. Balinese often cite this as an example of how 'development' affects religious activity.

The realm of Nusa has been different ever since the reign of His Royal Majesty, who was crowned Sri Aji Palaka. (May I be pardoned for my boldness in mentioning His name!) Well, the land of Nusa is <u>well known</u>, it's <u>famous</u> for being dry. But ever since He came it's changed and the country is different. Before you couldn't get anything to grow, now the landscape in Nusa is green.[80] Apart from that people have developed and have all been enthusiastically pursuing knowledge, which is the reason that schools have sprung up all over Nusa in the villages. That's why now everyone is equally clever. It fills my heart with pride and happiness to be a retainer in the court here....

2. On following one's own religion

(An exchange between the two court retainers about one's religious duties.)

Old Retainer   This is the reason that now...

Young Retainer   That it's (fitting to harmonise)...

Old Retainer   **One's own religious duties** with **one's personal obligations to the state**.[81]

Young Retainer   Everyone who is ruled by the king in the land of Nusa is free to follow their own religion?[82]

Old Retainer   What is right should be taught and broadcast to the whole of <u>society</u>.

Young Retainer   The basis of the religion we share is in philosophy. Having a philosophy doesn't produce results by itself. There should be a moral code to bring implement that philosophy in practice.

Old Retainer   But not even that's enough.

---

[80] This was clearly an indirect praise of the then President, Soeharto, who has laid great emphasis upon technological development. In Bali village society, this is reflected in improvements in agriculture and irrigation. The opening flattery runs directly counter to the *Panasar*'s, and the other actors', drift.

[81] It is left open which religion is being discussed. The commentators said they understood this as signifying that in every region people should be free to worship according to individual proclivity or local cultural usage.

[82] This is a rhetorical question: 'Is it right or is it not right?' The implication is that it should be so.

Young Retainer	That's not yet all that's appropriate. There needs to be art and there's something else, which we call 'rites'.
Old Retainer	Indeed so.
Young Retainer	(*He starts a folk etymological analysis of the word 'upacara', rites.*[83]) What's the significance of '*upa*'?
Old Retainer	What does it mean?
Young Retainer	'*Upa*' is like what we call 'energy', '*cara*' means 'each in his own way'. The ways we achieve it are different, but the aim for all of us is to serve Almighty God.[84]
Prince	So the world will be prosperous.
Young Retainer	Good Lord, yes!
Old Retainer	That is why good actions in this world and in the other depend, of course, on **the proper conduct of the one in command of the country**.
Young Retainer	Of course.
Old Retainer	That's the proper way to keep things in order, so that the world experiences peace.
Young Retainer	This is of course what we should strive for.
Old Retainer	If you're talking about nowadays, it's how <u>leaders</u> should **exert themselves** so that one can have a <u>society</u> which is <u>just</u> and <u>wealthy</u>.

---

[83] Significantly, in *kawi* the primary sense is 'requisites, accessories, paraphernalia, the proper adorn-ments,, insignia' and so 'the proper conduct, rites, etiquette' (Zoetmulder 1982: 2128). We misunder-stand Balinese ideas about religious action if we impose our own heavily loaded term, 'ritual'. That said, Balinese are adapting their exegesis of their own religious practices to fit other people's ideas of what religion is supposed to be about.

[84] The point is the one recognised in Pancasila, the principles of the Indonesian state, which was elaborated into an extraordinary ideology of the New Order régime. The first principle is that there are different, but equally acceptable, ways of worshipping God according to different religious traditions. Mutual religious recognition slides easily into mutual ethnic recognition, especially where certain eth-nic groups become closely associated with religious affiliation. Of nowhere is this more striking than Bali, where to the majority to be Balinese is to be Hindu(-Buddhist). For a different account from the small community of Muslim Balinese, see Barth (1993).

3. On modern fashion

(Joking between the princess [who is always portrayed as slightly crazy] and the two retainers. The princess has just done a mad-cap dance round the floor and fallen over.)

Princess	Do you know the latest dance?
Old Retainer	No. What is it?
Princess	The one where you jump about, do you know that one?
Old Retainer	Oh! An earthquake dance.
Princess	Yes. <u>It is</u> '*break dance*'.
Young Retainer	Uh! Is this the one they now call '*berek dén*'?
Old Retainer	No one here knows about it except for <u>the gentleman</u>. (*She points at me and then at my companion.*) He knows too. The two of them, <u>Madam</u> too.
Young Retainer	Oh! It's true. (Only foreigners know about that dance.)
Old Retainer	The '***Break dance***'.
Princess	That's it, but you say '***break dance***' not '*berek dén*'.
Old Retainer	What did I say?
Princess	'*Berek* dance'.[85]
Old Retainer	Huh!
Princess	(*Switching to speak like a garage mechanic looking at a vehicle in need of repair.*) How come your mouth's so clumsy? Hey! Tomorrow bring your mouth back here. It needs massaging to make it supple.
Old Retainer	Take your mouth in for repair tomorrow.

---

[85] *Berek* is Balinese for rotten – so 'rotten dance', which is what many more elderly people felt.

4. On Indonesian bureaucracy

(The princess has been talking about why the prince married her although she was ugly, and expatiates on what is required of a good wife. She speaks in the officialese beloved of the more self-important Indonesian bureaucrats.)

Princess	If I <u>did not fulfil the specifications,</u> no one would have wanted to take me. I wouldn't have looked for a man. Do you know what <u>the first requirement is</u>?
Young Retainer	Indeed, what?
Princess	<u>Submit a letter of request!</u>[86]
Young Retainer	Huh!
Princess	<u>Second be prepared to submit to a trial period of three months.</u>[87]
Old Retainer	It's very tough to apply for a job on the condition that one must <u>submit to a trial period of three months</u>!
Princess	<u>Be prepared to take up any possible position.</u>[88]
Old Retainer	Carry on.
Princess	Do you know what '<u>be prepared to take up any possible position</u>' means? Did you think it was <u>in the whole of the archipelago</u>?
Old Retainer	Isn't it '<u>in the whole of the archipelago</u>'?
Princess	No!
Old Retainer	What is it then?
Princess	'<u>Be prepared to take up any possible position</u>' means '<u>on the right, on the left, on top or underneath</u>'!
Old Retainer	Oh dear! I thought it was to agree to go wherever one was posted.

---

[86] This is a delicious send up of the Indonesian bureaucracy. Her remark refers both to the formal protocols, which government officials love. It also suggests a love letter to woo her.

[87] 1. It has become practice in some organisations to engage staff on a trial basis in the first instance.

2. This also refers to the increasingly common practice, especially in towns of a couple sleeping together fairly openly before marriage.

[88] 1. Be prepared to go on a posting anywhere within Indonesia. This is a standard requirement of official postings.

2. Be prepared to have to adopt unusual sexual positions.

5. On peaceful co-existence

(A discussion of the importance of the thumb in Bali, between the two retainers and the princess.)

Young Retainer   I remember when our parents used to give us advice in the past. 'My dear, in the

                      future, when you learn about (Balinese) custom, it is **like** a <u>symbol</u>.'

Old Retainer   Yes.

Young Retainer   Like a <u>symbol</u> of our religious feeling, our wish to have genuinely good relations

                      with other people. This. (*He holds up his right thumb.*) It's true. Is it not used to

                      greet guests? 'Please, go ahead.' It's true. This is what you use.[89]

(*The princess starts to walk backwards across the stage with arms outstretched, farting intermittently.*

The young retainer, who is facing the other way, does not see her at first.)

Old Retainer   Danger!

Young Retainer   Oh! What's the danger?

Old Retainer   This is fine behaviour, walking backwards. Only in a tourist area would an arse

                      go '*please*'![90]

6. On fulfilling your promises

(The prince has been granted an heir after going to many temples on the island to pray for an heir. He must now fulfil the terms of the promise, which were to build a temple, if his wish was granted.)

Village Elder   (He had) exhausted the temples in Nusa, including Sakénan, including Pulaki. He

                      had prayed everywhere, as far as all the temples of the *Dang Kahyangan.*[91]

---

[89] When indicating something to guests or superiors, or simply as a gesture of respect in Bali, it is proper to point with the thumb of the right hand, the remaining fingers being closed as in making a fist. One may even nest the right hand in the left, or support the right wrist with the open left hand, to be politer still.

[90] The Old Retainer treats the sound of farting as the English word 'please', pronounced '*plis*'. The usual onomatopaeia for farting is *prut* or *prit*. In High Balinese, or when needing to refer to the sound of a person of high birth farting, it is *priit*.

[91] The *Pura Dang Kahyangan* are temples which have a special history of importance to the most important kinds of religious functionary in Bali. Which precisely are the temples sufficiently important to be listed differs somewhat from kingdom to kingdom.

Analysis

The play works by setting up a complex interplay between the present and past. The present is not simply represented as a decline from a golden past (cf. Geertz 1980). The old retainer notes how much better life is now, not just materially, but in terms of people's opportunities, educational and otherwise. Rather the imagined differences open up extensive possibilities for commentary.[92] Quite what kind of commentaries depends largely upon the circumstances of the performance, what has happened recently, who the audience are, whether government officials are present who can serve as targets and so forth. Also actors can run greater risks in live performances than, say, on television, which, being recorded, provides evidence which can be produced against them more easily.

In other words, the play involves a fairly intricate 'double-voiced discourse'. That is the author makes use of someone else's discourse for his own purposes by inserting a new semantic intention into a discourse which already has, and which retains, an intention of its own (Bakhtin 1984: 189).

The ostensible world of events in the distant past in Nusa Penida is infused with quite different significance by virtue of the juxtaposition of the activities of two different sets of ruling élites. And different members of the audience may choose to appreciate the parallels in different ways. To this the actors each add their own spin.

In this sense then the play appears to work within the two rival hegemonic articulations of Balinese society. That is ways in which cultural elements are brought together, so as to appear necessary, essential, even absolute, but which are in fact the result of practices of mediation.[93] The first is the New Order discourse of development. The second is a discourse of 'traditional' cultural, religious and moral values – note the reiteration of the centrality of art and culture, the significance of religious practice and the moral obligations on leaders. It is of course a tradition which is being constantly revised and updated. However the play also situates itself *between* these two articulations. By contrasting the worlds which they present and, while seeming to pay deference to both, they point to crucial differences and defer the possibility of neat resolution. In so doing, they create a barely discernible counter-articulation, but one which inquiry shows the older members of the audience, at least, are quite clear about.

Let us see what is at issue in closer detail.

---

[92] The actors were elaborating a widely-held view that, while under the New Order régime people were on the whole significantly more prosperous than before, among the downsides were the encouragement of unbridled greed, the failure of political leaders to act morally, to attend to the needs of their subjects, or even to set a good example personally. The corruption of the President Soeharto's children was pretty widely recognised even in rural parts of Bali by the late 1980s.

[93] On the use of the notion of articulation in cultural studies, see Hall (1986); Slack (1996). For a theoretical exposition, which was adapted in cultural studies, see Laclau & Mouffe (1985). For the relevance of articulation to the study of Indonesian media, see Hobart (1999).

*Excerpt 1*The old retainer started by describing the gathering with the Arabic word <u>umat</u>, rather than with one of the Balinese words which are available. He followed it with a reference to the desirability of praying for peace. His prayer was directed towards Divinity in Its Hindu form of Paramawisesa, 'Most Excellent', a common way of designating the supreme deity, Ida Sang Hyang Widhi Wasa (Divinity as the power of fate, **widhiwasa**). He linked this reference by juxtaposition to Bali's artistic and cultural life, using Indonesian. The unstated, but obvious, reference was to the threat of violence. As there were no strong grounds at the time for violence between Balinese, the implicit referent (alluded to in <u>umat</u>) was religious and, at the same time ethnic, because Balinese widely feared they were the object of envy, and sometimes hatred, by their Muslim neighbours in Java and Lombok. Significantly though the actor avoided the sort of closure implied in notions of ethnic identity at several points. The stress was on whoever was living in Bali, whoever was listening to the performance, whoever cherished a rich artistic and cultural life. There were non-Balinese policemen and traders listening to the play (even if the latter from the street where they were doing business) and they were part of the sizeable non-Balinese population living on the island.

When the old retainer turned to religious *barong* processions, he was making an implicit criticism. In the past, for a month in the New Year, Balinese used to travel from village to village with *barong*s. The practice was dying out, because villagers were too concerned nowadays with making money and were not prepared to take the time off. He then moved onto the theme of our presence in the audience to indicate that it is the excellence of Balinese arts, which attracts visitors. He broke into English to address us directly, before using us as a way of commenting on the failure of Balinese to support their own cultural activities, such as theatre. He then started to introduce the background to the plot and neatly wove in what more experienced and interested members of the audience took as praise of the President for his successful development policies in bringing prosperity and education to what was a very dry and impoverished island.

Some of the themes should be fairly self-evident. I wish to comment on four. First, the choice of <u>umat</u> as the term for congregation has the effect of identifying Hinduism as a recognised and approved religion in the language of the dominant religious group in Indonesia, namely Muslims. The old retainer was implicitly appealing to the first article in the constitution, which recognises the different accepted faiths as paths towards God. Second, he was identifying Bali with its artistic and cultural life, based (here implicitly) on religion (on the articulation of culture, tradition and religion, see Picard (1996 a). Significantly he used Indonesian here. In part this may have been because the words for culture and art are loan words from Indonesian anyway. It was also that the problem of identity, and its representation as to do with culture, were more part of contemporary Indonesian discourse, than Balinese. Third, his praise (albeit indirect) of the President's policies set the stage for criticism later of how those policies have been implemented locally. Finally, in a plot ostensibly set in the remote past, he incorporated the presence of tourists in Bali (which he took us for at the time). He did so not as disruptive, nor even just as a source of money, but as highlighting what was uniquely valuable to Bali and which even foreigners could appreciate.

He thereby treated Balinese culture as something which was sufficiently commensurable with other peoples' cultures (or at least their acquired tastes) that they could enjoy - if not understand - it. The tone throughout was to treat differences, not as a source of antagonism or antipathy, but as overlapping. Followers of different religions each have their own way to Divinity, appropriate to their social and cultural circumstances. Balinese culture, which was presented as a highly self-conscious notion, could be and is appreciated by others, without detracting from them being Javanese, Minangkabau or English.

Excerpt 2   The retainers later took up the theme of religious observance and the relation of one's personal religious duties (**swadharmaning agama**) with one's duties to the state (**swadharmaning nagara**). It was not initially clear what the old retainer was referring to, but his younger brother specified it as the obligation - and the right - to follow whatever religion one pleased. He went on to identify each religion as based on its own philosophy. The implication is to shift the stress away from credos, beliefs and non-believers, to the variety and profundity of human thought with the consequent entitlement to mutual respect.

What followed was a common Balinese argument: thought without action however is not enough. It must be given form. And the young retainer gave a folk etymology of the root for rite or ceremony (*upacara*), which ended in a more or less explicit reference to the right to religious worship in the constitution. With the growing overlap in public discourse of religion and ethnicity in Bali, the actors were simultaneously producing an implicit parallel reading of the constitution as underpinning the right to ethnic distinctiveness. Such difference is quite distinct from the simulacra paraded by the New Order, where difference is reduced to iconic, and toothless, variations in dress and material culture, an example being the theme park in Jakarta, *Beautiful Indonesia*, inspired by Madame Soeharto's visit to Disneyland (for a somewhat condescending account, see Pemberton 1994). The possibility of ethnic or religious violence is never stated. The possibility and the danger are however the constitutive condition of the play as a whole.

Human prosperity and peace (the avoidance of conflict and war) was then linked to the activities of a good ruler. The reference was neatly double-edged. It both praised the then rulers of Indonesia and warned them of the need to 'exert themselves' in order to maintain this state of affairs among the populace. It did so by representing the order in Nusa Penida as that of a just king whose subjects were happy, prosperous and free to follow their religious inclinations. At a time when President Soeharto was widely thought in Bali to be leaning increasingly heavily towards Islam, the rebuke was evident.

Excerpt 3   The rôle of the mad princess in Arja includes making fun of Balinese good manners. The Liku had just been rolling around on the floor, slightly extreme even by the standards of the part. Then again, this was not a usual *Liku*. Refined male rôles like the prince have long been conventionally played by women. Unusually the princess, however, was played by a strapping male who had previously had a great reputation as a comic character in another genre, *Drama Gong* (see deBoer 1996; Picard 1996 b). The effect was to add a further twist and irony to what was already a complex double-voiced discourse.

The extract is from the *Liku*'s warming up her audience with various routines – many of which, as far as I know, were original and subsequently widely copied. Here she asked her servants whether they were up on the latest international fashion, breakdancing. While the resorts and big hotels in Bali may be part of the international circuit, things still take a little time to reach the further away Balinese villages. Once again we, as tourists, were woven into the narrative, as the princess turned to us to confirm what break-dancing was. She then castigated her servants for their ignorance (they could not pronounce the English properly) and wove in another idiom, that of the garage or repair shop, when she talked about their clumsy speech. Once again the effect was to situate Bali firmly as part of the modern world. The issue of modernity in Bali is an important and complex theme (see the contributors to Vickers 1996). Here the references seemed to be several. Bali, its art, culture and religion, are objects of appreciation to a metropolitan Indonesian and international élite. In contrast perhaps to most other parts of Indonesia, Bali can no longer be assigned the inferior status of 'underdeveloped country'. On the contrary, Balinese are active, autonomous and creative participants in processes of globalisation, choosing and adapting new ideas and practices to their own ends. The twin criteria of the élite connoiseurship and vulgar marketability of Bali are neatly brought to bear to underwrite the case for allowing, even encouraging, Balinese ethnic and religious – also known as 'cultural' – difference.

Excerpt 4   This exchange is from a long scene in which the princess had earlier run through a whole series of government development programmes, simultaneously explaining them and making fun of them. Having launched herself on debunking government and officialdom, she then turned to how one should set about finding a husband. This was followed by an account of a wife's duties in contemporary Bali, which brought the house down. Several spectators confessed afterwards that they had wet themselves laughing.

The excerpt rests upon a sustained use of *double entendre* between applying for a job, later specified as in the Indonesian civil service, and satisfying a sexual partner. First she treated love letters as like letters of application for a post. She then played on a trial period of employment to highlight the practice of young people sleeping together before marriage. While this has been common in Bali for a long time, semi-formal cohabitation was a relatively new phenomenon of town life. The rest of the excerpt consisted of the two senses of 'be prepared to take up any possible position'. The result was to poke fun at what villagers considered the officious self-importance of bureaucrats' presentation of self in public. While Balinese have to submit to the dictates of these officials in everyday life, the absurdity of the imagery was not so much, I would suggest, about, say, relieving anxiety through laughter over what one cannot confront, but was a more radical caricature of those in high office. It is difficult to take too seriously – at least for the moment – officials, however intimidating they may be in public life, when they are revealed by the demands placed upon their mistresses to be venal creatures engaged in sexual (and by inference, financial) athletics.

The other obvious venality, the notorious corruption of such officials, was left nicely implicit. It was there though, as the actors and spectators I spoke to made clear. Here the mockery of language is double edged. Everyone knows that officials often speak the supposedly impartial and high-flown (or overblown) language of bureaucracy as a cover for illicit demands. There is a more direct attack. This kind of officialese, at least among the Balinese I know, is considered a hallmark of the New Order régime, and indeed of the former president, Soeharto, himself. Indeed at one time imitating the President's speech mannerisms was treated as a criminal offence.[94]

Excerpt 5   This excerpt is taken from a long scene in which the princess compared the five principles of the Indonesian state with the functions of the five digits of the hand. Needless to say, each of the functions had a further and obscene reference. She had just been talking about the use of the thumb (to put money into, or get it out of, banks, by validating the transaction with one's thumbprint). The young retainer took up another use of the thumb, namely as a polite way to indicate something to someone. (It is vulgar to point with the forefinger.) He also introduced the idea that the thumb was a symbol - using the Indonesian loan word from the Dutch simbol.[95] He was making at least two points. First there are proper ways of addressing people, which are distinctively Balinese, inherited from their forefathers and to be retained. (The unspoken alternative, considered inappropriate by most village Balinese, is the two hands brought together on the chest in a prayer-like gesture, which was in fashion among Indonesians and townspeople.) Second he was showing how imported concepts like 'symbol' could be used to illuminate traditional Balinese practice.

The princess broke into his exposition by farting, which the old retainer turned neatly into a reference on the use of English in Bali. With the advent of mass tourism, there has been great demand among Balinese to learn English. Development in Bali

---

[94] In this exchange, the actor playing the *Liku*, plays elegantly with an unstated theme: class. The play, to a village audience, contrasts their position, as ordinary people with much in common with other people throughout Indonesia, with senior officialdom, the bosses. Certainly the people I spoke to afterwards saw him as speaking for the masses everywhere, not for Balinese in particular. If it is a favourite ploy of élites to foster conflicts along lines of ethnicity or religion as a means of diverting attention from the common class, or structural, position of most people, then the actors were being sociologically acute in taking issue with such strategies.

[95] As he specified it, it might to be considered closer to a sign (Sperber 1975; Todorov 1982).

has now reached such a pitch that in tourist areas of the island Balinese even fart in English!

Excerpt 6   This brief passage was the fourth time in the play that the cast referred to the prince having exhausted the temples in Bali. The sentence was ambiguous in each case. The word used, *telah*, may mean just a completed action 'he had been to all the temples', or to have finished something. However *telah* often carries the strong connotation of 'finishing off, exhausting, running down'. Members of the audience with whom I spoke agreed that either, or both, were possible and that the repetition of the formula several times did not look coincidental. When I had a long discussion about various parts of the play with the actor who played the old retainer, I asked whether the second sense was intended. He said it most certainly was, even though it was not he who had said the words. Behind this lies an interesting story.

A few weeks before the play was performed, a large decennial festival had been held at what has come to be known as the central temple of Bali, Besakih. Central government is notionally committed, through the Ministry of Religious Affairs, to provide funds for all religions towards the upkeep of religious shrines and towards major ceremonies. According to what was being said at the time, and from what I had been able to gather, very little money indeed was forthcoming for Hindu shrines. Certainly much of the cost of upkeep of the major temples on Bali, let alone the costs of ceremonies, has come from Balinese grouping together to pay from their own pockets, which was particularly evident as the costs of the decennial festival had to be met. What seemed to heighten awareness of differential treatment was the amount of money, which Balinese said was being put into building mosques for the minority of Muslims in Bali, as well as the right being given them to use loudspeakers to broadcast the calls to prayer. These echo across Balinese compounds each day and, more seriously, across temples during festivals.

The sub-text, as it were, of the play is that the ruler should keep his promises to his populace and that this had not been done. 'The temples are run down' - the village elder started to list some of the great temples of Bali in a state of disrepair - because of the ruler's neglect of his people and the breach of his promise to them. If a ruler breaks his promises and neglects his subjects, does he deserve to stay in power? How long can, or will, officials and cronies prop him up?

Conclusion

In a play seemingly about events sometime in the distant past on the small off-shore island of Bali are themes about how Balinese are to deal with events in the contemporary world and how they constitute themselves in the prevailing circumstances. The opening speech in most forms of theatre is important, because it sets the frame for subsequent events. The old retainer starts by setting out what it is to be Balinese in religious terms, but ones which are not confrontational or based on a dichotomy between Balinese-as-Hindus and other Indonesians-as-Muslims. Instead he describes the relationship as one of overlapping categories between the different paths to Divinity, and actually incorporating Hindu congregations as one kind of *umat.*

This should not necessarily be interpreted as a strategy born simply of the vulnerability of a religious minority surrounded by ethnically different and preponderantly Muslim peoples. Balinese embrace actively the view that different ways of life are appropriate to different circumstances and histories, not just between Balinese and others, but between people from different parts of Bali. If a Muslim woman marries a Hindu Balinese man, she is expected to become Hindu for the duration of the marriage and *vice versa* if a Hindu woman marries a Muslim. One follows one's husband's customary way of worship. Nor is this view necessarily new. Vickers points out that the Dutch had long hoped that the Balinese would prove allies against the Muslims in Indonesia. And 'a Dutch embassy of 1633 seeking allies against the Javanese kingdom of Mataram floundered on the fact that the Balinese did not shape their political enmity solely on the basis of religion' (1989: 14).

If the notion of identity as we usually understand it has any applicability to Indonesia, it would seem that, for a long time, it has not been simply along lines of ethnicity, religion or culture. Nor was an appeal to identity as a closed construct a feature of the play. To the extent that the play was about what it is to be Balinese, it was about how you do things and what you appreciate. And these are as rapidly changing behind the labels as is 'tradition' (Hobsbawm & Ranger 1983). This relates to a logical problem in the notion of identity as used in the social sciences. The only thing identical with something is precisely that thing itself in the same place at the same moment. Representing that thing, giving it an identity, by definition defers and imposes a difference. As with the broader process of representing, identifying requires exclusion, transformation and closure. You cannot represent or identify something as it is, in its fullness, but only as what it is not. There is a double displacement. You have to strip and simplify, to dispose of the accidental to reveal the essential, which effectively requires prejudging what you consider essential. Anyway identity depends upon what it is not, upon a 'constitutive outside', which is the subject of denial and erasure (Staten 1986; Laclau 1990). The only case for using the term at all is when it has become part of the discourse of the object of study. As an analytical notion it is vapid.

What then are Balinese attitudes to tourists, as expressed in the play? Well over a million foreigners and a similar number of Indonesian visitors a year visit this small island of some three million people. How this impact was represented in the play was interesting. Balinese culture was portrayed as something which has self-consciously to be maintained, as if it were no longer a set of practices which people did and which inevitably changed as it went along. Culture is valued in itself and is therefore labile. It is something, though, which Balinese are presented as having uniquely and defined in terms of their art and religion. Europeans are constituted as interested in this culture, which in turn is evidence of its unique value. Why else do they come to Bali?

Balinese culture, now a distinct entity or set of practices, is the source of attraction to others; but Balinese can be equally interested in these other cultural practices like break-dancing. The fun poked at the Indonesian bureaucracy and development projects both recognises their power and, at times, efficacy; but it seems to me not to be escapist fantasies of a successfully pacified proletariat. The actors were indeed themselves members of this bureaucracy, by virtue of working for the national radio station. It might seem to an anthropologist that Bali is being overwhelmed and its culture in danger of disappearing, except as a Baudrillardian simulation of itself, as it is turned into Indonesia's premier theme park. However, in the play at least, Balinese were still able to represent themselves as agents, who had truck with outsiders and new ideas on an equal basis. Ten years on, my impression from more recent Balinese theatre and television is that this optimism has lost its edge.

The ostensibly clear-cut differences of ethnic and religious difference obscure both the complex ties between people and how such differences are construed. Balinese see their aristocracy, after all, as mostly coming from Java. And Balinese have ruled over parts of Java, as Javanese have at times over parts of Bali. We are dealing here in part with the difference between two quite distinct conceptions of the polity. One is the nation state with unambiguous boundaries, prescriptions of citizenship, organised as a system of control over political subjects. The other is what Inden has characterised as the nature of an imperial formation in India, as

> a complex agent consisting of overlapping and contending polities. These more or less successfully relate themselves to each other in what they consider, or at least concede as constituting, a single way of life... Following a universalising strategy, it may claim to involve local and relatively isolated communities within 'its' imperial formation', while they themselves, opting for what I refer to as peripheralising or localising strategies, may attempt to deny or resist inclusion (Inden 1990: 29).

On a smaller scale, Inden's description of polities in India seems much better to describe the complex overlapping links which comprised, as far as we can tell, Balinese polities before conquest.

What Balinese expressed fear about, although not expressed in these terms, was a change in how differences were being construed. Is a dialectical relationship between different groups and polities being gradually replaced by an 'eristical' one, aimed at eliminating, or destroying, all others? At this point difference threatens to engender a kind of categorical hatred, which denies any coevalness or shared humanity between the parties concerned. I am not suggesting people have not disliked, sought to subjugate and kill others; but the mode of dealing with difference is different. It is the distinction between the challenge to an enemy of lances greased with pork fat and the promise of annihilation of whosoever is perceived as different, which has become so depressing and regular a concomitant of that wonderful invention, the nation state.

Postscript

Since May 1998 Indonesia has been in a state of turmoil. This followed riots, which led to the resignation of President Soeharto. Since then it has become clear that there has been a long history of military brutality against imagined enemies of the régime, in many cases where ethnicity is arguably an issue. The most publicised example is East Timor, with Aceh and Irian Jaya following closely behind. There are also reports of attacks by Dayaks and Malays on Madurese in Kalimantan, and of bloody clashes between Christians and Muslims in various parts of Indonesia, including Ambon. The difficulty is deciding in any instance how to determine when, and for whom, ethnicity, religion, class, economic or other motives is the 'real' cause and when the idiom for something else. Beyond a certain point though I suspect that it becomes impossible to pin down unambiguous causation in processes, which are evidently underdetermined and open to rival interpretation.

Such conflicts do not occur in a vacuum, but in a world where traditional and modern mass media are far-reaching and extremely important. Pretending, as do most scholars of development, that you can ignore the impact of such representations seems naïve to me. A review of Indonesian mass media in the last year suggests that much of the informed commentary in the print media and television have argued a similar case to the actors in the play discussed above. These commentators are, it seems to me, arguing against the simplistic use of categorical distinctions, which make for easy - and inflammatory - assertions about 'us' *versus* 'them', good and bad, and so forth.[96] At the time of writing, with a Muslim President and nationalist Vice-President just elected, there is hope that the recognition of, and a degree of respect for, difference may prevail. One can only hope.

References

Anderson, B.R.O'G. 1983. *Imagined communities: reflections on the origin and spread of nationalism*. London: Verso

Bakhtin, M.M. 1984. *Problems of Dostoevsky's poetics*. Trans. C. Emerson, Minneapolis: University of Minnesota Press

Barth, F. 1993. *Balinese worlds*. London: University of Chicago Press

---

[96] Like a number of Indonesian commentators in the mass media, I have been struck by how forebearing, sensible and reasonable the supposedly volatile Indonesian 'masses' have been. The problem seems to have been far more with the political élite, many of which appear still trapped in the strange world of the New Order.

Boon, J.A. 1977. *The anthropological romance of Bali 1597 - 1972: dynamic perspectives in marriage and caste, politics and religion.* Cambridge: University Press

Boon, J.A. 1990. *Affinities and extremities: crisscrossing the bittersweet ethnology of East Indies history, Hindu-Balinese culture, and Indo-European allure.* London: University of Chicago Press

Collingwood, R.G. 1933. *An essay on philosophical method.* Oxford: Clarendon Press

Collingwood, R.G. 1942. *The new Leviathan or man, society, civilization and barbarism.* Oxford: Clarendon Press

deBoer, F. 1996. Two modern Balinese theatre genres: *Sendratari and Drama Gong. In: Being modern in Bali.* (ed.). A. Vickers, New Haven: Yale University South East Asia series, No.43

Geertz, C. 1980. *Negara: the theatre state in nineteenth-century Bali.* Princeton, N.J.: University Press

Giddens, A. 1984. *The constitution of society: outline of the theory of structuration.* Cambridge: Polity Press

Hall, S. 1986. On postmodernism and articulation: an interview with Stuart Hall. *Journal of communicative inquiry 10*, 2: 45 - 60

Hobart, M. 1991. The patience of plants: a note on agency in Bali. *Review of Indonesian and Malaysian affairs.* 24, 2: 90 - 135

Hobart, M. 1999. The end of the world news: articulating television in Bali. In: R. Rubinstein and L. Connor (eds.). *Staying local in the global village: Bali in the twentieth century.* Honolulu: University of Hawaii Press

Hobsbawm, E.J. & Ranger, T. (eds.) 1983. *The invention of tradition.* Cambridge: University Press

Inden, R. 1990. *Imagining India.* Oxford: Blackwell

Kemp, J. 1989. Peasants and cities: the cultural and social image of the Thai peasant village community. *Sojourn.* 4, 1: 6 - 19

- 1991. The dialectics of village and state in modern Thailand. *Journal of Southeast Asian studies.* 22, 2: 312 - 26

Laclau, E. 1990. The impossibility of society. In: *New reflections on the revolution of our time.* London: Verso

Laclau, E. 1996. Universalism, particularism, and the question of identity. In: E.N. Wilmsen and P. McAllister (eds.). *The politics of difference: ethnic premises in a world of power*. London: University of Chicago Press

Laclau, E. and Mouffe, C. 1985. *Hegemony and socialist strategy: towards a radical democratic politics*. Trans. W. Moore and P. Cammack, London: Verso

McLuhan, M. 1964. The medium is the message. In: *Understanding media: the extensions of man*. London: Routledge

Mink, L. O. 1969. *Mind, history, and dialectic: the philosophy of R.G. Collingwood*. Middletown, Conn.: Wesleyan University Press

Pemberton, J. 1994. Recollections from 'Beautiful Indonesia': somewhere beyond the postmodern. *Public culture* 13: 241 - 262

Picard, M. 1996 a. *Bali: cultural tourism and touristic culture*. Trans. D. Darling, Singapore: Archipelago Press

Picard, M. 1996 b. Dance and drama in Bali: the making of an Indonesian art form. In: A. Vickers (ed.). *Being modern in Bali: image and change*. New Haven: Yale University Southeast Asia Studies No.43.

Slack, J.D. 1996. The theory and method of articulation in cultural studies. In: D. Morley and K-H. Chen (eds.). *Stuart Hall: critical dialogues in cultural studies*. London: Routledge

Sperber, D. 1975. *Rethinking symbolism*. Cambridge: University Press

Staten, H. 1986. *Wittgenstein and Derrida*. London: University of Nebraska Press

Todorov, T. 1982. *Theories of the symbol*. trans. C. Porter, Oxford: Blackwell

Vickers, A. 1989. *Bali: a paradise created*. Ringwood, Victoria: Penguin

Vickers, A. (ed.) 1996. *Being modern in Bali: image and change*. New Haven: Yale University Southeast Asia Studies No.43

Wessels, C. 1923. Ein Portugese missiepoging op Bali in 1635. *Studien* 99: 433 - 443

Zoetmulder, P.J. 1982. *Old Javanese-English Dictionary*. 2 Vols (with S. Robson), The Hague: Nijhoff

ABSTRACT

The chapter considers critically how Balinese 'reproduce' their own social and cultural institutions under conditions of very rapid development. A major problem in Indonesia is strict government censorship of any debate critical to the state ideology which enshrines a particular view of development through modernisation. Balinese regard theatre both as the most important way in which they rework their society and as the main source of critical social commentary.

In the excerpts the theatre play together with comments afterwards both by the actors and by members of the audience are analyzed in detail to examine their views of what was going on. A major theme was the right of different recognised religions to practise freely under the Indonesian constitution. Religion is the most widely adopted idiom of ethnic difference and conflict. So the extensive references to religion in the play made all sorts of statements about the nature of the development process in Indonesia, about the relative access of different groups to resources and the dangers of growing ethnic division, the jealousy of their Muslim neighbours of Balinese growing affluence and the hatred of which Balinese feel themselves the target. Using the example of a past Balinese king who, although Hindu, promoted the welfare and religious freedom of all his subjects equally, the actors were arguing for a beneficial model of mutual tolerance against an implicit antagonistic and destructive one. They were also being directly critical of government for failing to acieve this on behalf of all the people concerned. In this analysis, it is ignorance, sloth and avarice which are the sources of hatred. Government officials were being accused of all three and warned of the dire long term consequences of not doing their public duty.

The argument in the play was an elegant reflection on the dangers of imagining differences as rival interests, not as complementary ways of living. What is distinctive though is that the idiom, the language and the moral argument were distinctly Hindu Balinese, but engaged the problem of development, ethnicity and hatred from a distinct and almost totally unknown point of view.

RELIGION, MODERNITY, TRADITION AND THE CONSTRUCTION OF DIFFERENCE INSIDE AN EGYPTIAN VILLAGE

Petra Weyland

The construction of identity and difference is a topic which often comes up when dealing with ethnic groups or nationalism. However, it seems that similar processes of construction of the self and the other can also be observed on the micro level of much smaller social entities. And if I am here putting forward the case of an Egyptian village community I am in fact not the first to deal with such an issue in a rural context. Thus, Israeli social anthropologists dealt with the phenomenon of Palestinian village societies being cut into two distinct socio-cultural sub-communities already some decades ago. These scholars, often departing from some modernisation theory inspired background – as was to be expected at that time – have not been spared by critical Middle Eastern scholarship in its objective to unearth inherent orientalist attitudes in academic discourse (see, e.g., Asad 1975; Haidar & Zureik 1987; Nakhleh 1977). They have been reproached for their preoccupation with culture, and especially with Islam, as the quasi primordial driving force behind village segmentation and of their essentialist and ahistoric analysis by which any potential agency on the macro-structural level, in this case Israeli military and political institutions, is faded out. On the other hand, religion definitely is an asset when it comes to symbolic struggles over power. Religion as a vehicle for the delimitation of boundaries definitely is not a fantasy of Israeli social anthropologists writing in the 1950s and 60s – there is something more to it.

What I am interested in here is to unearth such elements belonging to symbol systems of difference and distinction. How are such sign systems created and established? Then, I want to point to the meaning social actors attribute to them. Lastly I intend to discuss strategies possibly pursued through the construction of identity and difference respectively.

In the lower Egyptian village I did my research in religious dichotomy is a fact. Approximately half of its inhabitants are Muslims while the other half are Christian. And *cum grano salis* one can say that large landowners are Christian while poor, small or landless cultivators are Muslim. But there are of course also poor members of Christian landowning families as there are some rich Muslim households. Thus religious affiliation mirrors class structure. The origins of this stratification are based in the history of village foundation, as in the 19th century, Muslim landless peasants in their search for work[97] settled on the estates of their Christian landlords.

---

[97] See Weyland (1993), and on the introduction and legislation of private landed property: Baer (1962), Cuno (1980) and Richards (1982)

In what follows I want to cite some examples from my field research to give an idea of emanations of such processes of self identification and construction of difference in the everyday life praxis of the villagers. In fact it was already from the very first hours of my stay in the village that I got a taste of it. Muna, an about 17 year- old girl from a Christian landless peasant household had been chosen to accompany me and to introduce me to the village families. On our very first walk through the village she presented me to her girlfriends, Christians like herself. Almost immediately the girls took over the initiative and managed to make religion the nearly exclusive topic of our conversation. They had even already asked the priest whether I was allowed to take Communion with them and so they proposed we visit the village's church and meet the priest. I was virtually bombarded by their inquiries into my religious practices and beliefs. With shining eyes Muna's friend related how Krullus (the spiritual leader of the Copts who is the most honored religious dignitary in the village) had performed a miracle on her when he let her pass her final school exams.

The entry in my field diary of what happened next on this very first afternoon in the village runs as follows:

> Later we had a walk through the fields and Muna surreptitiously drew my attention to houses inhabited by Muslims who seem to be living more or less in a quarter of their own. According to the girl's descriptions Muslims seem to be stupid and limited. Muna is angry that the ^{c}umda (the village headman) chose a veiled *mutadayyina* (religious Muslim woman) of all people, as another research assistant.

Another example conveying the same message is the exclamation of a woman from the Christian household I was staying in when she heard that I was about to go and visit some Muslim families:

> Oh, don't you go to visit them, they are so hostile towards us, don't you know that in this quarter of the village only Muslims live? They won't treat you in a gentle way and you will certainly catch lice there!

I have heard Christians clandestinely referring to the Muslim quarters as *harat al-^{c}abid,* the "quarter of the slaves" or "black". There are in fact some black families in the village whose presence which give us hints of the village foundation, its linkages to agricultural slavery and expanding market production.[98]

These examples stress the importance of religion in the imaginative worlds of these Christian women. They highlight the overriding priority religion has for the mapping of their practical everyday lives. The very first message these women – and

---

[98] According to Baer (1969: 165-166) in "(L)ower Egypt agricultural slavery was the temporary result of the sudden prosperity in the 1860's which lead to the acquisition of new land and to a tremendous expansion of agriculture." These black slaves originated from different parts of Africa, especially from Sudan and Nubia.

in fact they were not the only ones to do so on my very first day in the village – communicated to me was their explicitly Christian identity (rather than their Egyptian, Arab, female, rural or what so ever identity). Then, their efforts to include me in this identity, to make me one of theirs, the Christians, was obvious from their insistence on meeting the priest (instead of, e.g. walking through the village and its fields, showing me its shops, the place where rice is milled or any other household). The existence of an Other within village society and its identification in religious terms became obvious right from my first moments in this village society, at least its female sub-section: confronted with me, the female foreign researcher who was to stay for some months in the village, a socio-cultural Other was constructed which first of all was Muslim (not, for example, villagers from neighbouring communities, other families, the landowners, the migrants…). Muslims, however, were not only described in religious terms. (In fact the only instance I remember when the Islamic system of belief and Islamic institutions were explicitly at issue, was when a Christian woman argued that Muslims were backward because their men were allowed to marry four women.) Being Muslim is rather brought into connection with slavery, dirt, poverty, illiteracy, even stupidity. It is quite clear: being Muslim is considered as the epitome of backwardness. It is not really hidden hate, but some sort of disgust and contempt which dominates the Christian women's attitudes towards their Muslim neighbours. Islam generally connotes "tradition" in the sense of backwardness whereas Christianity is linked to enlightenment, modern life and progress.

This kind of imagination of difference struck me because I myself had some difficulties to make out any differences at all, as both groups actually share the same socioeconomic background. The families of the Christian girls were in fact involved in just the same harsh everyday life struggle for survival, for the securing of a meager subsistence base as their Muslim neighbours were. What was even more astonishing was that this *Mutadayyina* was no "fundamentalist" at all and besides she, that, was the only girl of the poor stratum holding a university degree from the renowned Al-Azhar university in Cairo while Muna only had an intermediate degree.

The construction of difference is not restricted to verbally expressed opinions, rather it is continuously channeled into inter-action. Looking back, much of what I experienced with these women on my first day in the village can be interpreted as their endeavor to draw me, the Christian woman from a Western, industrialised and "modern" country, onto their side, to make me 'one of theirs'. Thus Muna eagerly tried to introduce me exclusively to other Christian families and to screen me from Muslim households, even to avoid to entering "Muslim territory" at all. Her persistence in this endeavour eventually was to develop into a major conflict and a struggle over power as I insisted on getting to know Muslim families, too – a crisis which I could only solve in my favour by taking recourse to the village headman who also was the head of the household of my host family.

There is another significant incident of which I want to give an account here. I eventually became aware of the fact that Muna always, when together with me, dressed in a ready-made, urban style *gallabeya* which is not very customary for the young fellah-girl from the village. Moreover, when I visited her at home I always found her dressed in the "traditional" *gallabeya* the village women usually wear. I actually became aware of this fact because Muna herself one day told me that she deliberately put on this dress when together with me. It is perhaps interesting to note in this context that I myself sometimes wore one of these urban style *gallabeyas* which, what was more, happened to be a dress brought back by a migrant from Saudi Arabia and was easily recognisable as such by the women. Not aware of any special signification of this dress within the village context, I frequently ware it for lack of other clothing I found to be appropriate. And I certainly favoured it over my blue jeans in my endeavor to "go native". I only then noticed that a number of women admired this dress, the signs of which conveyed a totally different meaning *to them*: while for me it meant "going native", for them it connoted urban-style, Saudi-Arabian, and made of a synthetic fibre instead of the "traditional" Egyptian cotton – this was modernity! By chosing a ready-made, urban-style dress when together with me, Muna stressed the similarity between us, the shared use of symbols of modernity and urbanity.

While at first puzzled by Muna's behaviour I eventually understood what a precious asset I was for the realisation of her own strategies. Being with me all day long, walking with me along the village alleys, visiting other households, and especially the ones she liked to chose, as was the case in the beginning of our relationship, was certainly more delightful than doing the household chores and agricultural jobs her mother ordered her to do on ordinary days. But there was more to it on the symbolical level. My body, my dress, my way of moving and talking, all conveyed the same message: I was the woman from the West; what was more, I was Christian, I was highly educated and I was free to determine my movements as I had come alone, without husband or family. I had knowledge of the outside world – in fact I was the very manifestation of this outside world: I was the image of modernity having turned up on the village stage, within the core of tradition. To get me on her side was an important goal for Muna as she could symbolically associate herself (and with her, the Christian members of the community) with modernity thereby at the same time enlarging the distance to the Muslim villagers. In this context her dressing in a similar way as I did – instead of the way village women usually do – became an important visual aspect of her self-stylisation.

Another aspect which is already apparent from my paper so far is that this kind of active involvement in the creation of difference has significant spatial dimensions, too. Village geography does not consist of distinct and homogeneous Christian and Muslim territories. Yet these certainly exist as mental maps and are actively created, as the term *harat al-ᶜabid* shows. Both religious communities engage in the occupation, in the construction and delineation of specific places out of shared village space. Walls and doors are decorated with crosses and circles made of straw. Garlands made from the pictures of Christian saints can be found hung across the street. There is the mosque's minaret and the church's tower competing with each other for height. Newspaper garlands are hung up during the month of Ramadhan. All these signs convey the same message: look how many we are, this is all our territory, we are omnipresent, we determine village geography!

Besides the spatial aspects, temporal dimensions are of equal relevance within the struggle over power and domination. *Time-Spaces, Zeit-Räume,* are the objects of competition. The Christian season is the *muled,* the commemoration of a Christian saint who is celebrated during a whole week in summer with long nightly prayer sessions. This event brings the old landholding absentee aristocracy back to the village and it is in these instances that the poor Christians can demonstrate their belonging to the rich and modern (the absentee women always came high heeled, with fashionable dresses, their hair curled by an urban coiffeur) by joining them in the church while the Muslims have to stay outside.

The Muslims have their turn during Ramadhan. Yet they occupy temporal spaces not only once a year, but every night as I came to understand right from my first night in the village which was rather brutally brought to an all too early end some time before dawn when the mosque's loudspeaker started to transmit the religious morning program of radio Cairo. A male voice read religious instructions for about half an hour at such a high volume that there was no thought of sleep anymore. This was eventually followed by the habitual call to prayer. I really felt terrorised by the noise, and I soon had to learn that this was no exceptional event. It took me some weeks to get used to these nightly religious lectures. The Muslims who during daytime definitely have to play the subordinate role in the village community, at nighttime and with the help of electricity and loudspeakers manage to get the state (in the form of its religious programme) on their side. As this incident superficially was religious and concerned religious duties, moreover those of the Muslims who are dominant in Egypt, nobody dared to speak out loud.[99] In these moments Muslims without any doubt were the ones disposing of absolute power.

The construction of difference then by no ways is an exclusively mental affair. In manyfold ways it is turned into action within what Stauth (1990 a: 356) has called the "Bürgerkrieg des Alltags", "civil war of daily life" raging in the village. All these undertakings with the aim of achieving legitimacy, marking boundaries, creating difference and excluding the Other do not go unnoticed and do leave their impact: the symbols, messages are read by the addressee and influence his/her actions. I got an idea of this reality when I went back to the village some years after my field research. As I had not been there for about three years I took another young Christian woman with me on my first walks through the village. I had previously known this Christian

---

[99] According to the Egyptian constitution "Islam is the religion of the State" and the Shari'a is a principal source of legislation. The state stateguards the freedom of worship

woman to be very active in the endeavor of creating distinction. We eventually reached the Muslim women I had worked with. I felt their (as well as my own) joy at meeting again after quite a long time. While embracing each other and exchanging news I was almost immediately struck by the intensity of the literally bodily reactions of my Christian companion. I really could see the disgust and hate in her eyes and I felt her tension. She vigorously tried to hurry me along, rationalising her behaviour by stating that everything was so dirty here and that there was not enough time to stay.

Yet, I really could feel the extreme unease of this Christian woman and that she actually was afraid to be here, in the Other's territory. Here, she was no longer the dominant actor excluding the Other from some kind of "imagined community" but she was the one intruding on the enemy's territory, the construction of which she had actively participated in. This was something very different from the stylisation of the self as Christian superior, this was almost fear. This incident was a very clear indication of the degree to which Muslims too are engaged in the creation of space. Here, I got confronted with feelings, behaviour and action in such "enemy's territory". Here I experienced that the construction of the other is no purely academic affair, is not something which is merely talked about, thereby defining the self – rather this construction of the self and other turned into a reality which actually was able to determine the feelings of its creators.

What are all these actions with the aim of creating distance and distinction all about? Why do all these (female) actors spend so much energy on the construction of difference? This is all the more a question since all of them belong to the same stratum of poor, landless or near landless peasant households. Why is the Other constructed in religious terms and why is the enemy not the village based large landowner concentrating the community's land in his hand and valuating their labour power and their products under market prices? Why does the stressing of religious affiliation matter so much and why is religion the focal point at all? In this context I might add that I think we are not witnessing the effects of recent Muslim fundamentalism nor some sort of Christian response in village society.

The prevailing system of agricultural production and the scarcity of resources of the poor peasant household give us a clue to an understanding. This village is typical of Egypt's system of agricultural production. Here again I do not want to go into historical details about the market integration of Egypt's rural areas and its specific system of production. It is sufficient here to emphasise that this distinct form was not accompanied by the creation of large agricultural enterprises and a full-scale proletarianisation of the peasant producers. Rather, until today, a combination of subsistence and market production prevails leaving the cultivator largely autonomous in his/her organisation of subsistence production. It is in this sense that Stauth (1990 b: 123) stated:

Thus, the *izba* system remained the form of keeping the small peasantry alive by incorporating their labour force into a system of internationally articulated commodity production and by externalising the networks for securing and distributing the necessary means of subsistence.

This situation has not been changed by the Nasserist land reforms of the late 50s and early 60s. While there was some improvement in the situation of many near-landless peasant households, access to land has been deteriorating again since the mid-70s and a concentration of land in the hands of the village-based middle size landown-ers is taking place. Given the powerless position of the small cultivators vis-à-vis the state, its representatives in the village and the large landowners, given also virtually non-existent social insurance systems, given the fact that off-farm employment is hardly available, the securing of the household's survival to a large extent reverts to the community and its networks of reciprocity. This brings us from the economic level and that of the organisation of production to the level of values, to the village commu-nity's moral economy delineated by the *taqlid al-qarya*, the "village traditions". Within this context the large landowners have the responsibility to protect their "cli-ents" by renting out land, by entering into share-crop arrangements, by giving them work, by selling them cereals and by mediating in conflicts. This is one side. The other is that, given the scarcity of resources through the monopolisation of land by large landowners, given also minimal opportunities for wage labour and off-farm employ-ment, a situation of competition among all the dependent cultivators inevitably occurs.

In this specific context religious belonging may well be brought to the battle-ground. Belonging to the same religion as the landlord certainly serves to justify claims as do kinship, or being a poor, distant member of the landowner's family. In this particular context the construction of differences on religious grounds definitely is a potential tool in the endeavour to exclude competitors from the scene.

Naturally, expressing identity in religious terms does not only serve the inter-ests of a poor peasant strata in defending and representing legitimacy in order to secure access to scarce resources. This would be too much of a functional or causal explana-tion. Rather, we must understand these religious symbols as signs of an underlying structure, belonging to a "generative (set of) rules and resources drawn upon by actors in the production and reproduction of systems of interaction" to put it in Giddens' terms (1977: 14). In the same vein I can refer to Geertz and understand my examples as illustrations of "the ways in which the world is talked about – depicted, charted, represented – rather than the way it intrinsically is" (Geertz 1983: 4). Within such a framework it is likewise important to see who is talking to whom about what and whom: in my examples Christian poor women interacted with me, the Western female outsider, out of their interest in drawing me onto their side in their daily struggle with those who are their competitors over scarce resources – that is the poor Muslim house-holds.

What I have done, then, is to single out some images of an underlying texture, of an "imaginative make-up of a society" (Geertz ibid: 5) – the ones I became aware of, because these were the ones imparted to me.

I have here developed the argument that in the village context belonging to the Christian religion as a way of representing the self is linked to modernity which is positively valued. On the other hand, constructing the other as Muslim is linked to the notion of tradition as a feature of backwardness, which is thus negatively valued. Yet, a reversion of values simultaneously is taking place."Tradition" may also have a positive meaning in the village context, as I have already shown. This is the case when poor village households lay claim to the benevolence of the rich and landowning peasant households with the argument that village tradition, the *taqlid al-qarya* obliges the affluent to do so. I here want to give another example which illuminates this shifting into oppositite valuation of both notions, that is, that villagers turn "tradition" into an absolute positive while a modern lifestyle is frowned upon, to say the least. This example again refers to myself and my identity as a Western female researcher. When I came to the village I was immediately integrated into a struggle over legitimacy and the hierarchy of symbols: my own legitimacy, that of the Christian village women in relation to me were at stake and negotiated from the very first day onwards. One of the pivotal symbols in these interactions was my own identity as the migrant, characterised as the urban, "modern" woman. Moreover, that I was a woman from the West, from West Germany, one of the major paradises of modernity, where virtually everybody wanted to go to and I had a university degree. I wore modern clothes, I had short hair, and I did not yet have children. But what, in the context described above, that is, vis-à-vis the Muslims, had been a positive value, in the direct interaction between these Christian women and myself definitely was no longer a point for admiration – rather, the contrary was the case. These women - as, by the way, the Muslim women, too - engaged in the deconstruction of my legitimacy and identity as a female. Their sceptical facial expressions, the doubt in their voices time and again reminded me that I was the one not conforming to the rules and values. I had come alone to do research work – but was I not married and where was my father and mother, my family? Did I not have any children yet despite already being in my early thirties? Why did I, a woman from the rich West, not wear any kind of gold or jewelry? What, to study migration? What for? Does that feed anybody? Yes, definitely I was a symbol of modernity – but I really did not feel that this was a point to be admired for these women. Here I was in another territory with other rules and female roles.

Again it was the duality of modern and traditional lifestyles which were played upon. In this specific interaction I became a mirror to reflect the "traditionalism" of the Christian rural women, their belonging to the "Third World", subsistence producing village community. In their endeavour to defend themselves it was exactly these signs of modernity they called into question thus underlining their own cultural and moral superiority as the ones conforming to gender roles and the superior community tradition. Here again, the *taqlid al-qarya*, village tradition, emerges as the positive value per se, justified by the fact that "things have always been that way", the "this is our village custom". I was the one to be pitied.

What I have been highlighting with these examples, then, is the active engagement in the construction of symbols and their valuation. What I consider most interesting in this context is that actors clearly appropriate elements of an ongoing, overall discourse – and one would not be wrong to call this a globally articulated discourse – and to probe and apply it for their own interests and the sake of their own, village society based strategies. They, furthermore, do so with a great deal of resilience as, with changing counterparts, meaning may turn into its opposite value: what with reference to the Muslim women had been very positive becomes negative when the hierarchy between me and the Christian women was at stake.

In the end, both kinds of construction of difference, both kinds of normative idealisation of village tradition and its symbolic defence, undertaken with the aim of creating a mental map of the world they are living in, as well as realising their own strategies, serve those of the large landowners who depend on the functioning of the *taqlid al-qarya* as a non-coercive means of securing their dominance and wealth, and ultimately of reproducing constraint (Giddens 1984: 89). It is here that we meet the second aspect of Giddens' argument of the "duality of structure": social structures are the medium of human agency, yet they are at the same time constituted by it (Giddens 1991) – and within this framework the construction and valuation of the self and the other is of pivotal significance.

References

Asad, Talal 1975. Anthropological texts and ideological problems: an analysis of Cohen on Arab villages in Israel. *Review of Middle East Studies* 1: 1 - 40

Baer, Gabriel 1962. *A History of Landownership in Modern Egypt, 1800 - 1950*. London: Oxford UP

Baer, Gabriel 1969. Slavery and its Abolition. In: Baer, G. *Studies in the Social History of Modern Egypt*, Chicago, Il.: Chicago UP

Cuno, K. 1980. The Origins of Private Ownership of Land in Egypt: A Reappraisal. *International Journal of Middle East Studies* 12, 3: 245 - 75

Geertz, Clifford 1983. *Local Knowledge. Further Essays in Interpretative Anthropology* New York Basic Books

Giddens, Anthony 1977. *Studies in Social and Political Theory* London: Hutchinson

Giddens, Anthony 1991. Structuration theory: past, present and future. In: Bryant, Christopher G.A. and David Jary (eds.). *Giddens' Theory of Structuration. A critical appreciation.* London, New York: Routledge: 201 - 221

Giddens, Anthony 1984. *The constitution of Society: Outline of the Theory of Structuration* Cambridge: Polity Press and Berkeley: University of California Press

Haidar, Aziz and Zureik, Elia spring 1987. The Palestinians seen through the Israeli Cultural Paradigm. *Journal of Palestine Studies* 16, No.3: 68 - 86

Nakhleh, Khalil summer 1977. Anthropological and Sociological Studies of the Arabs in Israel: A Critique. *Journal of Palestine Studies* 6, No.4: 41 - 70

Richards, Allan 1982. *Egypt's Agricultural Development, 1800 - 1980. Technical and Social Change* Boulder, Colo.: Westview Press

Stauth, Georg 1990 a. Die Modernität des Dorfes. In: Georg Stauth, Christoph Reichert, Petra Weyland, Renate Albrecht: *Fellachen zwischen Überlebenssicherung und Modernität als Lebensstil. Strukturelle Unterentwicklung, Migration, Geschlechterverhältnis und Islamisierung: die Konflikte der ländlichen Gesellschaft Ägyptens 1986 - 1988.* Projektabschlußbericht Bielefeld: 353 - 357

Stauth, Georg 1990 b. Capitalist Farming and Small Peasant Households in Egypt. Glavanis and Glavanis: *The rural Middle East.* London: 122 - 141

Weyland, Petra 1993. *Inside the Egyptian Village* London, New York: Routledge

ABSTRACT

This article is a female Western anthropologist's account of the faces identity and difference take in a small and relatively poor Christian and Muslim Egyptian village in the late 1980's.

Christian and Muslim villagers until then lived together peacefully and generally uninfluenced by fundamentalist racism. Still, religion is the main currency when Christian village women depict, to the outsider woman, their mental maps of identity and difference, of who belongs to the self and who is part of the other. In this mental map the Muslim landscape is generally linked to backwardness and a traditionalist attitude.

The article gives empirical evidence of the symbolic expressions this dichotomy of Muslim backwardness and Christian superiority finds in the built environment, how it is translated into action and informs discourses, and also how the researcher is incorporated in this construction of difference.

While the imagination of the self and the other is a fundamental human fact and as such does not call for explanation, the question of why the construction of difference takes on a particular form rather than another one is relevant. Here, socio-economic issues come in as one possible explanation. As these Christians and Muslims share poverty and landlessness, denomination may be turned into a valuable asset in a situation of competition over scarce resources. Here, being Christian may serve to back up the claim for preferential treatment by the Christian patron towards his Christian clients in the allocation of work, gifts, land and favours.

THE MULTIDIMENSIONALITY OF OROMO IDENTITY
Georg Haneke

Introduction

In the years 1995 and 1996 I did research in southern Ethiopia[100]. The topic was *Points of Intersection of Power in the South of Ethiopia*, which was supposed to be a kind of follow-up project on research a colleague and myself had carried out in Kenya, between Nairobi and Moyale, in 1991[101].

At the time when I started my research in the project area between Addis Ababa and Moyale, I did not know that all native researchers of the University of Addis Ababa had already been withdrawn from that part of the country for "security reasons". Some were even arrested while they were visiting their home towns or villages.

Nevertheless, I got the research licence, the affiliation to the *Institute of Ethiopian Studies*, and tried to start my investigations by travelling around by public transport to get into contact with people along the road, like we had done some years ago in Kenya. After some journeys I found out that no-one wanted to talk to me, because I was always followed by some people. The only chance to get rid of these governmental intelligence agents who followed me, was to buy a four wheel drive car.

During the field work government officials confiscated all my official papers such as the affiliation, my passport, my Ethiopian ID-Card, they imprisoned me and my field assistant, they examined me in dark back rooms several times and, as we found out later on, they planned an attempt on our lives when we came back from Negele (Borana) to Moyale. Fortunately, and just by chance, we took another way going back. Finally, after giving a lecture at the University of Addis Ababa, where I was not allowed even to mention the name of a single ethnic group or place of my research, they put me under house arrest and told me not to leave Addis Ababa any more, because no-one could guarantee for my security any more. Even in my house I was no longer secure and I had to leave the country after nine months.

The circumstances mentioned above show the situation in the south of Ethiopia in 1995 – 96 very clearly. On one side the Tigrean dominated central government in Addis Ababa feared the struggle for independence specifically of the *Oromo Liberation Front* (*OLF*) and, in general, of the majority of Oromo people. On the other side many Oromo suffered under the socio-economical, political and military pressure of the government. The whole situation led to new discussions about being Oromo, self-consciousness and self-determination.

---

[100] The research was sponsered by the German Research Board and embedded in the Graduate School *Market, State and Ethnicity* of the University of Bielefeld.

[101] see Haneke & Stahl: 1994.

This paper considers this development and wants to contribute to the discussion of identity in the case of the Oromo.

Finding out an identity in a historical perspective

After the fall of the communist Mengistu-Regime, the TPLF (*Tigrean People's Liberation Front*) were the first to enter Addis Ababa with the help of the USA, though some other large armed opposition groups like the OLF fought against the regime. After a short period of time the common government of all opposition groups failed, mainly because of the domination of the Tigre who captured most of the former regime's weapons.

> (...) the EPRDF guerilla army was made the official, national defense force, replacing the demobilised, huge army of Mengistu Haile Mariam. Not only did this action render these ex-soldiers and their families destitute almost overnight, but it also made the armies of other liberation fronts illegal. The result of this was the further heightening of tension and potential conflict. Actual conflicts did occur between this new government army and the armies of OLF, IFLO, SLF, ALF, and a number of other isolated groups. Wherever it went, the TPLF/EPRDF army began to be seen not as a national army but as an occupation force. (Makonnen Bishaw 1995: 16f).[102]

It seems to be obvious that a strong political opposition is built, if an ethnic minority dominates a country and blocks access to nearly all resources. The preconditions for such a strong opposition movement are not only existential fears of individuals but also the consciousness of belonging to a group, e. g. an ethnic group – in this case even one which is numerically predominant - which is placed at a disadvantage. So, the first complex which should be focussed on, is the creation of the self-consciousness of being Oromo.

It might be helpful to have a look at the history of Oromo people. Today it is sure that the Oromo were already mentioned in the 16th century, but, until one or two decades ago, they featured under the name of *Galla*, which has really bad connotations today.

Ethiopian history, like so many other histories, has been "a narrative of the winning side" (Baxter et al.1996: 15), as Paul Baxter, Jan Hultin and Alessandro Triulzi pointed out in 1996. This means it is the history of Amhara kingdoms, expan-

---

[102] EPRDF = Ethiopian Peoples' Revolutionary Democratic Front, OLF = Oromo Liberation Front, IFLO = Islamic Front for the Liberation of Oromia, SLF = Sidama Liberation Front, ALF = Afar Liberation Front, TPLF = Tigray Peoples Liberation Front.

sions, civilisation and Orthodox Christianity. In Ethiopian history books the Islamisation of the 16th century is described as "fire", the Oromo migration as "water" flood-
ing the civilised Ethiopia. The Amhara were seen as the Christian rescuers of the civilised Occident from the dangerous *Galla*. Even western scientists cultivated this prejudice until the late 60s. As Ullendorff wrote in 1965:

> The Galla (...) had nothing to contribute to the civilisation of Ethiopia;
> they possessed no material or intellectual culture, and their social organi-
> sation was at a far lower stage of development than that of the population
> among whom they settled. They were not only cause of the depressed
> state into which the country now sank, but they helped to perpuate a
> situation from which even physically and spiritually exhausted Ethiopia
> might otherwise have been able to recover far more quickly (Ullendorff
> 1965: 76).

Proceeding from the identity-discourse, that "any identity needs the presence of
other comparable identities in order to define itself" (Baxter et al.1996: 15), the *Galla*
were seen as:

> a dark untamed force of Nature which, like a human deluge, could have
> spilled over Abyssinia, Egypt and the rest of the civilised world if the
> Amhara had not stopped them. The Emperor and his Amharic speaking
> followers were represented as having been given the historical mission to
> conquer, domesticate and christianise the 'Galla'. The northern colonial-
> ists used this mythical construction to justify their monopoly of power
> (Baxter et al.1996: 15).

How widespread this prejudice is even nowadays is shown by a remark made
by a former German Minister for Economic Cooperation, who emphasised the importance of development aid for Ethiopia. He spoke about Ethiopia as a Christian island in
an ocean of Islam. I have my doubts whether he knew that he was ignoring about 40 %
of the Ethiopian population.

Though the Abyssinian kingdoms could only occupy large territories by promoting an aggressive policy of expansion, massive imports of weapons and long wars
of conquest, history is not seen in a political or economical context, i. e. the competition over trade routes and production areas. Instead, it is usually only seen from a
moral point of view. A tale of Amhara modernity and progress was written and until
recently has been taught in schools everywhere in Ethiopia. Oromo history was left out
of consideration. For more information about the debate on historical research in
Ethiopia see Lewis (1993) who has pointed out that the Ethiopian empire was formed
in the same way as other Western colonial empires, and Gashaw (1993) who has underlined the existence of the Ethiopian state, including a distinct national identity for
over three thousand years.

The permanent discrimination of being Oromo has two possible solutions: firstly, consciousness of belonging to a discriminated group can lead to a strong self-identity in opposition to the ruling elite or ethnicity. Secondly, Oromo people try to become integrated into a Greater Ethiopia and wish to be accepted as equal members of a greater unit.

Many Oromo, especially educated ones, try to follow both ways. One expression shows the conflict very clearly:

At daytime we are Ethiopians, at night we are Oromo.

In the recent history, for a very short period of time, there was the possibility of connecting both identities as an Oromo Ethiopian or an Ethiopian Oromo. After the fall of the Mengistu regime there were plans to change the old Ethiopia into a federative republic with administrative, political and economical independence for every region. For such an identity without either polarisation or switching between being Oromo and Ethiopian it would have been necessary to gain access to all resources including the participation in political power, administrative structures, economical self-determination and executive control. As is known, the plan failed very soon after a national conference held in July 1991, when nearly all sectors of society started to be occupied by the Tigrean government. However, the aims were already formulated and lead to an Oromo self-consciousness.

Criteria of an Oromo identity

In the Oromo case, not just for scientific purposes, there still remains one main problem: to extract the actual definitions of being Oromo or belonging to the Oromo nation, otherwise books like *Being and Becoming Oromo* (Baxter et al.1996) would not have to be published. In order to find out aspects of this self-identity I just asked many people in my project area from Addis Ababa to Moyale. I did not only talk to OLF-members, fighters or political and military leaders or their sympathisers but also to OPDO[103]-officials, District Officers, as well as Amhara and Tigre so as to draw a picture of the non-Oromo view of being Oromo. After many interviews, discussions and reading published articles with and by Oromo, the following criteria should be mentioned:

- a common language (*oromiffa*)

- a common history

- a common system of social stucture (*gada*)

- a common consciousness of belonging to a discriminated group

---

[103] OPDO = *Oromo Peoples' Democratic Organisation*. The only legal Oromo party is government-controlled and -sponsered.

- a common demarcation of others (*Abyssinians*)

Let us have a differentiated and critical look at these criteria. I start with the common language.

The common language

Until recently, Oromo was only a spoken language and dialect differentiation within it was so considerable that my Boran field assistant had communication problems when we travelled to other areas.

But even the absence of dialect differences does not necessarily lead to the feeling of belonging to the same group. This is shown by the case of the Boran and the Gabbra in the South of Oromiya. Both ethnic groups speak the same language even without dialect differentiation. Nevertheless, there were and there still are many tribal clashes between the Boran who are mainly cattle herders and Gabbra camel herders, especially if there is a shortage of resources. The common language is not able to solve any of the problems they have with each other.

The adoption of the Latin alphabet by the Oromo movement in the 90s has been celebrated as an achievement on the way to nationhood. It remains to be seen whether this step will lead to processes of standardisation and unification of the language.

The common history

A common history seems to be the basis of a common identity. Only with a common and internalised history are political aims like an own nation-state acceptable today. That means if a nation-to-be does not have a common history, it must create one.

At any time and everywhere one can find such constructed histories of a people or of a nation, and there is definitely no need to go to Africa for this:

> (...) the ethnic principle (...) now is used to redraw political maps, a process which is accompanied by different levels of violence, ranging from the atrocities in former Yugoslavia to peaceful seperations like that of Czekia and Slovakia. (Schlee & Shongolo 1995: 7).

Creating an own history does not always mean fighting. Famous poets like Goethe and Schiller, philosophers like Kant and Schopenhauer or composers like Mozart and Bach are claimed as outstanding creators and bearers of a common German culture. What is faded out is the fact that none of them lived in a nation-state Germany, as it is defined today. They lived somewhere in the middle of Europe in different feudal countries or independent towns but definitely not in a common nation-state.

In the context of a nation-building process and of defining the Oromo as one people with a common and clear history, especially by members of the OLF, the historical ethnogenesis is faded out. The Oromo, and that might be a proud difference to many other peoples, are distinguished by the permanent adoption of individuals and foreign groups. Different Oromo groups had different varieties of the *gada*-system, some of them even lost it through their history (see Schlee 1998). Identity is an ongoing process on the basis of complicated reciprocal interactions.

As, among others, Paul Baxter has pointed out:

> Personal and ethnic identities are the products of culturally shaped public words, rather than membership of easily isolable and enduring social or political groupings (Baxter in Kaarsholm & Hultin 1994: 248).

Also, as mentioned above the history of pre-colonial times is quite different from the one published in Ethiopian history books and adopted by some European scientists until twenty years ago. The Oromo created many different political formations, from nomadic groups of hunters and gatherers to farmers and centralised mercantile states with a highly qualified bureaucracy and custom posts at their borders, sometimes even controlling the long distance trade. Based on traditional modes of thought and customs they were economically and socially very successful, but not as powerful as the Amharic Christian states of Northern Ethiopia (see Baxter in: Kaarsholm & Hultin 1994: 255).

The main constant of Oromo history and identity is openness. "One became an Oromo by becoming an accepted member of an Oromo community or becoming a client" (Baxter in: Kaarsholm & Hultin 1994: 248), which means an active involvement in Oromo cultural values through local ritual and social performances. "The incorporation or adoption of strangers, individually or in groups, has been constant throughout Oromo history" (Baxter in Kaarsholm & Hultin 1994: 248). This is quite the opposite of what is propagated by parts of some Oromo elites.

The common, sometimes invented history can also be seen in a symbolism which suggests historical continuity. Entirely

> new symbols and devices came into existence as part of national movements and states, such as national anthem (...), the national flag (...) or the personification of 'the nation' in symbol or image (...) (Hobsbawm & Ranger 1999: 7).

The following are two remarks on the case of the Oromo in Ethiopia in the context of inventing national continuity and the symbols which stand for it:

the historical fact that many Oromo fought side by side with the Abyssinians to conquer and occupy the southern part of the present Ethiopia, including the Oromo tribes living in that area, is ignored and never mentioned again in Oromo history. If one asks officials, the stereotypical answer is that they were only a few individuals, who were so called left-handed, but mostly this part of the history does not exist.

There is competition for the legitimate use of the same symbols. The *oda*-tree is to be seen on a flag with the Ethiopian colours. It is used by the OLF as a symbol of identity for a new nation and by the OPDO, the Oromo organisation of the Tigre-dominated government, as a sign for taking care of Oromo people and legitimising their own authority. So, the same symbol is adopted by both of the opposed sides, just to show that each of them is the one and only true representative of the people.

The common system of social structure

As already mentioned, *the* common social structure does not exist in the Oromo case. Although the *gada*-system is discussed as a potential form of a social and even political system it should be acceptable to ask which kind of *gada*-system is meant. Often the *gada* is described as a traditional system, but we face the same problems as mentioned above under "The common history".

One may get the impression that there is a religious dimension to the *gada*-system, though varying local conditions have led to different shapes (see Schlee 1994). This might be connected to a very uncertain memory of a mythical origin and a value-system. Other processes, like the permanent denial of resources and political power in Ethiopia or the definitions imposed by others might also play a big role.

The traditions, or rather *invented traditions*[104], are one important basis for justifying the Oromo struggle for freedom in Ethiopia. Of course, it is not only the struggle for independence, but also the fight for a central nation-state, a "Free Oromiya"[105]. This includes an own definition of an Oromo nation-state. Authors like Hobsbawm & Ranger already warned in the early 80s:

> (...) one must beware of making the further assumptions, firstly that older forms of community and authority structure, and consequently the traditions associated with them, were unadaptable and became rapidly unviable, and secondly that 'new' traditions simply resulted from the inability to use or adapt old ones. Adaptation took place for old uses in new conditions and by using old models for new purposes (Hobsbawm & Ranger 1983: 5).

---

[104] "'Invented tradition' is taken to mean a set of practices, normally governed by overtly or tacitly accepted rules and of ritual or symbolic nature, which seek to inculcate certain values and norms of behaviour by repetition, which automatically implies continuity with the past" (Hobsbawm & Ranger 1983: 1).

[105] "(...) whatever today, (...) has been re-emerging for the past decade from oblivion and historical irrelevance, in terms of state formations is not so much a rebirth as a new birth (despite all the more or less artificial "renaissances", through which national mysticism attempts to build connections between the present and the past)" (Allemann 1955: 236) (Translation by Elizabeth Ewart).

And in fact, the *Oromo Liberation Front*, as the intellectual and ideological spearhead of the Oromo movement, is discussing a future nation-state structure, which can be based on the *gada*-system, where the final authority is given to some special elders of a special age-set. But the structure of an Oromo nation-state as well as the internal and secret structure of the OLF itself, are not identical with the structures of any *gada*-system. All members and officials I talked to, carried out an intellectual balancing act by transferring the structure and names of the traditional organisation principle onto the structure of a future Oromo nation-state.

If one has a closer look at the planned structure of a future Oromo state it does look less like the realisation of any *gada*-system but more like a borrowing from a former socialist nation-state (see figure).

The following figure is an organigram of the future Oromo state as it was envisioned by the OLF in 1995.

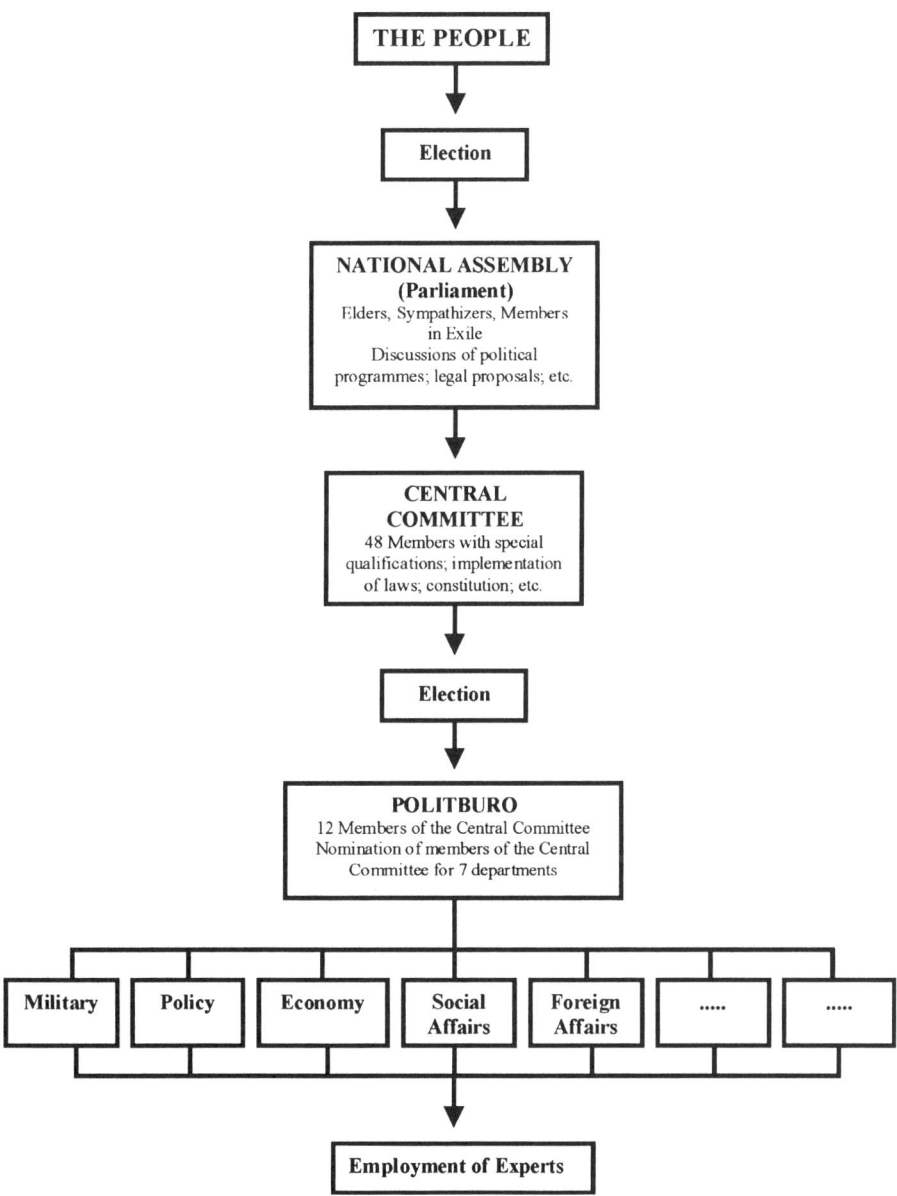

In this system it seems to be very doubtful whether political parties are able to participate. Although political discussions are embedded in this system, the political philosophy behind it is: one people, one party, one central nation-state.

One interesting question should be how the *gada*-system functions in general in the varying shapes in which it has existed for centuries. It not only provides the rules for participation in political power but it isalso the central organising principle as an age-set and generation-class-system. As such it does not construct ethnicity or even national consciousness, but builds *"we-groups"*[106] (see Elwert 1989). The membership in an age-set and the patrilineal descent line regulate the formal *rite de passage,* in the socialisation process, defining the military organisation, marriage options and special participation in social life. The simultaneous membership in a lineal descent group which includes women, regulates exogamy and defines ownership rights and the access to resources.

The combination of all these different processes leads to the strong stability of these *we-groups*.

The common consciousness

Before we come back to the case of the Oromo I should describe what is meant by a common consciousness. For instance, soccer-fans of a national team develop an emotional consciousness of belonging to the same group or nationality, although they might subscribe to completely different political ideas.

Another reason for a common consciousness is even more simple. The criterion might be a phenotypic appearance like skin. Communication might be made easier in a foreign country if one meets a person of a similar colour.

These brief examples should make clear the problem of a common consciousness. They show very easily how a common consciousness of belonging to a special group or set is often defined by the situation.

In the case of the Oromo, Thomas Zitelmann (1994) described the situation of Oromo people in exile, especially in Sudan, Somalia and Europe (see also Baxter in: Fukui & Markakis 1994: 171). After losing the relations to their families on the basis of reciprocity, economical support and their identity in smaller units like families, sub-

---

[106] "By nationalism we mean social movements with communicative or ideological references or with economically relevant commonalities which refer to the creation, consolidation or defence of an own nation according to a commonly shared definition" (Elwert 1989: 449);
and:

"The criticism of domination and exploitation with an emphasis on economy can initiate class war, with a moral emphasis it can lead to the formation of a religious community or it can constitute nationalism or nativism when the criticism of domination and exploitation is made by strangers" (Elwert 1989: 450). (Translation by Elizabeth Ewart)

clans or village communities, the refugees were open to ideologies, which provided an alternative identity with the suggestion of greatness.

This situation was used by the founders of the OLF. Financed by other members in European exile, the leaders started an education programme. Alphabetisation, the implementation of a common literary language and the teaching of a common history were the main contents of the programme. Access to food was not independent of the education programme. Almost everybody who needed food-aid was recruited for the programme. Especially those Oromo, who lived in Sudanese or Somali exile became members of the OLF and later on even teachers of the education programme. Even today they travel through the country and teach people, especially elders, how to be an Oromo.

In such a situation the connection of a political organisation to strong symbolic expressions is very attractive. Elwert pointed out that the lost home (in the sense of native place) is replaced by one's country (in the sense of "fatherland"). The damaged individual identity is upheld or replaced by the magic formula of national greatness (see Elwert 1989 b: 34).

OLF-propaganda makes Oromo identity sound very essentialised, as follows:

> *Oromumma*, derived from the name Oromo, refers to all those elements that constitute the Oromo personality. This personality is shaped by all those features of the internal and external environment that bind Oromo to their land, with its mountains and rivers, its plants and animals, ist seasonal patterns and the other cultures with which it interacts. (...) In other words, in Oromo, as opposed to other cultural and religious groups, the cultural boundaries of personhood, nationhood and religion are so coextensive that they are rendered practically interchangeable. (...) In short, for the Oromo, the belief system, ethnicity and identity are given with birth. An Oromo person does not become a member of a believing community through a formal rite of incorporation such as baptism. An Oromo is born with *Oromumma*. Thus, the simplest definition of an Oromo would be that he/she is born of an Oromo father (Gemetchu Megerssa in Baxter et al.1996: 92 - 94).

Though Gemetchu Megerssa also intends to show the connection to customs, he presumes that Oromoness, with all its implications of nationalism, is always given to everybody who has Oromo blood in his veins. By the way, it must be the blood of the father, which gives us a deep impression of the role of women against the background of modernity. Günther Schlee strongly criticised Gemetchu's ideological article:

> Where Gemetchu is heading with his deeper essence and uniqueness of Oromo identity is clear from the following definition: '...the simplest definition of an Oromo would be that he/she is born of an Oromo father.'

He is heading towards biologically self-reproducing social unit. Here the thin line between nationalism and racism has been crossed. (Schlee 1997: 235, Schlee 2000: 9)

Günther Schlee and Abdullahi Shongolo (1995), Mario Aguilar (1998) and other international reseachers recently have shown that a common identity acknowledged by all Oromo in general does not exist. Schlee and Shongolo, a Boran man from Moyale, remark:

> It may have become clear from our historical sketch that the heavy *gada* symbolism of the OLF (...) is hardly suitable to evoke feelings of belonging among those groups, like the Garre and Gabbra, who perceive themselves as the offspring of the victims of these traditional institutions glorified by the OLF. (Schlee & Shongolo 1995: 7).

As is known, the Boran have shared a ritualised killer complex with other Eastern Cushitic societies for centuries.

> Killings have to be performed in connection with certain promotion ceremonies. While among the Rendille this requirement can be fulfilled by shooting birds with bows and arrows and the Gabbra youths hunt small rodents (...), the Boran *raaba* used to go on war expeditions which aimed also at raiding cattle but primarily at obtaining the severed genitals of slain male enemies (of any age size from an embryo or baby to an old man) as trophies (...). (Schlee & Shongolo 1995: 10).

Only thirteen years ago, in a *Gumi Gaayo*, a *gada* assembly held in 1988, the Boran started to discuss how to abandon the requirement to kill and how to replace it with other proofs of manliness (see Shongolo 1992).

In this context an interview I recorded during my research in 1995/96 with an intelligence coordinator and officer of the OLF, underlines this problem. The question was how the OLF could win the support of other ethnic groups. He replied:

> In fact the effect of the recent ethnic clashes is still fresh in the minds of all Boran enemies. This has to a great extent hindered our plans to introduce our objectives into these communities. However, by now, we have managed to get symphatisers from among them. We have recruited our own agents from their own people and these agents are still recruiting more and more members, though the process is slow. Our effort to restore good relationships between the Boran and the others is still in progress and hopefully we shall succeed. (...) We are still trying to change the people, family by family (anonymous 1995).

This quotation does not seem to support Gemetchu Megerssa's suggestion that an Oromo is born with *Oromumma*. Their history, their situation and last but not least their common consciousness seem to be more complicated.

The common demarcation of others

In the most accepted theory (developed by Barth 1969) ethnicity does not articulate itself at the centre of an ethnic country, in the most homogenous area, but at the borderlines in touch with other ethnicities as it was underlined by Schlee & Werner (1996:10). That can lead either to conflicts or to peaceful co-existence of the different groups. In recent history we have many examples, for instance the peaceful separation of the Czech Republic and Slovakia. On the other hand we have the cruel example of former Yugoslavia.

> The focus shifts from the surface to the border, from the two-dimensional formation to the one-dimensional. Social identities, state claims to control, and economic areas are examined at the spot where they enter into contact with one another and react to one another (Haneke & Stahl 1994: 2).

The common demarcation is not necessarily defined by membership in one nation or by belonging to one ethnicity, as another African example can show very clearly. I only know of one African country which seems to have the precondition for being a homogenous nation-state. There is only one country with a high degree of cultural, linguistic and ethnic as well as socio-economic homogeneity: Somalia. Unfortunately, this nation-state has ceased to exist and has even lost its borderlines as tey appear on the world map. Somalia has been "fragmented along clan and sub-clan lines, well below the level of integration commonly referred to as national" (Schlee & Shongolo 1995).

Another interesting example is the recent conflict between Eritrea and the Tigrean-dominated Ethiopia. They speak the same language, they have a common history, their leaders fought against the same enemy, Mengistu, they cooperated intensively in military matters, they even allowed one another to control their borders, as I realised in Moyale when I was checked by Eritrean soldiers. Nevertheless, the two countries started fighting each other in 1998.

Former Yugoslavia, Somalia, Eritrea and Ethiopia show that even a close cultural, linguistical, ethnical, economic or social neighbourhood or homogeneity do not protect against wars or clashes.

Although the common point of reference of the Oromo are the Abyssinians, I made some interesting observations in Moyale, where different borderlines can be found. The first borderline is between different ethnicities like Boran, Garre, Gabbra, Burji, etc. which lead to ethnic clashes from time to time, especially over access to resources like water, grazing areas or settlements.

The second borderline is the official border between Kenya and Ethiopia, although the same ethnicities and even sometimes the same families live on both sides..

Nevertheless, one is able to perceive some differences. When I visited a bar on the Kenyan side of Moyale, all the Kenyan guests, mostly Boran, started laughing at midnight, because one could see the lights being switched off on the Ethiopian side of the town. The comments were full of irony like *"that is a strange country over there"*, *"they have no food besides bloody injerra, they have no lights, they have no schools, they only have guns"* or *"at daytime they will rob you, at night they will kill you"*. Let me underline that these statements were made by the Kenyan Boran about their Ethiopian brothers living some hundred metres away.

Indeed, there are some big differences between the two sides. The whole infrastructure like the school-system, the hospital and medical treatment, the food and the eating habits and so on are quite different among the Kenyan and Ethiopian Boran respectively. The pride and sometimes the arrogance of those living on one side of the borderline towards those who live on the opposite side reveal the wish for another demarcation. If there is already a demarcation between Boran and Boran one can imagine how difficult it will be to integrate different traditionally hostile ethnicities in one nation. So far it might have been possible to use stereotypes of the Abyssinian enemy, as a uniting force, but there might be the danger of internal conflicts once this enemy picture ceases to be strong enough to support identity.

Summary and prospects

Summary

Oromo identity is not as clear and well-defined as it seems to be.

A common language might be a good precondition for building a nation-state or for a common consciousness but it is not absolutely necessary nor is it a protection against conflicts as can be shown easily by the clashes between Boran and Gabbra or Garre.

The common history, not only in the context of the Oromo, is often created or re-written in a heroic way. Many differentiations fade and facts are deleted. Instead of growing by using their historic abilities to integrate and assimilate, nowadays a strong and simplistic nationalism which only appeals to some "original" Oromo, is propagated among different Oromo groups, especially in exile.

The common system of social structure had and has more importance in the sense of forming *"we-groups"* such as age sets, descent lines, defining the internal social organisation, marriage rules and possibilities to participate in social life, than as a practicable model for a nation-state.

Common consciousness has its limits depending on situations, as I explained using some examples, and is based on close relations within a group or between groups, which will be described in the next section.

The common demarcation is connected to consciousness. It depends on the group someone belongs to. It might be easy to draw the demarcation lines in respect of an enemy but, as I showed, demarcations also happen within one group, ethnicity or society.

Prospects

None of the criteria of being an Oromo, which were mentioned above, can on its own explain Oromo identity. But that is not a specific problem of being Oromo. Nearly everywhere at any time we may face such problems, either here in Germany or in Europe, Africa or Oromiya. In spite of these problems, the model of a centralised nation-state seems the only strong option for any movement or liberation front. In order to reach that aim they need simple and clear strategies, and it does not matter whether they ignore parts of their own history or cultural differences or similarities.

One of the main results of my research in 1995/96 is that in southern Oromiya an Oromo consciousness and history is created. When I came to that area for the first time in 1991and I asked people around Moyale who they were, they answered me '*I am a Gabbra*' or '*I am a Boran*', no one answered '*I am an Oromo*'. In 1991 I also asked them who and where the Oromo were. The answer was very clear given by all people in that area: "*the Oromo are living somewhere in the north; they speak a strange dialect or even another language*".

Four years later the situation had changed. Suddenly they became Oromo, but, and that is very important - although not surprising - only under special circumstances. If you ask the same question '*who are you*' usually the same answer will be given today: '*I am a Boran*' or '*I am a Gabbra*' but in a political discussion the same people would claim an Oromo identity for themselves. This seems to be one result of the education programme of the OLF, but also implies that no one had the feeling of being Oromo before.

It might be useful to create a triple division, a macro, a meso and a micro level of identity. Then, the main questions are how to determine, to characterise and to embed them, because the aims of every level are different. On the micro level, in small units, the belonging to a family, sub-clan or lineage and the access to water, grazing areas and other natural resources is more important than anything else. On the meso level demarcations between different tribes, their specific traditional, religious and socio-cultural distinctive features might be the focus of attention. The consciousness of being Oromo is only important, if fightings start between them. But even then, hierarchical structures, like elders and religious leaders with their instruments are able to solve the problems of neighbouring tribes who avoid toll or punish crime, as has already been described very often. If a problem cannot be solved by those decision making processes, it might become important to make an appeal to a common Oromo origin to avoid bloodshed.

The consciousness of being Oromo is specially important on the macro level, where the battlefield for the central nation-state is placed. Oromo nationalism plays *the* decisive role in the demarcation of Abyssinian dominance. The development of well-known strategies and slogans like 'one people', 'one history', 'one ground', 'one origin' or, in short, the use of invented traditions, is understandable from an outside point of view. So as to counterbalance the Amharic and, in recent years, the Tigrean domination, the OLF has started to argue in a very western way.

On the other hand, how can you claim a leading political role nowadays, if you cannot explain for whom you claim it, where the country and the borders are located exactly, which understandable political structure it should have and who your political partners should be outside the country?

But all these questions are nearly exclusively the focus of interest of Oromo living in exile and some few in Oromiya. They have established a strong *we-group* with a high intellectual level. *We-group-processes* in Oromiya are less distinctive on this level, of course and less stable, because identities can shift between the three levels very easily. Depending on the level, a co-operation between one identity and nation-state-based institutions, like the administration, are possibly easier, as was the case in the Boran society recently. Now the Tigrean-dominated central government started to build new roads, schools and a hospital after some talks between the governmental administration and Boran representatives. That does not mean that the Boran would deny being Oromo, but it is less important on two of the three levels, which are closer to their essential daily life problems than an uncertain nation building process in the future.

Finally, I want to come back to the topic of this paper, the "Multidimensionality of Oromo Identity". As I stressed critically, I cannot follow such simplifying and sometimes artificial identity patterns as the five criteria of being Oromo. The discussion of identity is more complicated. Until now, most of the identity patterns have not been discussed or even mentioned. Let me point out some usual examples.

People send thousands of children to schools, in this case on the Kenyan side of the Moyale District, because the school system in Ethiopia is really poor. Kenyan Oromo send them to different schools, catholic, protestant, public or Islamic schools. It depends on their religious beliefs. It is easy to understand that another consciousness will be born there. School classes are formed mainly by Boran pupils, which means that ethnicity can be stressed. In addition to that, they are also of the same age set, hence underlining the *we-group-feeling*, which is also supported by distinctive marks like school uniforms. It seems to be doubtful whether anything can create a stronger feeling of belonging than becoming a member of an age grade like *Kommicha*, *Yuba*, *Dabela* or *Jara* by a special ceremony (*rite de passage*) at the same time. And last but not least, they are on the way to be well-educated in the Kenyan school-system with foreign languages, which makes them more qualified than others. In the future they might have a closer relation to their colleagues at the workplace than to any idea of being Oromo.

Another example is the background of religious beliefs. In the last few years strong Islamic ideas have come to the area. One sign is that more and more women are fully veiled, though they are only few in comparison to other places. But those who do wear the veil, and of course their husbands or fathers might have interests other than becoming or being Oromo. They are more focused on identities which are closer to Mekka than to Finfinne. Every religious denomination builds another interesting group in the game of identity patterns.

The next illustration comes from Yabelo. I was really surprised to meet a Tigre man there, and he was neither a soldier nor a policeman. He was an owner of a small hotel. Many years ago his parents came to Yabelo sent by Haile Selassie. He was born in Yabelo and has never taken up residence anywhere else. Of course, his mother tongue might be Tigrinya and he is Tigre by origin, but he has been living in a Boran society since he was born, speaking the same language like everybody around him. Besides, he was grumbling about the Tigrean government far away in Addis Ababa, because everybody had started to suffer under the pressure. His small income had dropped by about 60 % and he feared that another Tigre would come and take his small bar away from him because of his increasing financial debts. For him it was very clear that he had to fight against the government, because of his decreasing income but especially because of the suffering of the people around him. There is not even a drop of Oromo blood in his veins, but he might be a better Oromo than some of his clients.

Another very shameful point is the use of identity for satisfying the chauvinist demands of Oromo men. A kind of slave-trade has been built up in recent years. Amharic girls and women can be ordered by Oromo businessmen or hotel-owners. The struggle for survival of these girls is used by Oromo bar-owners and, of course, their clients for their purposes.

That leads to another complex, namely the role of women in Oromo societies. My informants were mostly men. When I made interviews with them nobody mentioned any woman who played any role in the struggle for a 'Free Oromiya', besides a well-known singer living in the U.S.. Not until I insisted talking about the role of women in the struggle for freedom did my informants start thinking about that topic and they found out that women cook food and occasionally bring information from one place to another. Barring women from participation means splitting a modern society for a long time.

Another very important pattern is the profession. I had to repeatedly take my car to garages for check-ups and found an interesting solidarity between the mechanics. If they could not find the problem or lacked spare parts they just contacted other garage-owners without any problem of getting in touch. The ethics of their profession and the anticipation of a good deal made them very cooperative.

The same can be said about the Kenyan education officers and many of the teachers.They frequently have contacts with their equivalents on the Ethiopian side, even if these were members of the OPDO. Their professional ethics were stronger than the dislike of the OPDO-members. Professional identity seemed to outweigh political affiliation and to provide common interest and a kind of solidarity.

More important is the way of life. In the whole area you find nomadic camel-herders, semi-nomadic goat and sheep breeders and settled people. Even without any ethnic differentiation it is very clear that this kind of setting invites many problems. Grazing areas are occupied, settlements are attacked, people are sent away or have to move to other places or even areas. Although most of the conflicts are solved peacefully, there is a strong tension in the area at all times. As was already mentioned, there are brutal clashes along ethnic lines from time to time. That means nothing other than a conflict on the meso-level, as I explained above.

One can easily find other criteria and dimensions of identity, like income, social acceptance, marital status, phratry, moiety or lineage which might be even more important for the consciousness and identity than a profession, education or religion.

At last one can come to the conclusion, that each of the five claimed criteria of identity, the common language, the common history, the common system of social structure, the common consciousness and the common creation of distinctive marks by itself is not sufficient for explaining an identity, though the role of all five together should not be underrated. But, as I tried to show, identity is more complicated, situationally determined and conditioned by different levels. Nearly everybody is placed in a multidimensional space of identity criteria, building clusters with other persons.

These complex interrelations leave many questions open. Does it make any sense to claim such a strong Oromo identity as the only possible future model? What does self-determination mean according to the different levels mentioned above? Is it just the struggle for a strong central nation-state? What are the hidden motives? Do any alternative identity models exist or are there even better ones for comprehending the differentiation in societies? What danger is there if the common demarcation of others no longer exists; won't there be any demarcation of insiders or members of the common constructed society? Is it possible to build up a common system of social structure like the *gada* for a whole modern nation-state and, perhaps more importantly, will it be accepted by all different parts of society, including every group, cluster, gender, age-set, ethnicitiy, clan, lineage, profession, education level, status, living conditions, political views etc.?

The outcry for one common identity might be understandable in a political sense but the answers to the problem of what "identity" is are more complicated and go deeper than they are expected to at first sight.

References

Aguilar, M. 1998. Being Oromo in Kenya. Trenton: Africa World Press

Allemann, F. R. 1955. *Nationen im Werden*. Frankfurt/Main: Büchergilde Gutenberg

Anderson, B. 1998. *Die Erfindung der Nation. Zur Karriere eines folgenreichen Konzepts.* (erw. Ausgabe) Berlin: Ullstein

Anderson, B. 1983/96. *Imagined Communities. Reflections on the Origin and Spread of Nationalism.* London, New York: Verso

Barth, F. 1969. Ethnic Groups and Boundaries: The Social Organization of Culture Difference. Bergen, Oslo: Universitetsforlaget

Baxter, P.T.W. 1994. The creation and Constitution of Oromo Nationality. In: Fukui, K. and Markakis, J. (eds.). 167 - 186

Baxter, P.T.W., Hultin, J., Triulzi, A. (eds.) 1996. Being and Becoming Oromo. Historical and Anthropological Enquiries. Uppsala: Nordiska Afrikainstitutet

Elwert, G. 1989. Nationalismus und Ethnizität. Über die Bildung von Wir-Gruppen. In: *Kölner Zeitschrift für Soziologie und Sozialpsychologie* (2): 440 – 464

Elwert, G. 1989b. Nationalismus und Ethnizität. Occasional Papers Nr.22. Berlin: Verlag Das Arabische Buch

Fukui, K. and Markakis, J. (eds.) 1994. *Ethnicity and Conflict in the Horn of Africa.* London: James Currey

Gashaw, S. 1993. Nationalism and Ethnic Conflict in Ethiopia. In: Crawford Young (ed.). *The Rising Tide of Cultural Pluralism: The Nation-State at Bay?* Madison, Wisconsin: University of Wisconsin Press

Gellner, E. 1995. *Nationalismus und Moderne.* Hamburg: Rotbuch-Verlag

Gellner, E.: *Encounters with Nationalism.* Oxford: Blackwell Publishers (1994)

Haneke, G., Stahl, C. 1994. *Infrastruktur und sozialer Wandel: Sozialanthropologische Beobachtungen entlang einer Straße im Norden Kenias.* Saarbrücken: Verlag für Entwicklungspolitik Breitenbach GmbH

Hobsbawm, E., Ranger, T. 1983. *The Invention of Tradition.* Cambridge: University Press

Kaarsholm, P., Hultin, J. 1994. Inventions and Boundaries: Historical and Anthropological Approaches to the Study of Ethnicity and Nationalism. *Occasional Paper No.11.* Roskilde: International Development Studies

Kurimoto, E., Simonse, S. (eds.) 1998. *Conflict, Age and Power in North East Africa.* Oxford: James Currey

Lewis, H. 1993. Ethnicity in Ethiopia: The View from Below (and from the South, East and West). In: Crawford Young (ed.). *The Rising Tide of Cultural Pluralism: The Nation-State at Bay.* Madison, Wisconsin: University of Wisconsin Press

Makonnen, B. 1995. The Ethnicization of the Ethiopian State. *Working Paper No. 223,* University of Bielefeld, Faculty of Sociology, Bielefeld

Megerssa, Gemetchu 1996. Oromumma: Tradition, Consciousness and Identity. In: Baxter, P.T.W., Hultin, J., Triulzi, A. (eds.). 1996: 92 - 102

Schlee, G. 1994. Der Islam und das Gada-System als konfliktprägende Kräfte in Nordost-Afrika. *Sociologus* 44, 2: 112 - 135

Schlee, G. 1997. Neue Literatur zur Ethnizität in Ost- und Nordost-Afrika. In: *Zeitschrift für Ethnologie*, 122, 2: 229 - 242, Berlin: Dietrich Reimer Verlag

Schlee, G. 1998. Gada systems on the metaethnic level. In: Kurimoto and Simonse (eds.): *Conflict, Age and Power in North East Africa.* Oxford: James Currey: 121 - 146

Schlee, Günther 2000. *Redrawing the map of the Horn: the politics of difference.* Contribution to the biennal conference of the German African Studies Association (VAD), Leipzig, 30.03.–1.04.2000. Conference Proceedings available on CD

Schlee, G., Shongolo, A. 1995. Local war and its impact on ethnic and religious identification in Southern Ethiopia. *GeoJournal* 36.1: 7 - 17

Schlee, G., Werner, K. 1996. Inklusion und Exklusion. Die Dynamik von Grenzziehungen im Spannungsfeld von Markt, Staat und Ethnizität. Köln: Rüdiger Köppe Verlag

Shongolo, A. 1992. The *Gumi Gaayo* Assembly of the Boran: A Traditional Legislative Organ and its Relationship to the Ethiopian State and a Modernising World. *Zeitschrift für Ethnologie*, 119, 1 - 33, Berlin: Dietrich Reimer Verlag

Ullendorff, E. 1965. The *Ethiopians. An Introduction to Country and People.* London: Oxford University Press

Zitelmann, Th. 1994. *Nation der Oromo: kollektive Identitäten, nationale Konflikte, Wir-Gruppenbildung.* Berlin: das arabische buch

ABSTRACT

This article argues that Oromo identity is multidimensional and can easily shift depending upon the size of social units and also upon other social criteria like profession, religion, education, social status, etc. The paper specifically shows that Oromo identity is more complicated than the criteria on the macro-level how would identity indicate. It is influenced by different levels, situationally and individually determined. Besides the macro-level, where the struggle for the nation-state takes place, there are also the meso- and micro-levels. These latter two levels are more important in terms of everyday identity. On the meso-level, clans and ethnicities, conceptions of 'ethnic' identity create the feeling of belonging to a social group, that regulate processes of negotiation with others as well as the access to resources. On the micro-level, domestic groups and sub-clans, identity markers create sentiments of belonging to, and getting support from, families or descent groups based on daily life processes. This article underlines that nobody's identity can be seen as fixed in a timeless context, because identity changes with place in a multidimensional space of shifting identity criteria, building clusters with other persons.

Part IV

Organising violence and constructing the nation state

WRITING THE NATION:

THE PRE-WAR INDONESIAN NATIONALIST NOVEL
Thomas Rieger

Human consciousness is, if not identical with, at least strongly determined by language.[107] What we can and are likely to imagine is thus something which depends quite heavily on our linguistic or cultural background. Among the many different categories of speech acts, literature stands out as one where imagination of a very systematic, carefully constructed kind is communicated to an audience usually consisting of a considerable number of persons of a certain speech community.[108] It is therefore by no means accidental that the emergence of literature as a discourse, as a particular class of speech acts[109], as well as of certain genres like the novel, has played a major role in processes of collective imagination aiming at the construction of collective identity as a class [110] or nation. For the latter case, Bhabha (1990) in a recently published collection of essays, has coined the term of *writing the nation.* As Bhabha points out, writing the nation always implies writing the nation's "Other", constructing identity by delineating it, by setting demarcations. Writing the nation in the sense of Anderson's *imagined community* (1983) thus inevitably implies the imagination of differences, more often than not by means of antagonistic semantic isotopies[111], consisting of a system of binary oppositions representing 'us' and "them", supplying fertile ground for the seed of hatred. Without denying the importance of phenomena like the canonisation of "national literatures" and its interaction with the formation of standardised "national languages"[112] in the following we will thus focus on the textual level as being of more direct interest to the subject of this conference.

Speaking of the Indonesian nationalist novel necessitates a number of clarifying introductory remarks. Using the term "Indonesian" may provoke criticism, as it might be perceived as anachronistic, at least with regard to the period preceding World War I. Without refuting this criticism as a matter of principle, I would like to point out that

---

[107] The argument of identity of consciousness, ideology and language, derives from the Russian linguist Volosinov, but the idea of determination of consciousness by language is also reflected in the so-called Saphir-Whorf theorem.

[108] Conceiving of literature as a particular sort of speech act has been most convincingly suggested by Pratt (1977). Pratts argument is not only supported by Volosinov's reflections on language, but also bears the possibility of an interesting interpretation of Foucault's concept of discourse: "literature" as a discourse of post-Romantic Europe can be conceived of as a class of speech acts, as the result of a shift within the system of classification of speech acts within major European languages.

[109] Genres can be, if one tries to integrate the notion into the concept outlined above (see note 2), conceived of as sub-classes of speech-acts. Such a concept combines a socio-linguistic framework of analysis with a systemic approach suggested by the Luhmann-inspired Köhler (1977).

[110] Cf. Watt's famous work on the novel and its role in the formation/constitution of the bourgeoisie as a class.

[111] The concept is part of Greimas' structural semantics.

[112] Balibar (1974) has aptly demonstrated this relationship in the case of France.

in terms of a new identity, an Indonesian identity, to be constructed, Indonesianness and participation in the national movement[113] have to be regarded as synonymous and, as I have argued elsewhere[114], the point of departure of that movement, the *pergerakan*, has to be the foundation of the Chinese reformist organisation TIONG HOA HWE KOAN in 1900. Using terms like "novel" or "literature" with regard to texts or groups of texts produced in an environment quite different from post-Romantic Europe seems to be at loggerheads with what Foucault has taught us about the historical contingency of what was once (and by some still is) regarded as an eternal and universal category: literature. Though, due to the specific socio-historic conditions under Dutch colonial rule, the transformation of Malay from a chirographic language at best into a fully fledged typographic one[115] under a variety of mainly external influences, a recomposition of the discourse structure took place in the latter half of the 19th century, producing, among others, a literary discourse in the (post-)Romantic European sense. The very existence of literature, its birth under the impact of broader socio-cultural changes induced by foreign domination, is certainly worth further reflection, however I have to content myself here with stating that the use of that notion does not spring from a simple Euro-centric transfer of concepts.[116] Finally, the notion of a "nationalist" novel needs some explanation. Without any theoretical pretension I suggest here as a working definition that a novel will be categorised as "nationalist" if: 1. one or several of its characters belong to the nationalist movement or an organisation of that movement is assigned a function within its narrative structure; and 2. that character or organisation is assigned a positive value.

It is worth noting here, that although an important proportion of the material to be presented is either completely new or has never received the scholarly attention that it seems to merit, things are changing in the field of history, linguistics, letters as well as political science concerned with Indonesia. Recent research into the history of the country's nationalist movement, such as conducted by Anderson (1990) and Shiraishi (1990), has started to move away from the classical approach which used to focus almost exclusively on "political" organisations, their leaders and publications along with the colonial authorities' answers to their actions.

The epoch of writing the nation can be roughly divided into two periods, the first stretching from 1905 to 1926, the second one from 1927 to 1942. This division is supported by general historical data as well as by the properties of the texts under consideration. The period from 1905 to 1926, Shiraishi's 'age in motion" is the time of the first wave of anti-colonial awakening and mobilisation which came to an abrupt end with the bloody repression of the communists' and Islamic left's uprising of late 1926

---

[113] In the broad sense in which Petrus Blumberger (1931/1987) used the term.

[114] Rieger (1991: IV).

[115] These concepts are Ong's (1982).

[116] I have elaborated this point further in my thesis (Rieger 1991: 20-54).

and early 1927. The texts produced during this period are marked by an attitude of searching, of assimilating concepts, of gradual emancipation from a too simplistically "progress-"oriented world-view. The second period, coming to an end only with the Japanese occupation in 1942, saw not only a dramatic geographic and quantitative expansion in the production of nationalist novels, but was also marked by much clearer textual strategies on the part of the nationalist writers. Nationalist discourse in literary works, evolving quite rapidly since the mid-1920s, had by the early 1940s been established as a fairly closed discourse.

To illustrate both periods and substantiate my general characterisation of them, in the following a number of exemplary works from both periods will be presented in more detail.

Relatively well-known among scholars, but usually dismissed on aesthetic grounds as "mere propaganda" are three novels by authors belonging to the Semarang-based milieu of the Islamic left, *Student Hidjo* [The student Hidjo] by Marco Kartodikromo (1919), *Hikajat Kadiroen* [The Life-Story of Kadiroen] by Semaoen (1920) and *Rasa Merdika* [The Taste of Freedom/ Feeling Free] by Soemantri (1924). Marco Kartodikromo, founder of the first Indonesian association of journalists and one of the principal figures of the pre-1926 left, tells the story of a young Javanese aristocrat sent to the Netherlands for study, having an affair with a Dutch girl but finally returning to Indonesia, marrying his Javanese fiancée and becoming an official of the colonial administration. Although a certain cultural opposition is constructed between the Dutch, rough and boorish, unable to control their emotions, and as for their women - of easy virtue, and the Javanese, polite and refined in their behaviour, always mastering their emotions and of perfect virtue in the case of women, this contradiction is never presented as an irreconcilable one: the very Dutch style of the letters exchanged between the two young women in love with Hidjo, and, in political terms, the eventual integration of the hero into the colonial apparatus, are clear indications of this.[117] Tickell (1982: 189) [no reference in bibliography. The Editor] is certainly right in stating that

> the overt political message of the novel sits squarely within the intellectual boundaries of early twentieth century Dutch "ethical" thought and echoes some of the major catch cries of the Dutch Ethici. There is a call for enlightened and educated rule by the Dutch.

The SAREKAT ISLAM, Indonesia's first modern anti-colonial mass-movement which gave birth both to a part of reformist Islam and the revolutionary left of Indonesia, is presented more or less as a cultural institution in the life of the elite, designed to ascertain a sense of Muslim identity and self-respect.

---

[117] For this paragraph I have drawn on Tickell's (1982: 60-70, 101-106, 186-188) [no reference in bibliography. The Editor] analysis of this story's narrative structure.

Somewhat more outspoken, but still very much with the same limitations, is Semaoen's *Hikajat Kadiroen*, which appeared a year after Marco's work. The author was at the time one of the principal figures of the nationalist movement, contending with H.O.S.Tjokroaminoto for the leadership of the SAREKAT ISLAM, leading the most militant and influential trade union (the railway workers' V.S.T.P.) and one of the founders of the Indonesian Communist Party in May of that year.

As Maier (1986: 106) has pointed out, in terms of structure Semaoen's novel is both a *Bildungsroman* and a *roman à thèse*. This is a crucial point: the relationship between the coloniser and the colonised, between Dutch and Indonesians, is still depicted in a very moderate way by using repeatedly the image of a parent-child relationship between the Dutch colonial government and its subjects. But the ultimate goal is "adulthood" on the part of the child, or independence on the part of the colonised. In the course of the plot Kadiroen becomes a former colonial official and turns leader of the communist party, whereas in Marco's novel the hero ends up as a colonial official. Semaoen's discourse does not construct any antagonism between Dutch and Indonesians in general, colonialism is in a very mechanistic interpretation of historical materialism (certainly not Semaoen's privilege at that period ...) explained as the simple result of an almost natural law and the colonial government is seen as some sort of arbiter above contending groups of society, to be aided by the Communist Party to "introduce" social justice to the colony. Universal brotherhood between the races and religions is suggested on several occasions in a fashion more reminiscent of contemporary theosophical discourse than of the Communist Manifesto. But the "child' has started to think about growing up, mass organisation is advocated as a means of strengthening the Indonesian's position in the competition with the governments other child, the Dutch capitalists, for the "parents'" favour. And a warning is issued: should all benevolent efforts of the government fail, the party would have to resort to "communist' action and a system of soviets (councils) is proposed as the adequate form of running the country's administration.

A qualitative leap forward towards a closed nationalist discourse is achieved by Soemantri's novel *Rasa Merdika* (1924). Soemantri was among the leaders of the PKI (Communist Party of Indonesia) in the mid-1920s and at times editor in chief of the party's paper (Shiraishi 1990: 242n, 246).

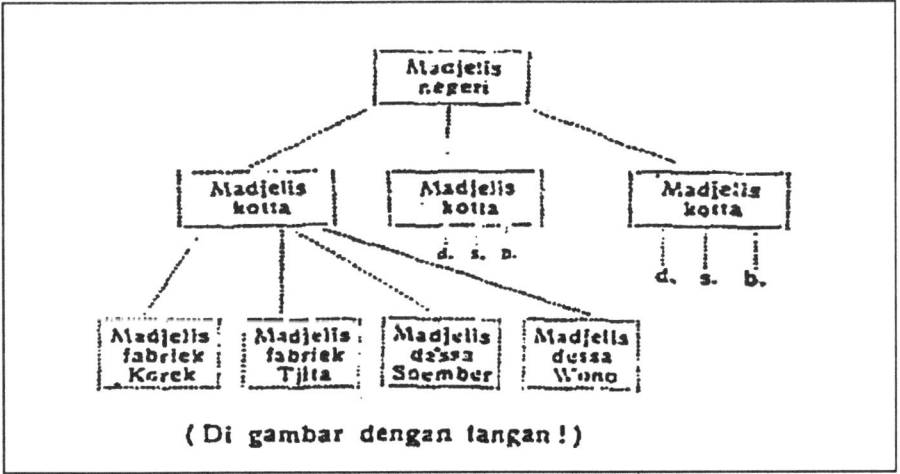

Figure 1: The novel's single illustration, the hero's design of a government of soviets.

Like the works of Marco and Semaoen, Soemantri's novel was composed in prison. In terms of its plot, on the verge of being a plagiat of Semaoen's *Hikajat Kadiroen*, the novel offers *nevertheless* several interesting aspects. First, the obvious integration of Partondo's translation of the Communist Manifesto, published a year earlier (McVey 1965: 433n) as an intertext contributes to a certain coherence of Soemantri's discourse, which is much more closed than Semaoen's. The notions of "means of production" [alat-alat menghasilkan, p.77], "capitalist exploitation" [penghisepan dari kapital, p.78] of "imperialism" [imperialisme, p.78], the "proletariat" [kaoem proletar, p.79; kasta proletar, p.80] and "class struggle" [klassenstrijd, p.81; interestingly enough borrowed from Dutch] are for the first time introduced into literary discourse. A Marxist analysis of the role of the state replaces Semaoen's quite conciliatory discourse on the colonial government:

> The capitalist class engages in systematic exploitation, protected by its organs, whereas the proletarian's lot is starvation. (Soemantri 1924: 86)
> [118]

The author also insists on the irreconcilable nature of the class antagonism between workers and capitalists (p.89).

Perhaps even more interesting than this radicalisation is the way in which the author's community's "Other", the Dutch, are presented. Contrary to the works of Marco and Semaoen, in Soemantri's novel we'll look in vain for a positive Dutch character. While the hero still is, at the beginning - of the story, a colonial official, his Dutch superior shows an almost pathological desire for displays of deference on the

---

[118] "Kasta modal mengisep teratoer dengen dilindoengi oleh alat-alatnja tetapi si proletar tinggal toelang dan koelitnia saja."

part of his inferiors (p.20). His second boss, after he has taken a job in the private sector, is apparently a gentle and generous person, but in reality a racist, greedy for profit, whose only reason for treating his indigenous employees well is to assure their working morale and maximum performance (p.58). The message cannot be clearer the Dutch are bad and if anyone among them seems to be alright, he certainly is a hypocrite.

Although the demarcation between "us" and "them" has thus become quite clear, we are still in a somewhat preparatory stage of the process of "writing the nation", as the discourse is still internationalist - a trait that both the Islamic as well as the socialist currents of the time bore - and it is more or less by the absence of Dutch workers and Indonesian capitalists from Soemantri's discourse, a certain congruence in the lines of class division with lines of racial division, that we can discern the germ of nationalism proper in this last text.

A fourth novel from this period, representing a current different from the Semarang left Muslim milieu, but as a part of the general social ferment certainly not entirely unrelated to it, is Kwee Seng Tjoan's *Tjerita Anak Prampoean Di Bikin Sebagi Parit Mas atawa Iboe jang Doerhaka* [The Story of a Daughter exploited as a Goldmine or The Cruel Mother] published in 1917. Unfortunately, only the first of the three volumes of this work seems to have survived, so we leave aside questions of narrative structure here. Nevertheless the limited part of the novel which has been at our disposal is interesting enough to take a closer look at it here. The story is set in the Chinese quarter of down town Batavia (Jakarta) in a milieu of ordinary local born as well as immigrant Chinese. It abounds in borrowings from Hokkian (Fujian) Chinese to an extent unusual even for the works of pre-war ethnic Chinese writers but contains - equally unusual for this period - almost no borrowings from Dutch, whereas the authenticity of the dialogues in Batavian Malay is most remarkable. The essential point however is the strong emphasis placed on Chinese education:

> After our people here in the Indies achieved unity and have recognised the primordial importance of education for enabling everybody to earn a living, the Tiong Hoa Hwee Koan was founded, because learning a foreign language first in order to be admitted to a [Dutch; T.R.] school is too difficult apart from the fact that their fees are prohibitive for everybody except the rich or those earning a top salary.[119]

(Kwee Seng Tjoan 1917: 23)

---

[119] "Tapi setelah kita poenja bangsa di ini Insulinde soeda bisa bersatoe hati dan dapet taoe djoega bahoewa pladjaran ada sanget bergoena boeat orang mentjari pengidoepan, sementara boeat bladjar bahasa asing terasa terlaloe soesa boeat bisa di trima didalem itoe sekola serta pembajarannja ada sanget mahal, djika boekan anaknja orang hartawan atawa orang jang dapet gadji besar soeda tentoe tida bisa dapet itoe pladjaran, maka itoe à orang soeda berdiriken Tiong Hoa Hwee Koan."

Apart from using the proto-nationalist "Insulinde" for referring to the Dutch East Indies, the perspective of the author is obviously sino-centric, the term *bangsa* already having undergone the semantic shift from its former "feudal" connotation[120] to referring to the Chinese as an ethnic community or even a nation, as the stress on "unity" suggests.[121] This point becomes even more obvious in the following quotation, an extract from the speech of the director of the TIONG HOA HWE KOAN school that the novel's hero frequents:

> You, the students, must not forget that we had to make a big effort to es-
> tablish this school and that we hope to see appropriate results in the fu-
> ture, that is to say that our people here in the Indies will know its lan-
> guage and its script. Only when all the overseas Chinese will be able to
> read Chinese, then the moment will have come that our love for our fa-
> therland can blossom and only then will we be able to re-establish close
> ties between us and China! Learn earnestly for your own and your peo-
> ple's sake![122] (ibid., p.77)

This is one of the finest examples of *Huaqiao*-nationalism in Indonesian literature: advancing the Indies' overseas Chinese lot by regaining Chineseness and re-
establishing ties with the land of the ancestors and becoming part of a (great) Chinese nation). All this is advanced by the diction used (Chinese borrowings), the setting in a Chinese quarter, the mixed personnage of *peranakan* (local born) and *totok* (immi-
grated) Chinese and not least the school which becomes almost a metaphor for the na-
tion in a sense quite similar to the way in which the *pergerakan* constituted something like the Indonesian nation *in statu nascendi*. An interesting feature of this effort of writing the (Chinese) nation is the virtual absence of all other ethnic communities of the Indies, where the Chinese constitute but a small minority. This symptomatic absence as well as any concrete reference to the situation in China are typical for a brand of nationalism which would soon undergo a grave crisis, giving rise to another phe-
nomenon, the one which Tan (1988) [no reference in bibliography. The Editor] has baptised "min-zhu nationalism", the retaining of cultural group identity within a multi-
ethnic nation, for the case of Malaysia.

---

[120] For a discussion of the semantic development of the term *bangsa* see Matheson (1979). [no reference in bibliography. The Editor]

[121] Conceiving the Chinese as one group and striving for unity is not as natural as it might seem to the external observer, only a few year before Kwee was writing, the Straits as well as the Indies had been the scene of sometimes bloody conflicts between different ethnic groups within the Chinese community.

[122] Dan sekarang moerid-moerid moesti inget, jang kita orang soeda berdiriken ini roema pegoeroean dengen soesa dan boewang banjak tanaga dengen harepan boeat dapetken boeahnja di kemoedian hari, jaitoe soepaja kita poenja bangsa di ini Insulnde bisa mengenal hoeroef dan bahasa sendiri. Djika se-
moewa Hoa Ki~ bisa batja soerat Tionghoa, di itoe waktoelah baroe bisa timboel kita orang poenja ketjintahan hati pada kita poenja tanah aer dan djoega kita orang poenja perhoeboengan dengen Tiongkok bisa djadi rapet kombali! Bladjarlah dengen soenggoe-soenggoe ini ada kebaekan boeat sekalian moenid-moerid poenja diri dan djoega boeat kebaekan kita poenja bangsa!

As we have remarked above, the period 1927 - 1942 was marked by the emergence of new centers of literary production, especially outside Java, as well as an overall quantitave expansion. From the enormous wealth of material we can present here but a few examples, considered to be the most representative of a number of features of nationalist novel writing of the time. The four works that we will present are *Roestam Digoelist* [Roestam, the Prisoner from Digoel[123] by D.E.Manu Tune (1940), *Teratai Terkoelai* [The Broken Lotus] by Merayu Sukma (1940), *Radiks Wikanta* [name of the hero] by Ifin (1941) and *Pendekar dari Chapei* [The Warrior from Chapei] by Kwee Tek Hoay (1932). [no references in bibliography. The Editor]

Chronologically the first one, Kwee Tek Hoay's voluminous work of roughly 800 pages was published after the Japanese aggression in Manchuria and the atrocities committed during the heavy fighting in the Chinese quarters of Shanghai in 1931 which stirred up considerable emotion among Chinese communities in Southeast Asia. It has to be seen in the context of the conflicts within the Chinese community regarding their role in the political life of Indonesia. Kwee Tek Hoay, a former supporter of *Huaqiao*-nationalism who had turned against this current in 1926 and had become an advocate of the pro-Dutch orientation, wrote the novel in order to expose the alledged weaknesses of the *Huaqiao*-nationalists grouped around the paper SIN PO. The third current, the Indonesia-oriented group led by Liem Koen Hian, appears in one of the other works that we will discuss below. These political conflicts had a violent and often personally insulting character.

The negative way the author presents two Chinese youth organisations is symptomatic for the erosion of the euphoria of only a couple of years earlier: these organisations are no longer seen as pioneers of Chinese nationalism but as vehicles for the private, primarily sexual ambitions of their members. *Huaqiao*-nationalism in general is ridiculed by presenting it as hypocritical: the novels's anti-hero, an ardent *Huaqiao*-nationalist who promised to sacrifice his life in the battle against the Japanese in Chapei is finally caught selling Japanese goods in the west-Javanese countryside. Strictly speaking, this novel does thus not fit into our definition of a nationalist novel, it is an example of "deconstructing the nation" rather than of writing the nation, but it is instructive as one of the possible conclusions of the development begun in the previous period. The same pessimistic tone can also be found in novels more sympathetic to the Chinese organisations, like Ong Siauw King's *Terloenta-loenta* (Suffering] published in Palembang in 1928. [no reference in bibliography. The Editor]

More representative of the general trend of the period is D.E.Manu Tune's *Roestam Digoelist* (1940). The short story was published in Medan, the most important among the new emerging centres of literary production at the time. It tells the story of

---

[123] Boven Digoel in the Dutch part of New Guinea was a notorious prison camp for political adversaries of the colonial regime, especially those members of left-wing organisations who could not be prosecuted on juridicial ground after the abortive 1926-1927 insurrection. Later, in the 1930s, members of the more militant wing of the nationalist movement were also banned to Boven Digoel.

the young nationalist Roestam, who, after being expelled from his school for insubordination, takes up a job in a plantation in the Simalungun region. Defending plantation workers against the physical harassment of their Dutch supervisor, Borsthaar, and organising clandestine education meetings he becomes popular among the workers. Borsthaar, hating Roestam for making him lose his face, spies on the young Indonesian and has him arrested by the colonial police at one of his clandestine meetings. In court Roestam admits to being a member of the illegal communist party and is banned to Boven Digoel. After returning to Sumatra some years later, he wants to marry his long-time fiancé, Tjindai, but only after a whole range of adventures are the two finally united. Apart from the fact, that this work is the only one dealing with real underground activity and one of the few daring to take up the problem of the deplorable situation in the plantations, the construction of Indonesianness in this novel is quite interesting. A double delimitation takes place: horizontally against the foreign, the Dutch: Roestam, the defender of the weak, brave and honest, the *ksatria* [knight, chevalier] to use the appropriate Indonesian image is opposed to the cruel and cunning Dutch, maltreating the weak and relying on the collective force of the colonial apparatus to confront his personal enemy. His name, which can be translated by "hairs of the chest", regarded by many Indonesians as a disgusting physical feature of Europeans, adds to this contrast. But the new Indonesia which the character Roestam embodies is also set up "vertically" against the backward, indigenous conservatives embodying the past. When Roestam and Tjindai try to enforce Tjindai's parents' permission for their marriage by resorting to the traditional custom of *kawin lari* (abduction of the bride), it is the old generation committing an infraction against the respected *adat* [customary law] and thereby discrediting themselves severely in the eyes of most Indonesians. It is this combination of rebellion and preservation of identity which is typical of most of the nationalist novels trying to construct Indonesian identity. Those who propose conservation of the old ways or advocate swallowing Western concepts of modernity hook, line and sinker (like St.Takdir Alisyahbana) find themselves in a more or less marginal position.

The novel *Teratai Terkoelai* by Merayu Sukma (1940) is interesting for two reasons. First it embodies, in the field of publishing, the growing interregional contact: the publishing company, DOENIA PENGALAMAN, originally founded in Medan, moved to Solo in 1940. Merayu Sukma, himself of Banjarese (Kalimantan) origin, wrote in Sumatran and later Javanese publications about his native region. The story is also a good example for a number of additional devices of defining Indonesian identity by delineating the imagined community against its "Other". The hero, a young man named Horman, quits his job as a teacher in a government school to become a small entrepreneur and advance the "national economy". His fiancée leaves him, because she has only contempt for his hard physical work as a petty merchant on the river. Horman finds new friends within the *pergerakan*-milieu and a new fiancée, active in the Islamic women's movement, explicitly called a *perempoean pergerakan* [women of the movement] (p.64). As his fame as a *pergerakan* leader rises the police becomes alerted and finally he is sentenced to a year and a half imprisonment for disturbing public peace. The values that Horman as the personification of the new "Indonesian" man embodies as opposed to his adversaries are listed in the following little table:

Horman	his former fiancée (and her friend and parents)
spirit of enterprise	servility to colonial official class
modesty	arrogance of the indigenous colonial officialdom
support for the *pergerakan*	hostility against the *pergerakan*
impeccable attitude with regard to traditional/Islamic norms and values with regard to sexuality	libertinage (or what ever the author took for this)

Finally, the novel *Radiks Wikanta* by Ifin (1941) paints the picture of the militant totally submerged within the *pergerakan*. This too is an important aspect of writing the nation: creating a micro-cosmos were the new Indonesia already seems a tangible reality, where the whole life of young people (the bulk of the authors as well as the readers of this kind of literature), their work, love, leisure is situated in a setting dominated by the struggle for the nation to be built. The story's hero, Radiks Wikanta, has barely passed from childhood to adolescence, when he becomes involved as a full time organiser in the youth movement, the workers' movement and the women's movement hurrying from one meeting to the next, providing that he is not serving one of his short prison terms. The novel is also remarkable for some allusions to the previous period, something almost totally lacking in the bulk of this literature.

Unfortunately, the bookcover of this, like many other works, has not survived. As an interesting example of the graphic support of the text and its images we reproduce the cover of another novel of the time, Synoe and Thomas' *Toekang Keboen Rahasia* [The Secret Gardener] (1941) below.

The subject has still to be explored further, but in view of the very limited numerical strength of most of the nationalist organisations, the limited circulation of party papers and the severe restrictions on public meeting and propaganda tours after 1933, it can be assumed that literature of the kind presented here, with most of the works printed in at least 5.000 copies had a more than marginal influence on Indonesian nationalism.

References

Anderson, B.R.O'G. 1983. *Imagined Communities. Reflections on the Origin and Spread of Nationalism.* London: Verso

Anderson, B.R.O'G. 1990. *Language and power: exploring political cultures in Indonesia.* Ithaca [u.a.]: Cornell University Press

Balibar, R. 1974. *Les Français Fictifs. Le Rapport des Styles Littéraires au Français National.* Paris: Hachette

Bhabha, Homi K. 1990 a. DissemiNation: time, narrative and the margins of the modern nation. In: Bhabha 1990 b: 291 – 322

Bhabha, Homi K. (ed.) 1990 b. *Nation and Narration.* London: Routledge

Köhler, E. 1977. Gattungssystem und Gesellschaftssystem. In: *Cahiers d'Histoire des Littératures Romanes*, No.1

Maier, H. 1986. Geschreven in het licht van de gevangenis. De Hikayat Kadiroen van Semaoen. In: C. M. S. Hellwig and S. O. Robson (eds.). *A Man of Indonesian Letters. Essays in Honour of Professor A.Teeuw (VKI 121)*. Dordrecht: Foris Publications 1986: 100 – 115

McVey, R. 1965. *The Rise of Indonesian Communism*. Ithaca, N.Y.: Cornell University Press

Ong, Walter J. 1982. *Orality and Literacy. The Technologising of the Word*. London and New York: Methuen

Petrus Blumberger, J.Th. 1987. *De Nationalistische Beweging in Nederlandsch-Indie* (reprint of the 1931 original). Dordrecht: Foris Publications

Pratt, Mary Louise. 1977. *Towards a Speech Act Theory of Literary Discourse*. Bloomington and London: University of Indiana Press

Rieger, T. 1991. *Le récit du mouvement nationaliste avant 1942 dans la littérature – indonésienne*. unpublished Ph.D. thesis. Ecole des Hautes Etudes en Sciences Sociales/Paris

Shiraishi, Takashi. 1990. *An Age in Motion. Popular Radicalism in Java 1912 - 1926*. Ithaca and N.Y.: Cornell University Press

ABSTRACT

"Writing the nation" in the sense of Anderson's "imagined community" has been an important element in many historical processes of constructing identities. Based on Indonesian popular novels written by pre-World War II nationalist authors as primary sources, the chapter explores textual strategies of constructing systems of imagined differences between "us" - the nation taking shape - and "them" - the colonial oppressor. It is found that a binary opposition is constructed between "good" = "our" and "bad" = "their" features. The "good/our" features are those accepted by and familiar to the community that is supposed to embrace the identity to be constructed. The "bad/their" features are the strange, reproachable or even disgusting behavioural or physical features of the "Other". Thereby hatred is evoked as a means of strengthening and stabilising the still shaky national identity.

POLITICS AND BERBER IDENTITIES IN MOROCCO

Bernhard Venema

Introduction

After having described the role of ethnicity in Nigerian society, Andreski concluded that it is but one of the elements along which society is organised. According to him, ethnicity comes only to the fore in the case of individuals identifying with it and, by so doing, separating themselves from others. In Nigeria there are many tribal groups with different histories and languages but they can only be conceived as ethnic groups if they coincide with in-groups and out-groups. These come into being if groups try to monopolise scarce resources. Ethnic identity develops as a consequence of conflicts of interests, with privileges going to one group rather than others (1970: 346 - 357; see also Barth 1969).

This political approach to identity formation is elaborated in this contribution, too, and I will argue that ethnicity is a result of shifts in the balance of power within the nation-state. Ethnic groups may come into being or play roles far greater than they did in the past because of changed options for monopolising resources or new opportunities. Such an analysis seems appropriate for Morocco.

King Hassan II frequently states that his nation is a unity and as a unity it has accepted his leadership in harmony. As a direct descendant of the *shurfa* Alawi[124], He is the Commander of the Faithful (*Amiir al mu'miniin*), and the symbol of the unity of the nation. As stated in the constitution, there is a holy pact between the King and His subjects, with the King representing the will of the population. Therefore, the Moroccan people will always agree that the Monarchy is a bastion against disorder and against enemies of the state (Maroc Soir, 7.11.1990).

Evidently, such statements have political connotations too. Shortly after the Berber riots, on which I will elaborate below, the king made another political statement making more sense to critical observers. He said: "For the works We are going to undertake, it is necessary that there is order and peace and that nothing is done to provoke insecurity and unrest among the people. I am convinced that My people will rally around My person with all their energy as they have done in the past, in order to obtain Our goals of a worthy and prosperous life" (Le Matin, 18.11.1988). Most observers argue that these goals have not been obtained and that the legitimacy of the state is rather weak. Consequently, it is stated that ethnic strife will become more apparent in Morocco because the Berbers have always been marginalised in Moroccan politics.

In this contribution I will examine whether unequal access to resources may open opportunities for the mobilisation of ethnic groups. More specifically, I will con-

---

[124] *Ashraaf*, descendants of Khalifa 'Ali and Fatima, the daughter of the Prophet

sider whether political developments in Morocco have changed access to resources and have initiated the emergence of Arabs and Berbers as ethnic groups. In the analysis of 'politisation of ethnicity' three closely connected issues seem to be important. In the first place it seems important to study what (backgrounds to) changes in the power balance at the national level have opened up opportunities for the monopolisation of resources by Arabs or Berbers. Has colonisation implied the creation of ethnic groups and a shift in the resource base of these groups, for example?

In addition, it seems worthwile to focus on the symbolic capital referred to by the Arab and Berber elite. Which elite has played an important role in history? History is often used as a touchstone to claim or deny political domination and access to resources. In Africa, as elsewhere, groups which have played a dominant role in the national movement have quite often acquired a prominent leadership role, for example. Are the representatives of this political elite still holding the reins of government?

The third issue I will dwell upon is the circulation of elites. Have elites, once they have come to occupy prominent positions within society, been able to make common cause with ordinary citizens, or have they merely pursued their own interests? The degree to which a larger category than a personal clientèle supports leadership has a major effect on internal ethnic loyalty and the appearance of an interest group in society. If established elites have engaged in patronage politics and machinations, have new elite groups come into existence in the decades after independence? To what symbolic capital could they refer to claim a special position for themselves? Have they been able to create a broad-based clientèle? Does it constitute an ethnic group or is the clientèle based on other identification criteria?

The 'politisation of ethnicity' seems therefore to be dependent on internal factors too, among them the legitimacy of leadership from the point of view of the common Berber or Arab citizen.

The role of the Kabyle myth

When the French colonisers arrived in Algeria they came across Berber tribes which, according to them, were governed independently by local councils rather than ruled by a central state. According to the French officials they were dealing here with egalitarian and democratic village societies applying customary law. These Berber societies were said to be quite distinct from the areas under Arab government, which were characterised by central rule, rigid stratification and elaborate occupational specialisation. The first anthropological fieldwork among Berbers took place at the end of the last century among the Kabyles, the most important Berber group in Algeria (Hanoteau & LeTourneux, 1893). This research did not contradict the view of the officials; in fact it strongly contributed to the creation of the Kabyles as a distinctive ethnic group and to a romantic and positive attitude of the French colonial government towards the Kabyle population in Algeria.

A very important side-effect was the development of the 'Kabyle myth', because it was assumed that all Berbers would have the same characteristics as the Kabyles that had been studied (see Burke 1972: 192). Because many French officials had started their career in Algeria but were then posted to Morocco or Tunisia, the Kabyle myth came to play an even greater role in colonial government.

As a consequence, the colonial government argued that in Morocco the Berber population was not embedded in the Arabic-Islamic culture but had been left untouched and therefore shaped by local Berber culture. However, their analysis was based on superficial facts. The Berber population lived in the countryside and had not frequented the Koran schools. They were not acquainted with all the formal Koranic laws and recommendations; for example they were not familiar with the rules of purity and did not pray at the required times. Neither were such practices in line with their agricultural way of life. For example, among the nomadic Berber population it was not very practical to construct a brick-built mosque and it was difficult to have the required number of participants for the Friday sermon. Because of the contribution of Berber women to agriculture, they were not secluded and veiled. The Berber way of life was indeed quite distinct from the urban elite, which was made up of mainly Arab middlemen, artisans and government staff.

However, for centuries the Berber population had felt themselves to be part of the Islamic community, though they did not deny that among the Arab population there was a more widespread knowledge of the Koran. In fact, many Arab religious specialists and Koran teachers had been received among them to help perform religious ceremonies. Religion was not a symbol of group differentiation between Arabs and Berbers. However, Berbers differed in their customs and behaviour from the Arab elite.

Being unaware of this fact, the French colonial government promulgated the 'Berber Dahir' of 1930. In this legislation the Berbers were no longer subject to Islamic legislation, but were obliged to maintain their own legal institutions. They were to apply customary law as regards personal, family and commercial affairs, while criminal acts would be dealt with by French criminal law. For centuries, however, the Berber population had acted according to Islamic law and customs, preferring local habits only in specific cases. Reading the reports of French officials, the endeavours employed in explaining away the Islamic institutions and Islamic religious specialists in the Berber areas are impressive (Archives Outre-Mer, Nantes: dossier Région Meknès, Maroc).

The emergence of an Arab nationalist elite

The introduction of the Berber *dahir* in 1930 emanated from the Kabyle myth, but would never have gained such importance if there had not been clear political issues at stake. By presenting the Berbers as a separate group, the colonial rulers hoped to create a solid barrier against nationalism. Nationalism had become important from 1930 onwards, mainly in the Arab inhabited cities. A new policy was required, of which the Berber *dahir* was only one element but a very important one. The first Resident-General Lyauty argued: "We must change the Berber language directly into French. The use of the Arabic language leads to islamisation because it is the language of the Koran. It is in our interest to educate the Berbers outside the Islamic culture" (Bidwell 1973: 52). By trying to assimilate the Berbers and by creating a distinct legal system and legislation, the colonial government hoped to create a distinctive Berber identity.

This policy was successful to the extent that many Berber tribal leaders were willing to co-operate because of the material advantages offered in exchange for loyal conduct. Those Berber leaders who succeeded in maintaining order and peace in their tribal areas and collaborated in the recruitment of labour for public works were awarded by increasing the area they supervised. This gave them the opportunity to increase their affluence by appropriating tribal land, forests and other properties. The French policy of co-operation with the Berber chiefs was widely applied and coined by the French officials as the *politique des grands caids*. At the end of the colonial era famous Berber chiefs such as Glaoui from Marrakech and Amharoq from Khenifra owned 15,000 and 56,000 ha, respectively, not to mention their access to common property and their stake in the trade sector. Even less important chiefs were able to make profits by appropriating collective land and wells and their use of duty labour (Venema 1992).

The enactment of the Berber *dahir* was promptly followed by the creation of the Comité d'Action Populaire, composed of representatives of the urban intelligentsia and members of the orthodox tendency within Islam (Salafiyya). Out of this committee developed the Independence Party, the Istiqlal, headed by Allal al Fassi, a Koran scholar from Fez. The members of the committee, and later those determining the direction of the party, were mostly Arabs from Fez (*Fassis*), for a large part teachers at the Quaraouine University.

Contrary to its intended purpose, the enactment of the Berber *dahir* served to initiate the development of nationalism, because the Arab elite conceived the *dahir* as an endeavour to shield the Berbers from Islamic culture and religion. Quite soon after the promulgation of the Berber *dahir*, members of the Arab elite travelled all over the country to convince their Berber brothers to make common cause with the nationalist movement and avert the efforts of the colonial rulers to 'convert them to Christianity' (Brown 1972: 208). As one Arab Koran scholar argued: "You, Berbers of the mountains, you are brave people but you are not educated and you are led by the French. Please, have confidence in us, shorfa and scholars from the town, because we defend the Islamic interests and we do everything to acquire the independence of Morocco" (Archives Nantes, région Meknes, Maroc; trad. B.V.). The Arab intelligentsia advanced a more orthodox form of Islam, unconnected to superstition and Islamic brotherhoods, but based on the Koran and Islamic tradition. The urban Arab intelligentsia thus presented themselves as the true representatives of Islamic culture and the future leaders of the nation.

It was only at the end of the 1940s that Berber teachers and students started to protest against the French policy of assimilation. They too supported the 'free schools' (*madaaris hurra*), created by Arab intellectuals, where the children were taught in Arabic. Until then they had sent their children to the 'écôles franco-berbères' established by the colonial governement where the pupils were taught in French. These Berber intellectuals gradually withdrew their support from the puppet Sultan Moulay ben Arafa, created by the colonial regime as an alternative to the nationalist leaders, among whom Sultan Mohammed V and his son Hassan II.

In Algeria the Kabyles have played an important role in the nationalist movement. From 1930 onwards they, together with Arab pioneers, struggled for independence. Their role in the resistance movement is still remembered today (Tabory / Tabory 1986). Contrary to the role of the Kabyles in Algeria, the Berbers of Morocco continued to collaborate with the French and just before independence the *grands caids*, in co-operation with the French, did their utmost to delay independence.

No accounts were settled in Morocco after independence. The Berber chiefs who had occupied administrative positions during colonial rule had to give up these positions, which were now occupied by the leaders of the independence movement (Hart 1972: 40). However, they were allowed to keep their land, cattle and other resources; only properties that had very clearly been obtained illegitimately were expropriated. Because the king was anxious to maintain order in the rural areas by every possible means, only about 10,000 ha of land was seized. He did not want to antagonise the Berber chiefs. As the traditional leaders of the rural population, their influence had to be taken into account; the forces they represented might come in handy later on.

The consolidation of the Arab elite and the emergence of a Berber elite

After Morocco's independence the most important administrative posts were occupied by the urban intelligentsia which had been active in the Istiqlal party. They belonged to the Arabic-Islamic elite and most of them were *Fasi*. They were able to monopolise these posts because of their role in the nationalist movement. In addition, the *Fasi* had been the economic elite for centuries and because of their economic influence they had easy access to spoils (Cigar 1981). They were appointed as ministers, governors and as district heads (Marais 1972: 278 - 81; Hart 1972: 40). Some positions were reserved by the king for the Berber leaders in order to maintain some balance of power.

However, this became more and more difficult. The upsurge of socialism in North Africa at the end of the fifties and in the early sixties meant that subsequent Moroccan governments were of a more leftist persuasion. Now the overwhelming majority of the posts in the cabinet were occupied by the urban elite: *Fassis*, supplemented by urban intellectuals who had studied in France and had become acquinted with socialism. From 1958 onwards, Berbers were only rarely appointed as members of the cabinet (Abou el Karam 1988). Because at the central and regional level the Arabs had monopolised state power, it was only at the subdistrict level (*caidat*) that Berbers who had not collaborated with the French succeeded in filling posts.

The Istiqlal elite made fairly extensive use of its position to appropriate all kinds of resources that became available after the French *colons* and Jews left the country from 1956 onwards. With regard to agricultural land, a little over 1 million ha became available. By 1960, 207,000 ha had already been acquired by individual Moroccans, most of it by the Arab Istiqlal elite (Swearingen 1987: 155). Besides the elite, a whole network of family members and friends was able to take advantage of various types of illegal transactions (Venema 1992). Apparently, short-term benefits prevailed over national commitments. The bureaucracy had become a system based on patronage and corruption.

Because most government posts had been acquired by Arabs, it is not surprising that the Berber chiefs found these developments quite unsatisfactory. Berber leaders, who were not too much under a cloud because of their stand in the colonial period, started to speak of 'Fassi domination' and began to claim government posts and economic prerogatives, too. Because these Berber leaders were large land and cattle owners, the *Fassis* referred to them as conservative 'Berber feudals', who, in addition, had never made an issue of the cause of independence. The spoils continued to be captured by the new political elite and at the end of the fifties this caused violent uprisings in the Rif and the Middle Atlas. Dissatisfaction among the Berber leaders was such that the army, headed by Hassan II himself, had to intervene to re-establish order (Gellner & Micaud 1972: 217 - 374).

In order to break away from the growing influence of the urban intelligentsia and not to lose his hold on the countryside, the King began to encourage the creation of the Berber party, the Mouvement Populaire. For the monarchy it was very important to avoid the situation of an Istiqlal one-party system or a party system in which Istiqlal was very dominant. This was especially important because the Istiqlal had been forced to follow a more leftist policy due to the radical stand of the Union Nationale des Forces Populaires (UNFP) which had seceded from Istiqlal in 1959 under the leadeship of Ben Barka. For the monarchy, then, it was very important that Istiqlal became encapsulated.

The friendship that King Hassan II had cultivated with the Berbers proved useful indeed. Friends of the King became the leaders of the new party. These leaders were Berber notables belonging to the landed class. It is no accident that just before the first local elections, held in 1964, the King promised that what remained of the land of the former *colons* could be distributed. The monarchy has been a vital element in the patrimonial character of the Moroccan state.

The Berber notables were thus quite eager to present themselves as candidates. The Berber party, together with some right-wing parties[125], emerged as election victors. After the election many administrative and political posts were occupied by Berbers (Kaddour 1972: 263). What remained of the estates of the *colons* and the Jews was quickly divided among the large land and cattle-owners. To the present day the Berber leaders have maintained their political influence in the rural areas where *Fassis* and their clients formerly held sway. Together with a number of friends and family members the Berber leaders exploit their domains for personal gain (Venema 1992). Here again there is little commitment to the common cause. The co-option of the Berber elites in government and the spoils they obtained have alienated them from the common Berber men and women.

Berbers of the Middle Atlas, the High and Anti Atlas and the Rif, share a distinct language and have a distinct culture as represented in Berber poetry, songs, marriage ceremonies and so on. As we have seen, their way of life is still quite distinct from that of the urban Arab elite because they live in the countryside. Berbers and Arabs have stereotyped images of one another. The fact is, however, that it has been both the Arab and the Berber elite that have appropriated land and forced common Berbers to migrate and struggle to survive in the poor quarters of the cities. Some of the Berber elite now live in towns, too. They have adopted the urban lifestyle of the Arab elite because this is seen as more prestiguous (Venema en Bakker 1994: 3 - 14). Berbers do not see themselves as a homogeneous group: some are rich, many are poor; many live in the countryside but some in towns, each operating in a different economy. Berbers, even those sharing the same dialect, do not see themselves as a separate group; within the group there are several horizontal divisions.

Developments since the seventies

Because of the kleptocracy in the national bureaucracy and in development administration, creation of job opportunities is lagging behind population growth. The total number of unemployed is estimated at 20 to 30 %, depending on the source of

---

[125] Right wing in the Moroccan context means conservative, opposed to political and economic reforms.

information. This means that of a total population of 24 million, 4 million are unemployed: they have great difficulty in eking out an existence. Many Berbers have left the rural areas and now live in the 'bidonville' section of the cities. According to Abouhani (1989: 26) about a quarter of the urban population is living in these sections. Migrants from the Rif are now populating the towns of Tanger, Tetouan and Fez, those from the Anti-Atlas the city of Casablanca; with the Berbers from the Middle Atlas still attached to their villages and local towns. For youths with primary or secondary school training it is very difficult to find suitable jobs, not to mention the drop-outs.

It is these young people who organised the riot of 1964 in Casablanca, in with several hundred children were killed, many other riots were to follow, such as the so-called 'bread wars' which broke out in many towns in 1981 and 1984. In a city like Fez since then there has never been a year without violence at the campus or in the city centre. In December 1990 there was a violent uprising too, in this case co-organised by the labour unions who wanted clear undertakings from the government as regards employment and minimum wages. What was clearly observable in Fez, but in the other centres as well, was that Berber and Arab youths alike participated in the demonstrations and strikes.

The common action of the young people, Berber or Arab, ensues from the fact that the lower class nationals never shared in the increase in national production or benefited from the government's development efforts. The standard of living or 'human development index' is far lower in Morocco than in other Maghreb countries (Venema 1993). Most development efforts focused on the implementation of huge irrigation schemes and, until recently, division of the properties left behind by the *colons* and the Jews. This was the case during the Istiqlal administration. However, this was also the case when the Berber Mouvement Populaire and other right-wing parties became able to occupy positions in the administration. The rural population, for the most part Berber, did not see any fundamental change when their own leaders came into power because all benefits were reserved for personal gain and for a small clique of friends. In fact, the Berber elite acted as they had done in the colonial period, appropriating resources for themselves. Moroccan youth therefore distrusts both the Istiqlal party of the Arab intelligentsia and economic elite as well as the Berber Mouvement Populaire. For them they are all alike: they lack a policy to tackle their personal and community priorities. Instead they conceive these parties as what we call 'political machines', distributing benefits in exchange for political support. If the youth revolts they do so beyond the framework of a party system. Even the leftist Union Socialiste des Forces Populaires (USFP, successor of the UNFP) did not succeed in capturing the youth. Neither youth nor elders participate in fundamentalist movements because these are under the complete control of the central government.

For the young people, ethnic criteria are not the most relevant. Their main opponent is the elite, which enriches itself leaving the young generation unemployed and without basic facilities. Because the elite is now from a different ethnic background, their frustration is not directed towards a particular group but towards the class of the well-to-do. The language and emotions refer to class. In Morocco it is not ethnic criteria that are important but differentiation into economic classes.

If the regime in Morocco collapses or has to yield to pressures, the main issue will be division of the nation's resources. Because the king and his family are by far the most prosperous, their position will also be undermined despite their religious aspirations.

Conclusion

The French colonial government in Morocco has tried to collaborate with indigenous chiefs and local councils in an attempt to facilitate control of the population. More specifically, the colonial staff acted on the belief that it was easier to control the Berber population than the Arabs because the former were believed to live in egalitarian and independent Berber communities while the Arab population was governed by a central state. Later on a policy to assimilate the Berber population was developed in an attempt to curtail the growing influence of the urban Arab elite and their nationalistic aspirations. The colonial state elite thus was concerned with the 'politisation of ethnicity' in order to maintain the status quo.

In 1980 the Kabyles of Algeria opposed the Arabisation of the educational system with strikes and demonstrations which were widely supported. The fact that in this case Berber leaders could refer to their role in the nationalist movement explains why Berber identity is more deeply rooted here compared with Morocco. In Morocco, Berber leaders collaborated with the French administration and endeavours of the latter to create a Berber ethnicity were therefore unsuccessful.

After independence the Arab-Islamic elite profited most from the political and economic positions that had become vacant. However, the legitimacy they had acquired from their role in the nationalist movement soon faded once they had acquired positions of influence. The 'political elite' has not remained a pioneer in nationalism in the sense of being committed to a more widely supported development policy.

When the position of this Arab elite grew too strong, a Berber party was created in order to curtail the influence of the Arab elite. So here again the central state elite was engaged in creating ethnicity, but in this case planned and executed by the post-colonial central elite. The leaders of the Berber party offered no alternative either, however. Being members of the landed aristocracy, they were not in a good position to assist the urban poor, but neither did they assist their Berber countrymen. Instead they engaged in 'machine politics' and in patronage, as the Arab elite had done before. When the youth revolts, they do so without the help of party organisations because they have no confidence in their leaders.

So there is no clear divide between Berbers and Arabs: Berber and Arab groups themselves are very hierarchical. Therefore Berbers living in the *bidonvilles* feel they have more in common with their Arab neighbours than with the Berber elite. This is especially true now that the Berber elite have adopted an urban life-style. Identification among the poor and among the rich is far stronger than that on the basis of ethnicity.

As long as regional and national political leaders are engaged in corruption and patronage, there is no future for ethnicity. Instead, if policies remain as they are, a class struggle will develop. The fact that the King is now encouraging the development of other parties and will reduce surveillance by the Ministry of the Interior is a sign that he is at last aware of this problem.

It is therefore true that ethnicity comes into prominence when central rulership favours one group over another, with implications for the resource base of these groups. This is not a sufficient explanation, however. The drive of the colonial government in Morocco to collaborate with the Berbers was based not only on political and economic motives but very probably also on anti-Islamic and anti-urban values. The application of these preferences by French officials contributed to ethnical differentiation. In addition, the Arab-Islamic intelligentsia's pursuit of nationalism cannot be explained merely as a reaction to the French policy to assimilate the Berbers. They were among the leadership of the wider anti-colonial movement in the southern countries, and the policy of 'divide and rule' should also be understood as a response to the important contribution of the Arab elite to nationalism and independence.

With thanks to Edien Bartels and Mayke Kaag for reading an earlier draft of this paper.

References

Abou el Karam, F. 1988. *Répertoire des Gouvernements du Royaume du Maroc.* Casablanca, Faculté des Lettres et des Sciences Humaines

Abouhani, A. 1989. L'état et le bidonville. *Al Asas*, 92: 26 - 31

Andreski, S. 1970. Kleptocracy as a system of government in Africa. In: A. J. Heidenheimer: *Political Corruption. Readings in Comparative Analysis.* New York: Holt, Rinehart and Winston Inc.

Barth, F. 1969. *Ethnic Groups and Boundaries: the Social Organisation of Cultural Differences.* Boston: Little Brown

Bidwell, R. 1973. *Morocco under colonial rule. French administration of tribal areas, 1912 - 1956*. London: Frank Cass

Brown, K. 1972. The impact of the Dahir Berbère in Salé. In: E. Gellner and C. Micaud: *Arabs and Berbers. From Tribe to Nation in North Africa*. London: Duckworth

Burke, E. 1972. The Image of the Moroccan State in French Ethnological Literature: a New Look at the Origin of Lyautey's Berber Policy. In: E. Gellner and C. Micaud: *Arabs and Berbers. From Tribe to Nation in North Africa*. London: Duckworth

Cigar, N. 1981. Socio-Economic Structures and the Development of an Urban Bougeoisie in Pre-colonial Morocco. *Maghreb Review*, 6 (2)

Gellner, E. and Micaud, C. 1972. *Arabs and Berbers. From Tribe to Nation in North Africa*. London: Duckworth

Hanoteau, A. and LeTourneux, A. 1893. *La Kabylie et les coutumes Kabyles*. Paris: Challamel

Hart, D. M. 1972. The Tribe in Modern Morocco. In: E. Gellner and C. Micaud: *Arabs and Berbers. From Tribe to Nation in North Africa*. London: Duckworth

Kaddour, Ben A. 1972. The Neo Makhzen and the Berbers. In: E. Gellner and C. Micaud: *Arabs and Berbers. From Tribe to Nation in North Africa*. London: Duckworth

Marais, O. 1972. The Political Evolution of the Berbers in Independant Morocco. In: E. Gellner and C. Micaud: *Arabs and Berbers. From Tribe to Nation in North Africa*. London: Duckworth

Swearingen, W.D. 1987. *Moroccan Mirages. Agrarian Dreams and Deceptions*. Princeton: Princeton University Press

Tabory, M. and Tabory, E. 1986. Berber Demands for Linguistic Rights in Algeria. *Plural Societies*, 16: 126 - 160

Venema, L. B. 1992. Het Ontstaan van een Lokale Elite in Azrou. De Relatie met Nationale Ontwikkelingen. *Sharqiyyat*, 4 (2): 145 - 160

Venema, L.B. 1993. Islamic Resurrection in North Africa: Backgrounds and Variations. In: M. Bax and A. Koster: *Power and Prayer, on Religion and Politics*. Amsterdam: VU University Press: 251 - 260

Venema, L. B. and Bakker, J. (eds.) 1994. *Vrouwen van de Midden Atlas: Vrij of Vroom?* Utrecht: Jan van Arkel

Journals: Le Matin, Maroc Soir

Archives: Archives Outre-Mer, Nantes, France

ABSTRACT

During the colonial period the French tried to play off the Berbers against the Arabs in an attempt to curtail nationalism led by the Arab urban elite. History has proven that this attempt was unsuccesful, Arabs and Berbers believing they were united in religion. Nevertheless, after independence the Arab elite occupied most of the positions in the bureaucracy due to their role in the nationalist movement.

It was the rise of socialism among the Arab elite which led the monarch to use ethnicity. In order to prevent the development of a socialist one-party state, he stimulated the creation of a Berber party and it was in 1964 that the 'landed aristocracy' was able to take over positions the Arab elite had been given before.

Since the eighties ethnicity no longer plays any role in Morrocan politics. The cooptation of the Arab and Berber elites in government and the spoils they obtained estranged them from the common population. Especially the educated population without suitable jobs turned away from the ethnic leaders and the political parties they were involved in.

Because the central government is well-organised and controls the fundamentalist movement as well as the socialist opposition parties, the only way open to this category is the participation in riots in which the hatred for the rich is the central element. The language is class and hardly any reference is made to ethnicity.

Not all the 'educated' unemployed participate. By granting favours to individuals the monarchy uses patronage to curtail political unrest. Among the less educated the monarch is conceived of as the 'Emir of the Faithful'. So the development of class is only partly occuring.

In this culture of cleptocracy, machine-politics, and patronage, domestic development is not possible. The future of the monarchy is therefore not bright and it might well be that class will become still more important in the future.

Part V

The politics of difference: escalating violence, shifting boundaries and the fragmentation of states

Exclusivist Rhetorics – The Constitution of Political Identities in Present-Day Algeria[126]

Birgit Mara Kaiser

Violence is like a raging fire that feeds on the very objects intended to smother the flames
René Girard

Questions on the relation of 'self' and 'other' have obtained enormous prominence during the last years and are constitutive of the equally prominent concern with questions of identity. In these recent discussions, the identity of the 'self' is seen as constructed through discursively externalising rejected characteristics of an 'other', which is thereby constituted as different, external, as 'other' to the conception of 'self'. This concern for the discursive representations of the 'other' and their crucial implications for the constitution of any identity has been sparked by Said's thesis on the effects of 'Western'[127] (orientalist) discourses on "oriental peoples" and on the constitution of Western identity itself. The discussion has therefore been intimately linked to the discursive interrelation of the notions of 'East' and 'West', notions that hold a central position in contemporary political discourses in Algeria and their attempts to forge an Algerian identity. The emphasis of a discussion of the discursive construction of 'self' and 'other' – a discussion this paper wishes to engage in with respect to two distinct political articulations in the present Algerian conflict – can be outlined in accordance with Norval:

> If identity requires the articulation of otherness, of frontiers in order to constitute itself as such, the issue here is the manner in which such an articulation takes place and the grounds on which political frontiers are to be drawn. The constitution of those frontiers, as well as the grounds on

---

[126] This paper – primarily its theoretical debate and its insights in the Algerian political situation - draws on my unpublished diploma thesis, Kaiser 1998. While the thesis discussed more extensively the relation between islamist discourses and political notions employed in Western discourses, most of the discourse analysis of this paper has been undertaken especially for this elaboration with its particular focus. The islamist discourses will be discussed on the basis of six journals published between 1992 and 1998 by Algerian islamist groups mainly in European exile. The republican discourses that will be juxtaposed can be found mainly in the publications of the RCD party and in the articulations of a few public figures that pronouce themselves in favour of the RCD. These figures (in particular the feminist Khalida Messaoudi, but also the writer Rachid Boudjedra) receive a fair amount of attention in the European reporting on the Algerian crisis and are taken generally as a trustworthy source in regard to the conflict.

[127] The term 'West' is not used as a description of a fixed unity, but rather as reference to an identitarian conception that is used in contrast to an 'Orient', or as in the case of the discourses discussed in this paper, to 'Islam'. The following reflections by Said on the notion of 'Orient' are therefore equally applicable to both of these prominent terms – West and Islam – and both are to be understood in this vein: "[T]he Orient is not an inert fact of nature. It is not merely *there*, just as the Occident itself is not just *there* either. […] Therefore as much as the West itself, the Orient is an idea that has a history and a tradition of thought, imagery, and vocabulary that have given it reality and presence in and for the West." (Said 1995: 4f) In the further course of the paper neither term will be put into quotation marks.

which they are being drawn, is *political* in the strict sense of the term. (Norval 1995: 43)

This paper will bear this political nature of the (never fully) established frontiers in mind, while following precisely the manners and grounds of their constitution.

The entanglement of 'other' and 'self' and the belief in their mutual discursive constitution implicates a dissolving of the formerly presumed underlying essences of identities. Such an anti-foundationalist understanding of identity is thus likely to enhance a crumbling of the belief in overarching narratives of an eventual fulfillment of the presumed essential qualities of man and the grand truths at the end of a unilinear historic evolution. In this sense, the debates on the relation of 'self' and 'other' go along with a conception of the present world as "postmodern", precisely marked by a dissolution of the belief in grand narratives. Apart from an agreement on these changes, however, the discussion about what follows from them differs widely. The quarrels over the "nature" of our present times (are we postmodern?) range from positions of a high or reflexive modernity (a position held for example by Giddens or Beck) over those of a globalised (post)modernity (assumed by for example Turner, Albrow, Stauth) to those of a hyperreal postmodernity (as held by Baudrillard). Correspondingly, the conceptions of 'self' and 'other' and questions of identity are addressed differently in the various approaches. Especially the debate of a globalised (post)modernity is concerned with the changes that are produced by the presumed processes of globalisation for the construction of identities. Focussing on the increase of a global awareness of other cultures, this debate tends to take the revelation of an intimate relation of 'self' and 'other' as a general opportunity for a better understanding between subjects from different identitarian backgrounds. The concern for the relation of 'self' and 'other' has become a primary issue in a globalised (post)modernity and emphasis is put on the endeavour of mutual tolerance. Yet, these hopes are shaken, if not shattered, by the enormous rise in conflicts which spark precisely along the lines of (ethnic, national, religious) identification.

Such a plea for tolerance is, however, not only disturbed empirically, but has also to be questioned theoretically. The idea of tolerance evokes an understanding of the notions of 'self' and 'other' that takes each to be a self-present entity confronted with an opposed one, conceptualising them as conscious subjects. Contrary to that, I prefer to picture the interrelation of the *concepts,* the *notions* of 'self' and 'other' as the relation of categories which are discursively represented as dichotomies, always precisely by way of naming and ascribing particular features and deliminating them from the non-desired or non-mentioned ones. These representations are not managed through conscious adherences to or decisions for one identity as against another. Rather they are placed within complex power relations and convoluted economies of representation. Such theoretical questionings of the self-present subject and considerations of the mutual dependency of the categories of 'self' and 'other' by no means intend to negate existing social, political, or cultural fractions – which would be a slap in present-day Algeria's face. But they call for a theoretically differentiated use of the crucial notions of 'self' and 'other', on which eventually the entire concept of discourse is built.

According to such an understanding – to be understood as critical engagement with the debate on globalised (post)modernity and its presumptions of a better understanding of 'others' in the future – I intend to focus this paper on the processes of conflictive othering in two of the most fiercely opposed political discourses in present-day Algeria and will examine the established frontiers and identifications in both of them. The paper opens with a discussion of the (theoretical) implications of the aforementioned debate on a globalised (post)modernity. It subsequently presents the identitarian discourses, by means of which two violently opposed sides are conjured up, fixed and deepened. Through their exclusivist rhetorics, both sides – one Islamist (*intégriste*)[128], one republican (*éradicateur*)[129] – refuse each 'other' as incompatible to true Algerianness, as incommunicably different and as legitimately eradicable. I hope to demonstrate not only the necessity of taking such an establishing of frontiers of identification into account as *political* – that means as anti-essential and therefore as changeable –, but also the necessity to closely regard the political context in which these frontiers are drawn. The fact of a *discursive* establishment of frontiers makes their establishment not only always fragile in the sense of the indispensable dependency of one on the other – and thus their traces within each category, their mutual contamination - but by means of the discursiveness of the categories, these also constantly run the risk of being conjured up in exclusivist terms. The interrelatedness of 'self' and 'other' is not *per se* a guarantor for an understanding or tolerance of the 'other', but needs to be embedded within a specific political context to allow such a desired form of dealing (cf. Norval 1998). In distinction to the theoretical implications of the (fairly popular) debate on globalised (post)modernity, a theoretical conceptualisation of the concern for the constitutive relation of 'self' and 'other' in identity construction needs to be found, one which allows me to address both the political character and the political context of the respective processes of 'othering'.

---

[128] The first term is the self-employed name of the fraction identifying by this category, while the bracketed one is their denomination in the discourses of "the other side". The term 'integrism' alludes to a totalitarian conception of society, integrally unified in its values, manners and identifications. The term derives from a Christian tradition of literalism and is clearly pejorative (cf. Burgat 1993: 38). It is also widely used in both Western and Algerian media coverage of the Islamist movement. In the following, the first one will be used for the general denomination of the fraction, while by the second term this fraction is designated in the adversary's discourse.

[129] The terms and their use in this paper will be handled in the same way as the terms 'intégriste/Islamist' explained above, 'republican' being the self-employed description of the fraction, 'éradicateur' their denomination in Islamist discourses. The term 'éradicateur' is also used in academic and media debates of the Algerian situation (cf. Roberts 1994; Mellah 1996) and refers to a group identified as the hardline anti-Islamists in Algerian government and administration, military and police forces, press and intellectual elite.

Debates on the 'other' and the 'hybrid' in an age of globalised (post)modernity

To view our present times as the epoch of globalised (post)modernity – as the age that results from the globalisation of modernity and is distinguished from the latter by the questioning of certainties so far taken for granted – is among the prominent academic approaches. This particular debate celebrates these changes as a "transformation" (Albrow 1996: 85). It presupposes that through an increase in contact between people from different cultural and personal backgrounds a mutual questioning of one's own certainties will be enhanced and identities will subsequently be understood as culturally constructed and thus as always exposed to (the possibility of) change (cf. Korff 1995: 4). This increase in cross-cultural contact is generally related to the process of globalisation. "Today we live in a global culture. The creative contribution of non-Western cultures in global modernisation becomes evident with Foucault's approach, which has made us aware of the significance of the 'Other' in shaping the discourse about the self and one's own identity." (Abaza 1991: 206) This awareness it, is hoped, will result in a greater tolerance of the 'other' and the plea for a greater emphasis on the "sameness" (Turner 1989: 635) that underlies this mutual construction of identities is made. The problem of former orientalist discourses is seen in their foundation on difference, which is portrayed as "the *problem* of difference (we versus them, east versus west, rationality versus irrationality)" (635, my emphasis). These problematic demarcations should be overcome in order to focus on the "continuities between various cultures" (635), a possibility which is seen to be most likely in the present world, since "the globalisation of cultures creates a greater reflexivity about personal and cultural identity" (Turner 1994: 202).

It is certainly relevant to describe 'globalised spaces' in 'global cities' as subject to change in the sense of an awareness of the increase of what Appadurai calls 'global flows' – the reduction of the time-spans and spaces through which people, finances, information, and ideas flow or float (cf. Appadurai 1999; Eade 1997). Such compression of time and space has shrunk the perception of the globe, as much as in the course of these changes the perception of the West as the ultimate and only evolutionary possibility for humankind has been shaken. However, to generalise the questioning of Western hegemony as the historical chance of a global "age" – an environment that necessitates both the stressing of "sameness" and the awareness of the contingency of one's own identity and subsequently is expected to lead to greater tolerance *vis-à-vis* the 'other' – strikes me as eurocentric and remains within an ontological dichotomy of 'self' and 'other'.

Firstly, it is precisely the reference to a "creative contribution" which insinuates that this perspective remains within the eurocentric tradition it intends to literally outdate.[130] With Abaza clearly alligning the "we" with 'a global culture' and with 'Foucault's approach', the 'non-Western cultures' are recognised as 'other' and are set off from "us" in a manner that again fixes their always derivative position through the acknowledgement of their contribution to "our" project. Doubtlessly, processes of 'othering' are grounded on an intimate intertwining of 'self' and 'other', but I intend to question whether this intertwining can be described as a "creative contribution". Precisely along with Foucault's concern for the relation of power and knowledge, power certainly needs to be considered in its productive operating, but knowledge also in its embeddedness in power relations. Therefore, I rather propose to picture the relation between "us" and "them" as a fixation of the 'other', an appropriation with colonising effects. The insight into the sedimentation of identities does indeed open possibilities for their de-sedimentation and therefore for change, but these possibilities are always embedded in hegemonic articulations which occupy social positions endowed with a specific power. However, presupposing an equal exchange (cf. Stauth 1996: 1) does not recognise these different articulatory positions and the contact is thereby ridden of the power relations underlying it. In this sense, Abaza appears to implicitly acknowledge the contribution from the *hegemonic* position, the position from which the "sharing" of possibilities to articulate or contribute is at stake, not the "achieving" of an articulatory position. And it is from this position that the debate on globalised (post)modernity pleads for a harmonious relation between differences, for tolerance of the 'other'. In my understanding, it thereby continues to perceive the notions of 'self' and 'other' as exclusive entities, as ontological beings – oppositions that can tolerate each other's differences. In this continuation of a dichotomous conception of self-containing units, the debate remains within a logic that reduces the 'other' to the 'same' (cf. Critchley 1992: 4 - 9).

A similar celebration of the 'other' can be found in Bhabha's treatment of the concept of hybridity, a concept which ensues from dissolving the conception of essentially fixed identities and which captures precisely the 'in-between' spaces of identities opened by diasporic or migrant experiences in a formerly colonial – and later globalised – world. Norval has argued against the celebration of the concept of hybridity as such, since firstly it has to be kept in mind that all identities are hybrid in the sense of unpure and are always only posited or sedimented as pure. Bhabha, however, attributes hybridity to minoritarian identities and blurs or fails to draw the distinction between an inevitable hybridity of any identity and the politics of subverting established identitarian conceptions by politisising this hybridity. Therefore, by celebrating the hybrid as *per se* predestined to a critique of an essential conception of identity, "Bhabha [...] moves almost seamlessly from a conception of hybrid identities [...] to a politics of

---

[130] I understand eurocentrism as the discourse which aims at sustaining the universality of the European (or in this regard interchangeably Western) project. "[T]he logic of eurocentism is currently hegemonic. Its hegemony has political/cultural significance for the planet. [...] With the dismantling of the overt means by which the West exercised *imperium* over the rest of the world, the logic of eurocentrism is the invisible empire which keeps the 'Rest' in its place." (Sayyid 1997: 129)

resistance" (Norval 1998: 9). However, if all identities are to be conceptualised as hybrid, it is precisely the "*intentional* hybridities" (Norval 1998: 10, my emphasis) that need to be stressed as *political* subversion of an established power relation. From this emphasis on the intentional character, it secondly becomes indispensable to consider the political context in which these identifications are cited (Norval 1998: 9f). Since the constitution of frontiers is always political, the question is whether the drawn and redrawn identities critique or support the established order. The citation of an identification, in its inevitable differentiation from an 'other', always runs the risk of constituting this identification "in narrow, exclusivist and identitary terms" (Norval 1995: 31). Therefore, it is essential for the examination of any form of identification to problematise the (political) context in which "difference" is evoked. Such contextualisation however seems to be overridden by celebrating the hybrid as subversion *per se* or a global culture as predestined for the "tolerance of difference". Such a celebration rather attributes to these hybridities *per se* a moment of resistance to hegemonic, essentialist conceptions of identity, or – in the case of the debate on globalised (post)modernity – to an increased contact *per se* a moment of reflexivity and understanding of the other.[131]

The present Algerian crisis, with which this paper is concerned, has lasted for more then ten years and its thorough socio-political alleviation in the near future is difficult to imagine. The crisis was sparked by the popular demand for democratisation in 1988, a process half-heartedly conceded by the ruling regime in 1989. The conflict developed into an increasingly open confrontation mainly between armed islamist groups and state forces after the abrogation of the parlamentary elections in 1991/92. Up until the 1995 conference in Rome[132] the conflicting camps seemed split in two – the ones not participating in the meeting and to a certain extent in accordance with the regime's policies, and the ones participating and opposing the regime. During the last years of the crisis, however, after the extensive armament of civilians, the lines of conflict have become opaque and the crisis has been led into an impasse – literally a dead

---

[131] Even if the threat that can result from the perception of the contingency of identity is not denied, the debate's stress on "tolerance" and "sameness" neglects the unequal power relations that determine the different discursive positions. Turner perceives 'fundamentalism' as one answer to this threat intending to build a "new *Gemeinschaft*, a new version of the traditional household which would close off the threat of postmodernity" (Turner 1994: 93). Taken out of their political context, the diverse identitarian discourses subsumed under the term 'fundamentalism' are thereby homogenised into a "traditional" reaction to postmodern uncertainties, and the specific and diverse manners of their identitarian discourses remain unexamined.

[132] The meeting was held in Rome on the 13/1/1995 and the *contrat national,* which proposed negotiations between the oppositional parties and the regime to resolve the conflict and pleaded for a political situation, was signed by the LADDH (*Ligue Algérienne de la Defense des Droits de l'Homme*), FLN (*Front de Libération nationale*), FFS (*Front des Forces Socialistes*), FIS, PT (*Parti Trotzkiste*), MDA (*Mouvement pour la Démocratie en Algérie*) and Al-Nahda (islamist party), JMC (*Jaza'ir musulmane contemporaine*).

end – with a degree of violence that Bensmaïa describes as generalised violence.[133] The exclusivist discourses that are examined in this paper are placed within this setting and can be understood both to provide the discursive climate for such a degree of violence and at the same time to result from it. After a decade of fierce fighting over the one legitimate definition of 'Algeria' the possible effects of the recent initiative towards national reconciliation by the newly elected president, Bouteflika, remain to be seen. But any such initiative needs to take into account the manners and grounds of the constitution of the opposing discourses. I intend to trace two of them in this paper.

Exclusivist rhetorics and conflictive 'othering'

> *The ongoing struggle in Algeria is between truth and falsehood,*
> *not merely between the government and the governed.*
> (E 3/6/94: 3)[134]

With regard to the presented debates on the relation of 'self' and 'other', the Algerian crisis is of particular interest in two respects. Firstly, the opposed discourses are expressed in a discursive tradition in Algeria which is marked by a predominance of unitarian conceptions of national identity and thus allows for little divergence from these holistic imaginations. The national identity, as it was forged by state discourse after independence, was seen as the fulfillment of a holistic entity with no divergences from the one authorised definition being neither desired nor tolerated. It was based on a specific combination of Islamic, Arab and socialist features, legitimised through the war of independence, authorised by the ruling regime and expressed in the state slogan "L'Algérie est ma patrie, l'arabe ma langue, l'Islam ma religion".[135] Oppositions to this unitarian definition have been most poignantly pronounced throughout the years of independence by Kabyle and feminist, more recently by islamist activists, and have consistently been put under constraint by the regime (cf. Knauss 1987). Parallel to the official neglect of any difference, political opposition has been subjected to persecu-

---

[133] Bensmaïa sees the form of generalised violence as the result of three traumatic "events" (the killing of soldiers at Guemmar in 1992, the demonstrations and subsequent killings of civilians in October 1988, the assassination of president Boudiaf in 1994) (cf. Bensmaïa 1997: 93f). I think this reference to *traumatic* "events" rightly draws attention to the gap between an exclusivist and denigrating 'othering' and the violence that possibly draws on such categorisations. The denigration of the 'other' does not compellingly lead to such violence as Algeria presently witnesses, their connection cannot be explained as a relation of cause and effect. However, this manner of 'othering' certainly provides an arena for the closing off of discursive possibilities and identifications – and it simultaniously flourishes in a (political) climate of closed possibilities – and provides the ground for a subsequent legitimation of violence against the anyhow closed off 'other'. But Bensmaïa's notion of generalised violence reminds us that it still takes "events" that are in one way or the other traumatic in order to spark the violent potential of such discursive arenas and to end in a spiralling "logic" of violence and counter-violence.

[134] The islamist journals will be referenced as follows: "The Enlightenment": (E date: page); "Echoes of Truth": (EoT date: page); "La Cause": (C number: page); "Al-Mounkidh": (M number: page); "Al-Ribat": (R number: page); "Algeria Salvation": (AS page).

[135] For a discussion of the conceptions of Algerian national identity see Abucar 1996; Bensmaïa 1997; Roberts 1984; Ruedy 1992.

tion and never been allowed to pronounce any deviance from the socialist conceptions of the Algerian state (cf. Hanoune & Mouffok 1997). It is in this tradition of silencing all difference that the exclusivist discourses of islamists and republicans have to be situated.

Secondly or correspondingly, a national dialogue has never been encouraged in Algerian political discourses and its resulting non-existance has increasingly manou-vered the crisis into a *cul-de-sac*, which appears not to leave – and to never have left – any room for negotiation, let alone for mutual understanding or tolerance. Maghraoui explicates this lack of dialogue by a profound doubt of the language, or the terms of reference, in which to engage in such a dialogue. He states that

> [b]oth the established order and the Islamic Salvation Front (FIS) *doubt* and *reject* each other's languages as a legitimate medium to engage in a dialogue. Each discourse imposes its own rules of debate, prohibits other rationalisations, and claims neutrality and universality in translating the 'real' problems facing Algerian society. (1995: 23f)

Although such a doubt and rejection is related in this quotation to the opposed discourses of the ruling forces and the islamists, both can equally be found in the op-position between islamist and republican discourses. Maghraoui sees a possible theo-retical framing of such a doubt and of an eventual lack of common terms of reference in Lyotard's notion of *différend* (cf. Maghraoui 1995: 24). "[A] differend [*différend*] would be a case of conflict, between (at least) two parties, that cannot be equitably resolved for lack of a rule of judgement applicable to both arguments." (Lyotard 1988: xi) The notion describes a conflictive situation in which no common point of reference can be identified, as a consequence of which there is no point from where the different discursive frames could be judged or an overarching reference could be found. A le-gitimate (meta-)language to which all different discursive frames could adhere is thus lost – if it ever existed in the first place. Relating this concept to the present Algerian situation, Bensmaïa holds that "we might say that in Algeria one is faced with four contradictions and [...] totally irreconcilable 'injunctions' [...] [I]t is not a matter here of a dialogue or even a discussion of ideas but, in the best case, of a 'differend' (in the Lyotardian sense)" (Bensmaïa 1997: 88)[136]. Regarding such a situation of *différend*, the demand for tolerance of the 'other' – apart from the discussed critical points that arise from this approach anyhow – runs short and a different conception of the relation of 'self' and 'other' is required. This point will be taken up towards the end of this pa-per. For the time being, the outlined political and discursive contexts have to be kept in

---

[136] Bensmaïa identifies four injunctions: the FIS, the governing forces, the civil society which he calls 'the Third Estate' in concordance with Derrida, and the intellectuals, which "could have played the role of intermediaries, 'translators', or producers of 'statements' that could serve as principles of arbi-tration between opposing points of view, principles shared by all that would have furnished the criteria by which to surmount differends and to impose respect of what the majority had decided on" (Bensmaïa 1997: 89). He sees this last injunction, however, as never having occupied any space in Algerian society.

mind for the following discussion of the exclusivist identitarian discourses of islamists and republicans.

In both of the opposed discourses underlying this analysis a clear determination of true and false in the struggle over the Algerian national fate can be found. A "bearable" solution to this struggle is strictly outlined and presented as the fulfillment of what is thought to be the correct definition of "Algerian". These definitions take shape in two socio-political projects that compete over an "Algerian future", and since the nation's fate is taken to be decided along these lines, no concessions are acceptable and no consensus desirable. Both sides entertain a rhetoric of all-or-nothing and accuse the other of being prepared to literally do away with half of the population in order to pursue their imagination of "Algeria", as can be seen in the mutual islamist and republican accusations:

> [L]es faux démocrates d'aujourd'hui [...] appellent à l'éradication (existe-t-il de mots plus forts pour désigner la violence) de toute une partie de la population. (C 24: 5)

> [T]he new F.I.S. spokesman in Algeria declared, in refering to professional people who refused Islamism: 'Personally, if I were them, I'd ship out. And we'll bring in shiploads of Muslim professionals. (Messaoudi 1998: 122)

In such a fixed definition of "Algeria" lies the crux of present Algerian political discourses, since it is precisely this fixation that encourages and nurtures the exclusivist discursive patterns this paper wishes to discuss. "Everything is happening as if, in Algeria, someone wanted to construct a system *without incompatibilities, without contradictions, without contraries.*" (Bensmaïa 1997: 91) The verbal and physical clashes of the last decade resulted from the heating of these two narrowed, exclusivist approaches to either of the projects, which can be ascribed to two fractions of political articulation. Before pursuing a more detailed discussion of the manners of 'othering', these fractions need to be shortly sketched.

One project - *le projet islamist* - is articulated by that part of the Algerian islamist movement[137] that organised around the FIS during its foundation in 1989 and largely remained adherent to the party's option for a legalistic, political course.[138]

---

[137] The islamist movement is unanimous neither in its political articulations nor in the forms of its political presence in Algeria. The multitude of islamist strands stretches from those holding seats in parliament, to the banned and exiled FIS, stressing its legalistic committment, to the openly militant GIA (*Groupes Islamiques Armés*), whose infiltration by the ruling forces is being increasingly suspected. Any serious engagement with islamist discourses in Algeria (and supposedly anywhere) needs to take this heterogeneity not only into account, but also allow it to disturb the implicit presuppositions about these discourses. I have tried elsewhere to grasp this heterogeneity of one of these islamist strands in Algeria, namely the FIS (cf. Kaiser 1998).

[138] In July 1994, the FIS formed the AIS (*Armée Islamique du Salut*) as the party's armed branch – in reaction to the increasing militant actions carried out by the GIA against the regime – in order to re-

Their discourses stress the fact of the party's commitment to an electoral system of proportional political representation and to the division and shifting of state powers, and they see all of this to be compatible with their definition of an Islamic State. In the further intent to unify 'Islam' "as *din* (faith), as *dunya* (complete way of life), and as *dawla* (a state or political order)" (Sayyid 1997: 47) they make of 'Islam' the master signifier of their political discourses (cf. Kaiser 1998: 44 - 87; for a discussion of the concept of master signifier in the context of islamist discourses see Sayyid 1997: 46ff). The FIS won a majority of 54.3 % in the municipal elections in 1990 and subsequently ruled over 32 of the 48 *wilayaat* (provinces). The regime's opposition to the party amounted to intents of boycotting and blocking islamist politics and the FIS in return, particularly in the course of the parliamentary elections in 1991, radicalised its political rhetorics calling for open confrontation and militant resistance to the regime and its allies. After the crackdown during the elections and the arrest or exilation of most of the FIS's members the party – and the islamist movement in general – was divided into various splintergroups which were increasingly militarised and engaged in violent confrontations with their adversaries (cf. Labat 1995). These adversaries are identified by the FIS's discourse with the regime, which does not concede to the FIS's electoral victory, and with the francophone Algerians, who refuse any negotiation with or participation of islamists in Algerian politics. Both are portrayed as internal colonisers, wanting to extinguish Islamic belief and practices in Algerian society (cf. M 9: 64).

The other project - *le projet républicain* - is primarily expressed in the discourses maintained by the *Rassemblement de la Culture et la Democratie* (RCD), one of the "democratic"[139] parties. The RCD was founded around Said Saadi in 1989, along with many other newly formed parties, after a revision of the constitution officially allowed political groups to form (cf. Burgat 1993: 271). It has its followers mostly among the population of the Kabyle region, the party itself coming from a

---

gain ground in the islamist struggle which it was afraid of loosing to the GIA. The discourses discussed here recognise the AIS as the legitimate armed force in the struggle with the regime and its allies and support the AIS's aims and methods, which are emphazised as being in concordance with Islamic Law. The analysis focuses on the islamist discourses maintained by the FIS and the opposed republican discourses – instead of a focus on the opposition of the regime's forces and the GIA –, because the latter opposition is too closely engaged in militant action and involved in a logic of force. The discourses that provide the terrain for such clashes by the manner of their mutual 'othering' (namely islamist and republican) seem to be – in the context of the questions this paper is concerned with – the ones that interest more than the ones that on the basis of the established categorisations of such an 'othering' are primarily engaged in militant conflict (namely the army and GIA). This distinction, however, is not intended to imply a division of the different discourses into primary and secondary ones. All need to be understood as secondary to the same extent, always only deriving from another one, but the manner of 'othering' can be more informative in one case or the other.

[139] The term 'democratic' is used in order to situate this fraction for the reader, who might be familiar with the popular threefold distinction between military forces, islamistes and a democratic opposition in Algeria. However, it is placed in quotation marks to express the need to differentiate this camp of opposed parties and their positions towards the ruling regime more carefully. To simply subsume all of them under the category of 'democratic' appears to spring too strongly from the wish to clarify (and simplify) a very opaque situation by finding at least someone, who is on the good, read: democratic, side.

background of concern for the extension of Berber cultural liberties. The RCD stands for liberal republicanism and wishes to fulfill "the separation of church and state, secularism, citizenship, a state based on rights, the repeal of the Family Code, the recognition of Algeria's Berber dimension, social justice, educational reform, and so on" (Messaoudi 1998: 94). The party participated in the elections of 1990 and 1991, obtaining 2.1 % resp. 2.9 % of the votes (Willis 1996: 393f). Measured by their little electoral support, the party and particularly the feminist Khalida Messaoudi[140] receive overdimensionally strong media attention in Europe and both are often portrayed as *the* democratic opposition in Algeria. With the prospective outcome of the parlamentary elections in 1991 – that is the prospective victory of the FIS – the RCD was one of the first to call for their abrogation. Ever since, the party holds strong convictions against any negotiation with the islamist fractions and it refused to participate in the Rome Accord due to this stance. In its uncompromising position towards islamist positions the RCD's republican discourse addresses the whole range of islamism as external, as wholly 'other' to the project of a republican, parliamentary, liberal Algeria. Islamist fractions are portrayed as wanting to establish a theocracy following the Iranian model and as willing to abrogate all liberal and republican rights (cf. Bulletin du RCD immigration: 2). Both this attitude and its support for an abrogation of the electoral process in 1991 (Messaoudi 1998: 122) positions the party's articulations in this respect close to the regime's hardliners ("our [army's and 'democrats'] interests converged circumstantially" (Messaoudi 1998: 125)) and in return makes it again the target for islamist accusations of collaboration with the "people's oppressors".

The divergent and yet similar portrayals of the opponents by either side speak for the exclusiveness and vigour with which the processes of mutual 'othering' are endowed. Both refuse to take the articulations of the 'other' into account and claim the adversaries are – to the extent to which they are conceded to exist – the mere outcome of plotting.

> Toutes ces déclarations de M Saadi ne doivent pas être prises isolément, mais comme un indice parmi tant d'autres, indiquant la conspiration diabolique qui se trame à l'encontre du peuple algérien. (M 4: 20)

> The 'Afghan' F.I.S. militants in the service of the United States cannot get along with the groups that are controlled by Qaddafi. Those who are financed by Saudi Arabia cannot work alongside those who are maintained by Iran or Sudan. (Messaoudi 1998: 136)

---

[140] Messaoudi is associated with the party and publicly supports its positions. The polemic that exists especially around her as a political figure polarises the positions taken on the Algerian crisis, as much in Algerian political as in academic discourses. Her person and positions are cited as *the* example of where the lines of conflict lie. I correspondingly will refer to her articulations which are pronounced in strong opposition to islamist positions. In some academic discourses she is taken as the example *par exellence* of the mediatic reduction of the Algerian situation, a reduction which presents her as *the* feminist voice of the country, embodying "the Algerian woman" endangered by islamist fanaticism (Burgat 1996: 249; Mellah 1996: 11).

In both discourses these plots are seen as supported by the ruling regime which is accused of doing anything in order to stay in power and which is described as being at the bottom of the conflict. Interestingly though, the denigration and demonisation of the 'other' is directed not at the regime, but at either one opponent, the islamist resp. the republican fraction. Both mutually describe each other as the regime's henchmen against their own project (projects which are on both sides perceived as contesting the regime), and while the regime is accused of a totalitarian rule and thereby urged to finally concede to the people's will, it is really the "acylotes" that are to be expelled from the definition of "Algeria".

The particularly fervent demonisation of this opposition – islamist and republican – employs a wide spectrum of ascriptions which will be discussed in detail below. One of these mutually employed denigrating ascriptions – namely 'fascist' – is striking for its parallel connotation in both discourses and shall be mentioned at this point, ahead of the more detailed analysis of the denigrating 'othering'. It not only categorises the 'other' in the same terms – this, as will be demonstrated later, is also the case with the mutual reproach of "foreignness", which however is explicated differently (as French or Iranian) –, but it also connotes the term in the same manner, namely as anti-democratic and totalitarian.

> Il y a ensuite un faux démocrate. Le S.S d'Algérie (Saadi). (C 30: 2)
>
> Ceux-là [les putschistes et les généraux dictateurs] sont les fascistes et les nazis d'aujourd'hui. (R 50: 2)
>
> On the F.I.S. side, an elderly spokesman named Mohamed Said, who had been in the Nazi S.S. [...]. (Messaoudi 1998: 122)
>
> Ils [les islamistes] pensent exactement ce que pensait Goebbels: 'Quand j'entend le mot culture, je sort mon révolver'. Les intégristes ont un slogan: celui qui nous insulte par la plume périra par la lame. (Boudjedra 1995: 25)

A closer reading of the opposed discourses will focus on both the rejection and absence of dialogue and the kinds of mutual demonisation. In the course of this reading I will present the two sides of the one process of mutual 'othering' – an islamist projection of *éradicateurs* and a republican projection of *intégristes*. Due to textual proceedings as well as for the sake of a clear argument I will have the discussion of one projection follow the other. I wish to stress, however, that this is not to reinscribe an understanding of such a process of 'othering' as occuring in two separate motions, located in pre-existant and self-present entities, but that I rather draw on the conception of 'self' and 'other' outlined above.

The islamist discourse and its 'other': the *éradicateurs*

The answer is that the junta are the criminals and the islamists are innocent.
(E 27/2/98: 1)

[L]es islamistes [...et...] leurs adversaires les éradicateurs...
(C 26: 8)

The Algerian islamist discourses discussed in this paper are maintained in journals and weeklies that are published on a regular basis by the part of the Algerian islamist movement adherent to the FIS and exiled in the aftermath of the abrogation of the parliamentary elections. These publications address an Algerian exile community as well as partly a Western, mostly European, audience. They vary in respect to the positions taken on different issues. However, in the representation of the political adversaries discussed here, all show a considerable unanimity which allows me to discuss these discursive features as relevant for all of the consulted journals.[141]

Most of the academic publications on islamism generally suggest as a main reference and a primary concern of islamist discourses the relation of Islamic societies with the West. Their demarcation from Western values and culture is taken as the principal referent of their political identifications, which draw on Islam as the civilisational alternative to the Occident. Thereby, islamist discourses reverse the orientalist representations of a dark, irrational, traditional Islam into a source of cultural authenticity (cf. Abaza & Stauth 1988: 345).

In the islamist discourses of the exiled groups adherent to FIS such a primary reference to the West can indeed be found. The West – taken as a complex of cultural identity and political and economic power – holds this prominent position as the 'other' of an islamist project. Much of the project's political legitimation, namely its proclaimed "difference" from all other societal alternatives, results precisely from being *different* from the *West* (cf. C 16: 5). However, the Algerian islamist discourses maintain a both ambiguous and differentiated position towards this 'other'. By no means is it dismissed as the "modern" adversary of an aspired traditional authenticity, nor as entirely "evil". To the contrary, they engage at length in discussing concepts of Western political liberalism and rule of law, and claim these societal and political principles for an Algerian Islamic state itself. They hold that only on the ground of these principles a modern societal order – to which they explicitly aspire – can be built (cf. C 23: 6; AS 27). The West is even approached as a possible partner in the struggle of the oppressed, of those striving for political and cultural self-representation. In this sense, an appeal is made to the proclaimedly Western principles of self-determination, liberty and justice (cf. AS 13). The discourses plead for mutual respect of differences

---

[141] The discursive variety of the journals regarding other issues is discussed in greater detail in my unpublished diploma thesis (Kaiser 1998) and interested readers are invited to consult there.

(cf. C 22: 2 - 4) and explicitly appreciate the principles of societal and political order considered to be Western (cf. M 4: 31; AS 23, 27).

The difference from a Western 'other' is seen much more strongly in cultural respects[142]. Algerian cultural features are perceived to be expressed mainly in the Islamic religion, belief and values (cf. C 22: 5). All of these are portrayed as homogenous, as timelessly given and *there* to recover.[143] "[D]espite all this scientific refinement to wiping out a culture of a whole society, in order to remove its identity, the latter still remained present and animated." (AS 5) If these Islamic features are neglected or dismissed, that is if for example a liberal form of political order is indispensably linked with secularism, this is suspected to be due to foreign cultural influence. This influence is generally described as Western. However, the term influence – as it is employed in the islamist discourses – alludes to *domination* by a foreign culture, to the *colonisation* or suppression of the authenic cultural features. In this connection it is mostly explicated as *French* cultural influence, perpetuating the colonisation of Algeria (cf. R 31: 3; AS 18f). The agents of this continued cultural influence are subsequently identified as the French speaking Algerians, especially those who *presently* form the political opposition to the islamist project of a society that draws its identity from its adherence to 'Islam'.

Keeping this demarcation from a present and political opponent in mind, it becomes difficult to maintain the abovementioned argument of islamism as the mere reversal of orientalist narratives. Firstly, the islamist discourses have to be seen as not merely reversing a projection, but as *presently* constructing a complex identity. This identity certainly and indispensably draws on established and perpetuated discursive regimes – as the orientalist ones that still inform discourses on 'Islam' –, but it is much more complex and ambiguous than is implied by the notion of a reversal. Secondly, this identity construction is embedded in a political context, and concerned with a particular political opponent, one that contests islamist aspirations more immediately than any orientalist discourses. This 'other' doubts the islamist societal project and struggles for a different one of its own. Yet, seen as the representative of Western influence *within* Algeria, this 'other' is the one islamist discourses cannot live with. Such an em-

---

[142] Western culture is represented as originating from judeo-christianism, but mainly built upon secularism, progress (measured as economic growth), and political freedom (cf. AS 10; C 19: 3; R 50: 2). It is seen as different from an Islamic civilisation, not necessarily opposed, but distinct.

[143] I wish to clarify that this understanding is maintained in the islamist political discourses, while my own is marked by the doubt of a recoverable 'origin'. Sayyid however describes to what extent 'Islam' – signifier in islamist articulatory practices – is likely to be refered to in terms of 'originality': "Islam does not only bear the marks of its previous interpretations, it also bears the marks of its current articulations in different discourses. Thus, the content of Islam is provided by the contestation between past and present reinterpretations. Behind these various articulatory practices, there is the trace of Islam's inauguration. This foundational moment continues to act as a call to 'return to the origins'. This return is inscribed in the possibility of recovering the 'original meaning' of Islam. This attempt to recover is never a recovery, for the attempt modifies what was to be recovered and forces us to question the status of this 'return to origins'." (1997: 43)

beddedness, however, is often neglected just as much in the mentioned discussions on islamism as in the discussed approach of globalised (post)modernity. In the following discussion, I wish to grasp both of these dimensions of identity construction in Algerian islamist discourses – its present character and its embeddedness in the political context.

The islamist discourses distinguish right – explicated as culturally authentic and self-determined – from wrong – correspondingly understood as culturally foreign and dominated – in the struggle over an Algerian political future. In this demarcation the right evolves around the islamist project and is marked off against "le projet laïco-communiste" (C 24: 2). By means of this distinction an enemy within the Algerian socio-political arena is established, one which is thought to undermine the self-respect of the Algerian people by denigrating 'Islam' as well as 'Algerian Islamic' culture, its values and beliefs. The adherents to the secularist project are equated with "éradicateur" (M 5: 26)[144] and the "éradicateurs" with the hardliners of an *Algérie française* (cf. M 4: 19). Those are perceived to be strongly represented amongst the French speaking parts of the society, primarily a circle of writers and intellectuals publishing in French.[145] The most vigorous opposition to the islamist project is considered to be expressed by this francophone elite associated with the secularist republicans, frequently referred to as the cultural spearhead of French cultural influence and associated with a group of francophone intellectuals.[146] Corresponding to the denomination as "éradicateur" or "pseudo" the secular tendencies are described as merely a residue of foreign influences and only minoritarian in extent.

> Le rejet massive par 91 % des suffrages exprimés de la laïcité et des thèses des éradicateurs qui se sont manifestés autour de Said Sadi [...] (R 78: 3)

---

[144] The designation of the opponents differs slightly in the various islamist journals underlying this analysis. Those laying emphasis on political self-representation and the lawful election of the FIS as representatives of the Algerian people employ "éradicateur", while those focussing on cultural self-representation and the cultural liberation of Islamic Algeria from the perceived French cultural distortion use "pseudo". Each designation is attributed to all presumably aligned groups, such as "les médias éradicatrices" (R 41: 4) or the "pseudo intellectuals" (C 16: 4).

[145] For the complexity of the language politics in Algeria, see Grandguillaume 1997; for the specific issue of publishing and censorship in Algeria, see Gafaiti 1997.

[146] The following argument is not to be misunderstood as supporting the often suggested islamist hate of anything intellectual in general due to islamist totalitarianism that is hostile to all reflection, but it rather examines their rigorous turning against this particular group of intellectuals. This particular group is linked with the regime – "en concubinage suspect avec la junte militaire" (C 16: 5) – and understood as the civil discourse against islamism, justifying the regime's policies. "De l'intellectualisme, les adeptes de cette mouvance [laïco-communiste] se sont réduits au rôle de justificateurs à postériori des décisions arbitraires et autoritaires d'une junte inculte." (M 5: 26) For a discussion of the mainstream suggestion of an islamist aversion against intellectualism, see Burgat 1996: 155-175.

La mouvance laïco-communiste, formée de résidues de marxistes-
léninistes et de régionalistes est réduite à un statut de sous-minorité idéo-
logique ne représentant qu'une partie infirme de la société et autopro-
clamée démocrate et parfois intellectuelle. (M 5: 26)

Subsequently, these tendencies are being disconnected from all popular support
– being no more than "une certaine minorité élitiste algérienne, déconnectée des réali-
tés nationales et partisans" (C 16: 5). Corresponding to this portrayal of the "éradicateurs", the "authentic"[147] is measured either by popular support (cf. E 30/5/97: 1) – a
factum very likely and promising to point out regarding the FIS' electoral victory – or
by adherance to an authentic Islamic/ist tradition (cf. AS 8). A total popular adherence
to the FIS in both regards – as voters and as Muslims – is reaffirmed in this vein, por-
traying the party as having emerged genuinely from amidst the Algerian people and
expressing its most pressing wishes.[148]

This direct opponent – compound of the laico-communist *éradicateurs* and the
francophone elites – represents the 'other' of Algerian islamist discourse, the one that
carries the traces both of a former French colonisation and of the social unequalities of
contemporary Algeria. Through the portrayal of this 'other' as foreign, fanatic, and
hateful an islamist political identification can establish a notion of 'self' that allows
them to represent just the opposite – authentic, reasonable and sincerely concerned
with an Algerian future.

The "Éradicateurs" – foreign to an 'Islamic-Algerian' identity

"According to islamist discourses, an Islamic tradition is historically rooted in
the Algerian society and provides the spinal bone of Algerian identity. French colonialism aimed particularly at uprooting this Islamic heritage (cf. AS 4; C 16: 6) and at
assimilating Algeria as part of the French motherland, namely as an *Algérie française*.[149] The foreign French rule was exercised in Algeria for over a century and has
implanted French culture into Algerian society. This influence still remains strong and

---

[147] In correspondance to the "authentic" there has to be a "non-authentic" a "false", which is identified
as "faux islamistes" (C 30: 2), "faux democrats" (C 24: 5) – all those pretending to be islamist or democrats, but not dedicated to "authentic" islamism – by definition FIS – or "authentic" demands for
democracy – by definition FIS.

[148] "The FIS is the people and the people are FIS." (EoT 1/91: 5) The discourse of the FIS shows a
gradual shifting in this measurement of "authentic" from the portrayal of FIS as *part* of the "true oppositional forces" (which include all non-parlamentary opposition with a certain popular backing and
historic legitimacy (cf. C 30: 2), to FIS as the *leading* force of the legitimate oppositional parties (cf. R
72: 2), to FIS as the *only* legitimate force due to ist adherance to divine truth and to Islam (cf. E
12/8/93: 1). For these gradual differences as well as the representation of FIS as the genuinely popular
force, see Kaiser 1998.

[149] This assimilationalist policy of French colonialism in Algeria is also widely agreed upon in academic discourse, cf. Lazreg 1994; Willis 1996.

promotes the diminishing of an 'Islamic-Algerian' identity. Its impact has to be reduced in order for these authentic features of Algerian culture to reappear (cf. AS 8),
an authenticity stressed by underlining the islamist adherence to Sunni Islam (cf. EoT
1/2/92: 15) and "la tradition des sunnites que nous sommes" (R 69: 3).

Parallely, the francophone 'other' – associated with secularism, socialism and
(neo)colonialism – is identified as being strongly influenced by French culture and
thus foreign to Islamic-Algerian values as well as alien to the Algerian people.

> La mouvance laïco-communiste, voilà un résidu du colonialisme et de la
> guerre froide, étranger aux valeurs ancestrales de pays, qui tente de pren-
> dre pied sur la terre islamique et combattante qu'est l'Algérie. (M 5: 26)

> [T]he secular movement imported from France […] does not match any
> reality in Algeria. (AS 8)

> [L]'intellectuel, trahi par sa culture dominante, vive dans un environne-
> ment virtuel très éloigné du sein. (M 4: 19)

In this respect, particularly the continuation of a French inspired educational
system is believed to lead to cultural alientation, only maintained "in order to perpetu-
ate the education of individuals alienated from their language, culture, values, religion,…etc. in a word, from their civilisations worldview" (EoT 3/4/93: 8). After this
distortion is once and for all set right, "afin d'endiguer une fois pour toute les racines
du mal" (C 16: 4), the 'Islamic-Algerian' will be recovered.

The political changes after independence are portrayed as a mere shifting of
posts, following the tactics of "il faut que tout bouge pour que rien ne change." (R 70:
3). This continued colonisation of Algerian society in a "pacte néo-colonial avec cette
minorité élitiste" (C 16: 5) is said to only have extended French (economic and cultural) interests. The socialist revolutionaries thus have proved to continue the same
mindset as the French ruler before them – "the coup leaders who were running Algeria
were following in the footsteps of the French colonial authorities" (EoT 2/94: 2). In
order to diminish this foreign influence, the islamist discourses announce their project
as a "real" break from post-independence politics, an alternative which all opposition
to the islamist project was and is unable to provide. The islamist movement is portrayed as taking up the torch of the people's revolution started in 1954 and as willing
to propose "*un projet de société en rupture avec celui prôné et appliqué par le pouvoir. Au contraire, l'autre opposition ne présentera jamais un projet fondamentalement différent de celui du régime algérien*" (C 24: 3). In this line of representation,
only the islamist project provides a viable alternative to the present situation and those
who disrespect it are thought to target not only the islamist project, but the whole of
"Algeria".

The fanatics I – lying, hating and killing

On the basis of this distinction between the "authentic" and the "pseudo" the *éradicateurs* are established as the counterpart of the islamist movement, representing a foreign and minoritarian fraction which is disconnected from the Algerian people and its values. The journals' readers are dissuaded from paying attention to the *éradicateurs'* positions, since "[i]t is no use listening to lies propagated by [a, BMK] minority that could not adapt to the political reality imposed by the FIS through its active participation and its presence at all levels" (AS 19). They are denied the honorability and the political realism to either talk to or listen to.

In the process of this 'othering' of the *éradicateurs* as the islamists' adversaries, whereby the features of the 'self' are carved out by fixing the 'other', the opposed fraction is contoured as motivated by fanaticism (cf. M 4: 20) and hatred. These "flots de haine déversés par les messaoudi et consorts" (C 28: 2) are said to be expressed in two directions – on the one hand against the islamist project, on the other hand as a republican self-hatred directed at their own "original" 'Islamic-Algerian' cultural background. The representation of the 'Islamic-Algerian' is thus again attributed to the islamist project.

> Nous avons vu à l'œuvre la haine qui anime ces éradicateurs tout-azimut [...] leurs attitudes hostiles et leurs manières ironiques (voire même im-polies). (C 26: 8)

> [T]hose in power are nothing more than a regionally affiliated, culturally self-hating elite that cares little for the ethical, moral, and civilisational dimensions of Islam. (AS 22)

Particularly in this respect, the targeted group of secular intellectuals is perceived as the ones that promote French culture and continue a close affiliation to the former colonial power, "ces intellectuels [...] ont une grande admiration pour le colonisateur et une grande haine contre leur peuple et principalement ses valeurs" (M 4: 18). This hatred is analysed as being caused twofoldedly, firstly by an education based on a French cultural background, which is said to have always given an inimical portrait of Islam, and secondly by personal interests endangered by the realisation of multipartism (cf. M 9: 62). The motivation of the *éradicateurs'* articulations of such hatred of everything Islamic leads them – according to the islamist discourses – not only to denigrate the islamist project, but also to call for the physical destruction of their adversaries. Due to this leap from verbal denigration to the call for physical extinction, the group of francophone intellectuals is ridden of any legitimacy and of their status as intellectuals. "Mais, de là à insulter, dire des mensonges sur les autres, et à appeler à leur éradications c'est se démarquer définitivement du statut d'intellectuel." (M 4: 18) They are neither suited to be called what they are called nor to be awarded the authority as intellectuals that they are awarded, "it is no use listening".

These exclusivist islamist rhetorics establish firm categories of what is described by an 'Islamic-Algerian' identity and what is to be considered foreign to it. Along those lines they demarcate the islamist project, presented in profound difference to the *éradicateurs*. As will be seen later, this second project, the republican one, offers an equally restricted, identitarian definition of "Algeria", and demarcates it from the *intégristes*. Both exclusivisms rest upon the conviction that the 'other' project must not be permitted any say in the future course of Algerian social, political and cultural affairs.

In the context of this exclusiveness, the present violence occuring in Algeria is described by islamist discourses as a "génocide, projet des éradicateurs" (M 6: 38).[150] At the same time, however, aggression is not disavowed in itself, but rather legitimised within a particular form. The Algerian political situation is said to have left no other alternative for the islamist opposition except the recourse to force. In the context of the violence exerted by the Algerian state, the islamist aggression and targeting of state institutions must be regarded as legitimate self-defense. "In the face of so much provocation, repression and abuse, the Islamic Front had no other alternative but to resort to the armed struggle to get rid of the military junta and to protect the people from its depredations." (EoT 2/93: 13) Furthermore, this "lutte du peuple Algérien" (M 7: 38) is explained as the Algerians' duty as Muslims to engage in a *jihad*[151] and oppose tyranny and oppression. The islamist self-defence against the ruling regime and its allies is depicted as limited to legitimate targets and to honorable ways of fighting in concordance with Islamic law. "[S]ans dépassement ni prétension outrancière l'AIS continue de mener le combat, pour le compte du peuple, dans le strict cadre stipulé par la loi islamique" (R 108: 2), since "le FIS est civilisé dans sa confrontation avec ses adversaries" (M 7: 44).[152]

---

[150] Along with the supposition of a profound hatred of the adversaries and the description of the present crisis as genocide, dubious comparisons are made with the Holocaust: "Comment le génocide d'Auschwitz, de Maïdanek et autres fut-il normalisé sinon par l'oeuvre de ceux qui banalisèrent le mépris et attisèrent la haine raciale et confessionnelle entre communautés. Cinquante année après ce drame humanitaire, l'histoire semble se répéter. Les victimes ont changé de faciès et de noms, mais elles sont toujours sémites." (C 22: 5) This comparison is made repeatedly in the journals, often directed at a Western audience, presumably in order to convince them of the gravity of the atrocities and their racist character. The disposition to such a comparison of different crimes and forms of violence corresponds to the mentioned emphasis on the relational character of the violence in Algeria – stressed as happening on both sides and therefore excusable – , and, to my mind, lies at the heart of this fierce conflict.

[151] The concept of *jihad* is explicated in this context at length as the Muslim's duty to strive for the good and just in all daily affairs, in order to differentiate it from its common representation as 'warfare in the name of God' (cf. EoT 3/2/94: 14).

[152] In this context, any contact or cooperation between the AIS and the GIA is denied and the GIA is disapproved of as much in regard to its methods as to its aims. "Quant à certains actes du violence et atrocités attribués au GIA contre les femmes et les civils, le Front Islamique du Salut ne peut en être le responsable pour les raisons évidentes à savoir qu'il n'y a aucun lien entre le FIS et le GIA." (M 7: 38)

The extreme violence of the present conflict is evidently a central concern in the journals' discourses. In accordance with the charge of (mis)representing anything Islamic in the media ("the so-called 'Islamophobia'" (E 21/3/97: 1)), the debates concentrate on two issues. Firstly, it is stressed that the violence does not occur unilaterally, but is suffered equally on both sides. The fact that it is given importance as a crime on one side, whilst not being mentioned at all or diminished in its criminal status on the other, is seen as *éradicateur* propaganda and largely supported by anti-Islamic/st media discourses.

> Revenons aux journalistes menacés, aggressés ou liquidés par l'un ou l'autre des protagonistes. Les comptes publiés par les médias éradicateurs laïco-communistes pour leur besoins de propagande et repris intégralement par la presse occidentale 'oublient' de tenir compte des journalistes du camp islamique, eux aussi menacés, aggressés et assassinés. (M 5: 26)

Secondly, the journals emphasise an "origin" of the violence, an initiation of the conflict by the state. This state aggression against the islamist movement is seen to be joined by the secularist tendencies, that pronounce themselves in favour of its destruction. Such an "original" violence has – according to the islamist discourses – only been responded to and countered by the islamist movement.

> Il est important de rappeler l'origine de cette violence politique afin de ne pas succomber à la propagande officielle du pouvoir en Algérie. En effet, cette violence politique, cette résistance populaire a vu le jour: après l'arret brutal du premier processus électoral libre de l'Algérie indépendante. (C 17: 7)

This implies that there was a determinable start to the violent confrontation, an origin, which – according to islamist discourses – must be located on the side of the state military forces and their allies. In this vein, the islamist discourses maintain a differentiation between state terrorism (cf. C 22: 4) and popular resistance (cf. M 7: 38f), whereby the first has caused the latter and the denomination of both insinuates the illegitimacy of the former and the legitimacy of the latter.

> En fait c'est bien le terrorisme initial du pouvoir et de l'État qui, après avoir fermé toutes les portes à une opposition saine et pacifique, a engendré une opposition d'abord radicale, puis violente, et enfin armée, appelée 'terrorisme islamique' mais qui n'est en fait qu'un parfait état de légitime défense. (C 22: 4)

This reference to an "opposition saine" that was prevented from developing and the implicit pathologisation of its present form can equally be found in the portrayal of the opponents: "[O]n est tenté [face à l'attitude de Saadi] à croire que 'parmi ceux qui choisissent les science de l'âme comme métier, nombreux sont ceux qui présentent une *pathologie potentielle*" (M 4: 23, my emphasis).[153] This pathologisation of the 'other' places it outside of liveable normality. By representing the 'other' as being in a state of "affolement et désordre" (M 4: 23) or setting it off from the normal (cf. R 41: 4) it is placed outside of the (aspired) normality, "no use listening to" (AS 19). This rhetoric turn provides the ground precisely for the portrayal of the 'other' as mad, irrational, and subsequently as fanatic and hateful – or follows from it, who is to decide(?).

This pathologisation works on both sides: "The pathological illness of the FIS is very deep and very serious" (Boudjedra 1993: 100, own translation).[154] Such parallelism of a denigrative 'othering' of the adversaries can equally be found in other characteristics employed by the republican discourses and will be explored in the following.

The republican discourse and its 'other': the intégristes[155]

> *[I]n my view: fundamentalism, like racism, is not an opinion, it's a crime.*
> (Messaoudi 1998: 135)

I will now juxtapose – as a *dépendant* to the islamist discourses – the articulations of a fraction of public discourse in Algeria maintaining an uncompromising stance towards islamist participation in political and social issues in Algeria. This fraction is less a fraction in the literal sense, but rather a conviction regarding the question of a possible solution to the current Algerian crisis which cuts through different social positions that would generally be identified as political agencies. It sees the building of an aspired to republican Algeria as intimately linked to an unyielding position towards islamist tendencies – uncompromising in regard to any negotiation with the latter and prefering their silencing to their participation – and can be found as much in discourses maintained by the military forces as well as by civilian agencies. This conviction can also be located in the political discourses of the RCD, which considers itself part of the democratic opposition – "the democrats who are leading the resistance in Algeria and who refuse any alliance with 'fascislamism'" (Messaoudi 1998: 141). The RCD, especially through some public Algerian voices that pronounce themselves in favour of its positions, presents itself as the protagonist of "le projet républicain incarné par le RCD" (Bulletin: 3). The party distances itself explicitly from the regime, which it renounces as having betrayed the Algerian people and the Algerian revolution, and it denounces the pact between the regime and the islamist movement (cf. Messaoudi 1998: 102). This unified aggression of both against the "truely democratic" forces is explained by their similarly totalitarian conceptions of power. "Tous deux [le pouvoir

---

[153] It has to be noted that Said Saadi works as a psychotherapist.

[154] Also: "Le RCD [...] a su faire émerger l'exigence d'une rupture *salutaire* avec le système qui a mené le pays à la faillite." (Bulletin: 2, my emphasis)

[155] Due to the fact that most of the following citations are in English, the French term *intégristes* itself will appear only rarely, the translation as "fundamentalist" being used instead. The French designation of the republican 'other' as *intégristes*, however, more richly alludes to the denigrating undertones of this 'othering' and is therefore adopted in this paper.

et les intégristes] donnent l'impression de se combattre. Mais fondamentalement tous deux épousent le même projet qui vise à imposer un système totalitaire broyeur d'intelligence." (Bulletin: 1) The writer Boudjedra – pronoucing himself in favour of republican interests and positions – does not spare the regime from criticism and sees the present crisis and especially the strength of the islamist tendencies in Algeria as the result of the regime's policies, which nurtured the latter for decades. The regime's alignment with islamist tendencies and its responsibility for their rise is expressed in the play of words in the title of his essay on islamism in Algeria. By entiteling it "FIS de la haine", he insinuates the FIS as sons (*fils*) of the hatred sowed by the political class of Algerian post-independence.

According to republican discourses, the present conflict results from this pact of the regime with the islamists against a liberal, republican Algeria. Both parties in this alignment are said to be predisposed by nature of their totalitarian conceptions of power to exert violence. Such totalitarian mindsets can only be countered by a truely democratic opening of the political sphere, and therefore the RCD offers the only alternative to the present situation. "Il reste le pôle démocratique et républicain dont le RCD est le chef de file. Il est déterminé à barrer la route au projet anti-national des intégristes et du pouvoir." (Bulletin: 2) This alternative takes shape in the republican project, which aims to "construire l'Algérie des patriotes et des républicains" (Bulletin: 2). Contrary to the otherwise stressed need for true democracy – contrary, if democracy is taken to be the struggle of controversial identifications and discourses –, "Algeria" is once again taken as the description of an identitarian whole and its future participants are designated by virtue of what they politically stand for. The RCD's project is not only presented as being radically different from the societal project aspired to by islamist tendencies, but also as decisively different from the ones proposed by the other political players. "Neither the social project espoused by the communists nor that of the F.F.S. was exactly the same as the project envisioned by the R.C.D [...] The major divergences arose, first of all, from differing interpretations of the phenomenon of fundamentalism." (Messaoudi 1998: 101) In respect to their position taken towards the islamist movement, all other opposed forces are designated as "fundamentalist negotiators" (Messaoudi 1998: 138). Parallel to the islamist discourse of the FIS, the republican rhetorics demand a real rupture with the present system, one which only the RCD – by virtue both of its denial of cooperation with the regime and its stern opposition to an islamist project – is able to provide. "La vraie rupture se fera avec Said Sadi et les démocrates authentiques, ceux qui n'ont rien volé au peuple algérien." (Boudjedra 1995: 25)

The RCD explains its demand for such a stern opposition to the islamist tendencies as mainly due to the islamists' totalitarian and anti-democratic conceptions of power and society. But this argument is overlapped by a rhetoric that depicts the *intégristes* as foreign and fanatical, a portrait which precisely feeds into the argument that islamist tendencies are anti-democratic and thus legitimately prevented from participating in Algerian political and social affairs. In the following I will focus on both of these overlapping dimensions – foreign and fanatic –, which match the axes of 'othering' discussed for islamist discourses.

The "Intégristes" – foreign to a 'Maghrebian-Algerian' identity

While in the islamist journals a common reference to the Islamic features of the identitarian category of "Algeria" was found, it is the 'Maghrebian', the mixture of Berber, Arab, African, and European influences that is stressed in the contouring of an Algerian identity in republican discourses (cf. Messaoudi 1998: 35). Although this divergence evokes different *images* of the same category, both employ a similar rhetoric in respect to their claim to exclusiveness. Just as the islamist discourses strive for an 'Islamic-Algerian' authenticity recovered from foreign influence, so do the republican discourses strive for an authentically 'Maghrebian-Algerian' at the cost of excluding certain other definitions of "Algeria" deviating from the 'Maghrebian-Algerian' – primarily the islamist in this case.

In their reference to such a 'Maghrebian-Algerian' identity and to the mixture of cultural influences that has nurtured this identity, the republican discourses do not reject as alien the traces of French cultural features, which this Algerian identity carries. Rather, those are seen as the imprints of a long duration of cultural domination and – in some important respects, as for example the republican political tradition – of cultural exchange that cannot be dissociated from Algerian identity any more. "[O]ur country was structured on French republicanism for a century, and our society was indelibly marked by that experience." (Messaoudi 1998: 142) In spite of this acceptance of French influence, an adherence to an Islamic tradition is nevertheless confirmed. This tradition is portrayed as authentically Maghrebian, in the sense that Berber traditions of worshipping marabouts intermingle with a more 'classical' Islamic tradition.

> We are at the heart of this brotherly, typically Algerian brand of Islam, which can be found in all regions of the country: it constitutes our true religious personality. [...T]oday it is the fundamentalists who have come to despise this form of Islam and want to eradicate it, on the pretext of 'returning to the basics.' (Messaoudi 1998: 11)

Such a conception of Islamic tradition is understood to be in opposition to the Islam promoted by the islamist movement, which is perceived as inspired by the Iranian revolution and Middle Eastern Muslim Brotherhoods (cf. Boudjedra 1992: 17). Particularly the enormous recruitment of Egyptian school teachers in the aftermath of national independence appears in this respect as an import of *foreign* conceptions of Islam. This import, paired with the regime's policies, has nurtured the rise of an islamist disposition among the Algerian population. "For the R.C.D., fundamentalism was not a product of Algerian society; rather, it was the monstrous offspring of a viola-

tion that the state institutions had committed within the school system, the state televi-
sions, the justice system, and so on." (Messaoudi 1998: 101)

Accordingly, the FIS is regarded as both religiously and culturally foreign to
'Maghrebian-Algerian' authenticity. The rigidity with which Iranian revolutionary Islam is associated and which the FIS is said to have imported into Algeria is perceived
as diametrically opposed to Algeria's gay and lively Islamic traditions (cf. Messaoudi
1998: 11f). The resulting distortion of these authentic traditions is perceived in the
changes in Algerian religious behaviour in favour of religious traditions from eastern
Muslim societies. Equally, the noticable change in attire during the last fifteen years –
"imported clothing from Arabia, Yemen or some miserable Sudan" (Boudjedra 1992:
68, own translation) – is seen as importing manners that have their cultural "origin" in
Middle Eastern Islamic countries (cf. Willis 1996). The replacement of the *haik*, the
Algerian headscarf worn by women, by the chador is thus seen as resulting from such
foreign influences.

Parallel to being disclaimed as foreign, the FIS is being disconnected from its elector-
ate by the portrayal of its electoral victory as resulting from mere frustration of the
Algerian population with the current regime, with the unfulfilled promises after independence, and with the deterioration of the standard of living during the 1980s. This
disposition of mere "protest-voters" to vote islamist instead of republican in order to
punish the regime is seen as the result of years of misguidance due to islamist influences in the educational system and the ranks of the regime itself.[156] "Les islamistes
aussi veulent se donner une image de respectabilité pour, espèrent-ils, tromper encore
une fois les électeurs." (Bulletin: 2) Accordingly, the islamist victory can only be explained (away) as betrayal of the Algerian people, taking advantage of a misguided
population, an attitude springing from the

> green fascism that only develops and moves through sadistic violence,
> barbarism and cruelty [...] the cowardly and pathological, that a minority
> wants to impose on a majority by trading upon the cowardice, the indif-
> ference or the equally naive and dramatic ignorance of most of the Alge-
> rians. (Boudjedra 1992: 65)

This portrait of the islamist disposition to betray and impose is taken further in
the second dimension of the establishment of an *intégriste* 'other' which I will discuss
in the following.

---

[156] Accordingly, the passing of the *code de la famille* (a legal code regulating and restricting women's
lives under the control of male guardianship, cf. Knauss 1987: 125f) in 1984 is seen not as an expression of the governments patriarchal and chauvinistic attitudes, but as a result of islamist influence.

The fanatics II – hating and killing

The most prevalent representation of islamists in the discourses of the RCD and its adherents is that of the bearded fanatic, willing to die and kill for the promise of martyrdom.[157] The notion of fanaticism is closely linked to the islamist totalitarian mindset. This perception of islamism as a "totalitarian religious vision" (Messaoudi 1998: 16) reflects in the French term *intégristes,* evoking a holistic, *intègre*[158] conception of society. Such totalitarianism is primarily noted in the islamist concern with women. Due to their holistic image of society, islamists target – according to republican discourses – all 'others' that could endanger these rigid conceptions of social and religious behaviour. They are said to perceive these 'others' primarily as women and intellectuals[159] and are described as "obsessed with the totalitarian will to domesticate women's sexuality absolutely, the better to control society" (Messaoudi 1998: 25). This portrayal is underscored by depicting the *intégristes* as fanatic "madmen of God" (Messaoudi 1998: 28) and as "égorgeurs" (Boudjedra 1992: 25). Both denominations render the islamist articulations irrational and thus the islamist movement neither suited to talk to nor to negotiate with. The frequent equation of islamist violence with the slitting of throats as the "preferred" method of assasination (*égorgeurs*) tops their violent disposition to an extent that insinuates a rituality in the killing. Thereby it is given an archaic flavour and feeds perfectly into the portrayal of irrationalism (Boudjedra 1992: 25).

Their irrationality is paired with the claim of islamist *hatred*, which according to republican discourses motivates their actions as much as it explains their attitudes.

> The F.I.S. hated them [the rai-singers, BMK] all [...] These singers expressed a popular Algerian culture that the islamists wanted to eradicate. (Messaoudi 1998: 104)

> [I]n addition, like all purifiers, they hate and persecute difference, which inevitably accompanies democracy. (Messaoudi 1998: 109)

---

[157] This portrayal of islamists as fanatics and adherent to a totalitarian logic matches the mainstream media coverage islamism receives in most Western societies (cf. Burgat 1996).

[158] Characteristically for the close reciprocity of the employed rhetorics of both 'sides', the term *intégriste* is equally used in islamist discourses for the RCD: "[C]e micro partie [RCD, BMK] marqué par son extranéité et son irrédentisme *intégriste* berbériste" (R 23/1/98: 3, my emphasis).

[159] These "groups" are said to endanger a totalitarian islamist conception by virtue of their *being* different – as women or as intellectuals, as thinkers. I find this portrayal problematic, because it essentialises both "groups" to an extent that leaves little room for the "difference" the republican articulations are concerned with. As women are implicitly perceived as different from their islamist representation by *nature* of being female, they are being essentialised as anti-islamist. I would hold against this that woman as category can be fitted to either imagination – islamist or republican –, but that the plurality of female identifications constantly escape both. Similarly, "the intellectual" is thought to oppose islamism by virtue of intellectual reflection, which is naturalised as *per se* secularist. The islamist discourses respond to this naturalisation with their primary concern with the quality of being intellectual and the disjunction of "intellectual" and "secularist", which has been discussed above.

In direct consequence of this portrayal of the islamist tendencies as hateful and archaically irrational, the republican discourses describe the present crisis as the outcome of islamist violence, exerted onesidedly and countered (or at best prevented) by the regime's forces. In the course of this argument, the islamist adversaries are essentialised as violent by nature, of being totalitarian. "I repeat that we are dealing with a brand of totalitarianism, and that violence is *consubstantial* with it." (Messaoudi 1998: 96, my emphasis) Violence is seen as identifiable with one group, "the group that was behind it [the violence, BMK]: the F.I.S." (Messaoudi 1998: 96). In this anticipation of islamist violence, which must be expected due to the perceived *nature* of islamism, state counter-violence is justifiable. "Je condamme moi aussi les excès et les bavures. Mais comment tenir des soldats qui savent que s'ils ne tuent pas les premiers ils seront égorgés ou émasculés?" (Boudjedra 1992: 25) Even if, at a first glance, Boudjedra condemns the violence exerted by the military forces, at a closer look it is only the violence against non-islamists that is addressed. "Ces actes [Mistreatment and executions of the parents of islamists by the military forces, BMK] sont intolerable[s]. Car de nombreux parents d'islamistes sont anti-islamistes." (25) This insinuates that, if the parents were adhered to islamist tendencies themselves, these acts would be tolerable.

Thus, this naming of the exerted violence and its implicit condemnation does not entail – parallel to the attitude towards violence in islamist discourses – a distancing from all exertion of violence. Rather a certain form of violence, namely the defence against a primary or "original" violence, identified as islamist, is justified. "Wherever it is, resistance has the same objective: to prevent pillaging, the kidnapping or raping of women, and assassinations, using weapons if necessary." (Messaoudi 1998: 143) In this context, the distinction between terrorism and resistance is introduced. According to the republican discourses, islamist violence springs from the islamists' terrorist disposition and is exerted upon an Algerian population. In opposition to such an "islamo-terrorisme" (Bulletin: 1) the republican cause and its adherents, caught between the two combattants of the same totalitarian mindset, represent a *resistance* to both the regime and the islamists. "[I]n Algeria, resistance is a popular reality that is directed as much against fundamentalism as it is against the regime." (Messaoudi 1998: 142) That same distinction between terrorism and resistance to terrorism had also been found in the islamist discourses, only with reversed addressees.

Conclusions

> *If politics is the moment of the decision – of judgement, of justice, of action,*
> *of antagonism, of beginning, of commitment, of conflict, of crisis*
> *- then how does one take a decision in an undecidable terrain*
>
> (Critchley 1992: 188)

What makes one particularly uneasy about the confrontation between the two factions whose discursive representations of their political adversaries have been discussed in this paper, is the *ambiguity* which was found in either position. The republicans strive for democratic pluralism, yet at the same time call upon the military regime to abrogate the first free elections after independence in order to save a democracy that was hardly existant. The islamists democratically win the elections and propose an Islamic state which claims to respect Algerians in their diversities. Yet at the same time they deny the francophone Algerians their "Algerianness", turning them into foreigners – "vivent l'exil culturel dans leur propre pays" (C 16: 4) – suited to be expelled to the country of their cultural "origin" (cf. C 16: 4). These ambiguities were found throughout the constructions of the political identities of both factions. Such a cutting *through* each of the various positions and not only *between* them makes it difficult to find a consistency in either position that would allow one to unproblematically side with one of them.

In addition to this ambiguity, it has been demonstrated how both factions reproach the other of similar faults, of being foreign to an authentic Algerian culture, of being fanatic and motivated by a hatred which lies at the heart of a onesided terrorist aggression against the people, against "true" Algeria. Throughout each of these processes of identification the 'other' is set off against the 'self' in narrow and *exclusivist* terms. It is precisely this exclusivist tendency in the Algerian struggle, nurtured and complemented by the repressive and identitarian political tradition of post-independence Algeria, that provides the arena for the clashes presently witnessed. The mere reference to an intimate relationship between 'self' and 'other' does thereby not result in a greater understanding of the "different", but leads in this particular political context to its demarcation and its exclusion from an aspired category (Algeria). Such mutual reduction to evil leaves little room for any consideration of the opponent's position, and the subsequent absolute rejection and assignment of guilt to the 'other' side was shown to result in a 'dialogue of the deaf'. As has been noted, a consensus is neither acceptable nor desirable to either discursive position, since each carries – metaphorically speaking – the full load of national fate on its shoulders.

Such a discursive situation, one which lacks a common point of reference from which a quarrel could be decided without overruling any one discourse or need, has been described by Lyotard's notion of *différend*. The *différend* precisely divulges the heterogeneity of discursive frames of reference and the absence of an *a priori* rule of judgement which, "for lack of a common idiom, makes consensus impossible" (Lyotard 1988: 55). Thus, a consensus in the sense of a mainly unquestioned political frame of reference can in this regard only be a hegemonically established and continually precarious one, one that rests upon a decision taken in an otherwise undecidable terrain (cf. Critchley 1992). As for the differing "genres" of discourse (with which the notion of *differend* is concerned), they can only be taken by the logic of their different rhetoric frames, which in their differences are irreconcilable. Such an understanding, however, does not fall prey to a relativism sometimes readily associated with such an argument. Rather, it intends to re-inscribe the role of politics in the sense that politics "[...] is the threat of the differend. It is not a genre, it is the multiplicity of genres, the diversity of ends, and par excellence the question of linkage" (Lyotard 1988: 138). Politics, therefore, would need to surpass the absolute imposition of one genre, and rather provide the arena for the linkage of their diversities.

In our case, however, the examined discourses intend to impose one genre, the one exclusively perceived as legitimate, "true", as almost naturally given, and set it off from their 'other', which is portrayed as illegitimate and detestably foreign. Their mutual attempts at providing the one and only solution to the Algerian national crisis via their one and only definition of an Algerian identity do precisely not acknowledge the political nature of a consensus, but are built on exclusivist rhetorics, which endow the identitarian features with a natural, self-understood flavour. The acknowledgement of politics as an arena of struggle over such definitions, however, implies an acceptance of both a plurality of social positions and the constant need to negotiate their articulations within a particular – in this case national – context.

For the discussed political identitarian discourses this would imply acceptance of a dialogue which disposes the very category of "Algeria" to persistent rearticulation, instead of struggling over the imposition of one exclusive definition. The reference to the notion of *differend* therefore does not imply a (relativistic) acceptance of the impasse in Algeria, as a dead end resulting necessarily from the lack of a meta-frame of reference. It rather calls for a re-conceptualisation of the very idea of a "solution", and thereby demands an understanding of the relation of 'self' and 'other' that outpasses the reduction of the 'other' to the 'same', and pays respect to the 'other' as 'other'. Such an understanding can be found in the work of the philosopher Emmanuel Levinas who provides an idea of a relation of 'self' and 'other' beyond their ontological distinction. An avoidance of such an ontological distinction which always inherently carries – taken to extremes – the possibilities for non-tolerance and exclusion pleads for an "ethics of deconstruction" (cf. Critchley 1992) that could live up to the indispensable relation of the 'self' with the 'other' and their mutual dependency, without reducing one to evil.

References

Abaza, Mona / Georg Stauth 1988. Occidental Reason, Orientalism, Islamic Fundamentalism: A Critique. In: *International Sociology*, 3/ 4: 343 - 364

Abaza, Mona 1991. The Discourse on Islamic Fundamentalism in the Middle East and Southeast Asia: A Critical Perspective. In: *Sojurn. Social Issues in Southeast Asia*, 6/2: 203 - 239

Abucar, Mohammed H. 1996. *The Post-colonial Society. The Algerian Struggle for Economic, Social and Political Change, 1965 – 1990*. New York: Peter Lang Publishing

Albrow, Martin 1996. *The Global Age*. Oxford: Polity Press

Appadurai, Arjun 1990. Disjuncture and Difference in the Global Cultural Economy. In: *Theory, Culture and Society*, 7: 295 – 310

Beck, Ulrich 1997. *Was ist Globalisierung? Irrtümer des Globalismus – Antworten auf Globalisierung*. Frankfurt am Main: Suhrkamp

Bensmaïa, Réda 1997. The Phantom Mediators. Reflections on the Nature of the Violence in Algeria. In: *diacritics*, 27/2: 85 - 97

Boudjedra, Rachid 1993. *Prinzip Haß. Pamphlet gegen den Fundamentalismus im Maghreb*. Mainz: Donata Kinzelbach

Boudjedra, Rachid 1995. Pas de compromis avec les égorgeurs! In: *Le nouvel Observateur*. Spécial Algérie: 25

Burgat, François 1993. *The Islamic Movement in North Africa*. Austin: University of Texas

Burgat, François 1996: *L'islamisme en face*. Paris: Editions La Découverte

Critchley, Simon 1992. *The Ethics of Deconstruction: Derrida and Levinas*. Oxford: Blackwell Publishers

Eade, John 1997. *Living the Global City. Globalisation as a Local Process*. London and New York: Routledge

Gafaiti, Hafid 1997. Between God and the President. Literature and Censorship in North Africa. In: *diacritics*, 27/2: 59 - 84

Grandguillaume, Gilbert 1997. Arabisation et Démagogie en Algérie. In: *Le Monde Diplomatique*, 2/97: 3

Hanoune, Louisa/Ghania Mouffok 1996. *Une Autre Voix pour l'Algérie.* Paris: Editions La Découverte

Kaiser, Birgit Mara 1998. *Identitätspolitik: Eine Analyse islamistischer Diskurse in Algerien.* unpublished diploma thesis, University of Bielefeld

Knauss, Peter R. 1987. *The Persistence of Patriarchy. Class, Gender and Ideology in Twentieth Century Algeria.* London and New York: Praeger

Korff, Rüdiger 1995. Globale Integration und lokale Fragmentierung. Das Konfliktpotential von Globalisierungsprozessen. *Working Paper 220.* Bielefeld: University of Bielefeld

Labat, Séverine 1995. *Les Islamistes Algériens. Entre les urnes et le maquis.* Paris: Seuil

Lazreg, Marnia 1994. *The Eloquence of Silence. Algerian Women in Question.* London and New York: Routledge

Lyotard, Jean-François 1988. *The Differend. Phrases in Dispute.* Minneapolis: University of Minnesota Press

Maghraoui, Abdeslam 1995. Algeria's Battle of Two Languages. In: *Middle East Report,* 192: 23 - 26

Mellah, Salima 1996. Algeriens Militärdemokratur. In: *Silsila. Zeitschrift gegen Rassismus und Imperialismus,* 6/7: 9 - 15

Messaoudi, Khalida 1998. *Unbowed: an Algerian woman confronts Islamic fundamentalism.* Philadelphia: University of Pennsylvania Press

Norval, Aletta J. 1995. Decolonisation, Demonisation and Difference: The Difficult Constitution of a Nation. In: *Philosophy and Social Criticism,* 21/3: 31 - 51

Norval, Aletta J. 1998. Rethinking Ethnicity. Identification, Hybridity and Democracy. In: Yeros, P. (ed.). *Ethnicity and Nationalism in Africa: Constructivist Reflections and Contemporary Politics.* Basingstoke: Macmillan Press

Roberts, Hugh 1984. The Politics of Algerian Socialism. In: Lawless, R. and A. M. Findlay (eds.). *North Africa: Contemporary politics and Economic Development.* New York: Saint Martin's Press: 5 - 49

Roberts, Hugh 1994. Algeria between Eradicators and Conciliators. In: *Middle East Report,* 189: 24 - 27

Ruedi, John 1992. *Modern Algeria. The Origins and Devolpment of a Nation.* Bloomington: Indiana University Press

Said, Edward W. 1995. *Orientalism. Western Conceptions of the Orient.* London: Penguin Books

Sayyid, Bobby S. 1997. *A Fundamental Fear. Eurocentrism and the Emergence of Islamism.* London and New York: Zed Books

Stauth, Georg 1996. Globalisation, Modernity and Islam. *Working Paper 249,* Bielefeld: University of Bielefeld

Turner, Bryan S. 1989. From Orientalism to Global Sociology. In: *Sociology,* 23/4: 629 - 638

Turner, Bryan S. 1994. *Orientalism, Postmodernism and Globalism.* London and New York: Routledge

Willis, Michael 1996. *The Islamist Challenge in Algeria. A Political History.* Reading: Ithaca Press

Materials

Bulletin du RCD immigration Belgique, Mai 1997, Trait d'Union.

Algeria Salvation

Al-Mounkidh

Al-Ribat

La Cause

Echoes of Truth

The Enlightenment

ABSTRACT

The prominent discussion in the social sciences and humanities around the construction of identities is taken as pivotal point in this article. In clear demarcation from a position which presumes an increase in tolerance of 'the other' due to intensified contact in (post)modern globalisation as well as in critical distance from a mere celebration of hybridity as such, this article not only stresses the discursive and thereby always only preliminarily closed character of any construction of identity, but it takes this argument further by outlining the necessity to account for the *political* dimension of such discursive constructions. Only by virtue of their mere constructedness, such identifications are no guarantor for the respect of otherness, but always run the risk of being established in exclusivist terms, disrespectful of the otherness they are always necessarily contaminated by. Focussing on two fiercely opposed political discourses in contemporary Algeria, one conducted by the islamist party FIS and one by the republican party RCD, both delineating themselves in such narrow and exclusivist terms, I wish to demonstrate the danger of discursive construction to violently denigrate the other. Against the background of a socio-discursive constellation such as the Algerian – which closely resembles that of the Lyotardian *différend* – this article wishes to take a stand by emphasizing the necessity of a particular *political* context for any identification, a context that accounts for the necessity to outpass the imposition of one side and affirms the very *struggle* over the disputed category – namely Algeria –, rendering any hegemonic sedimentation of one particular content of this category always preliminary and precarious.

COMBAT MODES, MIMESIS AND THE CULTIVATION OF HATRED:
REVENGE/COUNTER-REVENGE KILLINGS IN SRI LANKA[160]
Purnaka L. de Silva[161]

Introduction

In deeply polarised and brutalised societies like Sri Lanka, landscapes of violence are experiential spaces, where struggles for political power and/or control of resources and their distribution take place. 'Victory' in the eyes of the strategists seems to be the capture of the high ground in popular imagination and culture, in combination with spectacular successes in the macho field of combat-related political violence. And all means, fair and foul, are used in order to achieve these ends.

'Hatred' and 'revenge' are almost synonymous with many of the political murders that have taken place in contemporary Sri Lanka and Northern Ireland. However it must be stated from the outset that in terms of the sheer scale of these actions, these two case studies are incomparable, though they certainly share common elements. For example, in Sri Lanka, inter-ethnic and internecine revenge/counter-revenge killings run into tens of thousands, with some daily casualties in the hundreds – e.g. the intra-Sinhalese killings (1987 - 1990) between state forces and the Janatha Vimukthi Peramuna (JVP or People's Liberation Front).[162] The same cannot be said of events in Northern Ireland with a total of approximately 3,300 persons killed – despite the existence of similar intense animosities – i. e. of wanting to 'hurt the enemy' by any means possible. In Northern Ireland, the tit-for-tat killings in South Armagh in the early 1970s are considered an extreme case, where it is alleged that Loyalist paramilitaries from the Ulster Defence Association (UDA) killed two Catholic brothers. As an act of counter-revenge it is alleged that the Provisional Irish Republican Army (PIRA) or a cover organisation carried out the "White Cross Massacre" where ten protestant workers were taken off a bus and shot (Harnden 1999). Other instances of localised revenge/counter-revenge killings would be the "Murder Triangle" in East Tyrone and North Armagh between the Loyalist, Ulster Volunteer Force (UVF) and the PIRA, and

---

[160] I would like to thank Dr Patrick Maume and Dr Sydney Elliott for their helpful comments with regard to the case of Northern Ireland.

[161] The author lectures at the School of Politics in The Queen's University of Belfast.

[162] The JVP is a predominantly Sinhalese paramilitary organisation, which challenged the regime of the late President Premadasa for state power in a second abortive insurrection (1987-1990) in the southern, central, and western regions of Sri Lanka. The JVP was crushed militarily, with the majority (12 out of 13) of its politburo members being extra-judicially executed and an estimated 70,000-100,000 Sinhalese killed or missing, the vast majority of whom were civilians. During this period extra-judicial executions were carried out by death squads, which were affiliated to the then government of Sri Lanka. For more details concerning the JVP please refer to the works by: Alles (1990), Chandraprema (1991) and Gunaratna (1990). For a sympathetic account see Gunasekara (1998).

the "Murder Mile" in North Belfast (near Ardoyne and North-west Belfast) where 20 % of all killings in the 'troubles' took place.

In Sri Lanka, while revenge/counter-revenge killings are more numerous and widespread, in Northern Ireland they are far less numerous and tend to be more local-ised to areas where Catholics and Protestants live cheek by jowl – which is why spe-cific actions have survived in popular memory through lasting nicknames. In Sri Lanka, brutalisation of civil society has been to such an extent that the 'place-names' of such killings tend to fade with time. Unless, they are particularly gruesome and the body count high, or if there are well-known politicians allegedly involved. An example being the "Batalanda killings" where forty schoolboys were abducted and killed, in relation to which the current leader of the opposition Hon. Ranil Wickremasinghe (who was in government at the time of the event) appeared before the Batalanda Commission.

In this chapter, I focus on the 'meanings' attached to or derived from actions re-lated to 'hatred' and 'revenge' in locations of political violence. And in particular, I examine relations between 'hatred' and situated practices of 'revenge/counter-revenge' killings in Sri Lanka during the period 1980 to 2000. It is these situated practices of 'revenge/counter-revenge' killings that are compared occasionally with similar prac-tices in Northern Ireland. Such comparative illustrations are but the tip of an iceberg and all kinds of 'revenge/counter-revenge' killings continue to take place within po-litically charged and polarised contexts of identity and resource-based conflicts in deeply divided societies. Here, I examine such actions in light of *internecine* warfare in particular (e.g. intra-ethnic or group strife) – a common feature of many revolution-ary and/or nationalist struggles. Ironically enough, such warfare is carried out more fiercely in many cases, than the 'business' of the nationalist war or revolution.

In fact in the Sri Lankan case, up till maybe the big set piece battles of the late 1990s, more Tamil paramilitaries and their civilian sympathisers or suspected support-ers have been killed or tortured and/or incarcerated by members of rival organisations during internecine warfare.[163] And in this context, male and female paramilitaries (which would include teenagers and children) belonging to the Liberation Tamil Ti-gers of Tamil Eelam (LTTE – the cadres of which are referred to as 'Tamil Tigers' or 'Tigers') remain unsurpassed as 'successful practitioners'. Conversely, more Sinhalese (civilians, paramilitaries and soldiers) were killed in the violent intra-Sinhalese power struggle between the JVP and armed units of the government of Sri Lanka (1987 - 1990), and it is the revenge/counter-revenge killings arising out of these two theatres of conflict, which warrant closer scrutiny. In this chapter, due to restrictions on length, I focus mainly on the ongoing separatist war being waged by the LTTE. Rather than simply listing a gory catalogue of tit-for-tat killings for the record (which one can find

---

[163] For more details read my article: "The Growth of Tamil Paramilitary Nationalisms: Sinhala Chau-vinism and Tamil Responses" in Gamage and Watson (1999).

for example in most Amnesty International or Human Rights Watch publications), I examine the process of cultivating hatred in a deeply divided society – in accordance with the theme of this volume. I identify agents of political violence here as being all members of anti-government (or pro-government) paramilitary organisations, as well as members of death squads and army, navy, airforce and police units, that are linked overtly or covertly to the state apparatus.

Ironically enough, the conflicts in Sri Lanka are portrayed on many an occasion in academic texts and the media, as simply being 'an ethnic conflict' between Sinhalese and Tamils. Similarly, the conflicts in Northern Ireland are portrayed often enough as being 'sectarian' – i. e. between Protestants and Catholics. Such oversimplifications ignore much of the complexities and ground realities of each situation. In the Sri Lankan case, this point is highlighted by the facts that:

1. There have been *two* major theatres of conflict in Sri Lanka (one ongoing in the predominantly Tamil speaking areas of the north and east and the other in the Sinhala majority areas of the southern, central and western provinces).

2. Not to mention all the *internecine* and *intra-ethnic* bloodletting.

Similarly in the Northern Ireland case, revenge/counter-revenge killings involve more than sectarian violence between Republican and Loyalist paramilitaries. A recent spate of tit-for-tat killings was between Loyalist paramilitary groups (1999 - 2000) – i. e. between the Loyalist Volunteer Force (LVF) and the UVF – which in the past used to be one organisation. Apparently these revenge/counter-revenge killings are part of staking out territory showing that 'territory can be defended' to avoid disintegration and allegedly involve non-political considerations, such as control of lucrative underworld networks and personal vendettas. These situated practices of political violence illustrate some of the complexities of the Northern Irish context. Similarly, there have been low-scale internecine clashes in the past between the PIRA and other Republican paramilitary groups like the Irish National Liberation Army (INLA). Bitter feuds among various INLA factions in the 1980s led the organisation to tear itself to shreds. The 'spill-over' effect of what has been a low-level index of violence involves killings that are simply *personal* as exemplified by one of the "Shankill Butchers," Bates. Other factors that also need to be considered are intra-organisational killings and punishment beatings of 'criminal elements' within the support communities of the respective paramilitary groups. Defections from the PIRA to splinter groups such as the Continuity IRA and the Real IRA (which are opposed to the now near-paralysed Good Friday Agreement of 1998)[164] and an alleged urban (e.g. Belfast) versus rural (e.g. South Armagh) split are important factors that further complicate the 'sectarian divide'. Nevertheless, it must be pointed out that as opposed to Sri Lanka, internal constraints in

---

[164] For the behind-the-scenes story of the negotiations that culminated in the signing of the Northern Ireland Peace Accord, which is written by the American Senator who served as independent Chairman of the talks, see Mitchell (1999).

the form of public pressure and other external factors restrict the extent to which re-
venge/counter-revenge killings can take place in Northern Ireland. For example, the
LVF scaled-down its attacks on Catholics in early 1998, leading to the declaration of a
cease-fire, which involved a combination of 'people-pressure' from within the Protestant community, alleged drug-dealing interests and the assassination of the hard-line
Billy Wright (also known as the "King Rat"). However, before I delve into the nitty-
gritty of who killed whom and why, where, how, when, etc., I clarify certain issues of
significance, that provide an overview of the 'troubles' in Sri Lanka.

Theoretical, Conceptual and Strategic Considerations

> [W]e may say that anger is an emotion, whereas hatred must be classified
> as a sentiment – an enduring organisation of aggressive impulses toward
> a person or toward a class of persons. Since it is composed of habitual
> bitter feeling and accusatory thought, it constitutes a stubborn structure
> in the mental-emotional life of the individual. By its very nature hatred is
> extropunitive, which means that the hater is sure that the fault lies in the
> object of his [*sic*] hate (Allport 1992: 31).

The concept of *hatred* and other related concepts like anger, fear, aggression,
terror and of course violence, are inherently problematic owing to their vagueness and
manifold meanings. However at the popular level, given their felt or emotive content
these concepts can be cultivated and channelled, especially through imagery of enemy
stereotypes and revenge/counter-revenge mentalities. The degrees or levels to which
emotive sentiments are felt in the "organisation of aggressive impulses" (Ibid), vary in
degree, intensity and meaning, and from individual to individual in any given context.
Nevertheless, when it comes to the question of organised political violence, hatred and
revenge complement each other and become useful tools in cultivating homogeneous,
mono narratives.

From a theoretical standpoint – while expressing dissatisfaction with problems
of inconsistency, definitions raised by relativity, ambiguity and diversity of meanings
– researchers should exercise caution when examining concepts like hatred or revenge.
The very inconclusiveness surrounding feelings, thoughts and conduct related to hatred or revenge, should serve to discourage premature and simplistic verdicts. Nevertheless in this chapter, for the sake of discussion, I use the outline presented by Gordon
W. Allport as a 'sounding board'.

My focus here is confined to *political violence* and its heterogeneous phenomena, which involve the performance (including theatrical and spectacular elements) of
violence as an explicit political tool (e.g. in order to communicate and carry out strategic and/or tactical manoeuvres). However, even in this context, it is difficult to avoid
inconsistent and misleading terms. Therefore, while expressing the need for a consistent and widely accepted analytic categorisation, the following tentative, working definition of political violence is presented. I define political violence as *a process where*

the deliberate use and/or the threat of force is carried out, with an intention to cause death, and/or injury, and/or destruction of person(s), property and interests, by organised groups or members of such entities, to their perceived political enemies. The term 'injury' (used in the definition), refers both to physical 'damage' or 'hurt' as well as to psychological 'trauma' (e.g. PTSD or post-traumatic stress disorder – which is brought about as a result of torture, and/or participation in/exposure to, 'violent' actions).[165] Such collective actions of violence within polities, involve electoral violence, riots, rebellions, civil wars, and the like (cf. Rule 1988:xi and 11).

My definition of political violence is designed to cover *politically motivated, violent acts carried out by members of judicially accountable (i. e. regular armed forces and police) and extra-judicial (i. e. death squads and irregulars) forces loyal to the state, private armies run by politicians, as well as those by anti-state (and pro-state) paramilitary groups, in the manoeuvrings for power.* Here, the use of weapons adds an 'armed' component to such acts. Political violence therefore, is always aimed to the *detriment* and *coercion* of perceived enemies. Furthermore, the objectives of political violence are *political* (insofar as they pertain to policies and intrigues of state and anti-state actors), and are continuations of political affairs by means other than dialogue, debate, discussion, accommodation and compromise. This definition of political violence also covers phenomena of *ethnic riots* and *political rape* (as observed for example in Bosnia-Hercegovina,[166] Bangladesh during the war of liberation and Pakistan, where female members of families belonging to perceived political opponents have been systematically raped). In the case of Sri Lanka, statistics on political rape have not been compiled in any systematic manner (either on a regional or island wide basis), which does not mean that it does not happen, though it is certainly not a systematic policy.

In addition, I reiterate that hatred and revenge are but two considerations, that need to be taken into account when analysing a problem as complex as political violence. The field of popular culture in particular remains a contentious battleground. 'Cultural constructions' of political violence for example, involve cognitive, mythical and popular aspects of physical practices. 'Cultural constructions' of political violence

---

[165] Buss notes that there are problems in defining harm, which includes both physical and psychological harm (Buss 1971: 7-18). These problems apply in turn to the element of 'injury', which in this paper refers to physical damage or hurt as well as psychological trauma. One of the methods of assuaging the problems that arise from such a definition as the one used in this chapter is to apply a legally accepted definition of the terms, 'physical damage' or 'hurt' and 'psychological trauma'. What is sorely needed is an international covenant that clearly defines such terms, especially in the context of civil wars.

[166] In this respect, the case of Bosnia-Hercegovina is unprecedented, where more than 20,000 Muslim women are reported to have been systematically subjected to political rape by Serbian soldiers and irregulars up to 1993 (Conclusion of a series of BBC World Service Radio Reports, on the findings of a Special Human Rights Commission, assigned to investigate the issue of political rape in Bosnia-Hercegovina). Also see the article by Silva Meznaric (1994) on 'Gender as an Ethno-Marker: Rape, War, and Identity Politics in Former Yugoslavia' in a volume edited by Valentine Moghadam.

also include, to a large part, violence perpetrated against the body and its demonstration. For a detailed theoretical analysis and discussion of political violence and its cultural constructions in relation to the problematic of representation and narrative 'realities' in times of war see de Silva (forthcoming). Through demonstration and display of 'end results' (i. e. through vivid imagery of real events and/or narratives of such events), cultural constructions of political violence are given meaning. Mutilation and dismemberment of the living and dead, torture, burning, beating, rape, and disappearance, are all situated practices of violence that involve the body in one way or another. Torture in particular, is a system of persecution that deploys organised violence as a tactical measure to extract truth and submission[167] (de Silva 1993).

The body is a site of violence – where political power is exercised through hegemony and contested through resistance. The living body can therefore be perceived as an 'animated text' where,

> [P]olitical power increasingly becomes a matter of regimenting the circulation of bodies in time and space in a manner analogous to the circulation of things. Power, as Foucault has amply documented, becomes spatialised. It is contingent on the command of space and the command of those entities that move within politically marked spaces. The body becomes a unit of spatial power, and the distribution of these units in space constructs sites of domination (Feldman 1991: 8).

To illustrate his point Feldman describes the German Jew who is paraded by the Nazis with a placard around his neck which reads: "I am a Jew but I have no complaints against the Nazis" (Ibid: 7). In Sri Lanka, Tamil paramilitaries, as well as the JVP and armed forces of the state, have used similar imagery to terrorise opponents and convey political threats or illustrate punishment through the medium of fear. 'Lamp-posting' (i. e. the tying of executed victims to lampposts with an accompanying placard) is an extreme variant, first practised by Tamil paramilitaries. 'Eternal fires' were another gruesome practice adopted by government affiliated death squads, where corpses of indiscriminately slaughtered "students, dissident monks, young men, intellectuals, human rights monitors, and the families of JVP suspects and sympathisers" (McGowan 1993: 374) were found smouldering in 'landmine' craters (that had been exploded by the JVP) or in prominently-located public spaces.

---

[167] As far as the government of Sri Lanka is concerned, torture is prohibited by Article 11 of the 1978 Constitution, the Penal Code and the Police Ordinance. In spite of these considerable legal safeguards, torture has been used and continues to be used by the country's armed forces and police with impunity. And as far as anti-state (and pro-state) paramilitaries are concerned, there is absolutely no convention (local or international) that prohibits the use of torture and or summary executions. This illustrates glaring deficiencies in the implementation of existing constitutional and legal safeguards. There is a dire need for an international covenant, that binds anti-state or pro-state paramilitary forces and auxiliary units to legally prescribed 'acceptable standards of behavior during armed conflict and civil war'. Failure to comply with such a covenant should be met with immediate, punitive sanctions.

In other words, the living and dead bodies that continue to litter the landscapes of political violence in Sri Lanka, are circulated as political statements. They are also intended in particular instances to facilitate the process of cultivating hatred and promoting revenge/counter-revenge actions, thereby effectively leaving the protagonists firmly locked in the 'combat mode' (de Silva 1995 a). Mimesis or 'creative imitation' in these rather gruesome revenge/counter-revenge actions plays its own part in the deadly dynamic (de Silva forthcoming). Two examples of many from Sri Lanka's recent past would include actions carried out by the LTTE, a paramilitary organisation that actively engages in the cultivation of hatred in Sri Lanka.

1. The massacre of 42 Sinhalese civilians (men, women and children) and the burning of their tiny fishing village of Kallawara in the east of the country. This is the first such large-scale action carried out against civilians since the October 1992 massacre of 146 Muslims in Palliyagodella, also allegedly by the LTTE.

2. The assassination of the chief Buddhist priest of Dimbulagala, Venerable Kithalagama Siri Seelalankara around the end of May 1995. He was especially popular among Sinhalese inhabitants along the border areas between Tamil and Sinhala domains in the East and had been a long-term, vocal critic of the LTTE.

It is very probable that the massacre of Sinhalese civilians in Kallawara and the killing of a very popular Buddhist priest were aimed at provoking a Sinhalese (Buddhist) majority backlash against the minority Tamils. Failing to obtain the necessary result – i. e. a Sinhalese-backlash since these and similar attacks – more recently, the LTTE has changed tactics and raised the stakes by carrying out spectacular operations against high-profile targets. There are two types of targets that have been selected.

1. Firstly, the commando-style paramilitary attacks by the LTTE on 'prestige targets' in Colombo with the attack on the Kolonnawa Oil Refinery on 20th October 1995 and the suicide-truck-bombing of the Central Bank on 31st January 1996, along with the World Trade Centre truck-bombing on 15th October 1997. These attacks should be considered as being primarily targeted against economic infrastructure, which have added political significance due to their prestige, location and high-visibility. The name of the game here is to advertise the LTTE's capabilities as a formidable adversary, while at the same time bolstering any sign of flagging support as a result of war-weariness and combat fatigue. Secondly, there are a number of 'very high-profile targets' that have been selected between January 1998 and March 2000, which are of even greater significance – particularly with regard to the cultivation of hatred – and would include:

• The *Dalada Maligawa* (The 'Temple of the Tooth Relic' in Kandy, one of the most sacred of sites for Sinhalese Buddhists) suicide-truck-bombing on 25th January 1998 – which left the temple complex needing structural repairs and leaving 11 dead and 20 injured.

• The attempted assassination of Sri Lankan President, Ms. Chandrika Bandaranaike Kumaratunga by an LTTE woman suicide-bomber 3 days before the Presidential elections on 18th of December 1999, at a public-rally in Colombo Town Hall. She
was re-elected for a second term having narrowly escaped death and losing her right
eye in the attack.

• The botched suicide-bomb attack on the government building in the heart of
Colombo by another LTTE woman suicide-bomber, shortly thereafter on 5th January
2000. Here the intended-target was allegedly the octogenarian Prime Minister Ms.
Sirimavo Dias Bandaranaike (the world's first woman Prime Minister, who performs a
largely ceremonial role given her ill health, and who happens to be the President's
mother).

The failed ambush of a high-level ministerial motorcade en route from the Parliamentary - complex in downtown Colombo on 10th of March 2000 by an 8 to 10
strong paramilitary commando unit of LTTE suicide-bombers. To give a sense of
scale: according to reports, in this attack 5 suicide-bombers blew themselves up and 3
were shot dead, while 8 policemen and 20 civilians caught up in the rush hour traffic
were killed and 74 injured. Apparently the Sri Lankan security forces recovered from
the scene: 1 GPMG, 1 MPMG, 3 (or 5) T-56 assault rifles (a Chinese derivative of the
ubiquitous AK47), 2 (or 5) disposable RPGs, 3 grenades and 1 suicide jacket worn by
one of the LTTE paramilitaries who was shot dead.

Apart from these high-profile spectacular attacks, which attract widespread media attention locally and internally, the LTTE has also carried out a series of bus-
bombings against civilians in the Sinhalese-majority areas (between March 1998 and
February 2000).[168] These actions are aimed at maintaining a constant level of attrition
– a mechanism for the cultivation of hatred and sharpening ethnic divisions in a deeply
divided society. It can therefore be argued, that the cumulative whole of these well-
planned and co-ordinated actions are certainly orchestrated by the LTTE, towards the
cultivation of hatred to the point of bringing about a Sinhala-backlash (majority ethnic
group) against Tamil civilians (minority ethnic group) living in Colombo. Such an
event, would in the opinion of LTTE strategic planners:

1. Create enough negative publicity for the Sri Lankan government and the Sinhalese so that it would hinder bilateral/multilateral relations and the maintenance of
good diplomatic ties with the international community and donor states – particularly
with Western states that are keen on the promotion of democracy.

---

[168] Bus bombings like the one in March 1998 with 30 dead and 256 injured were occasional attacks. In
February 2000 however, indicating a change in tactics of the LTTE, there were six bus bombings with:
3 wounded in Colombo; 20 wounded in Kurunegala (70km north-east of Colombo); 10 injured in Ka-
dawatte (15km from Colombo); 35 wounded between Bibile and Moneragala; 3 killed and 43 injured
in two separate incidents in Colombo.

2. It would also create a different dynamic, where albeit in negative fashion, the LTTE's pariah status internationally as a blacklisted terrorist organisation (as per the US State Department) could be reviewed.

3. Thirdly and *most importantly*, a Sinhala-backlash against Tamils living in southern, central and western Sri Lanka would multiply support for the LTTE through increased Tamil chauvinist nationalism, obviously in fierce opposition and hatred towards Sinhalese chauvinism (that would be illustrated by the Sinhala-backlash). Such a dynamic would enable the LTTE, through an induction of new resources – both human and material – to continue along its well-honed militarist strategy. It would also weaken any alternative to the LTTE's hegemonic grip over the Tamil polity, given the supreme leader Velupillai Prabhakaran's (also spelt as 'Pirabakaran') obsessive antagonism towards any challenge to his authority – whether it be from within or without, however big or small. A fact, that is borne out by the substantial number of Tamil politicians and paramilitaries (anti-LTTE as well as LTTE) who have paid the ultimate penalty.

4. Last but not least, all types of spectacular attacks are a means of fuelling the LTTE's military campaign. Particularly by showing off the capabilities of its paramilitaries to the organisation's cadres and support base within the country, and more importantly to the Tamil Diaspora in Western Europe, North America and Australasia. This stratagem is a little like that of a trader 'rolling' his/her money in order to keep the trading concern on a 'good enough' operational footing, that is capable of convincing the customers that it remains a safe investment despite the fluctuations of the market. In other words, the LTTE has invested *all of its albeit finite resources and efforts* in convincing the Tamil polity and the government of Sri Lanka of its *total hegemony* and in showing that "there is only one show in town". Meaning that supporting the LTTE is the best bet for the Tamil polity, given that the path to the future is only via the fulfilment of the organisation's separatist-nationalist aims and objectives. Further, as far as the government of Sri Lanka is concerned, it is only by seriously engaging *with* the LTTE and providing the organisation and its leader with "satisfaction" that the future can be made secure. Thereby, this gambit of the 'rolling' metaphor is also a tactical means of undermining opposition to the LTTE – both from within the Tamil polity and from without.

History as memory

On Saturday, July 23, 1983 there was an ambush on the Palaly road in the northern peninsula town of Thirunelveli, carried out by paramilitaries of the LTTE. Thirunelveli is on the Jaffna peninsula, in the far north of Sri Lanka. And the target was a detachment of Sinhalese soldiers travelling by truck, who belonged to the First Battalion of the Sri Lanka Light Infantry (SLLI) regiment of the Sri Lanka Army (SLA). The overwhelming majority of the members of the government of Sri Lanka's security forces (i. e. the Army, Navy, Air Force, Police, and Homeguards) are Sinhalese. Thirteen soldiers died on that day when an improvised explosive device (IED) was set off.

Despite the subsequent casualties incurred by the Sri Lankan armed services (some of which have run into the thousands in recent years), this particular ambush has an important place in the history of Sri Lanka's political violence. It set the stage, in a manner of speaking, for the worst inter-ethnic riots ever witnessed. Stories and narratives in the form of rumours play a large part in the normative spread of violence at the level of popular culture. And an infamous example of its effects are the events that took place in the days prior to and on 'Black Friday' (the 29th of July 1983). These events, referred to as inter-ethnic 'riots', are situated practices of political violence. Anthony Giddens defines a riot as "an outbreak of illegal violence, directed against persons, property or both" Giddens 1991: 748). The 'riots' of July 1983 provided a justification at the time, for Sinhalese mobs to wreak havoc on their Tamil fellow-citizens, some of which I witnessed firsthand (managing to get Tamil office-colleagues to secure lodgings after running the gauntlet of rampaging mobs). Given the scale of violence and the lack of any law enforcement (confirmed by a senior Tamil police officer who said that he had instructions from the 'top' to confine himself to the premises of his police station), it is clear that there was a tacit, though never adequately proved government hand in giving the 'go ahead'. The 'mob violence' had an organised component reported by many witnesses. In my area, local members of the ruling United National Party (UNP) led the mob with a voters list, identifying and attacking practically every Tamil house in the neighbourhood. In some rare cases, the houses of the friends of the rioters were left untouched. The political fallout of this catastrophic phenomenon was that it swelled the ranks of the Tamil paramilitary organisations. The new recruits came from among the thousands of alienated and vengeful Tamil youths, who had lost family, friends, property, jobs and schools (many books were burned during the rioting), and become internally displaced persons (IDPs) in the space of a week and subsequently many becoming refugees in southern India. In the aftermath of the riots, recruiting was at its height in the refugee camps in the southern Indian state of Tamil Nadu, thus substantially strengthening the paramilitary groups.

At a more theoretical level, it can be observed that in such situations of conflict, essentialised popular cultural images and stereotypes are intertwined with situated practices of political violence. Here, violent actions of state security forces and para-militaries have an important impact on the local population, which in turn can be channelled into popular violence, as demonstrated by the inter-ethnic 'riots' of 1983. Situated practices of political violence also involve an *interaction* between the major combatants, which involves *mimesis*. In this context Allan Feldman makes an astute observation on the mimesis of the British state's militarism by paramilitary forces in Northern Ireland.

> The emergence of local paramilitary forces presupposed the fragmenta-
> tion, inversion, and internalisation of the social rhetoric of populist ag-
> gression historically promoted and centralised by the state. These groups
> emulated the state's fusion of repressive and ideological apparatuses and
> implemented programs of somatic regimentation and aggression antici-
> pated by state militarism. Today the mimesis between paramilitary
> groups and the state is still evident, though it has shifted to the parami-
> tary emulation of the manner in which violence is bureaucratised and ra-
> tionalised by the state's counterinsurgency apparatus (Feldman 1991:
> 41).

This observation is relevant to the case of Sri Lanka as well. In the early days (1972 - 73) of the rebellion in the north and east (during the embryo stage of the pre-sent day Tamil paramilitary groups), the main sources of *mimesis* for paramilitaries was the Sri Lankan police, American action movies and the failed JVP insurrection of 1971. By mimesis I do not mean, a mere aping (i. e. as a copy, reflection, replica or however else one might wish to refer to it) of 'militarisms' (represented by the state, foreign movie moguls or the JVP). Instead, I mean a *reproduction which is adapted to suit the particularistic needs* of the paramilitaries, what Ricoeur calls "creative imita-tion" (Ricoeur 1991: 138 - 139). This 'creative imitation' enabled the paramilitaries, who were in the process of organising and gaining knowledge about weaponry, tactics and strategies, to develop their capabilities qualitatively with each new confrontation with the police, as time went by. While JVP experiences, learned through narratives and discussions with JVP prisoners when held in custody together in Jaffna prison (in the early 1970s), brought new ideas of confronting and resisting the hegemony of state forces, it had only a marginal effect. The same applies to action movies, which also contributed only to the background experiences of early Tamil paramilitaries. Con-frontations with and brutal 'encounters' at the hands of the Criminal Investigation De-partment (CID) of the police, were much more important in their mimetic 'educational process', which brutalised and strengthened the young paramilitaries and their organi-sations at a tactical level. The Bastianpillai murder was also an important milestone and turning point in this process. This police officer of Tamil ethnic background, with an infamous reputation among the paramilitaries, was ambushed and murdered. This provided a symbolic victory and an example of success, at a time when the paramilitaries numbered only a handful, were relatively unknown and even unpopular. This 'un-popularity' led them to be derogatorily referred to at times as "the boys". A nickname and image which stuck for a long time. Later it turned into (our) "boys". The Bastian-pillai killing also served as an example to other Tamils who 'collaborated' with the police (and later army) in the government's crackdown on paramilitaries.

Justification

The LTTE's main argument/justification for pursuing its military strategy has been:

The *Sinhalese* government would never give us a just settlement, even if they [the current regime led by President Ms. Chandrika Bandaranaike Kumaratunga] would wish to, the *Sinhalese* opposition [led by Mr Ranil Wickremasinghe] would never permit a just settlement. And even if both the *Sinhalese* government and the opposition would wish to provide a just settlement, the *Sinhalese* Buddhist *Mahasangha*[169] would block such a move, as has been the case historically. **Therefore, we have but no other option** than to gain the undeniable rights of the *Thamil makkal* [Tamil people] by force of arms – the only message that is understood loud and clear – where all means justify the ends [which is the separate state of *Thamil* Eelam][170] – (Personal interview, March 2000).

How is it possible for cadres of the LTTE to carry out all types of actions as a means to an end without due regard to moral values and human considerations? This by-passing of traditional value systems and the creation of 'new morals' is the other side of the coin, which many analysts tend to overlook. The LTTE, which is a very successful organisation by its own grim standards, produces battle-hardened cadres who have been trained in carrying out the most desperate of actions, including the phenomenon of suicide-bombing. To achieve this level of dedication to a cause cer-tainly needs different stimuli. While actions of Sri Lankan armed service units play an important contributing role, at an immediate level on the battlefield, in maintaining the level of attrition, there are other factors which are carefully crafted in the cultivation of hatred for 'enemies' of the LTTE.

---

[169] The *Mahasangha* is the main order of Theravada Buddhist monks in Sri Lanka, which is made up of two Chapters, namely, Malwatte and Asgiriya, which are led by two Mahanayakas or Chief Priests.

[170] Interestingly enough, the word *Eelam* in Tamil is a reference to Ceylon. However in its contempo-rary, post-Indo-Sri Lanka Peace Accord usage (post-1987), it refers to an independent, sovereign and exclusively *Tamil* state of Eelam, that Tamil separatist-nationalist paramilitaries from the LTTE and their supporters (at times referred to as Eelamists) want to establish in north and east Sri Lanka. The LTTE's conceptualisation of "*Thamil Eelam*" (Tamil Eelam) is by definition chauvinist. While the LTTE continues to maintain its separatist stance, other erstwhile 'Eelamists' from rival paramilitary groups, have softened their hard-line position in order to pursue more Federalist options of coexistence vis-à-vis the hegemonic, (majority) Sinhalese social formation. In exchange, the government of Sri Lanka has made a commitment to devolve powers and resources, which is in the process of being fac-tored into an amended constitution.

The historical memory of the deep injustice of the anti-Tamil riots of 1983 forms one of the primary bases of hatred that many members of the LTTE have for the Sinhalese. These riots, which were carried out during President J.R. Jayawardene's regime against non-combatant Tamil civilians by Sinhalese mobs, while the armed service and police stood idly by or gave support, is frozen in time and used in the indoctrination of new cadres. Memories of previous anti-Tamil riots (1956, 1958, 1977 and 1978) further reinforce this one-sided stereotypical image of the Sinhalese state and people. These memories are combined with other injustices suffered by 'the Tamil people', such as university entrance requirements where Tamil students had to score higher grades than their Sinhalese counterparts, lack of sufficient employment opportunities in the government, most official correspondence with Tamil citizens being in the Sinhala language, etc. Once this base is laid, it is added to by shared individual experiential knowledge of the cadres (including that of their immediate family and friends) during the combat-training period, which could range from detention by Sri Lankan armed services to torture, rape, murder and destruction of property. The cultivation of hatred from within, which together with good organisational and logistical networks, has provided the LTTE with an added edge and momentum in the field of warfare. Generalised ethnic hatred and Tamil chauvinism as described in this context are a product of memory as history involving anti-Tamil riots, discrimination on ethnic grounds, Sinhalese chauvinism and the presence/conduct of the Sri Lankan armed services on the battlefield. Further validating the LTTE's main argument/justification, are public statements made by influential sections of Sinhalese civil society, in particular those made by the *Mahasangha*.

Let us briefly examine each of the recent high-profile cases aimed at provoking a Sinhalese-backlash that have been categorised above. All of these have been calculated attempts to fan flames of hatred and deepen the polarisation between the Sinhalese and Tamil ethnic groups. The bottom line of the LTTE position is that "we cannot live with the Sinhalese, therefore we need to live separately" (Ibid), so any means that justify this end are acceptable.

• The *Dalada Maligawa* truck-bombing is an interesting attack since it was aimed at a venerated site which is a repository for a sacred relic, reputed to be the tooth of the Buddha. The strategy here was to jolt the majority Sinhalese Buddhists into a spontaneous attack meting retribution upon Tamil civilians living amongst them, which was almost sparked off by localised rioting in Kandy. President Kumaratunga put a timely stop to it with media announcements and security measures preventing such an occurrence.

• President Kumaratunga as head of state and a leading politician has a fiercely loyal constituency, particularly in her family's strongholds of Attanagalla and Gampaha. The LTTE's attack on her could very well have led to a Sinhala-backlash, had the President not made an urgent personal appeal from her hospital bed to prevent this.

• Given the combination of age, gender and a fiercely loyal constituency which she shares with her daughter, the alleged attack on the octogenarian Prime Minister Bandaranaike was like attempting to assassinate the Queen Mother in Britain. Had the attack been successful it could well have precipitated a Sinhala-backlash.

• And most recently, the failed ambush on a ministerial motorcade came at a time when the government of Sri Lanka has officially requested the assistance of Norway as a third-party mediator between the LTTE and the government. The abortive attack came a day after the President and the leader of the opposition agreed to a consensual approach to resolving the national question at a high-level meeting between the government and opposition.

Given that the Norwegians were playing a behind-the-scenes role for some time, these recent actions might point to the fact that the LTTE seems particularly nervous about a negotiated peace settlement. In other words, it illustrates a worry that peace could potentially jeopardise the LTTE's hegemonic one-party hold over 'the Tamil polity', which it maintains by making recourse to warfare and its concomitant siege mentality. While this might be the case, recent statements in the press give credence to the LTTE's firmly held conviction that the *Sinhalese* Theravada Buddhist establishment would in the final analysis block a just settlement. To quote one headline: "**Mahanayakas say 'no' to reforms**: Buddhist groups rise against Norway's facilitating role in Lankan conflict", where it is stated that,

> The Venerable Mahanayakas of the two leading Chapters – Malwatte and Asgiriya and other leaders of the Buddhist clergy have decided to launch campaigns to prevent the Government introducing constitutional reforms and using Norway as a facilitator for a negotiated settlement of the ethnic conflict (Front page of *The Sunday Times*, 5 March, 2000).

In the revenge/counter-revenge 'discourse' of Sri Lankan politics, described above, macabre messages are exchanged/delivered repeatedly through terrifying imagery. Such 'communiqués' are exchanged between agents of political violence and also 'delivered' by them to respective 'target audiences' among the general public, in their struggles for power and hegemony (de Silva 1993, 1995 b).

A brief commentary on power here will give an idea as to why hegemonic and counter-hegemonic manoeuvrings take place, between/among parties involved in political conflict and violence (including their civilian target populations). In a general outline of this concept, Anthony Giddens notes:

By power is meant the ability of individuals or groups to make their own interests count, even where others resist. Power sometimes involves the direct use of force, but it is almost always accompanied by the develop-ment of ideas (ideologies) which **justify** the actions of the power-ful...Power is a pervasive aspect of all human relationships. Many **con-flicts** in society are struggles over power, because how much power an individual or group is able to achieve governs how far they are able to put their wishes into practice at the expense of those of others (Giddens 1991: 52, 729).

What is at stake in the current conflict between the LTTE and the sovereign state of Sri Lanka/rival Tamil paramilitary groups, is hegemony over *geographical territory or space*, and monopoly over *power and resources* (including human). And in order to achieve these ends, all parties concerned have at one time or another used the option of political violence, in opposition to dialogue, compromise and negotiated po-litical settlement.

Internecine Warfare, Hatred and Revenge/Counter-Revenge Kill-ings

Ours is a national liberation struggle, a struggle for freedom to shape our political destiny, a struggle waged with courage, heroism and sacri-fice, a struggle soaked in blood and tears, a struggle built on the ashes of several thousands of martyrs (Political Committee of the LTTE in Seevaratnam 1989:v).

The Tigers' history, their theoretical vacuum, lack of political creativity, intolerance and fanatical dedication will be the ultimate cause of their own break up. The legendary Tigers will go to their demise with their legends smeared with the blood and tears of victims of their own misdo-ings. A new Tiger will not emerge from their ashes. Only by breaking with this whole history and its dominant ideology, can a new liberating outlook be born (Rajani Thiranagama in *The Broken Palmyra*).[171]

The manner in which hatred and revenge are understood and acted upon, differ from culture to culture. In the Sri Lankan situation, not exceptionally, it also differs according to sub-culture. In Tamil paramilitary sub-culture, the violent settling of scores *within* and *between* organisations is well defined – to the extent that in 1995 a former bodyguard of the late PLOTE leader "Uma Maheswaran" was murdered along

---

[171] Dr. Rajani Thiranagama, a well-known South Asian feminist (with a PhD in Anatomy from Uni-versity College London), was a former member of the LTTE and a prominent member of University Teachers for Human Rights (Jaffna). While serving as a senior member of staff in the Jaffna Univer-sity Medical Faculty, she was murdered by LTTE gunmen – who shot her five times in the head at close range - while cycling home from the university, on account of her anti-paramilitary writings and human rights oriented activities.

with his wife in Zurich, for allegedly participating in the 1988 assassination of "Maheswaran". Whereas, when Sinhala civilian victims (members of another sub-culture) lost sons, daughters and loved ones to government sponsored massacres against suspected JVP cadres, the calls for justice and revenge have been more tame and uncertain, and generally confined to within the boundaries of the law. Here, the attitudes of civilian victims are clearly different from those of paramilitaries. For a detailed discussion of Tamil paramilitary perspectives on internecine warfare and the fate of the Tamil polity, refer to the verbatim narratives in my chapter on "Sri Lankan Futures" in Munck and de Silva (2000).

From a human rights perspective, the University Teachers for Human Rights (Jaffna) published an insightful catalogue of horrors of political violence in North-East Sri Lanka in 1994, entitled: *Someone Else's War*. According to the anonymous authors (for reasons of their personal safety), the most recent violations against the civilian population had been perpetrated largely by the LTTE. In areas controlled by the LTTE, anyone suspected of disobedience or 'working against the interests of the LTTE' (however innocent) is liable to be arrested, incarcerated, interrogated, tortured and/or executed. Most of the LTTE's prisoners are either members or sympathisers of rival Tamil organisations and their relatives, or LTTE cadres suspected of internal dissent. Captured servicemen from the Sri Lankan armed services form another category of prisoners. Here is an excerpt, concerning the fate of a Tamil prisoner held by the LTTE.

> Members of the LTTE intelligence unit worked with the wardens in some camps to extract information...Kanthi, nicknamed 'The Butcher', a member of the intelligence unit...once went berserk when he discovered that a torture victim who fainted had been given medical attention and ripped off the bandages before killing the victim with a pick-axe handle (University Teachers for Human Rights-Jaffna 1994: 100).

How is it possible, that Tamil paramilitaries torture and kill one another with such ferocity? As far as political rhetoric in the North-East goes, the LTTE categorically states that it is fighting a liberation struggle to establish a separate, sovereign Tamil state called 'Tamil Eelam'. According to this logic, are not all Tamils then 'the sons and daughters of Tamil mothers' and is their no 'unity in struggle'? It is paradoxical that since 1984/85, an openly chauvinist Tamil paramilitary organisation such as the LTTE has been *systematically* targeting the members of other Tamil paramilitary groups – in a violent bid to become the sole representative of the Tamil people. The stratagem behind this recourse to internecine warfare must be attributed in the first instance, to the 'brains' behind the LTTE.

The LTTE's supremo, Velupillai Prabhakaran, is an interesting and almost Macbethian figure – with blood on his hands and ghosts looking over his shoulder. He systematically murdered, exiled or 'got rid of' through convenient 'missions impossible', the second tier of leadership within his own organisation, on a variety of trumped up charges. One casualty being Mahendraraja, better known as 'Mahaththaya', who it is rumoured was executed in January 1995 after a secret 'trial'. Mahaththaya had been the LTTE's long standing number-two man and former commander of the Wanni sector, with a loyal following of his own. Most of his followers were sent on the first wave of a subsequent assault on the Sri Lankan military base in Pooneryn, where many lost their lives. Therefore, it comes as no surprise that members of rival Tamil organisations have been and are ruthlessly crushed. Since the founding of the LTTE, political killings of Tamils, Sinhalese, Muslims and Indians (combatants and civilians alike) paved the way in one way or another, to power enhancement and consolidation, as well as *de facto* control over geographical and politico-cultural space. As far as Prabhakaran is concerned, there is absolutely no question of power sharing in relation to the affairs of the Tamil polity.

Given such a state of affairs, it becomes necessary for an organisation such as the LTTE to adopt various stratagems, in order for the will of Prabhakaran and his lieutenants to be carried out by the rank and file. My hypothesis is that 'hatred' of all forces (political and/or military) other than the LTTE is actively cultivated among the rank and file. And furthermore, this process is facilitated through the inculcation of pre-emptive and revenge/counter-revenge killings as a political and military solution. In other words, there has been and continues to be "an enduring organisation of aggressive impulses" (Allport 1992: 31) toward persons deemed to be and therefore, labelled as 'enemies'.

The manipulation of this stratagem in combination with others – particularly, the use of suicide operations, cyanide capsules, and notions of self-sacrifice and martyrdom – have given the LTTE a tactical edge not only on the battlefield but also in popular imagination (de Silva 1995 a). The LTTE "supremo's thoughts for the week" (in Tamil language script) on the Internet (photographically recorded in Gunaratna 1997: 56), actively cultivates such imagination and motivation. *"Fear is the outcome of weakness. The coward's friend. The enemy of courage. The root of fear among humans is the fear of death. The one who destroys the fear of death, is victorious over himself. He is the one who liberates himself from the inner prison"* (Velupillai Prabhakaran – my translation). Despite its tactical edge, the LTTE's violent efforts at hijacking the Tamil national liberation struggle also resulted in fierce counter-hegemonic reactions from rival Tamil paramilitary organisations. And in this bloody internecine warfare, hatred and revenge/counter-revenge killings became the norm.

Driven by these events, 'doing one better' than the Tigers and exacting revenge, became of paramount importance for rival Tamil paramilitaries – thereby effectively de-railing a united Tamil national liberation struggle once and for all. It is hardly surprising therefore, to find Tamil paramilitary organisations such as the PLOTE, EPDP and TELO fighting side by side with military units of the government of Sri Lanka against the LTTE – proving right a derivative of the old Kautilyan adage, that 'an enemy's enemy is my friend'. And in the 'extropunitive gaze' of many of those involved in internecine warfare, 'enemies from within' are definitely seen as 'the cause' for the failure or corruption of the Tamil separatist-national liberation struggle.

Nevertheless, the question of why internecine warfare between rival Tamil paramilitaries has been carried out more fiercely *and* effectively – than between Tamil fighters and predominantly Sinhala soldiers on the government side – is only partially answered through a discussion of hatred and revenge killings. The question of internecine warfare and combat should also be addressed through an examination of other important issues pertaining to agents of political violence, such as;

(1) Logistical Capabilities;

(2) Labelling/Disinformation;

(3) Power/Hegemony.

Logistical capabilities – such as familiarity/knowledge of enemy strengths, weaknesses, movements, mobility, support, resources, the ability to discern fact from disinformation, combined with a thorough understanding of terrain/politico-cultural space – provide an enemy from within (i. e. rival Tamil paramilitaries in this case) with far more opportunities to inflict more severe casualties than an enemy from without. Therefore it becomes paramount (whenever possible), in military terms, to completely wipe out opposition or enemies from within – which in turn leads to ever spiralling, vicious and no-holds-barred combat. In Sri Lanka, such characteristics of internecine warfare could also be observed in the mainly intra-Sinhala conflict (from 1987 to 1990) between the forces of the government and the JVP (see footnote 162 for references). It also explains, to some extent, why the predominantly Sinhalese Sri Lankan military forces have fared badly in Tamil districts but were successful against the JVP in Sinhala districts.

Labelling/Disinformation – in situations of extreme ethnonationalist conflicts there are increased chances for xenophobia to exist within a given community or group. Xenophobia and/or siege mentality, enable easy labelling of 'traitors' and 'fifth columnists', who are given short shrift. Time and time again in Sri Lanka atrocities have been committed against such perceived 'traitors', who on many occasions have later turned out to be innocent civilians or persons targeted as a result of private quarrels. In all warfare, as in internecine conflict, labelling and disinformation go hand in hand. Therefore, when LTTE commanders identify members of other Tamil groups as 'traitors', 'perpetrators of atrocities' or 'corrupt elements' (e.g. thieves, robbers, drug dealers) bringing discredit to the Tamil nation, it becomes easier for the rank and file to justify their actions as well as to nurture hatred. The same is true for the LTTE's rivals (i. e. Tamil paramilitaries and members of the Sri Lankan armed forces). who use a similar logic in their military and political campaigns.

Power/Hegemony – another aspect of internecine struggles for power and hegemony is to illustrate in no uncertain manner that 'we' are more powerful than (rival) others. Myths of superiority/inferiority fuel heightened competition between rival paramilitaries, who exert tremendous efforts to either 'prove' or 'disprove' the myth concerned – since capture of the high ground in popular imagination and culture is all important. All these complex factors then combine into a highly explosive cocktail, which fuels the passions, hatred and energies that revolve around revenge/counter-revenge killings and constructions of political violence – illustrated here by the case of Tamil paramilitaries.

Conclusion

If we believe in absurdities we shall commit atrocities – Voltaire.

In all the internecine warfare and revenge/counter-revenge killings between Tamil paramilitaries, 'hatred' has been an important galvanising and motivating factor. Hatred towards enemies makes it easy for commanders to order rank and file into the fiercest of action and to commit atrocities at will. This explains the LTTE's need to cultivate hatred at an organisational level and on its adoption of pre-emptive and revenge killings as an effective stratagem of conquest.

The political culture propagated by the LTTE prevails unchallenged, particularly in contemporary Jaffna society. Since the early 1980s the organisation has made more and more determined efforts to cultivate hatred directed at 'rival Tamil organisations' and 'the Sinhala dominated Sri Lankan state'. Thus far, the organisation has succeeded in achieving certain limited politico-military-cultural objectives, and appears to be reasonably well established for the time being – at least in the eyes of Prabhakaran and his field commanders.[172] The costs of such successes, both in human (e.g. in terms of distress, grief, suffering, morality, culture, etc.) and economic terms, have never been calculated. It is highly doubtful whether such considerations would be of major significance given the resumption of hostilities, to an organisation that is governed by military doctrine. In fact at present, 'the costs of waging war' are portrayed through images (e.g. propaganda videos, spectacular operations) in order to generate more support in monetary terms for 'the war effort', both within and outside Sri Lanka (e.g. Europe, North America). Nevertheless, the most important question being asked in Sri Lanka today is whether the LTTE has the vision and fortitude to change course from its well honed routine of hatred, revenge/counter-revenge killings and political violence.

---

[172] For a different albeit critical perspective on this issue, see de Silva (1995 a)

From a global perspective, a handful of revolutionary, liberation-oriented and nationalist organisations – such as the African National Congress (ANC), Palestine Liberation Organisation (PLO) and the PIRA (to some extent) – have shown the willingness and long-sightedness to cope with the exigencies of peacetime politics, in opposition to the prolongation of war. True enough, there are many obstacles and frustrations along the way, in opting for long term solutions, ending bloodshed and coming to negotiated political settlements. On the other hand, there is the chaos, carnage and lawlessness of contemporary Chechnya, Kosovo, Bosnia-Hercegovina and Sierra Leone, to name but a few random hot spots in this post-Cold War globe.

What the final outcome will be for the long suffering peoples of the North-East and rest of Sri Lanka, remains open to speculation. Peace remains an option in the rest of Sri Lanka, only if there is the political will and conviction *simultaneously*, on the part of both the LTTE and the present government, supported by the opposition and significant sections of civil society, including the clergy. And as far as the North-East *per se* is concerned, long lasting peace will only be an option once:

1. The LTTE and its Tamil rivals are able to 'bury their hatchets' and accommodate each other's point of view.

2. As well as being able to accommodate the perspectives of the Muslim and Sinhala polities living in the Northwest and East.

3. A follow-up step to backup détente between Tamils, Muslims and Sinhalese, would be the development of a sustainable framework of economic policies – i. e. to re-develop the North-East, so as to return it at least to the level of successful production in existence before the war.

From a broader perspective, the partitioning of Sri Lanka along ethnic lines is a recipe for 'disaster waiting to happen', as has been the case elsewhere in South Asia, when 'British India' was carved up by the departing colonial power. Today we have two sovereign states, India and Pakistan, that are armed to the teeth and have developed tactical nuclear weapons programmes that have destabilised the whole region – with a seemingly 'intractable problem' over the fate of a relatively minor territory called Kashmir. From a territorial perspective Sri Lanka is far too small a place to sustain a hypothetically unstable border partitioning two 'hostile neighbours'. Realistically, neither the Sinhalese nor the Tamils can tolerate the costs of future, long-term bloodletting. Some cynics on the other hand would argue, looking at the ethnic conflict from a 'numbers game', that over the long-term there would be far fewer Tamils to fight for the LTTE. But if America's experience in Vietnam is anything to go by this is another recipe for 'disaster waiting to happen'. And neither can Sri Lanka afford the scarce resources that are currently being squandered by pursuing an ill-conceived military option, which calls for more and more 'blood sacrifices' from the protagonists, with no positive returns or a resolution in sight. Sri Lanka, which was the envy of its

East Asian neighbours like Singapore and Malaysia at the turn of independence cannot afford the costs of the cultivation of hatreds and militarism – which are quite obviously at the expense of long-term peace, stability and economic development. In the long run survival for the Sinhalese, Tamil and Muslim social formations on this fairly small island, requires the politicians of all three ethnic groups to hold a steady course geared towards the peaceful resolution of the ethnic conflict. And here if Norway's or any other third party's mediating role is proved to be a useful strategy then by all means such options should be utilised. Needless to say, the negative stimuli provided in this process through the provocations of those actors trapped within the 'combat mode', who cultivate hatred in order to fuel their path to an imagined future, must be overcome through disciplined but constructive engagement. An example of good faith based on such engagement could be the provision of tangible benefits to victims of ethnic conflict, such as tangibly improving the living conditions of internally displaced persons (IDPs). Ultimately, Sinhalese, Tamil and Muslim politicians must develop the institutional structures, policy frameworks and constitutional safeguards, that would create a viable entity that is capable of catering to the preferences of all three ethnic groups, while maintaining mutual co-existence.

As I have argued elsewhere (de Silva 1995 a), the 'Tigers' have attempted over a long period of time to maintain a continuum between the emotional bonds that enable large sections of the Tamil people to empathise with the 'Tamil Liberation Struggle' and the organisation-centred activities of the LTTE. This effort is conducted both at the national and transnational[173] levels. In the representations of the LTTE, both phenomena are mutually inclusive. The principle problem with this stratagem, which has become more sophisticated over time, is the fact that the 'Tamil people' are *not* a homogenous entity. Despite linkages, which occur through the usage of a common language and cultural heritage, there are myriad differences and oppositions, at regional, local, politico-ideological and cultural levels.

In the long-term, this variety of interests disables the project of the 'Tigers' in maintaining an emotional continuum, between their organisation and 'the Tamil people'. Therefore, the LTTE has been obliged to adopt the strategy of short-term *spectacular* actions.[174] Through such short-term measures attempts are made to rekindle the 'emotional continuum', whenever it is at low ebb. Another reason, which calls for such spectacular *situation-specific* and *response-specific* actions, is the inconstant na-

---

[173] By transnational I refer to the Tamil diaspora of Sri Lankan origin, that is spread across the globe. In this categorisation, I also include 'Tamilians' sympathetic to the Eelam national liberation struggle. These are Tamils who live in the southern Indian state of Tamil Nadu and who share a sense of community and ethnic identity with their counterparts in Sri Lanka, through linguistic, cultural, and religious affinities.

[174] Such spectacular actions are conducted always within the ambit of the 'combat mode' (de Silva 1995 a).

ture of populist emotion-based support.[175] By situation-specific actions, I mean *proactive actions* that correspond to the dynamics of *context-specific* or *particular* military operations and/or political situations. And by response-specific actions, I mean *reactive actions* that correspond narrowly to the dynamics of *responding* (sometimes in "knee-jerk" fashion) to a specific or particular military campaign by the Sri Lankan armed services and its auxiliaries/irregulars. Of course, spectacular action is not the only important strategy adopted by the 'Tigers' in the planning and implementation of their military campaign. They have, for instance, succeeded in presenting the LTTE as the only obstacle to the total defeat and destruction of 'the Tamil people' by the Sinhala state and its armed forces. In fact, a senior Tamil police officer once remarked that: "We [Tamils] can walk in the streets today with our backbone held erect because of the 'Tigers'" [Personal field-notes 1998]. Given the bloody history of the Tamil national liberation struggle, such apocalyptic visions generate a degree of appeal even among those who are either politically or morally opposed to the unpalatable and unsavoury practices of the 'Tigers' (Manikkalingam 1992).

It should be kept in mind that all wars do end for a variety of historical and existential reasons. And in Sri Lanka, the task at hand is to cope with or muddle through the short-term problems of warfare, of which the cultivation of hatred is but one negative consequence. Building a genuine consensus between all the parties represented in parliament, is an absolute prerequisite for a long-term settlement. Based on the legitimacy of such a multipartisan and unified consensus, the representatives of parliamentary democracy in Sri Lanka can then move on to the next stage and deal with the demands of the separatist-nationalist paramilitaries of the LTTE in a more professional manner. Attempting to fulfil the self-interest motives of most, if not all the parties concerned is one concrete measure that can eventually help overcome societal polarisation and the consequences of cultivated hatreds by changing the focus of engagement. Failure to initiate such a process effectively is in my opinion, one of the biggest stumbling blocks to a long-term and stable peace in Sri Lanka.

---

[175] Problems of support and mobilisation occur due to the effects of waning support, indifference and skepticism, which accompany initial enthusiasm among a populist support base. These practices include – summary executions, prolonged periods of incarceration and semi-starvation in communal pits dug into the ground for political prisoners, frequent use of torture, the use of 'soft' civilian targets (similar to the much publicised 'ethnic cleansing'), etc.

References

Alles, A.C. 1990. *The J.V.P. 1969 – 1989.* Colombo: Lake House

Allport, Gordon Willard 1992. The Nature of Hatred. In: Robert M. Baird and Stuart E. Rosenbaum (eds.). *Bigotry, Prejudice and Hatred: Definitions, Causes and Solutions.* Buffalo, New York: Prometheus

Buss, A.H. 1971. Aggression Pays. In: J.L. Singer (ed.). *The Control of Aggression and Violence.* New York: Academic Press

Chandraprema, C.A. (Jr.) 1991. *Sri Lanka: The Years of Terror – The JVP Insurrection 1987 – 1989.* Colombo: Lake House Bookshop

de Silva, Purnaka L. (Forthcoming) *Political Violence and Its Cultural Constructions: Representational and Narrative 'Realities' in Times of War.* London: Macmillan and New York: St. Martin's Press

de Silva, Purnaka L. 2000. Sri Lankan Futures: Conflicts, Alternatives and Possibilities in the 21st Century. In: Ronaldo Munck and Purnaka L. de Silva (eds.). *Postmodern Insurgencies: Political Violence, Identity Formation and Peacemaking in Comparative Perspective.* London: Macmillan and New York: St. Martin's Press

de Silva, Purnaka L. 1999. The Growth of Tamil Paramilitary Nationalisms: Sinhala Chauvinism and Tamil Responses. In: Siri Gamage and Bruce Watson (eds.). *Conflict and Community in Sri Lanka.* New Delhi and London: Sage

de Silva, Purnaka L. 1995 a. The Efficacy of "Combat Mode": Organisation, Political Violence, Affect and Cognition in the Case of the Liberation Tigers of Tamil Eelam. In: Pradeep Jeganathan and Qadri Ismail (eds.). *Unmaking the Nation: The Politics of Identity and History in Sri Lanka.* Colombo: Social Scientists Association

de Silva, Purnaka L. 1995 b. Studying Political Violence and Its Cultural Constructions. In: *FOLK – Journal of the Danish Ethnographic Society,* Vol.36: 61 - 89

de Silva, Purnaka L. 1993. How Ethnic is the Ethnic Conflict in Sri Lanka?: Complexities of Heterogeneity – Unpublished paper presented at Workshop II: *Ethnicity, Politics and the State* at the Conference *The Anthropology of Ethnicity: A Critical Review.* University of Amsterdam, December 14 - 19

Feldman, Allen 1991. *Formations of Violence: The Narrative of the Body and Political Terror in Northern Ireland.* Chicago: The University of Chicago Press

Gamage, Sri & I. B. Watson 1999. *Conflict and community in contemporary Sri Lanka: 'Pearl of the Indian Ocean' or 'the island of tears'* New Dehli: Thousand Oaks, Calif.: Sage

Giddens, Anthony 1991. *Sociology.* Cambridge: Polity Press

Gunaratna, Rohan 1997. *International and Regional Security Implications of the Sri Lankan Tamil Insurgency.* Colombo: Alumni Association of the Bandaranaike Centre for International Studies and St. Albans, Herts: International Foundation of Sri Lankans

Gunaratna, Rohan 1990. *Sri Lanka: A Lost Revolution? – The Inside Story of the JVP.* Kandy: Institute of Fundamental Studies

Gunasekara, Prins 1998. *Sri Lanka in Crisis: A Lost Generation – The Untold Story.* Colombo: S. Godage and Brothers

Harnden, Toby 1999. *Bandit Country.* London: Trafalgar Square

Hoole, Rajan., Somasunderam, Daya., Sritheran, K. and Thiranagama, Rajani 1992. *The Broken Palmyra: The Tamil Crisis in Sri Lanka – An Inside Account.* Claremont, California: The Sri Lanka Studies Institute

Manikkalingam, Ramanujam 1992. *Tigerism.* Colombo: Social Scientists Association

McGowan, William 1992. *Only Man is Vile: The Tragedy of Sri Lanka.* London: Picador

Meznaric, Silva 1994. Gender as an Ethno-Marker: Rape, War, and Identity Politics in the Former Yugoslavia. In: Valentine M. Moghadam (ed.). *Identity Politics and Women: Cultural Reassertions and Feminisms in International Perspective.* Boulder, Colorado: Westview Press

Mitchell, George J. 1999. *Making Peace.* New York: Knopf

Munck, Ronaldo and Purnaka L. de Silva 2000. *Postmodern insurgencies: political violence, identity formation, and peacemaking in comparative perspective.* Houndmills, Basingstoke, Hampshire: Macmillan Press; New York: St. Martin's Press

Ricoeur, Paul 1991. In: Mario J. Valdés (ed.). *A Ricoeur Reader: Reflection and Imagination.* New York and London: Harvester Wheatsheaf

Rule, James B. 1988. *Theories of Civil Violence.* Berkeley: University of California Press

Seevaratnam, N. (ed.) 1989. *The Tamil National Question and the Indo-Sri Lanka Accord.* Delhi: Konark Publishers Pvt Ltd

University Teachers for Human Rights (Jaffna) 1994. *Someone Else's War.* Colombo: Movement for Inter Racial Justice and Equality

ABSTRACT

This paper focuses on 'hatred' and its relation to situated practices of revenge killings, in the context of the Sri Lankan embroglio - which forms part of a wider ethnographic study on political violence. It starts by laying out briefly, the historical and contextual backdrop to these situated actions of political violence and then goes on to argue that political violence is a construction of sorts, where *culture* plays an important role. In this context the concept of 'hatred' and its impact on the identities of paramilitaries and soldiers alike (i. e. agents of political violence) - as well as its relations to the rather specific phenomen of revenge killings are examined. Revenge killings take place within politically charged and polarised contexts, as in Sri Lanka, and other such deeply divided societies. Such actions are analysed in the setting of *internecine* warfare in particular (e.g. intra-ethnic or group strife), a common situation in many revolutionary and/or nationalistic struggles. Ironically enough, such infights are carried out more fiercely than the 'business' of the nationalist war or revolution.

TARGETING THE VICTIMS OF VIOLENCE:

THE ROLE OF FOLK HISTORY AND VOLUNTARY ASSOCIATIONS IN THE CONSTRUCTION OF HATRED IN NORTHERN IRELAND

Mary C. Kenney

Hatred and difference are always constructed but not everywhere in the same way. How differences are differently conceptualised in various parts of the world has implications for patterns of conflict and communal and political violence examined cross-culturally. In many European settings, in the border zones and multi-ethnic regions created by processes of state formation and internal colonialism in Europe, difference is largely constructed in terms of history, and the importance of language and religion are understood in folk historical terms. More precisely, it is oppositional versions of folk history (local, regional and national) that primarily define the relational identities of rival ethno-religious communities living intermixed in politically contested territories.

Peter Sahlins, discussing concepts of ethnic and national identity, stresses the role of local versions of history and "the oppositional character of identities and loyalties, particularly visible in the Catalan borderland and found more generally throughout Europe (1989: 111)". Northern Ireland represents a violent exception to the majority of the ethnically complicated border disputes in Western Europe, most of which are now politically dormant within the EU. This focus on local and regional history (as part of the construction of collective hatreds) is one of the major differences between ethnic conflict and racism since ethnic conflict is constructed mainly in reference to historical and religious distinctions while racism is constructed mainly by means of biological metaphors.

In Northern Ireland these folk histories are part of the ideological and ritual property of major political organisations such as the Orange Order and the Provisional IRA. The social construction of difference is essential for defining the complex relation between inter-personal (or psychological) hatred and the collective hate that constitutes the theme of this volume. Collective and communal hatreds are more than just personal hatreds multiplied and mobilised. The case of Northern Ireland shows how the primordial hatred, to borrow a term from Clifford Geertz (1963), between Catholics (Republicans) and Protestants (Loyalists) can be seen to be constructed primarily, not by the ethnic group in general, but by certain social clubs and political organisations that play a central role in day to day life and in the maintenance of ethnic identity.

Ethno-religious prejudices, and hostile attitudes toward the others, are acquired by individual members of the rival groups mainly through the process of socialisation of children and youths as active participants in these organisations and also through their influence on family and neighbourhood traditions. Through this structuring of everyday life on the local level, these organisations have largely determined the public life of Protestant and Catholic communities in Northern Ireland. Through the operation of what Roy Rappaport terms a 'cybernetic system' (1979), the ethnic conflict promoted by the organisations reinforces the autonomy of the locality in Northern Ireland and thus of local influences on the individual. Hatred, which is focused on specific others who are seen as a threat to the welfare of one's own group and to personal identity, is thus perpetuated in the normal processes of socialisation.

Recognition of this aspect of the social and political organisation of ethnicity in Northern Ireland, and of so-called ethnic conflict, is important because it helps to explain the different patterns of political and communal violence typical of Protestants and Catholics there. The two rival folk histories of Northern Ireland differentially identify the "legitimate targets" of political and communal violence in Northern Ireland and actors, organised as particular voluntary associations and local social groups (the paramilitary organisations on both sides, "Orange" and Republican mobs) carry it out. Evidence from Northern Ireland suggests that ethnic violence is not usually randomly directed at anonymous members of the other groups but is patterned by specific cultural scenarios (Turner 1974). These metaphors and scenarios, which structure emotions (including political hatred) on the levels of the individual and the group, are closely associated with certain social organisations which include churches and men's' clubs.

Even the nature and degree of violent acts in Northern Ireland are characteristic, one might say traditional, of locally based political organisations. Seen in terms of the theory of social organisation, ethnic violence is patterned by feud-like interactions between locally based rival parties. In Northern Ireland, the political rivalry of "the Orange and the Green" represents an interrelated system of Protestant and Catholic symbols and parallel social organisation (Leyton 1974). Seen in terms of social processes, however, it is not a system that is strictly balanced in a Levi-Straussian sense.

Ulster Protestant history is primarily defined by the customs, rituals and politics of the Orange Order which targets Catholics as the enemy. No one really knows the exact membership of this semi-secret men's' organisation but the local Orange Lodge remains a focus of social life in working class and lower-middle class Protestant residential districts, urban and rural, in Northern Ireland. Formally an adult male social organisation with affiliated roles for boys and women, estimates by outsiders credit the "Orangemen" with around 100,000 active members out of a total Ulster Protestant population of close to one million. The organisation has informal (and unacknowledged) links with the loyalist paramilitary groups, mainly through overlapping patterns of membership (Kenney 1991).

Catholic folk-history, on the other hand, mainly targets the British as the enemy. Thus, political violence, organised by the Republican paramilitary groups in Northern Ireland, has been focused on the Northern Irish police (as the local representatives of the British state), on members of the British military in Northern Ireland and against the British public and government in the form of terrorist bombings in London and other mainland British cities. Attacks against Ulster Protestant civilians have been exceptions in the Republican campaign of organised political violence. The loyalist paramilitary organisations, on the other hand, are infamous for their kidnappings and murders of unarmed Catholics. Loyalists typically consider ordinary Catholics to be their enemies. The victims are usually abducted from the streets of Protestant or mixed areas of Belfast and murdered, or are shot down in Catholic districts by loyalist gunmen coming from neighbouring Protestant residential areas. Thus, Protestant violence (and hatred) tends to be defined as sectarian while Catholic violence is usually seen as being political in nature.

In terms of the theme of this volume, however, I will claim that typically (and in terms of folk history and political ideology) Catholics in Northern Ireland hate the British, while Ulster Protestants typically hate their Catholic neighbours. Seen as a personal lack of religious tolerance, defined in a modern social and political sense, Northern Irish Catholics are frequently as sectarian as Ulster Protestants and their Church is just as capable of advocating sectarian social and political policies as Ian Paisley or the Orange Order. Sectarianism in Northern Ireland, however (and therefore hatred), is officially associated with the Orange Order as the promoter of an explicitly anti-Catholic ideology. This "Orange" ideology is based on, and legitimised by, a version of Irish history that stands in opposition to the Irish nationalist version and upholds Protestant dominance.

The point is to focus on local social organisation as the proper sociological approach to the question of how religion is related to ethnic conflict as well as how ethnic differences are actually constructed in real situations of conflict in various parts of the world. Although differences, and hatreds, are indeed constructed, and operate as forces influencing culture and society, this historical process of the construction of ethnic and racial differences reflects material and political struggles for control over economic and political resources. This usually happens in post-colonial settings like Northern Ireland. Oppositional forms of social organisation, including ethnic identities, reflect competitive economic and political strategies in which the construction of differences and the construction of collective hatreds play a crucial organisational role.

The conflict in Northern Ireland has often been ridiculed as anachronistic. A joke, no doubt of English origin, has a British Airways pilot announce over the Irish Sea, "The temperature in Belfast is 60 degrees and the local time is 1690". Religion is not supposed to be a major political issue at the end of the twentieth century and outsiders often comment about the conflict that "it's really not about religion at all, you know". By this they mean that it is really about economics and class differences. Examining the role of secret societies and men's' clubs, evident on both sides in Northern Irish local and regional history, reveals the relationships between religion, ethnicity and class that structure collective hatred and determine the patterns of political vio-

lence in a particular divided society. Attention is usually focused on the relations between Catholics and the British state or, less frequently, between the Protestants and
the British state. The focus is on the power of the state in macro-level studies, as in
Marxist analyses of Irish history such as Michael Hechter's book (1975).

While this perspective is important, a complementary focus on the development
of regional political and cultural forces like the Orange Order and the Provisional IRA
(as regional and local structures of power with a complex relation to the state and class
systems) clarifies the causal influence and role of religion in the Northern Irish conflict
today. Thus, the attention needs to be shifted on to the issues of regional history, locality and identity.

The Bright Orange Heroes of Comber

On the twelfth day of July last,
as we went walking past
to Kirkcubbin where we did assemble
the rebels they did pray
for a curse on us that day
for we're the bright Orange heroes of Comber.

As we walked down Shuttle Row
(its a rebel place you know)
thinking that we were useless lumber,
they swore they'd break our drum
if we up to them did come
but we're the bright Orange heroes of Comber.

O'Connell he did boast
of his great big rebel host,
he says they are ten millions in number.
But most of them you'll find
they are both lame and blind
and we're the bright Orange heroes of Comber.

So here's a loyal toast,
may all base traitors roast,
confound the foes of the Orange Order.
May we give blow for blow
while sweet Boyne waters flow,
for we're the bright Orange Heroes of Comber.[176]

This traditional Orange song describes a situation from the nineteenth century
in County Down that helps to explain the motivations of the Orangemen who continue

---

[176] This Orange song was sung for me by Jon Allison, now Professor of English at the University of
Kentucky, on the front porch of a house on West Huron Street in Ann Arbor, Michigan. He says that it
is his favorite Protestant song from his boyhood in Bangor, County Down.

to insist on marching down the Garvaghy Road in Portadown, County Armagh every year on the Twelfth of July. It explains too, the response of Portadown's Catholic residents to the annual Orange invasion.

As the song shows, the symbols of conflict in Northern Ireland refer to folk history. The "heroes" are members of the Comber Orange Lodge. The "rebels" are the residents of a Catholic locality. The Twelfth of July is the anniversary of the Battle of the Boyne, the day when the membership of the Orange lodges parade with banners, to the music of marching bands, throughout all of Northern Ireland. The holiday celebrates the victory of the Protestant King William of Orange over the Catholic monarch James II. The song refers disparagingly to Daniel O'Connell and his followers. O'Connell, the great "emancipator" of the Catholic peasantry in the mid-nineteenth century, was famous for organising mass demonstrations of enormous size.

The failure to achieve a democratic solution to the problems of Northern Ireland has been popularly attributed, at least by those reluctant to blame Britain, to an Irish obsession with history. This inability to forget the past allegedly leads to a failure to pursue politics in modern terms, which is thought to be characteristic of the Irish of both persuasions. Political scientists and sociologists, on the other hand, tend to ignore preoccupations with history. Both attitudes reflect a lack of understanding of the meaning of history in Northern Ireland and how folk history as rhetoric is tied to other major aspects of Irish culture and social organisation. These aspects include locality (Arensberg 1959), the ethno-religious basis of communal identity and the political role of marching groups like the Orange Order and their Catholic equivalent, the Ancient Order of Hibernians, as well as the present day paramilitary organisations on both sides.

The voluntary associations, which play a key role in the symbolic elaboration of conflict and the construction of hatred in Northern Ireland, are locally based and are actively involved in maintaining or disputing the local (micro-territorial) ethnic boundaries that mirror the main border dispute in a partitioned Ireland (Boal / Livingstone 1984) and the invasion of Catholic areas by Orange processions is just the most famous example of this function of voluntary associations in Ulster. These are also the organisations that sponsor the public rituals that dramatise folk historical themes and keep them current in popular imagination. The intensity of historical and territorial preoccupations can partly be attributed to the persistence (as politically powerful) of the "semi-masonic" type of organisation that Eric Hobsbawm calls the "secret revolutionary brotherhood".

The period between 1789 and 1848 saw a development of the ritual organisation which is of considerable importance in the history of social
movements. Throughout the period of the   three French revolutions
the secret revolutionary brotherhood was by far the most important form
of organisation for changing society in Western Europe, and it was often
ritualised to the point of resembling an Italian opera rather than a revolutionary body. Similar brotherhoods have remained politically important
elsewhere and some are still important (1959: 162).

The most famous secret revolutionary brotherhood in the history of Northern
Ireland were the United Irishmen[177] who organised an uprising at the end of the eight-
eenth century, but a number of organisations that remain politically active in Ireland,
North and South, exhibit major elements of the secret revolutionary brotherhood.

Because of their emphasis on ritual and symbolism, masonic-type organisations
(with their levels of secret initiation) serve as ideal originators and repositories of my-
tho-historical lore in early modern and modern societies. On the local level they exert
a historical emphasis on the interpretation of current political events because members
seek organisational and communal legitimation through links with a glorious and heroic past. The major masonic-like groups in Northern Ireland today are, strictly speaking,
not fully secret revolutionary brotherhoods in the eighteenth and nineteenth century
sense. But the Orange Order (and to a lesser degree the Ancient Order of Hibernians) are
certainly semi-secret, politically powerful and heirs (on both sides) to the tradition of
vigilantes and rebellion in Ireland[178]. The roots of the paramilitary organisations of today
also lie in this tradition.

The masonic-like groups, that carry on the marching tradition in Ireland, were
not the only type of eighteenth and nineteenth century organisations to influence the
modern paramilitary organisations of today in Northern Ireland. Another type of organisation, important in Irish political and social history, the agrarian secret society or
"Whiteboys", adopted secret brotherhood customs and practices in their violent campaigns to protect the economic rights of the rural poor against richer tenants, the landlords and the law of the land.

Members of these bands of marauders swore oaths, used secret passwords and
signs, and sometimes wore costumes and other disguises in their nocturnal raids on

---

[177] The United Irishmen joined many Ulster Presbyterians with rebellious members of the Catholic
peasantry throughout Ireland in an attempt, inspired by the political ideals of the then recent American
and French revolutions, to overthrow English tyranny.

[178] The Orange order was founded during the same period of political history as the United Irishmen
and Miller (1983) sees the different attitudes toward Catholics, characteristic of the two organisations,
as reflecting different economic and political forces influencing Protestants in Counties Antrim (the
center of the United Irishmen movement), Down and Armagh (the birthplace of the Orange Order) at
this time.

neighbouring farms and estates. Whiteboys also engaged in rivalries and ritualised battles, so-called faction fighting, with other local groups and predatory bands (Roberts: 1983). Early nineteenth century faction fighting fights in Ulster also had a sectarian dimension. The Orange Order was founded by a group of (Protestant) "Peep of Day Boys" who defeated a band of "Defenders" (Catholics) at the "Battle of the Diamond" in County Armagh in 1795. The fact that the major Orange "battles" of the 1990's have taken place in Portadown, located in County Armagh, is not a coincidence but rather another example of the spirit of historical re-enactment in Northern Ireland.

Both the Orangemen and the Hibernians today celebrate their organisational identities as heirs to this era of agrarian violence in Ireland and have incorporated symbols and rituals, referring to this tradition, into their official collections of cultural and historical lore. These oppositional collections of cultural and historical artifacts constitute the signs and symbols of ethnic identity in Northern Ireland and outline the general patterns of modern communal and political violence. Among Catholics and Protestants, the organisational forms of the past heavily influence the attitudes and even the political strategies of the present day.

On the Protestant side, bands of rural marauders and armed secret societies were often legitimised in their violent activities against their Catholic neighbours through their covert or overt inclusion in militia and other legal paramilitary bodies. This practice continued past the mid-twentieth century with the infamous "B-Specials", former auxiliary units of the Royal Ulster Constabulary that had links to the Orange Order. It persisted until very recently in the form of the Ulster Defence Regiment of the British army. This regiment was permanently stationed in Northern Ireland during the 1970's and 1980's and was made up of members of the local Protestant communities. The UDR was frequently accused of harboring active members of the loyalist paramilitary organisations and of allowing their attacks and harassments against the IRA (and the Catholic population in general) to take place under the cover of British army operations.

A historical conviction of the right to and the necessity for mutual protection, by means of local strength of arms rather than a belief in impartial law, in Northern Ireland (Miller 1983: 188-189) remains the popular bedrock of support for secret organisations and paramilitarism in Northern Ireland among Catholics and Protestants. The modern paramilitary bodies operating in Northern Ireland today also display the stamp of their descent from the eighteenth century brotherhoods by their participation in the marching tradition. The paramilitary groups have also inherited the local violent functions (both defensive and offensive) of the agrarian bands and have adopted the public rituals and customs historically related to social dynamics of micro-territoriality.[179]

---

[179] The adoption of marching by paramilitary groups in Northern Ireland explains a puzzling aspect of secret brotherhoods in general. Why do "secret" (and sometimes illegal) organisations ritually expose

While the Protestant paramilitary groups have marched openly, if sometimes wearing masks, the Provisional IRA does not parade under its own name. However, uniformed and armed Republican paramilitaries regularly appear at Sinn Fein sponsored marches (and especially funerals) where they perform ceremonial roles such as taunting the army with their open presence and firing salutes over the coffins of comrades "killed in action". As I have claimed elsewhere, the function of the local Republican paramilitaries to defend Catholic residential enclaves, against invasion by the police and loyalist mobs, is the most crucial factor in their high level of acceptance among Northern Irish Catholics (Kenney 1991). The popular support for the defensive functions of the IRA may be quite high at the same time as their terrorist activities outside the neighbourhood are generally met with disapproval.

One manifestation of this social organisational legacy is the political culture of marching and mass political display shared by Catholics and Protestants. Another can be observed in the particular and varied uses of history characteristic of Northern Irish life. The political ideologies of individuals, including their political and ethnic hatreds, reflect their participation in a variety of common Western European organisations (churches, men's' clubs, musical bands, local militia etc.) which have special ethnic and sectarian significance in the context of the social and political history of the North of Ireland. Organisational connections and relationships are demonstrated in the variety of historical references and allusions overheard in everyday talk, especially political talk (or, as is common in Ireland, in political song). One particular use of history is the construction of differences between Protestants and Catholics (claimed by the Comber Orangemen to be "both lame and blind"), and between the Irish and the British that basically patterns ethnic and political violence, and in the justification of collective hatreds and acts of violence by means of interpretive and interactional frames that are constructed basically in folk historical terms.

References

Arensberg, Conrad 1959. *The Irish Countryman: An Anthropological Study.* Glouster, Mass.: P. Smith

Boal, Frederick W. and Livingstone, David N. 1984. *The Frontier in the City: Eth-nonationalism in Belfast International Political Science Review.* 5: 161 - 179

---

esoteric symbols and organisational information in regular public displays? Hobsbawm comments that "members were pleased and edified...non-members impressed and entertained" by the annual processions and other public ceremonies of these groups (ibid: 160-161). While this is undoubtedly true, as an explanation it hardly conveys the implications of power and threat implicit in mass demonstrations by the Orange Order and the paramilitary organisations (including the Provisional IRA) in Northern Ireland.

Roy Rappaport's idea (1968) that public rituals transmit information about the numbers and readiness to fight of native groups in highland New Guinea is useful here. Parades in Northern Ireland are certainly displays of strength performed to intimidate enemies and impress friends.

Geertz, Clifford 1963. The Integrative Revolution: Primordial Sentiments and Civil Politics in the New States. In: *Old Societies and New States.* London: The Free Press of Glencoe

Hechter, Michael 1975. Internal Colonialism: The Celtic Fringe. In: *British National Development.* London: Routledge and Kegan Paul

Hobsbawm, Eric 1959. *Primitive Rebels.* Manchester: Manchester University Press

Kenney, Mary Catherine 1991. *Neighbourhoods and Parades: The Social and Symbolic Organisation of Conflict in Northern Ireland.* PhD dissertation, Department of Anthropology, University of Michigan

Leyton, Elliott 1974. The Orange and the Green: Opposition and Integration. In: *Ulster.* Man 9(2): 185 – 198

Miller, David 1983. The Armagh Troubles, 1784 – 95. In: Samuel Clark and James S. Donnelly Jr (eds.). *Irish Peasants: Violence and Political Unrest, 1780 - 1914.* Madison. University of Wisconsin Press: 155 - 191

Rappaport, Roy 1979. *Ecology, Meaning and Religion.* Berkeley: North Atlantic Books,

Rappaport, Roy 1968. *Pigs for the Ancestors.* New Haven: Yale University Press

Roberts, Paul E. W. 1983. Caravats and Shanavests: Whiteboyism and Faction Fighting in East Munster, 1802 - 1811. In: Samuel Clark and James S. Donnelly Jr (eds.). *Irish Peasants: Violence and Political Unrest, 1780 - 1914.* Madison. University of Wisconsin Press: 64 - 101

Sahlins, Peter 1989. *Boundaries: The Making of France and Spain in the Pyrenees.* Berkeley: University of California Press

Turner, Victor 1974. *Dramas, Fields and Metaphors.* Ithaca, New York: Cornell University Press

ABSTRACT

Hatred and difference are always socially constructed realities. However human differences and conflict are not constructed everywhere in the same way or by the same cultural agents. Viewed cross-culturally, certain localised organisations and voluntary associations play a major role in defining and interpreting human differences and sometimes in targeting the so defined "other" as a target of political and ethnic hatred and even violence. In Northern Ireland, Republican paramilitaries (Catholic) have tended to target "the British" (Northern Ireland police officers, British soldiers and the English public) as victims of political violence. In contrast loyalist paramilitaries (Protestant) mainly target their Catholic neighbours as victims of political murder. This paper, which describes the historical role of men's organisation like the (Protestant) Orange Order in local Northern Irish interethnic relations, shows how this particular regional pattern of hatred and ethnic violence has developed.

REGULARITY IN CHAOS:

THE POLITICS OF DIFFERENCE IN THE RECENT HISTORY OF SOMALIA

Günther Schlee

Introduction

In poststructuralist anthropology kinship and lineages are no longer fashionable. This paper, however, seeks to explore the constant elements, the patterns or "structures" so to speak, and, the lineage factor prominent among them, in connection with new and more variable factors in recent conflicts in Somalia. In order to clarify the lineages and the contractual elements employed in their mobilization it focusses on the best known example, the rivalry between the two pretenders to the presidency of the country, namely Aydid (killed in 1996 and succeeded by his son) and Ali Mahdi, along with their respective allies. In the 1990s each one was in control of a part of the capital city. It deals with old and new forces in Somali politics. Examples from other parts of Somalia and of Somali in other countries (Kenya, Europe ...) are used to illustrate one or the other point but are not explored systematically. The paper starts with a summary of the history of Somalia and continues with an analysis of the forms of conflict extant there. [180]

Somalia, as it appears on the map today, has only existed since 1960. Or to be more precise, this construction existed from 1960 until it broke up towards the end of the 1980s, when ever larger parts of the region came under the control of competing militias. For roughly three decades though, a unified state did exist, not only on paper, but as a political reality. As used here, however, the term "the history of Somalia" includes both the period prior to and in particular the period following this approximately thirty year interlude. Because directly or indirectly, the problems that led to costly, futile interventions by international agencies and to an ongoing refugee problem all ultimately have something to do with the breakdown of this state.

"Somali" was of course the name of a people long before the states which Somalis live in today (Djibouti, Ethiopia, now once more fragmented Somalia and Kenya), and these countries' colonial forerunners, took shape. The Somali language belongs to the lowland branch of the East Cushitic languages, the neighbouring languages to the west: Afar, Saho, Oromo and Rendille. The internal dialect differentia-

---

[180] There are early German versions of this paper (Schlee 1995 and in Schlee / Werner (eds.) 1996.) Some of the materials used here have also been included in a more comprehensive publication in Spanish (Schlee 1998). The present version has been expanded and updated with regard to recent events. (The emphasis here is not on these events, however; the focus is rather on the identification of patterns, and these can be illustrated just as well with reference to what happened some time ago as to very recent events.) I have also attempted to take the latest literature into account, in the notes at any rate. I thank Adam Kuper, Stephen Reyna and Patty Gray for comments.

tion is strong, and even more pronounced in the south than the north, which seems to indicate that these people have had a longer history in the south.[181] The nucleus from which the Somali-speaking groups spread would appear to lie in the south-west of the area they currently occupy, probably in the southern part of the Ethiopian highlands or in what is today the Kenyan-Ethiopian border region (Schlee 1987 a). The thesis, that there was a general tendency to migrate from north to south arises from an unjustified generalisation of recent migrations of certain clan groups.[182] Nevertheless, this strong emphasis on north-south migrations, also found in oral accounts, ties in very well with pious legends of genealogical origins in the *quraysh*, the tribe of the Prophet, and descent from migrant Arab sheikhs. Were one to subscribe to these legends, it would mean that all Somalis were Arabs by patrilineal descent. The origins of their distinctive language and characteristics - of everything that makes Somalis Somali - are not explained in these traditional accounts. Moreover, different versions of these genealogies contradict one another (Schlee 1987 b, 1989: 214).

As an ethnic category, "Somali" is not clearly delineated. Certain groups have increasingly come to see themselves as Somali in the course of Islamisation. There are also transitional linguistic and cultural areas between Oromo and Somalis in which groups may define themselves more as one or the other depending on what happens to be politically opportune.[183] The first attempts to colonise Somali territories were made from 1884 onwards, when the European countries divided Africa up amongst themselves at the Berlin Conference. Since the building of the Suez Canal, Aden had been of extreme importance to the British as a base due to its position on the sea route to India. In 1885 and 1886 British negotiators entered into various agreements of mutual assistance with Somali chiefs on the coast across from Aden. If one reads these agreements carefully, there is no mention of handing over territory; but since the rival European colonial powers needed no particular legitimation for their conquests in Africa anyway, this was of little consequence.[184] In 1885 France took Djibouti, and in 1887 the Ethiopian emperor Menelik captured the Muslim city of Harer in the east of the country, driving a wedge deep into Somali-speaking territories. In the same year, Ethiopia signed a border agreement with the British. Already at this point, then, the British must have felt entitled to dispose of Somali territories.

Italy completed its takeover of Italian Somalia only in the 1920s; the territory finally took on the form it was to retain in 1925, when Jubaland, formerly part of Brit-

---

[181] See Lamberti (1983) on Somali dialects, Dyen (1956) on the relationship between language distribution patterns and the history of the spread of people.

[182] As recently as 1980 Lewis (1980: 22-3) still subscribed to this thesis. Though often repeated, it has little historical foundation.

[183] Schlee / Shongolo 1995, Schlee 1994 a.

[184] FitzGibbon (1982: 15-20) quotes some of these agreements verbatim; see also Hamilton (1967). On the further dynamics unleashed by the border drawn between Ethiopia and north Somalia, see Djama (1993).

ish East Africa, was conceded to the Italians. The British, having had unpleasant experiences with the Aulihan Somalis at Serenli in 1916 (Schlee 1989: 44f), were undoubtedly happy to comply with the Italians' desire to expand their territories in this area. Since one of the arenas of the Second World War was the Horn of Africa, the development of colonies was interrupted during this period. After the war, the Italians regained their lost colony in the form of a UN mandate. From the British-controlled north, however, the Somali Youth League (SYL) articulated ever more pressing demands for independence; and since the British and Italian Somali territories became independent in 1960, with their unification into a single state ensuing a few days later, it can be said that in effect the colonial period lasted barely a generation. That the colonial states did not last long does not mean that the Somali had no experience of statehood as such. Just to their west there were sultanates like the one of Harrar and the Ethiopian empire. Djama (1997 a: 403 ff.) is right in underlining that it would be a simplification to describe Somali society as a pure and non-state lineage system. Mainly on the coast nuclei of centralised power, the emergence of a commercial class and links to the world market could be found. These rudimentary states and commercial networks were penetrated by the lineage mode of organisation, and that applies also to the postcolonial state and later its fragments. Even if Djama puts the stress on the differences between his analysis and the "functionalist model" of segmentary lineages, his description is full of references to the latter. His final and concluding example of a chief who was originally elected by his lineage and who later managed to find all sorts of arrangements with external powers and kept an elevated position through all political upheavals, shows, according to Djama, that "the dynamics at work in the local political field can no longer be read along the old segmentary grid" (1997 a: 425). From this example one can also draw the opposite conclusion: the persistence of choosing of a leader by a lineage council indicates the continued importance of lineages. Even if the "old segmentary grids" are no longer the only elements necessary to understand local politics (if ever they were), it continues to be true that these latter cannot be "read" without reference to them. *(The translations of citations are all mine.)*

What Djama's analysis shows is that instead of playing out the "lineage" against the "State" (like the classical British authors did), and instead of playing out the "modern" forces and the "State" against the "lineage", one has to study the interpenetration of the two.

For a long time after independence Somalia was regarded as the only true nation state in Africa, and given extensive linguistic and cultural unity. Together with the fact that all Somalis locate themselves in a common genealogical system, and the almost one hundred per cent Islamisation, the view seemed justified. Here and here alone in all of sub-Saharan Africa the European idea of a 'nation', implying something more than just a common state, had found organisational expression. However, the question of what all Somalis really do have in common will be addressed further on. From the outset there was also the problem that although almost all the inhabitants of

Somalia were Somalis, by no means all Somalis lived in Somalia. Right from the start there were demands for the annexation of the Somali territories in Djibouti, Ethiopia and Kenya, and in the 1960s a guerrilla movement in the north of Kenya, the so-called *Shifta*, fought for the annexation of north and east Kenya with support from Somalia.

Perhaps 1977 can be regarded as the peak of the Somali state's power. At this point democracy had long given way to a dictatorship which was supported by a clan alliance whose core consisted of only a minority population group. Nevertheless, Somalia had never been closer to achieving its military objectives. The *Western Somali Liberation Front* (WSLF), militarily supported by Somalia, had brought large areas of east Ethiopia, the *Haud* and the *Ogadeen* under its control. In 1978 though things changed. Ethiopia regained its eastern territories, and in Somalia the refugee camps filled up. The USA had been supporting Ethiopia for decades, whereas Somalia had been relying mainly on the Soviet Union for the preceding ten years. A change of alliances occurred in 1977, with the Soviet Union henceforth supporting Ethiopia, whilst the USA half-heartedly turned to Somalia. Prior to this, the USA had acquired the Indian Ocean island of Diego Garcia as a strategic base, which meant that Kagnew, its base in Eritrea had ceased to be of much significance.[185] The use of this Eritrean base had been agreed with the central government in Ethiopia.[186] Thus although the USA had up until then had a very concrete interest in Ethiopia remaining a centralised state, this interest now sunk considerably. In addition, the Carter administration was facing growing criticism for supporting a regime responsible for the bloody suppression of the Eritrean liberation movement. When the revolution in Ethiopia led to imperial rule being replaced by a regime with Marxist-Leninist proclivities, it was no big deal for the Americans to end the alliance. The Russians were able to exchange a small ally in the Horn for a big one, thus making a significant advance as far as influence in Africa went.[187]

---

[185] Lewis (1981: 14) infers this connection.

[186] According to Matthies (1987: 105) the American military's rights in Ethiopia, particularly the use of the Kagnew base, were granted in return for extensive military and economic aid. "The USA saw in the Ethiopia of the time a stable, conservative and anti-communist bulwark ..."

[187] This view, that the Soviets simply exchanged a small piece of Africa for a larger one (about ten times larger in terms of population) may appear too simplistic to some analysts. Prunier (1997: 394) attributes ideological motives to the Soviets "...Somalia... saw its Soviet protectors abandon her in the middle of the conflict to join in a decisive way the side of the much more credibly Marxist-Leninist revolution which was taking place at the time in Ethiopia" (all translations of quotations are mine). The credibility of Marxism-Leninism in Ethiopia in the dergue/Mengistu period (1974-1991) may appear doubtful to others (not to speak of its credibility in Russia itself during that period). In response to this footnote in an earlier version, Gérard Prunier sent me the following comment: I do agree with you that the primary motive of the Soviet alliance reversal of 1977 was a desire to ally themselves with a stronger power in the Horn. But please try to deal with complex advanced/bureaucratic societies with the same degree of understanding and sophistication you display when dealing with the Gabra or the Aulihan. During the Brejnev era Soviet Marxism was sick (as you rightly point out). I did not mean that everybody in Moscow was cynical about it. Many would have liked to revivify it. I have been a long-time student of left-wing movement (although never a Marxist

Somalia had also gained sympathy in the West when Mohammed Siad Barre's government allowed a unit of the German Federal Border Guard to storm a Lufthansa aircraft hijacked and held at Mogadishu by Arab terrorists on October 18, 1977. The Somali government expected, and received, Western support as a reward for their co-operation in what the Germans code-named "operation fire magic" ("Aktion Feuer-zauber"). However, this support was not sufficient to ensure Barre's victory in the *Ogadeen* war.[188]

In the context of the superpowers' change of alliances in the Horn of Africa, Somalia and Ethiopia totted up some staggering arms-related statistics. The Soviet Union's military aid to Ethiopia in 1977 and 1978, more or less equalled its imports to Somalia over the entire preceding decade. In 1977 the value of arms imports to Ethiopia was 132.3 % of the total value of that country's exports, and in 1978 the figure was 358.3 %. Note that this does not refer to the profits made over and above the rest of the country's foreign trade, but to the total value of all products Ethiopia exported in this period. In Somalia too, the value of arms imports exceeded the total value of exports in 1974, 1976, 1977 and 1978 - which, at 158.9 %, reached its peak. Already in the 1970s, then, there was no hope whatsoever of these countries ever being able to pay back the loans taken out on the basis of their own economies to buy arms. Nor indeed could those who delivered weapons to the Horn on credit have possibly expected payment (Henze 1984: 651) . There are rumours though that in the years that followed, the Russians had direct access to goldmines in southern Ethiopia, and that gold deliveries that do not appear in the foreign trade statistics were made to the Soviet Union.

When the tide of war turned against Somalia in the *Ogadeen* war, there was a massive flood of refugees. It was never possible to establish exactly how many were

---

myself, more of an Anarchist which predisposes me to work among Somali) and I had long conversations with Russians and others (East Germans, Bulgarians) in Addis-Ababa in the mid-1980s. Many told me that they thought that Ethiopia's was a genuine Marxist revolution, because of the land issue, the class struggles and so on. They were even fascinated by the parallels between Russian and Ethiopian revolutions and I remember a Soviet diplomat telling me with great enthusiasm: "This is their 1919". On the Ethiopian side there was a certain amount of cynicism and *realpolitik* but there was also genuine enthusiasm for the revolution. And quarrels about its course, up to and including violent confrontations between supporters of various revolutionary tendencies. I know that they all had their regional/ethnic dimensions (i.e. the "Oromo Mei'son", the "Amhara EPRP") but such ethnic descriptions were definitely short of the reality even if they did have some relevance. At a time when official Soviet Marxism was intellectually, politically and emotionally exhausted the Russians found it romantic, challenging and refreshing to be helping a "real revolution". They even would tell me: "We know very well that those niggers in Congo-Brazzaville, Benin, Mozambique and Angola are not serious; but these fellows here (meaning the Ethiopians) *they* are the genuine article". One Russian even added the strange opinion that "only they can become good Marxists in Africa because they are Orthodox Christians". He did not explicit the cultural or intellectual connection between Orthodoxy and Marxism, although a person with such an evil anarchist mind as mine could probably supply the missing link.

[188] Development cooperation in the civilian sector was also intensified after "Mogadishu". For instance, the German Organisation for Technical Cooperation, GTZ, was running one of its biggest programmes worldwide in Somalia in the 1980s, with 22 projects and 50 experts (Conze / Labahn 1986: 7).

involved, since the Somali government systematically hindered or manipulated censuses. In any event, the government wanted to present high numbers to ensure a constant flow of aid. Thus from time to time refugees were moved from one camp to another by truck, to be counted several times. In the end a figure of 700,000 was agreed upon - a number which must be regarded as politically motivated, and the result of negotiations.[189] The country's dependence on the international community rose due to the refugee problem, which was also perpetuated and exacerbated by the Somali government itself impeding remigration and integration. The numerous UN officials who lived in a select quarter of Mogadishu earned on average 45 times more than a Somali minister.[190] Given this kind of imbalance, it is not hard to imagine that a Somali minister would scarcely be content to live on his salary alone; instead, Somali bureaucrats made the food aid industry and other charitable institutions pay for allowing them to help the country. The representatives of the aid agencies, who were often on temporary contracts and anxious to have one project phase after the other implemented, were often only too willing to pay such bribes. Through this type of corruption and via other mechanisms such as the disappearance of goods, allocation of posts in projects etc., the state rapidly turned into an instrument for accessing help from the outside and for creaming off external resources.

At the same time the development of internal resources, in particular the pastoral economy, was increasingly neglected. This was because, even though this view had long since been refuted by science, there was a "conviction on the part of officials in the local government and also in the international development organisations that it [i. e. mobile livestock husbandry, G.S.] is an anachronism, a sign of backwardness" (Stern 1991: 124). Similarly, Baas notes: "The rural regions, which is the area where foreign exchange income originates, are ignored, the nomadic life is branded primitive and unproductive" (1991: 234). State measures, ostensibly aimed at improving grazing conditions, led at best to the elites privately acquiring the choicest cuts to be had in the pastoral system: an "expression of political calculation aimed at self-enrichment on the part of the government" and material considerations paid to "financially powerful persons" (Stern 1991: 126, see also Janzen 1984).

Yet over the years that sector of Somali society which could reckon with obtaining benefits from the state shrank ever more. In spite of making the clan structure a taboo - under Siad Barre it was officially forbidden to ask anyone what their clan was – this same clan structure has always remained the power base of each Somali gov-

---

[189] Waldron 1984: 673, similarly also Negussay 1984: 665.

[190] Using the Somali Shilling's black market exchange value, which is a truer reflection of its buying power, the difference is in fact 1:90 (Hancock 1991: 198). Anna Simons who witnessed the end of that first (non-military) UN invasion of Somalia in 1989 describes the way of life and the stereotypical convictions of this subculture of American and European "experts" and the relationships of their Somali employees and counterparts with them. By calculating domestic budgets of the Somali, she also shows that for them the search for more or less illegal supplements to their salaries was a question of survival (Simons 1996: 124 ff.).

ernment.[191] The prohibition on speaking about clans was linked to the impossibility of discussing this power base, or indeed of questioning its legitimacy. Whereas earlier Somali governments had co-opted elements of various clans to widen their power base, Siad Barre's government was known as 'MOD': the 'M' stood for his clan, *Marehan (Marexan)*, the 'O' for the *Ogadeen*, the President's mother's clan (or as one would say in Somali, the clan of his mother's brother: *reer abti*), and the 'D' for *Dulbahante*, the clan of his son-in-law, who was head of State Security.[192] As the Barre regime went into decline, ever larger parts of the *Ogadeen* and *Dulbahante* began to pull out, and eventually Barre was left with his own clan *Marehan* as his only power base. On the other hand, during the final stages, the *Marehan* were almost entirely militarised or otherwise incorporated into the state.

This process whereby large parts of the Somali population broke away from the state until only the *Marehan* were left within it, began in the north, where the second largest of Somali clan families, the *Isaaq*, had long felt excluded from power. The city of Hargeisa was bombarded, wells poisoned, and millions of landmines were planted in north Somalia.[193]

As Mohamed Siad Barre's power dwindled, so the armed opposition to him grew, until finally on Jan. 27, 1991 he was forced to flee Mogadishu. While the exiles' organisations were still awaiting consultation, Ali Mahdi promptly declared himself interim president two days later. The north reacted on May 18, 1991 by declaring the independence of 'Somaliland' within the borders of the former British colony. In the south of the country, those forces denied a share of the power by Ali Mahdi took up arms against him. On Sept. 10, 1991 the UN announced that it was pulling out of Somalia, although it remained active in the northern Republic of Somaliland (Eikenberg / Körner 1993: 34 - 45). The reason for the helpers' withdrawal was the civil war unleashed when Ali Mahdi proclaimed himself president. This self-proclamation was contested by the other movements that had ousted Siad Barre. Within a short time, famine broke out as a result of the war.

The USA, presumably motivated amongst other considerations by the desire to improve its image in the Islamic world in the wake of the Gulf War by appearing in an Islamic country in the role of helper, not enemy, felt obliged to intervene in the name

---

[191] It is evident that this taboo on speaking about clans – which here even takes the form of an official interdiction – is an indicator of the importance of these clans in games of power. It is therefore strange to see anthropologists who have come to analyse these very power games obey this taboo. Anna Simons (as Djama 1997 b: 525n has noticed) never gives the names of clans in her case histories. I thought this was political (over-)"correctness" on her side, but she later told me that nobody volunteered clan names to her. And she might not have pushed. In Kenya, where there are no such political sensitivities, people would often ask for somebody for his clan affiliation before they even knew his name.

[192] Lewis 1981: 16. The *Dulbahante* son-in-law was Mohamed Seleban Abdallah. More will be said about another son-in-law of Siad Barre's below.

[193] Africa Watch Report: Somalia, a government at war with its own people 1990.

of the United Nations. On Dec. 9, 1992, during peak television viewing time in America, US troops landed in Mogadishu. Some months later, and also on camera, the corpses of Americans were maltreated by an angry mob in the streets of Mogadishu. As a result, the USA left the country again, the last of their troops pulled out on March 25, 1993[194], ahead of other intervention forces – of which the Pakistanis had suffered the most losses. Here the chronological overview comes to an end. Looking back, one has to see the United Nations intervention in Somalia (UNOSOM), in which the US played a prominent part, as a failure that cost billions of dollars, and incurred even greater costs in human and political terms. Various reasons as to why this happened will be addressed below in relation to a closer analysis of forms of conflict and organisation in Somali society.

Forms of conflict in pre-colonial and colonial Somali society

At a conference on the Horn of Africa in December 1993 at the Institute of African and Asian Studies of the University of Khartoum (Sudan), a representative of the Somali National Alliance (SLA), the faction under General 'Aydid', one of the former presidents of Somalia, took the floor frequently and at length. His thesis was that before the intrusion of Europeans into the Horn of Africa, the Somalis lived together in peace and harmony. Only outside interventions, first the colonial conquest and all it entailed, then the American intervention, were able to destroy Somalia's peace. This myth of a pre-colonial idyll was widespread in sub-Saharan Africa in the 1960s, when decolonisation was at its peak. However particularly with regard to Somalia, this assertion of pre-colonial tranquillity is nothing short of absurd.[195]

Somalia is the only country in Africa in which the majority of the population still consists of nomadic pastoralists. Even today, the one-sided orientation towards livestock products for specific markets remains a problem for the export economy.[196]

---

[194] For a chronology see Ruf 1994: 165. Ruf discusses legal aspects of the UN intervention.

[195] Absurd as it may be, this myth about the pacific character of pre-colonial Somali society seems rather wide-spread. Prunier has also come across this "construction, most often of Somali origin" (1997: 375) which he contrasts with his own finding that "violence is a fact which is inseparable from the life of segmentary groups" (p. 383).

[196] According to Janzen (1987: 17), over 50 % of the Somali are nomads. About 25 % live in towns, and the remaining 25 % are sedentary farmers. Sedentarisation has increased recently (Aden 1986). The dominance of the livestock economy is most obvious in the profits from export (in times of peace, figures from 1982). The livestock economy's share was 93.9 %; agriculture on the other hand made up only 1.3 % (Janzen 1987: 22). One problem with the livestock exports was Saudi Arabia's purchasing monopoly (monopsony) and the one-sided orientation of the trade structures towards this (Janzen 1986: 22, 38; Hummen 1987: 120; Aves & Bechtold 1987: 155). Abdullahi (1991: 262) shows the cyclical nature of this trade with Saudi Arabia in a graphic model. The *hajj* season is the high point of this cycle. This contradicts the image of nomads constituting a traditional society producing only for their own needs. Somali nomads are market-dependent and react to market trends by adapting their production to meet the demand. As to the export situation, the mid-nineties presented the following picture: the prices for small livestock, which make up the majority of the exports, were low. The Saudi-Arabian purchasers were in a strong bargaining position. Busy shipping had resumed around

The picture handed down from pre-colonial times is dominated by the notion of martial pastoralism. Narrower and broader solidarities and alliances were created according to the principle of patrilineal clan organisation in small units and also in larger units of the same kind (Schlee 1989: 26 - 29). By tracing back the father's line to specific apical ancestors, every Somali was able to evoke numerous patrilineal units, some more restricted, some more expansive. Smaller units of limited genealogical depth were included in the larger units calculated from more distant apical ancestors. One of these units – larger units of several thousand members were chosen for the purpose – was defined as the unit that had to pay wergeld. If a member of such a group killed a male outsider, then a fine of 100 camels had to be paid to prevent retaliation. For a woman the payment was 50 camels, and there was also a whole catalogue of different grades of compensation payments for injuries. Such payments are termed *mag* in Somali, but are more frequently referred to by the Arabic term *diya* in the literature. They are a component of *adat* law, which is recognised in the Islamic legal system as local law albeit with a lower status than the *shari͑a* and provided it does not conflict with the *shari͑a*. A larger *diya*-paying group had a double advantage over a smaller one. Thanks to its own potential strength, it could assume with greater confidence that the opposing group would not attempt to take vengeance and would withdraw from a disputed territory. Even in the event of the larger group agreeing to pay wergeld, the individual members each had to pay a smaller contribution.

The rules about compensation are based on the right to retaliate because one pays compensation to avoid vengeance. If one calls this a form of justice, one might just as well call it a form of injustice. Other legal systems, may, of course, also produce injustice and they may be sensitive to force and bend the law. In the Somali case no force is required to bend the rules: force underlies the rules; the rules themselves provide the space in which force is exerted. If vengeance or acceptance of bloodwealth are equally legitimate options, it is always the party which is in a position to exert vengeance that can shape the outcome of the negotiations by an effective latent threat of violence. Therefore one can defend one's rights just as well as one's wrongs through this system. Below is an example of what happens between a small and weak group and a large and powerful one as a result of purely bilateral negotiations about compensation without judge or arbitration.

In northern Kenya in 1990 I was present at a meeting between Degodia, a large and well armed clan which affiliates itself by a uterine link to the Hawiyye clan fam-

---

many small harbours on the Somali coast. On the Saudi side, a harbour specially for the livestock transports from Somalia had been created near Jidda. Here the market was subject to somewhat different practices than elsewhere; the suppliers were exclusively Somalis, and they were disadvantaged - with official support. Payment was made in goods, for example in sugar! Though Somalia did export to other countries on the Arabian Peninsula, Saudi Arabia is the major customer, on account of the *hajj* (Ahmed Farah Mohamed, personal communication, Bielefeld, 16.7.1995). In 1997, Saudi-Arabia once more banned the import of meat from Somalia after an outbreak of Rift Valley fever in Kenya (IRIN, May 13th, 1999).

ily, and Sakuye, a group of some one thousand islamised speakers of the Oromo language. The Sakuye had suffered a heavy loss of lives and property during the *shifta* emergency of the 1960s when they had taken up the cause of Somali irredentism.

A young Degodia had raped a Sakuye girl who was tending animals in the bush. He left her disfigured and almost without a voice as a result of stabs wounds to the face and neck. The Sakuye demanded five camels and the Degodia agreed perfectly that that would be a *diya* payment justified by the rules. "But, if you demand *diya* now," the Degodia went on, "what would you do in the inverse case, if, for example, one of your youths killed one of ours? Would you be able to pay one hundred camels as *diya* for him? Certainly not. You would ask us not to insist on *diya* and to accept the sort of present one would give inside one's tribe, in a brotherly way, to mollify us. Now it is your turn to waive *diya* and to accept a gift. Let us be brotherly!" In the end the Sakuye accepted a single camel. However, it is doubtful whether the Degodia would have shown the same degree of brotherliness, had a Sakuye man raped one of their women. More likely they would have committed a revenge massacre, or, if the Sakuye had persuaded them to accept compensation, they would have insisted on one hundred camels. The Sakuye are too prudent to put this to the test.

This system of justice gives those the freedom to defend themselves who are able to do so. It knows no other equality but that of balanced forces. But what about the third part of the motto of the French revolution, namely fraternity? This system dictates to everyone not strong enough to stand on his own to become someone's little brother as soon as he can. So, in this system one needs to be strong, and strength depends on numbers and cohesion. If the numbers of people linked to oneself by ties based on patrilineal descent are not sufficient, they need to be complemented by contracts.

Let us first focus on the patrilineal descent groups in which smaller ones are nested in larger ones that have greater genealogical depth but are of the same kind. As far as the recruitment of military strength and organisation of social solidarity along patrilineal lines is concerned, the Somali are by no means unique. The model of segmentary lineage systems once was a standard one (particularly in British anthropology: e. g. Evans-Pritchard 1940, Middleton & Tait 1958). In fact, for a time, it was used to such an extent that it has occasionally aroused criticism when applied all too mechanically to where it was not appropriate, or when other elements of social organisation (Big-Man-ship, age-groups etc.), also present and making the picture seem more complex, were neglected due to an overly one-sided accent on the segmentary lineage system.[197] The argument was less concerned with the question of whether the segmentary

---

[197] Indeed, descriptions of those societies upon which the development of the segmentary lineage model was based are the ones most intensively re-analysed to find out if other models could not be used for them. In the early 1980s there was a major *Nuer* debate raging in *Current Anthropology* (Karp / Maynard 1983 with eight commentaries, Bonte 1984, Glickman 1985), with a smaller one in *American Anthropologist* (Verdon 1982, Kelly 1983). Kuper (1988) is often understood as considering the

lineage system could be seen as an instructive model – that much was granted by most – but rather what it was a model *of*. Did it model an emic social construct, or a behavioural reality? Whereas for example Peters (1967), writing on the Bedouin of Cyrenaica, believed that their form of organisation was actually based on local units, and that the lineage genealogies were mere ideology, Salzman (1978, field research in the Iranian part of Baluchistan) objected that the lineage system was by no means a folk ideology. Instead it was rooted in the reality of actual behaviour; and this reality was given in the case of the Bedouins of Cyrenaica as well. Even if from time to time the lineage system might be of secondary importance to territorially defined units, Salzman argued, it remained in reserve until the next territorial shift or next migration, when it would re-emerge as a functioning structure. Later the model of segmentary lineages was washed away altogether by an anti-structuralist wave along with all other concepts relating to social structure. It was done away with on the grounds of principle, not on empirical grounds. This later criticism did not distinguish between cases where the model is more appropriate and where it is less so. Those who discarded this model often did not replace it by one which explained the data in a better fashion. Many of them appear not to be interested in explanations at all (the *Writing Culture* crowd). Now the time has come either to give up the anthropological enterprise altogether as a vain effort or to take up the struggle with empirical data and model building once more. I opt for the latter. We can distinguish between cases where the segmentary lineage model is an artificial imposition, others, where it works but neglects further important aspects[198], and yet others where it fits rather well. To a large extent, the Somali – and not just their folk ideology or image they themselves have of their society – correspond to this model, even if a few amendments are made below. This is not to imply that they are helplessly subjugated to these lineage structures. Even "descent" is not pure fate, but subject to political and religious influences; in other words, to human ambition. (On the influences affecting the formation of Somali genealogies cf. for example Schlee 1989, Chapter 5.)[199] Obviously, the ties and bonds that arise

---

entire lineage model to be an anthropological illusion. In a personal conversation, however, he told me that he regards it as overgeneralised and too mechanically applied but fitting some cases better than others. This would not amount to a rejection on principle. Johnson (1991: 116) keeps himself aloof from this debate, declaring that all those involved have completely misunderstood the history and ecology of the Upper Nile region and that no one has a solid empirical basis. In part, he asserts, the issue is nothing more than selective readings of E.E. Evans-Pritchard (1940).

[198] I criticised the model whereby clans and subclans are regarded only as subunits of larger units and interethnic clan identities are neglected (Schlee 1998: 1).

[199] To claim that they *are* a segmentary lineage society seems problematic only in terms of principle. Because if there are such things as segmentary lineage societies, then they constitute one. One can of course hold the view that it doesn't make sense, or is potentially misleading at least, to apply adjectival characterisations of this kind to *societies*. The line of thought being pursued here is analogous to Needham's, when he also asserted that there are no patrilineal and no matrilineal societies, but rather at most patri- and matrilineal forms of transferring rights and affiliations. If one applies characterisations like "segmentary", "caste", "modern", "organic", "class" etc. to entire societies rather than to forms of organisation and internal differentiation which may also co-exist and interact, then societies end up all too quickly in different pigeonholes, or even in different disciplines: the segmentary ones end up with the Africa anthropologists, and the caste ones with the Indologists. Yet some elements of

from the obligations imposed by common linear descent or from the transfer of these reciprocal obligations to adopted "brothers" were not "discovered" by modern anthropologists. Indeed, according to Ibn Khaldun, blood (including pseudo-kinship based on the model of consanguinity) was the only kind of bond which could serve as a basis for power at all. For Ibn Khaldun, who analysed Muslim societies in the Maghreb and the Mashreq with astounding perspicacity in the 14th century, it was nomadic herdsmen, and also farmers, who had the necessary tribal cohesion to allow them to take power in the Muslim state. Ibn Khaldun was also familiar with the complex urban type of society with its division of labour; this functioned according to completely different principles from the communities of equal-ranking nomadic pastoralists, but in Ibn Khaldun's view lacked the vital element of cohesion. (Here he differed from Durkheim, who saw the division of labour as the root of modern, higher "organic solidarity" as opposed to the earlier "mechanical solidarity" of segmentary societies.) For Ibn Khaldun, the city was at most a useful site where sophisticated objects were produced, and one which was worth ruling over – but it was never a source of power.

Thus Ibn Khaldun's theory is a theory of the state. He is interested in how segmentary structures form the basis of power in the state (or as we would say today, in a particular kind of state). Segmentary societies can of course manage very well without the state (and unlike Ibn Khaldun, one would say today that states can also manage without segmentarily organised conquerors).

This independence from the state, and the possibility of organising life without state and centralised governments, was what fascinated modern ethnologists about segmentary societies. Book titles like "Regulated Anarchy" (Sigrist 1967) and "Tribes without Rulers" (Middleton & Tait 1958) reflect this interest (Leverenz 1987).

But while modern ethnologists come from societies organised as states, and thus thematise the potential distancing from the state demonstrated by segmentary societies, Ibn Khaldun is coming from the opposite direction: his starting point is the segmentary society, and he is interested in explaining how the power to rule is constituted in the state. This power, he observes, changes hands cyclically. Nomads conquer the cities and "go soft" so rapidly that within approximately four generations they too become the victims of the next wave of nomadic conquests, and become part of the subjugated urban population themselves (Gellner 1981). According to Ibn Khaldun, critical urban Qur'an scholars, tired of the corrupt rule of pampered sultans, enter into alliances with as yet untainted tribal warriors, and together periodically renew Islamic society. Ibn Khaldun is an analyst rather than a moralist. Yet to the extent that moral evaluations shine through, the nomadic warriors can be seen to have the more positive role. Obviously, Ibn Khaldun's theory cannot be transferred indiscriminately from the

---

caste thinking (and the practices which accompany it) such as endogamy/hypergamy, or else differentiation on the basis of status or occupation in the case of the "segmentary societies" (for example the sacred lineages of the Bedouin of Cyrenaica, Evans-Pritchard), would not fit into a framework of this kind.

14th century Maghreb to the Horn of Africa at the end of the 20th century. Perhaps, though, the same cohesive forces of tribal organisation as described by Ibn Khaldun are at work in today's Somalia, and the youthful, qat chewing[200] militia members, harassing the civilian population of Mogadishu from their jeeps with their mounted machine guns, are in fact a degenerate form of Ibn Khaldun's pure, unspoilt Bedouin warrior. Whereas they resemble the latter in their tribal cohesion, they contribute neither to the renewal of Islam nor indeed to any kind of social order.

If it was impossible to recruit a big enough group along patrilineal principles – whether due to the distance from other segments of one's own clan, or to its limited demographic growth – there was still the option of forming *diya*-paying groups with segments of other clans in the same position on a contractual basis. The principle of *tol*, of patrilineal descent, or the segmentary lineage system, and, the principle of *xeer (heer)*, the association by contract, were the two recruitment mechanisms used to constitute the divisions of Somali society; divisions which were internally peaceful, but tendentially aggressive towards outsiders. *Xeer* were contracts between equals. Groups that were too small or weak to present themselves as independent partners in a contractual arrangement could also enter into pseudo-kinship-relations with stronger groups. These relationships are called *sheegat* from the verb *sheeganaya*, "I name". In this case one names the forefathers of another group as one's own, that is, one subordinates oneself to it in terms of genealogy. In any event, one's chances of survival depend on support from a powerful group. This principle is aptly reflected in the Somali motto, "either be a mountain, or else lean against one" (Lewis 1961, 1962, 1972).

Cunning is a highly-valued cultural attribute among Somali. And it is regarded as highly cunning to break a contractual agreement, whether it be based on *xeer* or on *sheegat*, at an opportune moment. Like the stories of the Icelandic Vikings or of Byzantine court intrigues, Somali history bristles with treachery and massacres of former

---

[200] Qat *(catha edulis)*, the leaves of which are chewed, is a mild drug and plays an important role as payment for militia members in Somalia at present. The health aspects of this drug consumption are probably insignificant compared to the political structures which arise as a result of its distribution, and the economic consequences of its being imported by air. Qat is grown in the highlands of east and northeast Africa. The best kinds come from Kenya, where it is known as *miraa*.

In the context of warlords, *qat* is often demonised as a drug (Elwert 1997: 89, 1995: 133). In the media it is sometimes even said to make people go mad. As it is consumed by militias, it is believed to make one aggressive. In fact, it has about the same hallucinogenic potential as chocolate or tea. At most, it deprives one of sleep. For this reason it is appreciated by long distance drivers and watchmen.

For unclear reasons, *qat* was forbidden in Germany where it was consumed only by immigrant circles, mostly Somali, in 1998. At the same time as the legalisation on strong drugs is proposed with good reasons to reduce Beschaffungskriminalität ("crimes of procuration", drugs related crimes) a very soft drug is being pushed underground. That may mean that Somali asylum seekers will be obliged to spend an even higher proportion of their welfare on *qat*. As to the role of *qat* in Somalia see also Heyer 1997: 29, 30; Pape 1998: 48

protectors. The latter are struck down and robbed of their women and herds the moment their dependents have grown strong enough under their protection.[201]

The ever-present threat of treachery restricted the growth of internally peaceful and cooperative groups. The tendency of groups to become larger, thus reducing the individual's risks vis-à-vis dangers from the outside, was countered by suspicion of distant clan kin and allies from other clans, which produced a tendency towards fission, and thus a reduction in group size.

However, a series of factors caused the tendency towards unity to outweigh the tendency towards division, and thus larger groups were formed. First of all, obviously, there was the threat from outside. Then the skill of politically gifted personalities also contributed. While simple Somalis often married within their own clans, and being relatives, were released from paying part of the brideprice, leaders often contracted strategic marriages across clan boundaries. Sayyid Muhammad Abdille Hassan, who defied several colonial powers at once from 1900 - 1920, made extensive use of this mechanism. Head of a "dervish" order, the *Salihiyya*, he was awarded the derogatory nickname 'Mad Mullah' by the British, and he contracted an impressive number of strategic marriages, both simultaneously and successively.

Battle lines and forms of conflict

In the turmoil after the expulsion of Muhammed Siad Barre, the following picture emerged: the country collapsed into numerous zones in which local power-elites tried to gain control of resources on the basis of clan membership and clan alliances. The capital, Mogadishu, split into two halves, one controlled by Ali Mahdi Muhammed, the other by General Mohammed 'Aydid'[202] until the latter died of the injuries received in an exchange of fire with followers of Osman Ali 'Ato', of whom more presently. A short time later his son Hussein took his place.[203] Both Ali Mahdi and 'Aydid' originally belonged to the United Somali Congress (USC). But since in this context important-looking abbreviations such as this have little substance, it is more productive to examine the power base of both pretendants to the presidency within the

---

[201] Cf. e.g. Turnbull 1955: 2 et passim, Schlee 1989: 46f. That the Somali place cultural value on cunning, and that a well-staged swindle is much admired, can be inferred from a series of folk tales collected by Muuse Haaji Ismaa'iil Galaal, edited by B.W. Andrzejewski, (1956). Cf. e.g. no. 4, p. 33, which is reproduced here in my own translation from the Somali:

Cousin, teach me cunning!

One day a man came to another. He said: "I would like you to teach me cunning." The other replied: "Milk your camel for me!" So the man milked his camel for him, and when he had drunk the milk, the one who had brought the milk said: "And now, teach me cunning!" Whereupon the other said: "I've done that already. I've had your milk, haven't I?" The man's mouth dropped open in surprise.

[202] 'Aydid' will be discussed here almost exclusively with reference to his clan affiliations. For a more detailed biographic appreciation see Dualeh (1994), and for an assessment in terms of the history of ideas, see Zitelmann (1996).

[203] Africa Confidential 37, no. 17, Aug. 1996.

Somali clan system. Overall, Ali Mahdi can count on the support of his subclan of the *Herab* clan, of the *Hawiye*, which is called *Abgal*. In the case of General 'Aydid', it is another *Herab* subclan, the *Habr Gidir*. The distinction, then, is at the subclan level.

It is clear from the news reports of the early 1990s that the division into *Abgal* on the one hand and *Habr Gidir* on the other must have been too rough from the start, or else that segmentary processes had taken place, splitting these subclans into even smaller parties along sub-subclan divisions (lineages). Up to two yet finer degrees of distinction below the level of *Habr Gidir* are mentioned in reports. For example, in June 1994 differences arose between 'Aydid' and his financial advisor Osman 'Ato', and both of them were sure of their respective subgroup's backing: 'Aydid's' being the *Jalaaf* subgroup of the *Saad* sub-subclan of the *Habr Gidir* subclan of the *Hawiye*, Osman 'Ato's' being the *Hilowle* within the *Saad*.[204] In August of that year there had been fighting at an airfield "belonging" to one of 'Aydid's' benefactors, Ahmed Dualeh (*Saad and Habr Gidir*). His airport guards had clashed with fighters recruited from a subgroup of the *Absiye*, who belong to the *Ayr*, who in turn are part of the *Habr Gidir*. This shows, according to "Africa Confidential", that the economic dominance of the *Saad* over the other groups belonging to the *Habr Gidir* continues to meet resistance. The reports also precisely locate Ali Mahdi, the rival president: he is a member of *Harti Abgal*, a subgroup of the *Abgal* subclan of the *Hawiye*.[205] But enough of names. The principle has become clear by now: in the current political and economic conditions, the patrilineal clan structures have a stronger tendency to divide than in the immediately preceding period. Solidarity is restricted to smaller groups of shallower genealogical depth.

Since both presidential hopefuls nursed the ambition to be more than simply ruler of a part of Mogadishu, each tried to extend his power base by means of alliances. General 'Aydid' had an ally amongst the *Ogadeen*, Ahmed Omar 'Jess', who named his faction the *Somali Patriotic Movement* and exercised a certain amount of control in Kisimayu and areas surrounding this southern Somali port.

On 22nd February 1993, shortly after the Belgians and Americans had marched into the town, rival clan groups drove Ahmed Omar 'Jess' out of Kisimayu. These were under orders from Mohamed Sa'id Hirsi, known as General Morgan, another son-in-law of ex-president Mohamed Siad Barre. Mohamed Sa'id Hirsi 'Morgan' is *Majerteen*[206], that is, a member of a clan group that lives mainly at the eastern most

---

[204] Africa Confidential 35, no. 12, June 1994. At a party conference on 12.6.1995 'Ato' replaced 'Aydid' as Chairman of the United Somali Congress, which did not prevent the latter from continuing to claim the state presidency. He was supported in his claim by businessmen from the *Nimaale* and *Ayanle* subclans of *Saad* (Africa Confidential 36, no. 13, June 1995).

[205] Africa Confidential 35, no. 20, Oct. 1994.

[206] According to Africa Confidential 34, no. 5, March 1993 and 35, no. 12, June 1994. The information that he is *Marehan* (34, no. 13) seems to be incorrect. The *Marehan*, the ex-president's clan, are

point of the Horn. Down in the south though there are still people who resettled here because of the drought mentioned above.[207] 'Morgan's' power base also rested on his brothers-in-law, the *Marehan* of ex-president Mohamed Siad Barre and on cooperation with General Adan Abdullahi 'Gebiyu' of the *Ogadeen*. The division into followers of 'Jess' and 'Gebiyu' is said to correspond to that between *Mohamed Zubeir Ogadeen* and *Aulihan Ogadeen*.[208] *Majerteen*, *Marehan* and *Ogadeen* all belong to the large *Darood* clan family. Those who take as their starting point the idea of the segmentary lineage system, in which more closely related groups cooperate against more distant kin, will not be surprised that in this case parts of these three clans should ally themselves with one another. The deviation from the model consists in the fact that they do this against parts of themselves, cooperating with parts of completely unconnected clans: 'Jess' with 'Aydid's' *Habr Gidir-Hawiye* and 'Morgan' and 'Gebiyu' at least de facto Ali Mahdi's *Abgal-Hawiye*, who were manning another front against 'Aydid' and his allies. Since 'Ato's' break with 'Aydid' and in the logic of such alliances it follows that he should join up with 'Aydid's' opponents. Accordingly there were reports [209] that he had had an arrangement with 'Morgan' and also one with Ali Mahdi, which confirmed that these two had an indirect alliance with each other – an alliance, note, with strangers to the clan and not clan "brothers".

Against this background, 'Aydid's' anger at the Americans is understandable. They had entered Kisimayu as "peace-bringers", started to disarm 'Aydid's' ally 'Jess', and then stood and watched his rival 'Morgan' take the town.

Transcontinuities

Elements of a social structure, or a political system, which survive revolutionary alterations and always re-emerge, albeit perhaps under a different name and guise, whatever social ruptures may occur, are termed "transcontinuities". No matter how much the *ancien regime* may have been based upon "divine right", and Napoleon's rhetoric been loaded with "republican" values, the historian still finds more similarities than differences in the organisation of power in both systems. The Stalinist system can be seen as by no means less autocratic than Czarist rule, although Czarist rule openly acknowledged its absolutism, and Stalinism (personality cult aside) professed to be based on rule by the social class constituting the majority of the population. Transcontinuities have also been much discussed with regard to the revolutionary upheavals in

---

his brothers-in-law, not his clan brothers. "Sa'id" and "Siad" are two different names. Tthey are occasionally confused by the press.

[207] Oral information from Feisal Hassan, Bielefeld, 16.5.1995. The spelling of names in this article tends to follow the forms used by the persons in question, rather than the Somali standard orthography, which would have Xasan for Hassan, Farax for Farah, Cabdille for Abdullahi. In many contexts Somali do not use their own orthography.

[208] *Africa Confidential* 35, no. 20, Oct. 1994.

[209] *Africa Confidential* 36, no. 13, June 1995.

Ethiopia, where – at least in the Christian heartland – the same centralist, hierarchical structures always triumph.[210]

In Somalia too it is possible to trace transcontinuities which span two radical historical changes. Patrilineal descent and clan alliances were basic social structures in the pre-colonial as well as colonial period, when the colonial rulers made good use of these very structures to demarcate grazing areas and arbitrate in conflicts. Indeed, they strengthened the structures further by codification; and by strengthening them naturally also changed them.[211] The principles of *tol* and *heer*, patrilineal descent and contractual alliance, also underlie the battle lines formed in the Somali civil war - despite the impressive-sounding names (containing programmatic elements like "National", "Salvation" and the like) used in rhetoric aimed at the outside world.

Like the colonial powers before them, UNOSOM has given in to the temptation of using clan proportion systems to help establish representation and control. In so doing, they have failed to recognise the changeable character of these divisions. Patrilineal units alter their function in accordance with demographic growth. Lineages become subclans, subclans become clans. This is why the Somali language declines to deliver more precise terms for these levels of clan division. Basically, they are always larger or smaller units of the same kind, with their functions depending on their size. And alliances are no less variable. Neither can be pinned down, both are subject to political opportunism, and both can be manipulated far better by Somalis than by rulers or mediators from outside.

Connections established through wives, i. e. in-law relationships, were just as important for Sayyid Mohammed Abdille Hassan at the start of the 20th century as for Mohammed Siad Barre, even though in other respects Somalis would quite rightly object to these two historical figures being put into one basket.

Transcontinuities are not only to be found in such areas as military recruitment or the formation of larger solidarity groups. The organisation of labour in the small family group is often characterised by diversification or spatial separation. In the nomadic herding sector, there is the camel camp, *geel her* or *geel jire*[212] for example; satellite camps at remote pastures, where the young men tend the camels far from the main camp, which is closer to the wells and where the women, children, older men and small livestock are to be found.

After the country suffered a severe drought in 1974, the Somali government developed programmes aimed at introducing other forms of production outside the no-

---

[210] In the ethnographic literature, "Political Systems of Highland Burma" (Leach 1954) is a good example of transcontinuities. The Ethiopian case is discussed by Janssen (1991).

[211] The most remarkable example of a genealogical survey in the colonial period is Hunt, 1951. On the use made of such genealogies cf. Schlee 1984 a: 156, 1989: 48.

[212] The former term is used by Lewis 1981: 23; the latter I heard in Kenya.

madic herding sector. There was a sedentarisation programme on land administered by
agricultural development projects, and fishing towns were established on the coast,
where former pastoralists were taught to fish and given boats and equipment. After a
certain time, a large proportion of the men returned to the nomadic sector, whilst
women and children frequently remained behind in the newly-established settlements
so as to have continued access to services such as schools and healthcare.[213] This pattern of families splitting up geographically on work-related grounds was extended with
the onset of male migration to the Gulf states. Today, with the internationalisation of
the refugee problem, the pattern can be discerned on a global scale: the men will be
working in the Gulf while their families are living on social security in Sweden or
Canada.[214]

With so many transcontinuities, one naturally has to ask what is in fact different
today. One major difference is the escalation of violence. There is a glut of weapons
originating from stocks built up in the course of the superpowers' arms race in the
Horn of Africa in the 1970s, which means automatic firearms are easily available everywhere.[215] Before and during the colonial period, particularly in the dry season, grazing was only available near watering places, and these could be the scenes of fierce
fighting. Occasionally one or two strange herdsmen might be killed at the well. Repri-
sals too, if not forestalled by wergild payments, could sometimes result in death. But
the current confrontations are taking place on a far higher level of escalation, and do
not only concern grazing rights, but also the control of the harbour, the airport, urban
areas and foreign aid deliveries. They go on all year, they are more anonymous and
also more numerous. In a reader mainly concerned with the Jubba Valley, a river oasis,
Cassanelli (Besteman & Cassanelli 1996) also underlines the importance of competi-

---

[213] Lewis 1981: 31; Farah Mohamed / Touati 1991: 100.

[214] The situation in the countries of asylum is not simply characterised by a transfer of old models into
new situations. In family relations there have been radical changes. The practice of the authorities to
count children with the mother and their perception of fathers as peripatetic and unstable elements –
realistic as it may be –led them to channel the financial assistance through the women and even to
register children under the name of their mother's father, may result in these children being regarded
as illegitimate if they ever return to Somalia. These practices contribute to the instability of Somali
marriages which in any case are of comparatively short average duration (ongoing research in cooperation with 'Isir Schlee née Hassan Musa and Saado ᶜAbdi about Somali migrants in Germany).

By marriage a Somali woman does not change her clan affiliation. Patrilineal descent applies to children of both genders, married or unmarried alike, even though it is, of course, only transmitted through
sons. Therefore to avenge a tort against a woman is primarily the responsibility of her brothers and not
of her husband. The double set of links of wives in exogamous marriages – by descent to one clan and
by marriage to another – predestines them for mediating roles. This task of Somali women is claimed
in even stronger terms in exile under the influence of western feminism (Sonja Heyer, report on the
"Seventh International Congress of Somali Studies, York University, Toronto, July 8 – 11, 1999, for
the Max Planck Institute for Social Anthropology, Halle/S.).

[215] On the glut of weapons in west Kenya, cf. Bollig 1992: 73, in north Kenya. Schlee 1994 b: 3,
which also discusses the knock-on effects of the dissolution of Mengistu's army on power relations
elsewhere, as weapons which had been abandoned, sold or exchanged for food were passed from hand
to hand.

tion for commercialised agricultural resources in this context. Indeed, he sees this as the underlying cause of the Somali crisis. In so doing he takes a sideswipe at unnamed earlier analyses which allegedly placed too one-sided an emphasis on clan structures. Focusing on the population of the Jubba Valley, who are crop farmers and partly of Bantu extraction, he argues that the population of Somalia is not only differentiated according to clan membership, but is in his words also "deeply divided by occupation, class, physical type and dialect", even if "journalists and pundits" should have failed to notice this (Cassanelli 1996: 14). To avoid landing in either of these objectionable categories, it is as well to consider this argument more closely.

To begin with the mere presence of occupational and status-related differentiations does not necessarily imply that there are unbridgeable rifts in a society. There are societies, among them the so-called "modern" ones, which are based on precisely such differences. Nor do variations in types of physical build and differences in dialect as such inhibit integration. For both features, the internal variation in Germany is undoubtedly greater than in Bosnia. Nevertheless Germany is enjoying internal peace at present, and Bosnia is not. Without getting side-tracked by the disparaging rhetoric, then, we need to consider what Cassanelli's perspective is capable of explaining, and what it is not.

As a result of discrimination against people displaying the features mentioned above, the "minorities" of south Somalia were particularly vulnerable', as Cassanelli demonstrates convincingly. Since the members of clans with pastoral roots were battling one another for land that had formerly been farmed by the "minorities" in their region, the latter were particularly badly affected by the war. Cassanelli and the authors contributing to his collection do thus partly explain what the war was about: it was amongst other things (in this region at least) about control of the labour power of these south Somali minorities, and of the land which they traditionally farmed. But they fail to explain the form of conflict or the fronts which emerged. The lines of conflict in fact run through the relatively homogeneous groups of the north and central Somalis, who are remarkably similar in "occupation, class, physical type and dialect", and who furthermore, as has been shown above, are frequently very close to one another in their clan affiliations.

Once again at this point it appears necessary to revert to the lowest segmentary level, and look at alliances in terms of the clan analyses of which Cassanelli is so dismissive. How little Cassanelli distinguishes between these two aspects is apparent from his analysis of Mohamed Siad Barre's success. He used, says Cassanelli, resources of whatever origin – foreign aid deliveries, profits from trade in livestock and *qat* etc. - to buy political support. "That he did this along lines of kinship and clientelism gave precedence to clan analyses of Somalia's plight, but in fact it was his control of resources that underpinned the system." (1996: 22) This is a false opposition. The resources named were the *object* of the transfer; clan structures and clientelism were the *formative forces*. The first is the answer to the question "what?", the second is the answer to the question "who to whom?" or "who with whom?" How one can construe a contradiction (*"but"*) between them is logically not altogether fathomable.

That the farmers of Bantu descent were the real sufferers in the war, rather than being main actors, is also confirmed by Menkhaus (1996: 150): "although the Gosha played no part in the fighting and had seemingly little stake in the outcome of this internecine war, they bore the brunt of the war's destruction."[216] In view of this increased level of violence and the broader spectrum of resources which are the object of competition it is highly questionable whether the traditional legal instruments for restoring peace, negotiations and compensation payments, will ever again be able to bring about some kind of regulation.

Somalia and the outside world

The UNOSOM intervention lacked funding, knowledge and goals. It may have been possible to overcome the country by military force, place it under a military administration and under its protection to build up the institutions of a civil society, an administrative apparatus, professional and other associations. It may finally further have been possible to found political parties and then, following elections, to restore the reins of government to the local people. However, in a country as fragmented and heavily armed as Somalia, this would have demanded such a degree of financial sacrifice and so high a loss of life that it is extremely unlikely that the parliaments of the industrial powers would have been prepared to release the necessary means. As it is, the intervention cost 1.6 billion dollars: more than the amount spent in the preceding decades on development aid to Somalia (ZDF, Bonn Direkt, 4.3.95). Yet it is hard to see how much sense an intervention that fell anything short of a complete takeover of the country and the establishment of a military administration could have conceivably made. At one point in the conflict, maps were drawn up in America with a view to dividing the country into 5 pieces, namely Somaliland within the borders of the former British colony, Puntland (imaginatively given an old Egyptian name) in the north east, central Somalia on the lower Shabelle, Upper Juba and Jubaland.[217] What was never explained when these plans were being made was how it could be assumed that these smaller units would not be subject to the same processes of fractionalisation as former

---

[216] As a bone of contention, just how important the role of agricultural resources (the other aspect mentioned by Cassanelli) is in terms of the bigger picture cannot be conclusively established here. The figures quoted above would seem instead to indicate the continuing dominance of pastoral nomadic livestock production. In another contribution to the collection, one focused more on the region of Afmadow, some distance from the Jubba Valley, there is no mention of crop farming. In Little's view (1996: 111), the conflicts described above with the protagonists 'Jess' and 'Morgan' have correlates in rivalries between clan-based networks of livestock traders.

Incidentally, it would be interesting to know why Little (or else his informants) describe the *Herti* as a subgroup of the *Majerteen*, when precisely the opposite genealogical view is more widely held (compare Little 1996: 95 with Coronaro 1925: 332).

[217] *Africa Confidential* 35, no. 11. Patrick Gilkes also commented on such plans at the aforementioned conference in Khartoum in December 1993.

Somalia as a whole. As has been pointed out, the current political fractionalisation is taking place at the subclan level, and all five areas accommodate hundreds of subclans.

UNOSOM was unable to provide backing for civilian political forces. On the contrary, they supported leaders of clan militias – urban business people and political entrepreneurs – who were by no means identical with traditional clan elders, inviting them to Addis Abeba for conferences, paying for their air tickets, and then artificially increasing their political clout with media coverage.

In an earlier version of this paper in German (Schlee 1995: 289) I concluded in the following way:

> In the current situation, one has to conclude that outside intervention failed, that internal forces of renewal are not to be discerned, and that the rekindling or continuation of the civil war is highly probable. In terms of the international refugee problem and debates on the right to asylum, including the one being conducted in Germany, this means that for the foreseeable future there are very real grounds for seeking refuge.

Recent reports which indicate that subsistence production and to some extent trade are functioning again in rural areas do give some grounds for hope, however. This is no thanks to the many political movements with their impressive acronyms. On the contrary, the indications are that it is distance from these movements, or indeed from any form of state at all, right down to the very idea of one, which actually makes it possible to function. Since these movements fought over the state as a resource until it fell to pieces (Simons 1994), it is only distance from them that allows a modicum of regulation reminiscent of peace, together with a modest degree of security. The segmentary lineage system, with its various forms of sanction and consultation, seems to be surviving well, as long as it is far from the state. The horrors in Somalia were never the result of the segmentary lineage system in its own right, but rather of the takeover of the state by segmentary lineage structures (and vice versa?) under Siad Barre and equally so under those who fought over his succession. Little (1996: 110) reports that the local economy has not completely broken down in south Somalia, only gone underground. With the warlords sitting in the harbours, though, the official marketing structures have collapsed. Saudi Arabia as a market has moved far out of range; instead, livestock are being smuggled over the nearby Kenyan border. From there perhaps it still finds its way to Saudi Arabia, and there is no question that the Kenyan harbours have profited from the collapse of Somali foreign trade. For the present then one has to trust in the healing power of local arrangements and the black market, since there are no political movements in sight right now that might have the ability and resources to re-establish a state, let alone a unified state, in Somalia. Even the colonial powers, who were squabbling over this corner of Africa with expensive intrigues a century ago, would not take on today's task even if you paid them.

In the meantime the "rekindling or continuation of the civil war" which I described earlier (Schlee 1994 b) as highly probable, has materialised. In 1999 there was
a new escalation. Hussein Aydid has formed an alliance with the Islamist movement
Ittihad which also operated in region 5, i. e. the Somali area of Ethiopia. This pro-
voked an Ethiopian invasion in the area of Baidoa. The Ethiopians supported the RRA,
the Rahanweyn Resistance Army, which took control of Baidoa in June 1999 (IRIN,
June 11, Aug 4, Oct. 10 1999) The Rahanweyn, like their Digil allies who have also
joined the battle, are southern Somali for whom agriculture is of greater importance.
At the early stages of the civil war they and their lands only figured as the bone of contention between central and northern Somali factions of pastoralists and former pastoralists. But ever since a bumper harvest in 1994 these southern agriculturalists have also
been in a position to acquire arms (Natsios 1997: 94).

For Ethiopia, Somalia was only the second front in this period. The principle
theatre of war was the Eritrean frontier. After the fall of the Mengistu regime the new
leaders of Eritrea and Ethiopia were initially on good terms. In the struggle against
Mengistu they had been comrades in arms. A war of independence which had lasted
thirty years now had come to an end. In 1992 Eritrea was formally established by a
referendum. But in 1999 a border conflict soon escalated into a full-scale war. Ever
since taking possession of the capital, the Ethiopian regime, of Tigray origin and
originally regionalist, combined regionalist rhetoric with more and more centralist
policies. In the course of this new conflict they now fully took up the unionist discourses of their predecessors and all the symbols they had formerly tried to dismantle:
a long Christian-Semitic tradition of Empire and the battle of Adawa against the Italians, the central symbol of Imperial military glory.[218]

In such a situation in which civil wars are superimposed on international ones,
it is logical to look for allies among all forces opposed to one's adversaries. Thus, a
triangle of support came about between the Somali forces of Aydid's alliance, Eritrea,
and the Oromo Liberation Front (OLF) which operated in southern Ethiopia from
bases in Kenya. The relations of these latter are the object of another study (Schlee /
Shongolo, work in progress). For a long time the presence of the OLF had been ignored by the Kenyan authorities, but this tolerance ended in 1999. Pressure by Kenyan
military obliged the OLF to leave Kenya in June (DAILY NATION, June 9, 1999).
Moving down to the coast in Somalia the OLF cleared the roads of the road-blocks of
rival Somali militias (BBC) and changed the equilibrium in favour of Hussein Aydid
for a brief period. But already by December, the OLF was (or should have been) dis-
armed and its leaders expelled from Somalia after Hussein Aydid was obliged to sign
an agreement to that effect in Addis Abeba (IRIN, Dec. 21, 1999).

---

[218] Dereje Feyissa, oral communication, Feb. 3, 2000.

One could go on indefinitely talking about Somali factions and their alliances. Also the relatively successful model of Somaliland or 'Northern Somalia'[219] would merit a discussion. But here we limit ourselves to our privileged case: the region between Mogadishu and Kisimayu and the alliances around Ali Mahdi and the Aydids, father and son. As far as these alliances are concerned, there was little change between 1992 and the time of writing (2000), apart from the just mentioned external extensions of these alliances and the circumstance that – at least at times – Ali Mahdi became isolated in his own movement and withdrew into Egyptian exile. But at a peace conference in Djibouti in May Ali Mahdi showed up again (IRIN, May 05, 2000) although the president of the host country had declared that "all those associated with violence, namely warlords" should be excluded from participation in the "national reconciliation conference" (IRIN, Oct. 6, 1999).

Apparently Hussein Aydid had also been invited but had refused to come (IRIN, May 5, 2000). But all this concerns persons and not structures. The model of alliances between Hawiye subgroups with Darood subgroups against other Hawiye and other Darood seems to have persisted throughout this entire period.

In some periods of the past – including the uneasy peace based on domination by a large alliance – the patrilineal groups among whom internal peace and solidarity against outsiders prevailed, were genealogically deeper and demographically larger than today. However, there is no evidence that in periods of stronger fragmentation, sublineages of as shallow depth as the ones we find as political units today have not forged cross-clan alliances in just the same way as in pre-colonial times. In other words: with minor variations the patterns have remained the same. In colonial times these variations included the fact that the colonial powers became part of the game and formalised lineage structures for administrative purposes. During this period the colonised and colonisers manipulated each other, both using the lineage idiom. Newer interventionists like the UNOSOM have unsuccessfully attempted to play this game as well. Inspite of these outside interferences, of exogenous and endogenous variations, however, the basic principles of group formation are those already described by I. M. Lewis back in the period of the pax Britannica: namely patrilineal descent and contract *(xeer)*.

References

Abdullahi, Ahmed M. 1991. Ökonomik und Bedeutung der nomadisch-pastoralen Betriebssysteme Afrikas. Das Beispiel Zentral-Somalia. In: Scholz, Fred (ed.): *Nomaden*. Berlin: das arabische buch: 253 - 264

---

[219] I. e. the former British colony. In the cases of Somalia and neighbouring Yemen the references to cardinal points in the names of political units do not quite correspond to geographical realities. In both cases the "southern" part has a north-eastern corner which extends further north than the "northern" part. Regarding Somaliland see Prunier 1996.

Aden, H. Abdurahman 1986. Kulturwandel im Prozeß der Entnomadisierung. In: A-ves, Maho A. and Karl-Heinz W. Bechtold (eds.) 1987: 44 - 60

Africa Watch 1990. *Somalia: a government at war with its own people. Testimonies about the killings and the conflict in the north.* New York, Washington, London

Aves, Maho A. and Karl-Heinz Bechtold 1987. *The Effects of the IMF Conditionality in Somalia.* In: Aves, Maho A. & Karl-Heinz Bechtold (eds.): 136 - 172

Aves, Maho A. and Karl-Heinz Bechtold, (eds.) 1987. *Somalia im Wandel. Probleme und Perspektiven am Horn von Afrika.* Tübingen: Institut für wissenschaftliche Zusammenarbeit

Baas, Stephan 1991. Endogene Entwicklung im nomadischen Produktionssektor Somalias und ihre ökologischen Folgen - Dargestellt am Beispiel der westlichen "Central Rangelands". In: Scholz, Fred (ed.): *Nomaden.* Berlin: das arabische buch: 233 - 264

Besteman, Catherine and Lee Cassanelli (eds.) 1996. *The struggle for land in Southern Somalia: the war behind the war.* Boulder (Col.): Westview, London: HAAN

Bollig, Michael 1992 (1990). Ethnic conflicts in North-West Kenya. *Zeitschrift für Ethnologie* 115: 73 - 90

Bonte, Pierre 1984. On reading The Nuer. *Current Anthropology*, 25, 1: 129 - 30

Bongartz, M. 1991. *Somalia im Bürgerkrieg. Ursachen und Perspektiven des innenpolitischen Konflikts.* Institut für Afrikakunde (No.74)

Bourgeot, André (ed.) 1999. *Horizons nomades en Afrique sahélienne.* Paris: Karthala

Cassanelli, Lee V. 1996. Explaining the Somali crisis. In: C. Bestemann and L. V. Cassanelli (eds.): 13 - 26

Clarke, Walter and Jeffrey Herbst (eds.) 1997. *Learning from Somalia: the lessons of armed humanitarian intervention.* Boulder: Westview Press

Clapham, Christopher 1988. *Transformation and continuity in revolutionary Ethiopia.* Cambridge: Cambridge University Press

Conze, Peter and Thomas Labahn (eds.) 1986. *Somalia. Agriculture in the winds of change.* Saarbrücken: epi

Coronaro, Ettore 1925. Le popolazioni dell'Oltre Giuba. In: *Rivista Coloniale.* Rom: 330 - 346

Djama, Marcel 1993. *Dynamiques sociales en zone frontalière: changement social et conflit dans une communauté somali de la plaine du Hawd (1900 - 1960).* Paris: Ecole des Hautes Etudes en Sciences Sociales, Recueils est-africains 3

Djama, Marcel 1997 a. Trajectoire du pouvoir en pays somali. *Cahiers d'Études africaines* 146, XXXVII - 2: 403 - 428

Djama, Marcel 1997 b. As reported by Simons 1995. *Cahiers d'Études africaines* XXXVII - 2: 523 - 526

Dualeh, Hussein Ali 1994. *From Burre to Aideed. Somalia: the agony of a nation* Nairobi: Stellagraphics Ltd

Dyen, Isidore 1956. Language distribution and migration theory. *Language* 32 (4): 611 - 26

Eikenberg, Kathrin, Peter Körner 1993. Bewaffnete Humanität oder Interessenpolitik? Militärinterventionen in Liberia und Somalia. In: *Afrika-Jahrbuch* 1992: 34 - 45

Elwert, Georg 1995. Gewalt und Märkte. In: Dombrowski, Wolf and Ursula Pasero (eds.): *Wissenschaft, Literatur, Katastrophe. Festschrift für Lars Claussen.* Opladen: Westdeutscher Verlag

Elwert, Georg 1997. Gewaltmärkte. Beobachtungen zur Zweckrationalität von Gewalt. In: Trotha, Trutz v. (ed.): Soziologie der Gewalt. *Kölner Zeitschrift für Soziologie und Sozialpsychologie,* Special Issue, 37: 86 - 91

Evans-Pritchard, E.E. 1940. *The Nuer.* Oxford: Clarendon Press

Evans-Pritchard, E.E. 1949. *The Sanusi of Cyrenaica.* Oxford: Oxford University Press

Farah Mohamed, Ahmed & Jasmin Touati 1991. *Sedentarisierung von Nomaden - Chancen und Gefahren einer Entwicklungsstrategie am Beispiel Somalias.* Saarbrücken, Fort Lauderdale: Breitenbach

FitzGibbon, Louis 1982. *The betrayal of the Somalis.* London: Rex Collins

FitzGibbon, Louis 1985. *The evaded duty.* London: Rex Collins

Gellner, Ernest 1981. *Muslim Society.* Cambridge: Cambridge University Press

Glickman, Maurice 1985. On rereading *The Nuer. Current Anthropology* 26, 2: 286 - 7

Gurdon, Charles (ed.) 1996. *The Horn of Africa.* London: UCL Press

Hamilton, David 1967. Imperialism Ancient and Modern: A Study of British Attitudes to the Claims to Sovereignty to the Northern Somali Coastline. In: *Journal of Ethiopian Studies 5*, 2: 9 - 35

Hancock, Graham 1991 (1989). *Lords of poverty.* London: Mandarin

Heyer, Sonja 1997. *Kontinuitäten von Staatsbildung und –verfall in Somalia.* MA-Thesis, FU Berlin, Ethnologie

Henze, Paul B. 1984. Arming the Horn 1960 - 1980: military expenditures, arms imports and military aid in Ethiopia, Kenya, Somalia and Sudan, with statistics on economic growth and governmental expenditures. In: Rubenson, Sven (ed.) 1984: 637 - 656

Hummen, Wilhelm 1987. Die Wirtschaftspolitik Somalias im Umbruch. In: Aves, Maho A. and Karl-Heinz W. Bechtold (eds.) 1987: 114 - 135

Hunt, J. A. 1951. *A general survey of the Somaliland protectorate 1944 - 1950.* Colonial Development and Welfare Scheme. D.484. London: The Crown Agents for the Colonies

Janssen, Volker 1992. Monopolmechanismus und "Transkontinuität" in Äthiopien. In: Hansgünter Meyer: *Soziologen-Tag Leipzig 1991: Soziologie in Deutschland und die Transformation großer gesellschaftlicher Systeme.* Akademie Verlag

Janzen, Jörg 1984. Nomadismus in Somalia. *africa spectrum.* 84/2: 149 - 171

Janzen, Jörg 1987. Kennzeichen und Tendenzen ländlicher Entwicklung in Somalia. In: Aves, Maho and Karl-Heinz Bechtold (eds.) 1987: 16 - 43

Johnson, Douglas H. 1991. Political ecology in the upper Nile: the twentieth century expansion of the pastoral "common economy". In: Galaty, John G. and Pierre Bonte: *Herders, warriors and traders: pastoralism in Africa.* Boulder: Westview

Karp, Ivan and Kent Maynard 1983. Reading *The Nuer. Current Anthropology*, 24, 4: 481 - 503 with comments by John W. Burton, Peter Harries-Jones, Robert W. Hefner, Richard Huntington, M.C. Jedrej, Philip Carl Salzman, Robert C. Ulin

Kelly, Raymond C. 1983. A note on Nuer segmentary opposition. *American Anthropologist* 85: 905 - 6, with a response by Michel Verpdon: 906 - 7

Kuper, Adam 1988. *The Invention of primitive society: transformations of an illusion.* London: Routledge

Lamberti, Marcello 1983. *Die Somali-Dialekte: eine vergleichende Untersuchung.* PhD-Thesis, Köln, Philosophische Fakultät

Leach, E. R. 1954. *Political Systems of Highland Burma.* London: Athlone Press

Leverenz, Irene 1987. "Segmentäre Gesellschaft". In: Streck, Bernhard (ed.): *Wörterbuch der Ethnologie.* Köln: DuMont

Lewis, I. M. 1961. Force and fission in northern Somali lineage structure. *American Anthropologist* 63: 94 - 112

Lewis, I. M. 1962. Historical aspects of genealogies in northern Somali structure. *Journal of African History*, III, 1: 35 - 48

Lewis, I. M. 1972 (1969). From nomadism to cultivation: the expansion of political solidarity in southern Somalia. In: Douglas, Mary and Phyllis M. Kaberry (eds.): *Man in Africa*, London

Lewis, I. M. 1980 (1965). *A modern history of Somaliland: from nation to state.* London and New York: Longman

Lewis, I. M. 1981. *Somali culture, history and social institutions: an introductory guide to the Somali Democratic Republic.* London: the London School of Economics and Political Science

Little, Peter D. 1996. Rural herders and urban merchants: the cattle trade in Southern Somalia. In: C. Besteman and L.V. Cassanelli (eds.): 91 - 113

Matthies, Volker 1987. Konfliktherd Horn von Afrika. In: Aves, Maho and Karl-Heinz Bechtold (eds.): 96 - 113

Menkhaus, Kenneth 1996. From feast to famine: land and the state in Somalia's Lower Jubba Valley. In: C. Besteman and L.V. Cassanelli (eds.): 133 - 153

Middleton, J. and D. Tait (eds.) 1958. *Tribes without rulers: studies in African segmentary systems.* London: Routledge and Kegan Paul

Muuse Haaji Ismaa'iil Galaal 1956. *Hikmad Soomaali*, edited by B. W. Andrzejewski, London, Cape Town: Oxford University Press

Natsios, Andrew S. 1997. Humanitarian relief intervention in Somalia: the economics of chaos. In: Clarke and Herbst (eds.): 77 - 95

Needham, Rodney 1974. *Remarks and inventions: skeptical essays about kinship.* London: Tavistock

Negussay, Ayele 1984. Somalia's relations with her neighbours: from "Greater Somalia" to "Western Somalia" to "Somali Refugees" to... In: Rubenson, Sven (ed.) 1984: 657 - 666

Pape, Nicola 1998. *Kriegsfolgenbewältigung in Eritrea und Somaliland im Vergleich.* Dissertation Thesis, University of Bielefeld, FSP Entwicklungssoziologie

Peters, Emrys L. 1967. Some structural aspects of feud among camel-herding Bedouin of Cyrenaica. In: *Africa 37,* 261 - 282 (reprinted in Peters 1990)

Peters, Emrys L. 1990. *The Bedouin of Cyrenaica: studies in personal and corporate power.* Cambridge, New York: Cambridge University Press

Prunier, Gérard 1996. *Somaliland: birth of a new country?* In: Gurdon Charles (ed.) : 61 - 75

Prunier, Gérard 1997. Segmentarité et violence dans l'espace somali, 1840 - 1992. *Cahiers d'Études africaines,* 146, XXXVII - 2: 379 – 401

Rubenson, Sven (ed.) 1984. *Proceedings of the Seventh International Conference of Ethiopian Studies,* Lund 1982, Addis Abeba: Institute of Ethiopian Studies, Uppsala: Scandinavian Institute of African Studies, East Lansing: MSU African Studies Center

Ruf, Werner 1994. *Die neue Welt UN-Ordnung: vom Umgang des Sicherheitsrates mit der Souveränität der "Dritten Welt".* Münster: agenda Verlag.

Salzman, Philip Carl 1978. Does complementary opposition exist? In: *American Anthropologist* 80 (1): 53 - 70

Schlee, Günther 1984 a. Nomaden und Staat. Das Beispiel Nordkenia. *Sociologus* 34 (2): 140 - 161

Schlee, Günther 1984 b. Une société pastorale pluriethnique: Oromo et somalis au nord du Kenya. *Production pastorale et société* 15 (autumn 1984). 21 - 39

Schlee, Günther 1987 a. Somaloid history: oral tradition, *Kulturgeschichte* and historical linguistics in an area of Oromo and Somaloid Interaction. In: Jungraithmayr, H. and W. W. Müller: *Proceedings of the Fourteenth International Hamito-Semitic Congress,* Marburg, 20 - 22 September, 1983: 265 - 315

Schlee, Günther 1987 b. Die Islamisierung der Vergangenheit: Von der Rückwirkung der Konversion somalischer und somaloider Gruppen zum Islam auf deren oral tradiertes Geschichtsbild. (bilingue: L'islamisation du passé: à propos de l'effet réactif de la conversion de groupes somalis et somaloïdes à l'islam sur la représentation de l'histoire dans leurs traditions orales. In: W.J.G. Möhlig, H. Jungraithmayr, J.F. Thiel (eds.). *La littérature orale en Afrique comme source pour la découverte des cultures traditionnelles.* Berlin: Reimer: 269 - 299

Schlee, Günther 1989. *Identities on the move: clanship and pastoralism in Northern Kenya.* Manchester University Press, New York: St. Martin's Press, paperback Nairobi 1994: Gideon S. Were Press, Hamburg, Münster: Lit Verlag

Schlee, Günther 1991. Les réseaux de relations intra- et interethniques chez les nomades du nord Kenya. *Bulletin des études africaines de l'INALCO,* No.16: 73 - 95

Schlee, Günther 1994 a. Der Islam und das Gada-System in Nordost-Afrika. *Sociologus* 44 (2): 112 - 135

Schlee, Günther 1994 b. Cross-cutting ties. Grenzen, Raub und Krieg. Universität Bielefeld: FSP Entwicklungssoziologie, Working Paper No.203

Schlee, Günther 1995. Regelmäßigkeiten im Chaos: Elemente einer Erklärung von Allianzen und Frontverläufen in Somalia. *africa spectrum* 95, 3: 273 - 279

Schlee, Günther 1997. Cross-cutting ties and interethnic conflict: the example of Gabbra Oromo and Rendille. *Ethiopia in broader perspective. Papers of the 13th International Conference of Ethiopian Studies* (eds. Fukui, K., E. Kurimoto and M. Shigeta), Vol.2, Kyoto: Shokado Book Sellers: 577 - 596

Schlee, Günther 1998. Identidades múltiples y *cross-cutting ties* (nexos transversales) en la teoría de los conflictos. *Revista Mexicana de Sociología,* 60, 3: 121 - 146

Schlee, Günther 1999. Nomades et l'État au nord du Kenya. In: Bourgeot, André (ed.): 219 - 239

Schlee, Günther and Shongolo, Abdullahi A. 1995. Local war and its impact on ethnic and religious identification in Southern Ethiopia. *GeoJournal* 36 (1): 7 - 17

Schlee, Günther and Shongolo, Abdullahi A. In preparation. *Islam and ethnicity in northern Kenya*

Schlee, Günther and Werner, Karin (eds.) 1996. *Inklusion und Exklusion: die Dynamik von Grenzziehungen im Spannungsfeld von Markt, Staat und Ethnizität.* Köln (Cologne): Rüdiger Köppe Verlag

Sigrist, Christian 1967. *Regulierte Anarchie: Untersuchungen zum Fehlen und zur Entstehung politischer Herrschaft in segmentären Gesellschaften Afrikas.* Frankfurt: Syndikat

Simons, Anna 1994. Somalia and the dissolution of the nation-state. *American Anthropologist* 96: 818 - 824

Simons, Anna 1996. *Networks of dissolution: Somalia undone.* Boulder, Colorado: Westview Press

Stern, Werner 1991. Mobile Viehhaltung als Wirtschaftsfaktor. In: Scholz, Fred (ed.): *Nomaden*. Berlin: das arabische buch: 113 - 130

Turnbull R.G. 1955. *The Darod Invasion*. Private edition

Verdon, Michel 1982. Where have all their lineages gone? Cattle and descent among the Nuer. *American Anthropologist* 84, 3: 566 - 579

Waldron, Sidney R. 1984. Is there a future for the Ogadeen refugees? In: Rubenson, Sven (ed.) 1984: 673 - 680

Zitelmann, Thomas 1996. Begegnungen im globalen Ideoraum: Mohammed Farah Aidid. Klan, demokratische Autonomie und die Apokalypse. In: H.P. Müller (ed.): *Weltsystem und kulturelles Erbe*. Berlin. Reimer

Press and electronic sources:
Africa Confidential, Oxford, Great Britain
BBC- British Broadcasting Corporation
Daily Nation, Nairobi, Kenya
IRIN: "irin-english" service of the UN's IRIN humanitarian information unit.
http: //www.reliefweb.int/IRIN

ABSTRACT

It is certain that the events in Somalia are influenced by external factors and that the civil war and the ways of coping with its effects cannot be explained in terms of an image of a "traditional society". However, some models of social organisation have been found in the present situation of conflict, models which have persisted since colonial and pre-colonial times. Among them, we find a complementary relation between agnatic and contractual affiliation, a general tendency for preferring opportunist economic strategies to recurrent activities and the spatial separation of units of production. Such separation entails networks spanning long distances. Some recent characteristics of Somali politics and of their current situation are described in terms of new transformations of old models.